11/4

Ruins in the Literary and Cultural Imagination

Efterpi Mitsi · Anna Despotopoulou ·
Stamatina Dimakopoulou ·
Emmanouil Aretoulakis
Editors

Ruins in the Literary and Cultural Imagination

Editors
Efterpi Mitsi
National and Kapodistrian University
of Athens
Athens, Greece

Anna Despotopoulou
National and Kapodistrian University
of Athens
Athens, Greece

Stamatina Dimakopoulou
National and Kapodistrian University
of Athens
Athens, Greece

Emmanouil Aretoulakis
National and Kapodistrian University
of Athens
Athens, Greece

ISBN 978-3-030-26904-3   ISBN 978-3-030-26905-0   (eBook)
https://doi.org/10.1007/978-3-030-26905-0

This Palgrave Macmillan imprint is published by the registered company Springer Nature Switzerland AG
The registered company address is: Gewerbestrasse 11, 6330 Cham, Switzerland

ACKNOWLEDGEMENTS

The inspiration for this volume came from a conference we organized in 2017 at the National and Kapodistrian University of Athens on the subject of ruins. The Athenian surroundings were particularly conducive to the theoretical and cultural approaches to ruin that were explored during three days of enthusiastic academic discussion. The essays collected here are substantially expanded and revised versions of the conference papers from which they originated. We would like to thank all the contributors for their dedication, generosity and shared commitment to the volume. We also gratefully acknowledge the reviewers who offered their time and expertise to assess submissions and provide feedback on the essays.

We are grateful to everyone at Palgrave Macmillan: to Ben Doyle, who first showed interest in the proposal and put it through the review process, and to Allie Troyanos, who moved the project forward; to the anonymous readers for their generous and constructive suggestions; and to Rachel Jacobe and the editorial and production teams for taking the volume through the publication process smoothly and for all their support.

We also wish to thank the Aikaterini Laskaridis Foundation, the Museum of the City of Athens—Vouros Eutaxias Foundation, Yiannis Mitos and Tom Burrows for allowing us to use the illustrations and photographs from their collections. Excerpts from Leonard Cohen's songs and "The Background Singers" are used by permission of The Wylie Agency LLC (© 1964, 1969, 1974, 1984, 1988, 1992, 2001, 2004, 2012, 2014 and 2016 by Leonard Cohen); Claude Pélieu's collage from

Bulletin from Nothing 2 (1965) is used by permission of the Claude Pélieu estate; Toyen's *Relâche* (Relaxed) (1943) is used by permission of the Artists Rights Society (ARS).

Thanks are also due to the National and Kapodistrian University of Athens and the Special Account for Research Grants, for its support of our conference and our research.

Contents

Notes on Contributors

Emmanouil Aretoulakis is tenured Associate Lecturer at the Department of Literature/Culture, Faculty of English Language and Literature of the National and Kapodistrian University of Athens, Greece. He teaches English fiction, poetry and contemporary theory. His most recent book *Forbidden Aesthetics, Ethical Justice, and Terror in Modern Western Culture* was published by Lexington, USA (2016). He has published three monographs and various articles in peer-and blind-reviewed academic journals such as *Katherine Mansfield Studies, Philosophy and Literature, European Journal of English Studies, Journal of Early Modern Studies* and others.

Adam Beardsworth is Associate Professor of English at Grenfell Campus, Memorial University of Newfoundland. His critical work on American and Canadian poetry has been published widely in journals and edited collections, including *Canadian Poetry, The Canadian Review of American Studies* and *Studies in Canadian Literature*. He is also a published poet and currently sits as president of the Canadian Association for American Studies.

Anna Despotopoulou is Professor in English Literature and Culture at the National and Kapodistrian University of Athens. She is the author of *Women and the Railway, 1850–1915* (Edinburgh UP, 2015), and co-editor of *Henry James and the Supernatural* (Palgrave Macmillan, 2011), *Transforming Henry James* (Cambridge Scholars, 2013) and *Reconstructing Pain and Joy* (Cambridge Scholars, 2008). Her articles on Victorian Literature and Culture have appeared in *Modern Fiction Studies, The Henry James Review, The Review of English Studies* and other journals.

Stamatina Dimakopoulou is Assistant Professor in American Literature and Culture at the National and Kapodistrian University of Athens. She has been Fulbright Visiting Scholar at New York University. Publications include articles on Surrealism, modernist magazines, US poetry and art. She is a founding member and co-editor of *Synthesis, an Anglophone Journal of Comparative Literary Studies.* Her current research focuses on US poetry, theory and art of the late 1960s and early 1970s.

Christina Dokou is Assistant Professor of American Literature and Culture at the National and Kapodistrian University of Athens, Department of English. She is the co-editor of two volumes of essays and has published book chapters and articles on her areas of interest, which include Gender Studies, Comparative Literature (specifically, Greek myth in modern Anglophone literature), Comics Studies and American Folklore.

Giorgos Giannakopoulos holds a Ph.D. from the National and Kapodistrian University of Athens. He has published essays in English and Greek on literature, film, and continental philosophy. His academic interests include American literature, deconstruction and psychoanalysis. He is currently working on a book based on his Ph.D. thesis.

Michael Hollington is a retired professor currently living in Scotland and Italy. He has taught on every continent, most especially Europe and Australasia, ending his career in 2007 in Toulouse. He is best known as a Dickensian, but has published widely on Renaissance and post-Renaissance writing in English and other European languages. He has written or edited several books on Dickens, Grass, Whitman, Katherine Mansfield and Milton.

Vassiliki Kolocotroni is Senior Lecturer in English Literature at the University of Glasgow. She works in the areas of international modernism and the avant-garde, theory, classical reception, travel and film. She is the co-editor of *Modernism: An Anthology of Sources and Documents, The Edinburgh Dictionary of Modernism,* and the European literature editor of *The Routledge Encyclopedia of Modernism.* She has also co-edited *In the Country of the Moon: British Women Travelers to Greece, 1718–1932, Women Writing Greece: Essays on Hellenism, Orientalism and Travel*, and has published journal articles and book chapters on Woolf, Freud, Conrad, Joyce, Eliot, H. D. Benjamin, Heidegger, Derrida and their engagement with ancient and modern Greece.

Apostolos Lampropoulos is Professor of Comparative Literature at the University Bordeaux Montaigne. He has published the monograph *Le Pari de la description* (2002). He has co-edited the volumes *States of Theory* (in Greek; 2010), *AutoBioPhagies* (2011), *Textual Layering* (2017) and *Écriture musicale, écriture picturale de la littérature et des arts* (2017) and the issue "Configurations of Cultural Amnesia" of the journal *Synthesis* (2011). He is currently completing the monograph *Histories of the Mouth* and is developing a project on critical intimacy.

Carl Lavery is Professor of Theatre and Performance at the University of Glasgow. He has published numerous texts on theatre and ecology, including *Rethinking the Theatre of the Absurd: Ecology, Environment and the Greening of the Modern Stage* (2015) and *Performance and Ecology: What Can Theatre Do?* (2018). He edited a special issue of the journal *Performance Research* on *Ruins and Ruination* (2015) and collaborated with the artist Lee Hassall on the film and performance "Return to Battleship Island," which deals with the abandoned island of Hashima in Japan.

Chryssa Marinou holds a B.A. in English Language and Literature and an M.A. in Literature, Culture, Ideology from National and Kapodistrian University of Athens. She is currently completing her Ph.D., a comparative reading of Henry James and Dorothy Richardson through the work of Walter Benjamin. She has published in *Synthesis: an Anglophone Journal of Comparative Literary Studies* (2013 and 2018), *Pilgrimages: a Journal of Dorothy Richardson Studies* (2015), *Mnimon: Society for the Study of Modern Hellenism* (2016), and has contributed to Arcades Material Yellow: Subterranean to Street, eds. Sam Dolbear, Hannah Proctor (Aldgate Press, 2019). Her research interests include comparative literature, modernity, modernism, political theory.

Efterpi Mitsi is Professor in English Literature and Culture at the National and Kapodistrian University of Athens. Her research and publications are on classical receptions in English literature, word and image, and travellers to Greece. She is the author of *Greece in Early English Travel Writing, 1596–1682* (Palgrave, 2017), the editor of *Troilus and Cressida: A Critical Reader* (Bloomsbury, 2019) and co-editor of a number of volumes, including *In the Country of the Moon: British Women Travelers to Greece, 1718–1932, Women Writing Greece: Essays on Hellenism, Orientalism and Travel* and *The Letter of Law: Literature, Justice and the Other*.

Simon Murray teaches contemporary theatre and performance at the University of Glasgow. Originally a sociologist "by trade," he was a professional actor and theatre maker for 10 years, specializing in physical performance. He has written on Jacques Lecoq, Physical Theatres, Lightness, Collaboration and W. G. Sebald. He is currently completing a book entitled *Performing Ruins* as part of a forthcoming series called *Performing Landscapes*.

Claire Potter is Tutor at the Architecture Association, London. She wrote her Masters thesis on psychoanalysis and tragedy at Paris VII, Denis Diderot, examining movement and desire in the body. Her published work includes three books of poetry, essays on Irigaray, Woolf, Hardy and Blanchot. She is a member of the Poetry Society London.

Jyotsna G. Singh is Professor of English at Michigan State University. Her books include *Colonial Narratives/Cultural Dialogues: 'Discoveries' of India in the Language of Colonialism* (1996), and *Shakespeare and Postcolonial Theory* (Arden Bloomsbury, 2019), and *A Companion to the Global Renaissance*, ed. (2009). Her research interests include early modern literature and culture, including Shakespeare, postcolonial theory, colonial history, and gender and sexuality.

Jeffrey L. Spear has recently retired from the English Department of NYU where he specialized in Victorian Literature and Culture, Visual Culture and aspects of British India. He has followed Leonard Cohen's career since 1967. His recent publications include articles on Nina Paley's *Sita Sings the Blues*, The South Kensington Colonial and Indian Exhibition of 1886, and the *devadasis* in the dance and performance history of British India.

Sheila Teahan is Associate Professor of English at Michigan State University. She is the author of *The Rhetorical Logic of Henry James* (a Choice Outstanding Academic Book) and of essays on James in *The*

Henry James Review, Arizona Quarterly, Henry James in Context (Cambridge UP), the Bedford/St. Martin's Case Studies of *The Turn of the Screw, Advances in Henry James Studies* (Palgrave), *Transforming Henry James* (Cambridge Scholars), *The Letter of the Law* (Peter Lang) and elsewhere.

Angeliki Tseti holds a Ph.D. in Anglophone Studies from the University Denis Diderot—Paris VII, in France, and the National and Kapodistrian University of Athens, Greece. Her research interests include photography and literature, word-image interactions, as well as trauma studies, memory, historiography, genocide and film. She has published articles on photo-literature, specifically the works of W. G. Sebald, Jonathan Safran Foer and Aleksandar Hemon, in academic journals and collective volumes. Her latest work includes articles on Claude Lanzmann and Susanne Khardalian and the photo-memoir of Daniel Mendelsohn, as well as the translation and editing of Liliane Louvel's *The Pictorial Third: An Essay into Intermedial Criticism* (2018).

Theodora Tsimpouki is Professor of American Literature at the National and Kapodistrian University of Athens. A graduate of the Department of English Literature and Culture, National and Kapodistrian University of Athens, she has also studied at the Sorbonne and holds a Ph.D. in English from New York University. Her research has centred on American literature and culture, visual culture and theories of space. Her work has been published in journals and edited volumes abroad and in Greece. Her recent published research includes articles on Constance Fenimore Woolson, Henry James, Edith Wharton, Stephen Crane, Anais Nin, Bertrand Malamud, Philip Roth, E. L. Doctorow, American Exceptionalism and American ideology of space. She is co-editor of *The War on the Human: New Responses to an Ever-Present Debate* (2017).

David Tucker is Associate Lecturer in the Department of Visual Cultures at Goldsmiths, University of London. He has published a number of books and articles on Samuel Beckett, including the monograph *Samuel Beckett and Arnold Geulincx: Tracing 'A Literary Fantasia'* (Continuum, 2012), as well as articles on Harold Pinter. Current work includes co-editing a critical edition of Beckett's non-fiction prose (Faber & Faber, forthcoming, 2021).

Maria Vara is Senior Teaching Fellow at the Hellenic Air Force Academy, a visiting lecturer at the Athens School of Fine Arts and secretary of the Hellenic Association for the Study of English (HASE). Her publications include chapters in *Metafiction and Metahistory in Contemporary Women's Writing* (Palgrave Macmillan, 2007), *Le Gothic* (Palgrave Macmillan, 2008), *Rewriting/Reprising: Plural Intertextualities* (Cambridge Scholars Publishing, 2009), *The Letter of the Law: Literature, Justice and the Other* (Peter Lang, 2013), *The Reception of Charles Dickens in Europe* (Bloomsbury Academic, 2013) and *Liminal Dickens* (Cambridge Scholars Publishing, 2016).

List of Figures

CHAPTER 1

Introduction

Efterpi Mitsi, Anna Despotopoulou,
Stamatina Dimakopoulou and Emmanouil Aretoulakis

In a footnote to the first stanza of *Childe Harold's Pilgrimage* Canto 2, Byron reflects on the meaning of the ruined Parthenon:

> We can all feel, or imagine, the regret with which the ruins of cities, once the capitals of empires, are beheld; the reflections suggested by such objects are too trite to require recapitulation. But never did the littleness of man, and the vanity of his very best virtues, of patriotism to exalt, and of valour to defend his country, appear more conspicuous in the record of what Athens was, and the certainty of what she now is. (Byron 1980)

The poet argues that the thoughts triggered by the sight of ruined cities, like Athens, where he arrived in December 1809, are "too trite" for explanation. At the same time, these reflections generate many lines of poetry, lamenting the ruination of the Parthenon not only due to the ravages of time but also because of the looting of conquerors and "plunderers." In stanza 6, the temple's "broken arch, its ruined wall, / Its chambers desolate, and portals foul" form a sad contrast to the glory of ancient Athens, where "this was once Ambition's airy hall, / The dome

E. Mitsi · A. Despotopoulou (✉) · S. Dimakopoulou · E. Aretoulakis
National and Kapodistrian University of Athens, Athens, Greece

© The Author(s) 2019
E. Mitsi et al. (eds.), *Ruins in the Literary and Cultural Imagination*,
https://doi.org/10.1007/978-3-030-26905-0_1

1

of Thought, the palace of the Soul" (Byron 1980, 2.46–9). Emphasizing the removal of the Parthenon sculptures by Lord Elgin as the worst kind of vandalism and imperialism, Byron recognizes that these "relics [are] ne'er to be restored" (2.132); the ruin cannot be recuperated, ruination as a historical and political act cannot be reversed. Sitting on "this massy stone, / The marble column's yet unshaken base" (Byron 1980, 2.82–3), Harold is not a mere ruin-gazer but a critical reader of ruins, connecting imperial with cultural politics and condemning the British as the "plunderers of yon fane" (2.91). In that same footnote, the poet suggests that the littleness and vanity of Byron's contemporaries have turned ruins into commodities, and Athens itself into "a scene of petty intrigue and perpetual disturbance, between the bickering agents of certain British nobility and gentry" (1980, 2. note p. 189). Moreover, in a note to the papers appended to the poem, Byron adds that Elgin could indeed "boast of having ruined Athens" ("Appendix to Canto the Second," Note [A]). Yet, in the midst of ruins, a new hope of recovery arises, the political renewal of Greece itself.[1]

On 20 July 2015, just over 200 years after the publication of *Childe Harold's Pilgrimage*, the cover of *Time* magazine showed an image of the Acropolis looming above Athens, with the Parthenon at the foreground. The headline "State of Ruin"[2] connected the topos of Byron's "Sad relic" with the condition of Greece as a failed state on the verge of yet one more economic disaster. The ruin, which in the early nineteenth century "nor ev'n can Fancy's eye / Restore what Time hath labour'd to deface" (*Childe Harold's Pilgrimage* 2.85–8), has become synonymous in the early twenty-first with the state itself. The subtitle under the headline, "The battle to save Greece, the euro and the dream of a united Europe," also evoked the philhellenic dream to liberate Greece from oriental despotism, linking it to the post-war ideal of a united Europe, itself emerging from the disaster and the ruins of World War II. Thus, the state of ruin forewarns of the ruin of a union which has been founded

---

[1] On Byron's thoughts on the Parthenon marbles and Elgin, see St. Clair (1998, 180–200), Leask (2004, 104–106), Esterhammer (2009), and Keach (2012).

[2] The article in *Time* was written by Simon Shuster, reporting from Athens after the rejection of the proposed bailout by a referendum which took place on 5 July 2015. On 13 July 2015, however, the Greek government reached an agreement with the European authorities for a 3-year-bailout with even harsher austerity conditions than the ones originally proposed.

on a common currency and shared political and social values. It is still uncertain whether the battle was victorious, with Brexit having replaced the fear of Grexit and with the rise of anti-European, far-right nationalism throughout Europe.

In the autumn of 2018, the 6th Athens Biennale, entitled "ANTI," used emptied and abandoned Athens landmark buildings to house its exhibits, which set "to challenge our faith in emancipation and humanism by doubting prevalent resurrections of ideas of the 'human.'"[3] In one of these venues, the Benakeios Library, located on the side of the Old Parliament of Greece and closed to the public since 2004, a video by Chinese artist Cao Fei shows the ruins resulting from the demolition of old buildings in China strangely reflected on the debris falling from the room's ceiling. The video, entitled *Rumba II: Nomad*, focuses on a group of vacuum cleaning robots navigating in a demolishing area in Beijing and vainly trying to clean the dust and rubble of urban destruction.[4] The surreal element of the cleaning robots is counterbalanced by a man collecting brick by brick the remains of the past. Will something new be built from the ruins of the past, or is his effort as futile as that of the wandering robots? Cao Fei, born in 1978 in Guangzhou and living in Beijing, reflects on the frenzied rhythm of destruction, construction and urbanization occurring in China today but also on the human obsession with progress and renewal concurrent with the fear of ruin, obliteration and oblivion. In the ruined nineteenth-century Benakeios library, different states of ruin come together, material and symbolic, local and global. The boundaries between rubble and ruin, between debris and monument are blurred, as viewers contemplate and recognize their own fascination with ruins.

Focusing on the ruin as metaphor and as a materiality that triggers appropriations and imaginings across different cultural experiences and forms of writing, the chapters of this volume seek to understand what determines a given object "as a ruin" and how it interacts with the past as a palimpsest, inscribed by the continuous attempts to assign meaning

[3] ANTI, 6th Athens Biennale, 26/10-9/12/2018, curated by Stefanie Hessler, Poka-Yio. Kostis Stafylakis, https://anti.athensbiennale.org/en/6th-athens-biennale-anti (accessed 8 December 2018).

[4] Cao Fei, *Rumba II: Nomad*, 2015, video 14 mins 16 secs, sound by Dickson Dee, commissioned by GUCCI, http://www.caofei.com/works.aspx?year=2015&wtid=3 (accessed 9 December 2018).

to its incompleteness. The ruin predominantly recalls a classical or distant past and is valued as a silent yet privileged ground for its reconstruction or continued influence. Ruins have enduring, interconnected, but also distinct legacies, as historical realities, material and/or aesthetic objects, and as categories of thought. Following the critical discourse on ruins, *Ruins in the Literary and Cultural Imagination* makes an original contribution to recent discussions on the significance of ruins and fills a gap in the existing scholarship. Despite important studies of the meaning of classical ruins in Western culture, from Rose Macaulay's *Pleasure of Ruins* (1953) to Julia Hell's very recent *The Conquest of Ruins: The Third Reich and the Fall of Rome* (2019),[5] as well as explorations of the idea of ruin in specific historical periods, the ruin as materiality and metaphor in British and American literature and culture has not been sufficiently discussed. In literary studies, scholars have mostly studied ruins in the context of Romanticism. Thomas McFarland (1981), Elizabeth Harries (1994), Gillen Wood d' Arcy (2001) and Sophie Thomas (2010) explore fragments and ruins as central notions in Romantic authors, centring on the crosscurrents between architectural ruins and textual fragments in Romantic literature and on ruins as expressions of the space between the visible and the invisible. More recently, Andrew Hui (2017) reflects on the shifting meaning of ruins in the Renaissance through readings of Petrarch, Du Bellay and Spenser. Both Macaulay and Hui have shown the genealogy of the "cult of ruins," emerging in the Renaissance through poetic collections such as Du Bellay's *Antiquités de Rome* (1558), which admired the greatness of classical ruins, while lamenting the fall of empires and civilizations. As Macaulay argues, "the Renaissance desire to build up the ancient ruins into their glorious first state" is counterbalanced by the lamentation over the ruin as "wreckage of perfection" (1953, 192–193). At the same time, according to Brian Dillon, already in the Renaissance the ruin was transformed from "a legible remnant of the past" to a "scattered cipher: a text that was alternately readable and utterly mysterious" (Dillon 2005 [2006], par. 1).

The moral reading of ruins, which made them emblems of the transience and temporality of human life and ambition, changed in the eighteenth century, as ruins became autonomous entities rather than enigmatic remains of an original work, testifying to their own survival

---

[5] Julia Hell's book was published in early 2019, after the chapters of this book had been completed.

from oblivion. As Maria Vara writes in Chapter 2, it is then that the Gothic becomes the main language of the ruin, paving the way for phantasmagoric spectacles set in ruined monasteries and castles. Also in the eighteenth century, replicas of ancient Greek monuments are reconstructed in Britain, aesthetically appropriating the ruins of Athens. Vara reveals how the ruins of a Capuchin monastery, in the heart of Athens, which had appropriated the Choragic Monument of Lysicrates and was destroyed in 1821 during the Greek War of Independence, became a key site of "ruin lust" from the eighteenth century to the nineteenth century, fusing antiquity, the Gothic and technology. And the fact that Lord Byron stayed for eight months there in 1810–1811, reading and writing within the monument, which had become the monastery's library, may further illuminate his reflections on ruins and their impact on the present.

The fascination with ruins during the long eighteenth century becomes more intense than in earlier periods. Since the Great Lisbon Earthquake of 1755—the first major event of ruination and catastrophe in modernity and a defining moment in the Enlightenment—the ruin has lent itself "to a monumental and memorializing panoramic aesthetic" (Feldman 2005, 203), thus arousing the suspicion that the ruin-as-monument and the catastrophic were one and the same thing. Significantly, the Lisbon Earthquake opened up new rationalistic roads that mitigated terror at the sight of catastrophe and ruins and, at the same time, encouraged the possibility of distanced, aesthetic appreciation of the ruin as something that appeals to the senses and individual imagination. It was in the immediate aftermath of the Lisbon disaster that waves of foreigners started pouring in from all corners of Europe to witness the newly created ruins in the Portuguese capital. Those people—whom we could call "disaster tourists"—had arrived on the scene to appreciate with their own eyes how an entire city turned, in just a few seconds, into debris and ruins. Those ruins were, fascinatingly, not ancient ruins but fully modern ones, which created the almost enthusiastic feeling that they (the "disaster tourists" themselves) were not just distant observers but actually participants in history-making.

Edmund Burke touched upon the fascination with ruins by making the hypothesis that had London suffered an earthquake of that magnitude, it would be turned into an exciting city, one full of new modern ruins, and a fascinating spectacle for all. In fact, he says, people who never cared to visit the English capital before would be exhilarated at such a prospect now, almost as if an interesting London were a *destroyed* one: "But suppose such a fatal accident to have happened, what numbers from all parts would croud to behold the ruins..." (Burke 1990, 44). The fantastic ruins of London that he has in mind would attract the human eye as something unprecedented, unexpected and utterly *real*.

Ruins evoke the grandeur and inevitable decay of cultures and civilizations in the distant past, while constituting the main vehicle of reconstructing that past in the present. It is in the nature of the ruin to always oscillate between the before and after, standing, both temporally and spatially, at a liminal point of in-between-ness. Ruins have always enthralled and mystified humanity as they point to something magnificent and glorious (or excessive) which was gradually or suddenly lost. From that perspective, they even evoke the fear of the future ruination of the contemporary, modern world. Shelley, in his celebrated poetic fragment "Ozymandias," alludes to the Romantic nostalgia for lost grandeur as a two-edged sword: on the one hand, the poet laments the evanescence of human power and authority, but on the other, he recognizes that mighty power contains the seeds of its own destruction. In a way, as Shelley might argue in the context of his sonnet, being in ruins—in the sense of being humbled—is (or should be) the natural condition of humanity.

In the early twentieth century, in his essay "The Ruin" (1911), Georg Simmel addressed the Romantic concerns about the precariousness of human power, by offering an ecological view of ancient ruins, which for him represented the eternal antagonism between nature and the human spirit. Simmel's view of ruins challenges humanistic and anthropocentric views of the dominance of man over nature, by suggesting that nature imposes its own "culture" on human products, transforming them into the raw material for its own constructions: "Nature has transformed the work of art into material for her own expression as she has previously served as material for art" (Simmel 1958, 381). While the human spirit is forever locked in an ongoing dialectic of the "not yet and the no-longer" (382), seeking to fulfil its utmost ambition but never reaching its peak, nature, which had been latent while humanity was creating, is reclaiming its materials, bringing them "home" (382), in a "peaceful unity of belonging" (383). Decay destroys a work of art's or a building's unity of form, but through nature's intervention a new whole emerges which "is entirely meaningful, comprehensible, differentiated" (381). Yet, for others, as William Keach notes, ruins are seen from a post-Romantic view, making "legible simultaneously natural and social processes." Keach distinguishes between "canonical ruin culture [that] transvalues fall, decay, collapse, disaster into sites and objects of positive aesthetic and ideological value" and "critical ruin discourse" which goes beyond the aesthetic transvaluation of ruins, disclosing meanings and historical circumstances that would otherwise remain hidden (2012, par. 8, 10).

In the modernity that begins from Romanticism as Theodor Adorno complexly suggested in his *Aesthetic Theory*, "the fragment is that part of the totality of the work that opposes totality."[6] It is perhaps at such a juncture that the continuity between Romanticism and modernism can be rethought in the context of a reflection on the trope of the ruin and on the legacies of ruin thinking. Like the fragment, the ruin may lead towards a more malleable notion of wholeness or totality. Philippe Lacoue-Labarthe and Jean-Luc Nancy point to a similar direction in an oft-quoted moment from the *Literary Absolute*: "fragmentary totality … cannot be situated in any single point: it is simultaneously in the whole and in each part. Each fragment stands for itself and for that from which it is detached" (1988, 44). The break that the thinkers evoke is not only aesthetic but also epistemological and is symptomatic of radically different experiences of historical time. Significantly, Linda Nochlin opens her study of "the fragment as a metaphor for modernity" through "the body in pieces" with Fuseli's *Artist Overwhelmed by the Grandeur of Antique Ruins*. Fuseli's artist represents a non-Adornian moment, as it were: "modernity … is figured as irrevocable loss, poignant regret for lost totality, a vanished wholeness. So devastated is the artist by this loss that he cannot even see; he is represented as self-blinded" (Nochlin 1994, 7). Fuseli's outlook on art will be forcibly offset by the momentum of the French Revolution which "was caught in the throes of destroying one civilization before creating a new one" (Nochlin, 10). Yet, as Nochlin's study also reveals, the political imperative of destruction and the cultural imperative to memorialize the present emerged in tandem, a dialectic that was annulled in the catastrophes of the two World Wars where the modern values and societies that emerged in the wake of the French Revolution were nearly annihilated.

---

[6]Also cited in Malpas (2003, 84). Malpas revisits Adorno in the context of a reflection on whether "artistic fragmentation is posited as a disturbance of or challenge to the closure and completion of systems of thought of politics" (2003, 84).

Walter Benjamin, whose critical view of ruins informs many of the volume's chapters, puts forth in his *Origin of the German Tragic Drama* (1977) as well as "Theses on the Philosophy of History" (1969) the concept of history itself as a mass of unconnected ruins and fragments. Nonetheless, as Vassiliki Kolocotroni argues in Chapter 14 of this book, "What Benjamin preserves ... is the destruction of an original vision, but also the conviction that amongst its ruins remain signs of a salutary witnessing, fragments of the past that may be defunct, but ripe for strategic reconstitution." Benjamin, in the very act of reflecting on meaningless ruins, discerns the possibility of a transhistorical envisioning: every time we look at ruins, that is, we are actually catching glimpses (or allegories) of historical processes. So, ruins are more than aesthetic objects: "they are allegories of thinking itself" (Benjamin 1977, 177–178). Kolocotroni's reading of Brecht with Benjamin and vice versa, reveals how, as Joanna Hodge puts it, "the notions of ruination, destruction and technique ... are simultaneously modal and critical" in Benjamin (2003, 223), and puts forward a crucial "counterpoint to the type of hubristic exemplarity and mimetic identification through myth envisioned by the fascist model" that Julia Hell has aptly analyzed (2010, 184–188).

As the twentieth century progresses, fragmentation and ruination become cultural forms, in which the fragment figures as a metonymy of nostalgic wholeness and a metaphor of a modernity that contemplates wholeness as irreversibly lost. In the wake of postmodernism, ruins and fragments may operate as tropes of uniqueness and multiplicity, open-endedness and incompleteness, or discontinuity and destruction. Julia Hell and Andreas Schönle's interdisciplinary collection of essays, *Ruins of Modernity*, offers such a mapping of the philosophical reflection and the political and cultural appropriations of ruins and ruination in distinct geographies from a transnational perspective. In her most recent book, *The Conquest of Ruins*, Hell examines the fascination with the ruins of Rome through the centuries, from Charles V and Napoleon to the Third Reich, and the ways in which Europeans connected empires to ruins, arguing that there is no "imperial imaginary without ruin-gazing scenarios" (2019, 3). In the British context, scholars have turned to the literature that records how artists responded to the ruins of wartime and to the aftermath of destruction. Chris Baldick in *Literature of the 1920s: Writers Among the Ruins* focuses on the "overlooked" 1920s and examines understudied British writers who experienced "the impact of the cataclysm" of World War I as "a sudden historic disconnection,

[a] disturbing discontinuity between past and present" (2012, 7). In a similar vein, Leo Mellor, in *Reading the Ruins: Modernism, Bombsites and British Culture*, takes as his point of departure the presence of ruins and fragments in much British literature of the 1920s and 1930s which, as the individual chapters demonstrate, has been "hauntingly proleptic" (2011, 5). Mellor's contention that "the British bombsite—as imagined in the years before the Second World War—was a complex place" that "was delineated … as a zone from which forces would emerge to destroy society—but as a space also ripe for hope of redemption and rebuilding" (12) is strikingly prescient of cultural discourses and literary responses to the real and epistemological ruins of World War II and of the nuclear age in its wake.

Unlike the aforementioned books as well as other examinations of ruins by Robert Harbison (2015), Francesco Orlando (2008), Robert Ginsberg (2004) and Christopher Woodward (2001), *Ruins in the Literary and Cultural Imagination* concentrates on the dialectics of destruction and recovery through original studies of predominantly literary texts from the Victorian period to the present day, thus drawing out the historical and affective power of textual representations and evocations of ruins. Organized according to a progressive reading strategy, and transatlantic in scope, the book begins from the era of industrial modernity, and moves onto the significance of ruins in the twentieth century, against the backdrop of conflict, waste and destruction; it concludes with current debates on physical and human ruins, touching on issues such as the refugee crisis that take the ruin beyond the text. The volume's contributors bring the ruin into the present through sustained reflection on its diverse legacies and conceptual resources.

In the nineteenth century, which is the focus of the first part of the book, ruins were antithetical to the modern obsession with progress and newness. Articulating the decay of former glory or defeat, ruins were often the unwanted material remainders of a regressive ideology that was hardly compatible with the world of science and technology that the Victorians actively developed. As can be seen in Chapters 3 and 7, large cities, such as London and New York, were resistant to ruins which scarcely survived the modernizing architecture aimed at planned urban growth and well-designed spatial organization. Ruins, old and new, threatened the discourse of progress and were often either ignored or wiped out to make room for buildings more conducive to commerce and business or for modern infrastructure such as railway lines and stations.

In Dickens's London, the ruins of old houses become homes for his pitiable slum-dwellers who live in urban squalor. For Dickens, such ruinous abodes could not but nurture revolutionary impulses in the poor, who would then, as if by a chain reaction, cause more ruin and degradation. The fictional area of "Tom-all-Alone's" in *Bleak House* (1996), physically located close to the Chancery, with the spontaneous collapses of its deteriorating houses, stands for menace and destruction at the very heart of the city; it "shall work its retribution through every order of society up to the proudest of the proud and to the highest of the high. Verily, what with tainting, plundering, and spoiling, Tom has his revenge" (710).

In New York, as Henry James noted in *The American Scene*, the city constantly purges itself of anything old and ruinous; old buildings are replaced by new ones, while even the new ones are under constant threat of demolition at the first sign of decay: "I build you up but to tear you down," is the motto of the perpetually new city with its fast pace of construction and destruction (James 1994, 86). Dora Tsimpouki in Chapter 7 examines how cultural and literary discourses capitalized on metaphors of creative destruction at the turn of the twentieth century against the backdrop of the urbanscape of New York City. Even though the creation of ruins was fervently anticipated in the wake of revolutionary change—and this feeling of expectancy was often entwined with a critique of industrial capitalism as Michael Hollington demonstrates in Chapter 3—the ruin was feared for it was "perceived as a threat to the Progressive era's project of modernization." Dickens and Henry James, as Hollington and Tsimpouki show, criticize harshly what Hollington terms "the transience of all human endeavour"; but in the case of modern buildings, their ephemerality is the result not only of time but also of a new mentality which favours haste, progress and novelty.

As the traces of the past were gradually replaced by a new architectural and social order, what Raymond Williams has so aptly called "a determining system" (Williams 1975, 154), the Victorian literary imagination was less concerned with material or architectural ruins and more with ruined reputations, fortunes and prospects. From Dickens to Hardy, ruined lives are juxtaposed with ruined buildings and monuments that become allegories of the human condition, so attracted but also overwhelmed and wrecked by progress and modernity. The haunting repetition of "The house is a ruin, and the rats fly from it" (Dickens 1969, 786), in one of the closing chapters of Dickens's *Dombey and Son*, aptly conflates the human with the material, the psychological ruin of Dombey with the decay and deterioration of his house and the collapse of his business. As Hollington observes, in his fascination with ruins, Dickens confuses the animate with the inanimate, as the anthropomorphic ruins acquire a levelling will and power of their own. Rather than evoking former success as enduring monuments, Victorian ruins come to represent not the relentless passage of time but the unredeeming forces of industry and urbanization which lead to human failures.

In the Victorian period, the metaphor of ruin was also commonly used to suggest the fallen state of a woman who had given into her sexual impulses and desires. However, authors from Dickens onwards used the trope of the ruin more critically to satirize or challenge the facile equation between ruin and female transgression. Female figures are thus placed against the ruins of prehistoric or classical ages which come to signify, by antithesis and correlation, the psychological condition of modernity: loneliness, alienation, fragility and fragmentation. Creating a dialectic between past and present, by which the historical becomes personal as Chryssa Marinou argues in Chapter 5, ruins for nineteenth-century women denote personal anxieties about ruined marriages or lives. For Hollington and Marinou, little Dorritt and Isabel Archer, respectively, among the Roman ruins, are able to contemplate two superimposed images of the past and the present which enable them to explore their own personal trajectories. So does Dorothea, in George Eliot's *Middlemarch*, who as a young bride sees her own "personal lot," her dejection, projected on the grandest of Roman ruins, which, like a magic lantern show, play "the oppressive masquerade of ages" that spreads "like a disease of the retina" (Eliot 1994, 193, 194). In such cases, conjured by the classical ruins that satiate the urban landscape and beyond, domineering institutions and restrictive ideologies survive and are perpetuated. At the same time, as Julia Hell suggestively argues, "[r]endering the Roman past newly visible, this specific kind of spatiotemporal imaginary produced a new-Roman time-space, a kind of shadowy twilight zone in which the world of imperial Rome is brought into close proximity to the imperial present" (2019, 20). Eliot emphasizes Dorothea's need to drive out to the Roman Campagna in order to avoid the imperial signification of ruins. Similarly, Hardy, for Claire Potter in Chapter 4, constructs Tess as a fragment that defies the wholeness suggested by the ruins; she goes beyond the ruinous context of Stonehenge which stands for centuries-old boundaries and confines. Through their subversive use of ruins, writers from Dickens to James unsettle the narrative tendency of framing women within such restrictive settings.

In this sense, the nineteenth century saw in the figure of the ruins the conflation of the public and the private. As Svetlana Boym argues, "In ruins, monuments become mortal. National and ideological symbols acquire a fragile body and a human scale" (2010, 80). Despite the growth of the tourist industry that promoted ruin-gazing by inviting the viewer to revisit the remnants of a collective past, authors emphasized the more personal appropriation of ruins, where the imaginative reconstruction of their missing parts became a means of reconfiguring the private present. Thus, the meaning of ruins becomes subjective and uncontrollable, and the institutions that they once symbolized are challenged by the individual will and imagination. Emphasizing a transient sense of self, which comes into being through their juxtaposition with the ruins, the fictional women of our chapters represent the modern, fragmentary consciousness that, in the words of Virginia Woolf, encompasses "the spasmodic, the obscure, the fragmentary, the failure" (1924, 24). Ruins, with their semantic instability, enable such a modern view of self which is derived from unassembled fragmentariness. In Daphne Du Maurier's *Rebecca*, as Sheila Teahan writes in Chapter 6, the ruins of a house, an allegory of a broken marriage, also represent this fragmentariness of the female self that returns as a spectral presence to challenge the male protagonist's experience of wholeness. The ruinous house, therefore, fills up with the fragmentary paratexts of Rebecca and *Rebecca* the novel, which multiply and stimulate an involuntary memory forcefully and subversively linking the private with the public. Thus, these female characters contest their political and cultural abjection.

In fusing the animate with the inanimate ruins, nineteenth-century authors, therefore, resisted the aestheticization of ruins that threatened to undermine the horrific human history that they often represented. As Schönle argues in an article on Tolstoy, in a political sense, ruins could become "a site invested with the power to call for resistance to a stifling contemporary political order" (2010, 98). Dickens, in Chapter 3, does grasp this political sense by projecting himself in the past and its bloody histories visible in the ruins, combining the "pleasure of ruins" with a relief that they are indeed ruins, as Hollington argues; the old order and tyrannies that they symbolize have collapsed, and the ruins become a warning against the inertia that might lead to a new restrictive political order. In Hardy's *Tess of the D' Urbervilles*, the eponymous heroine, for Potter, resists the moral and political stagnation of Stonehenge, paradoxically, through sleep which enables her to dream of a mental freedom, denied in her conscious, embodied life. And Isabel Archer, for Marinou, while drawn to the petrified, static ruins, animates them with her own epiphanic flash of self-knowledge. Thus, the dialectic between stasis and mental movement emphasizes Isabel's conjunction with as well as defiance of the wider social and historical order. In all the Victorian novels examined, the authors thereby use the ruins as a means of linking an age of tyranny with the characters' mental and emotional loss of innocence. With their emphasis on the moral and social incoherence that ensues the contemplation of ruins, these authors, Du Maurier included, as Teahan argues, offer fragmentation as an antidote to the condition of ruination; fragmentation becomes the means by which the past may endure but in a revised, modern way, not merely as a triumph of life over death, but more poignantly as the triumph of the subjective consciousness and story over the totalizing force of history. The nineteenth century and early twentieth century therefore saw the ruins as both a return and a departure, an enshrined heritage as well as an open arena of unpredictable impulses and desires.

The second part of the volume focuses on the ways in which the ruin becomes a metaphor and a reality of destruction in history, in the catastrophes of the two World Wars, the Holocaust, and the Cold War, just as it may be a point of departure for a reflection on the process of writing. Twentieth-century poststructuralist thought raises issues that bear on the fundamental impossibility of communicating the real through human, symbolic language. Postmodernism emphasizes the sublime unrepresentability of such manmade disasters as the Holocaust and the nuclear destruction of Hiroshima and Nagasaki—the two major events that Jean-François Lyotard calls unpresentable in history. Therefore, their memory can only be preserved through silence—negative presentation—because no words or human articulations are able to do justice to them.

One cannot afford not to think of the unpresentable in terms of a "language scepticism" that poisons, yet fascinates major twentieth-century figures such as Beckett and Pinter, as David Tucker demonstrates in Chapter 8. Unlike postmodern thinkers like Lyotard, who phenomenologically look to the notion of the unpresentable for resurrecting the idea of the inaccessible *other* (which is always elusive), Beckett dismisses the possibility of there being any meaning or *other* at all. For Lyotard, ruins are indications of something far too remote, but for Beckett they are self-reflexive, that is, they speak to themselves almost in an aesthetic, self-centred mode, while continually reproducing themselves in a chaotic, erratic way. Tucker shows that Beckett does not theorize but rather *performs* ruination. He communicates that he has nothing to communicate by building ruins upon ruins that make up for the lack of an entire, self-sustaining edifice of meaning. Along similar lines, communication in Pinter's world is made up of a formless body of pointless information meant to create the appearance of a real communication between two persons. In this sense, Pinter's idea of communication without communication can approximate the Lyotardian and Derridian conceptions of *difference* in linguistic communication—an unbridgeable gap between two people, which creates a fundamental non-communicability.

Unlike Fuseli's artist who was incapacitated by the sight of "antique ruins," North American poets and writers in post-World War II period find themselves debilitated by the sightings and the experiencing of the ruins of an all too recent history. In Chapter 9, Giorgos Giannakopoulos examines the workings of trauma "out of the ruins of Dresden" in Kurt Vonnegut's *Slaughterhouse Five*. As the ruins of war give way to a ruined psyche, Giannakopoulos aptly maps the topography of psychic destruction and ruin in Vonnegut's novel in dialogue with Catherine Malabou's destructive plasticity. Responding to the aftermath of World War II, Robert Lowell and Anne Sexton bear the trauma of a nuclear age in which as Reiko Tachibana puts it, the "ruins of Hiroshima and Nagasaki" "displayed the feasibility of annihilating humankind" (2009, 137), while Leonard Cohen, as Jeffrey Spear demonstrates in Chapter 11, navigates the post-war era from the 1960s onwards by bearing the trauma of a Holocaust that he has neither witnessed nor experienced. Unlike Vonnegut, Lowell, Sexton and Cohen are survivors of destructions from which they have been spared, as well as of destructions that have not yet taken place. Therefore, they experience and also ponder on ruins of a different order that are those of a fractured psyche.

In a special issue of *Cultural Anthropology* on *Imperial Debris*, Joseph Masco asks whether "any nation-state invested as profoundly in ruins as Cold War America?" (2008, 361). The nuclear ruin-mongering that so pervasively defined Cold War America is a dark irony vis-à-vis the ruinophobia that Tsimpouki examined in Chapter 7. As Masco ironically states, "it took American ingenuity to transform ruination into a form of nation-building" (2008, 361). "Nuclear fear," according to Masco, "colonized" everyday life and existence. "Postnuclear ruins" became "a new American frontier" (367), and because of the fact that the fantasy became so ingrained, Masco argues, "the September 11, 2001, attacks on New York and Washington, D. C., felt strangely familiar to many U.S. citizens" (388). In resonance with Masco's analysis, Adam Beardsworth in Chapter 10 shows how nuclear fear was played out in the sphere of the poets' own intimacy and examines how Lowell and Sexton "probe the epistemological uncertainty generated by the atomic ruin." The two poets dramatize their own aesthetic resistance through a poetry that displays how they internalize and confront the nuclear fear through their affect, while positing their suffering as a form of resistance. Against the backdrop of World War II, Leonard Cohen's lyrics, as Spear argues, also dramatize a fractured world and a fractured psyche. His songs often perform his own injunction—"steer your way through the ruins"—and reflect the trauma of the Holocaust that affected both his life and the fragmentary quality of his lyrics.

In the post-war period, the ruin as a metaphor of history also appears "as an aesthetic trope that condenses images and ideas from different genres, as an invitation to thought and as the site of a sublime (though also sometimes comical or even kitsch) haunting," as Brian Dillon notes in his introductory remarks to the anthology of writings on ruins (2011, 11). Such a "comical haunting" is at work in Mel Brooks's *The Producers*, where, as Christina Dokou argues in Chapter 12, historical atrocity and human ruination are represented in the form of entertaining simulacra which end up ridiculing the very concept of ruin and ultimately obliterating the ruin as well as the memory of atrocity that is connected with it. In Mel Brooks's comedy, historical trauma is repackaged as a hilarious product to be innocuously consumed by complacent viewers. Dokou further qualifies the inherent aestheticism of treating ruins in American culture by alluding to the tendency to ridicule past atrocities in a decontextualized fashion—presenting, for instance, Nazis as grotesque and mentally challenged persons—as symptomatic of uncritical historical revisionism and a celebration of surface over depth. In this lens, collapsing together ruins from distinct historico-political periods, thus creating a spectacular postmodern pastiche, implies that not a single ruin seems important as a synecdoche of the real but rather as a fascinating fragment to be admired and enjoyed in itself.

If Dokou's point is that a sheer aesthetic appreciation of decontextualized fragments of the Nazi horror engenders political apathy and leads to unhistorical revisionism and the blurring of memory, in a similar vein, Angeliki Tseti, in Chapter 13, questions the very legitimacy of recognizable, symbolic sites bearing witness to Nazi atrocities. The underlying poststructuralist assumption here is that the presence of scattered Nazi ruins would only tell "half the story," so to speak, leading eventually to the blurring or even erasure of memory concerning the Holocaust. Tseti reflects on a dialectics of remembering of a different kind in the wake of an ineffable destruction that was engineered so as to obliterate its ruins. By examining how in Daniel Mendelsohn's *Lost: A Search for Six of Six Million* and Claude Lanzmann's *Shoah* the memory of atrocity is paradoxically preserved through the absence of mnemonic sites, she shows that the invisibility of ruins in historical sites further entrenches the feeling of horror and, in the final analysis, the memory of atrocity through the activation of imagination rather than grand or "official" narratives of commemoration. Arguably, the disappearance of tangible ruins of mass murder opens up non-symbolic spaces of commemoration—what Tseti calls the "non-sites of memory"—that constitute instances of negative presentation.

In the third part of the volume, the chapters go beyond the boundaries of Anglo-American literatures, reflecting on the evolving idea of the ruin in the continental philosophical tradition. In Chapter 14, Kolocotroni shows how Benjamin and Brecht conceive the ruin as a form of refuge and radical edification against "dark times" within a period of displacement and personal and political catastrophe, while in Chapter 15, Carl Lavery and Simon Murray engage in a dialogue on what it means "to think like a ruin" in present times. Referring to both concrete and artistic ruins, from Gibellina in Sicily to St. Peter's Seminary near Glasgow, and from Andy Goldsworthy's *Stonehouse Bonnington* to Kris Verdonck's *Conversations at the End of the World*, Lavery and Murray ruminate on the materiality of the ruin, its crumbling and entropic decay and the human agency which produces ruination; they view ruins as "possessing a possibility for forms of resistance, ways of becoming other, of abandoning the present, remaining true to their eventual charge." Thinking like a ruin opens up ways of revisiting the "state of ruin," leading us back to Athens, which figures again in Chapter 16 by Apostolos Lampropoulos. Here, Derrida's definition of "unconditional hospitality" is rethought in terms of fragments of hospitality in a landscape of physical and human ruins evoked by the recent refugee crisis in Athens. Focusing on examples relating to modern Athens, this chapter places emphasis on the fact that, if ruins maintain elective affinities with the renegotiation of the past, they also spell out the conditions of survival of people, spaces and objects. As Lampropoulos implies, today's artistic responses to the recent refugee crisis attempt to bring to the foreground "authentic" remnants of a shattered life: clothes, shoes and lifejackets. However, can those "authentic" ruins truly tell the story of people's real displacement and forced immigration? In essence, Lampropoulos would agree that neither satirical appropriations of tragedy (Dokou, Chapter 12) nor symbolic spaces of commemoration (Tseti, Chapter 13) could safely lay claim to an authenticity or historical reality that is no longer there.

Also situated in the Greek landscape, Athens and Epidaurus, the Afterword by Jyotsna Singh (Chapter 17) concludes the volume by offering a reflective response on ruins and fragments in relation to the question of memory and hospitality. Focusing on the emotions kindled by the sight of ancient monuments, such as the Parthenon and Epidaurus, Singh wonders if these scattered stones may lead us to an understanding of life through a connection with the dead that transcends time and otherness. By beginning (Chapter 2) and ending in Greece, the volume finally links the ruin with time and contingency; in *Time in Ruins*, Marc Augé argues that the contemplation of ruins is in fact the experience of pure time, since ruins allow us to grasp the notion of time beyond the one recorded in history books, "pure time, not dated." For Augé, only art may sometimes find this "lost time" within our contemporary "world of images, simulacra and reconstitutions," "a violent word in which rubble does not have the time to become ruins" (2003, 10).

The pure temporality of past ruins is thus opposed to the "ruins of the present," created by humanity's perennial destructive impulses and facilitated by technology, as Augé has pointed out. Produced by post-industrial capitalism, technological progress and urbanization, contemporary ruins, like those filmed by Cao Fei in Beijing, are not about loss but about waste, complicating the notion of the ruin. Ultimately, there arises a sense of ruin as "not only an endpoint," but also as a wellspring of inspiration through which humanity's condition may be reconceptualized. The literary and philosophical shift, at the end of the twentieth century, from postmodern unpresentability (what we call "negative presentation" or the "anti-aesthetic") to a rethinking of the aesthetic and the image potentially gives us the opportunity to revisit the "ruin" both as a politico/historical and an aesthetic signifier, capable of bearing witness to history and memory, not despite but *because of* its aesthetic powerfulness.

Positing "authentic ruins" as "products of modernity," Huyssen proclaims that "the age of the authentic ruin is over. We can write its genealogy, but we can't resurrect it. We live in the age of preservation, restoration, and authentic remakes, all of which cancel out the idea of the authentic ruin" (2010, 70). Huyssen is addressing pressing questions raised by the ruins that have been generated in recent historical catastrophes. His question as to "where do 9/11 and the bombing of Baghdad and Falluja figure in" the long history of the "imaginary of ruins" (69), can be related to Dillon's notion that ruination was and still is integral to our history, and all the more so since our sense of history has become increasingly globalized. But if we have always lived in a time of ruination, is the ruin ultimately tautological or can it be reenvisioned as a redemptive trope? If the latter is the case, then it is imperative to think of our relation to the ruin as a condition of a "critical intimacy," as Lampropoulos proposes. A reflexive perspective on our in/ability to comprehend and empathize with ruination also raises the question, suggested by Lavery and Murray, of whether "the ruin [can] ... disclose alternative possibilities for living differently on the earth." If such possibilities inhere in ruination, then the ruin is "a fragment with a future; it will live on after us despite the fact that it reminds us of a lost wholeness of perfection" (Dillon 2011, 11).

Whether literal or metaphorical, ruins bear dualities that are continually recuperated and revisited as they speak of creation and destruction, recovery and silence, memory and forgetting, visible and invisible vulnerabilities. At a time when conflicting notions about shared pasts may be seen as tokens of a shared despair, and the tension between the timeless and the crumbling is becoming all the more manifest, thinking rigorously about ruins in the past and present is both urgent and generative of new critical resources.

References

Augé, Marc. 2003. *Le temps en ruines*. Paris: Galilé.

Baldick, Chris. 2012. *Literature of the 1920s: Writers Among the Ruins*. Edinburgh: Edinburgh University Press.

Benjamin, Walter. 1969. Theses on the Philosophy of History. In *Illuminations: Essays and Reflections*, ed. Hannah Arendt. New York: Schocken.

Benjamin, Walter. 1977. *The Origin of German Tragic Drama*, trans. John Osborne. London: NLB.

Boym, Svetlana. 2010. Ruins of the Avant-Garde: From Tatlin's Tower to Paper Architecture. In *The Ruins of Modernity*, ed. Julia Hell and Andreas Schönle, 58–85. Durham: Duke University Press.

Burke, Edmund. 1990. *A Philosophical Enquiry into the Origin of Our Ideas of the Sublime and the Beautiful*, ed. Adam Phillips. Oxford: Oxford University Press.

Byron, George Gordon, Lord. 1980. *The Complete Poetical Works*, ed. Jerome J. McGann, vol. 2: *Childe Harold's Pilgrimage*. Oxford: Oxford University Press.

Dickens, Charles. 1969. *Dombey and Son*. London: Collins.

Dickens, Charles. 1996. *Bleak House*. London: Penguin Books.

Dillon, Brian. 2005 [2006]. Fragments from a History of Ruin. *Cabinet* 20. http://www.cabinetmagazine.org/issues/20/dillon.php. Accessed 8 Apr 2017.

Dillon, Brian. 2011. Introduction: A Short History of Decay. In *Ruins Documents of Contemporary Art*, ed. Brian Dillon, 10–15. London: Whitechapel Gallery, The MIT Press.

Eliot, George. 1994. *Middlemarch*. London: Penguin Books.

Esterhammer, Angela. 2009. Translating the Elgin Marbles: Byron, Hemans, Keats. *Wordsworth Circle* 40 (1): 29–36.

Feldman, Allen. 2005. On the Actuarial Gaze. *Cultural Studies* 19 (2): 203–226.

Ginsberg, Robert. 2004. *The Aesthetics of Ruins*. Amsterdam: Rodopi.

Harbison, Robert. 2015. *Ruins and Fragments: Tales of Loss and Rediscovery*. London: Reaktion Books.

Harries, Elizabeth. 1994. *The Unfinished Manner: Essays on the Fragment in the Later Eighteenth Century*. Charlottesville and London: University Press of Virginia.

Hell, Julia. 2010. Imperial Ruin Gazers, or Why Did Scipio Weep? In *Ruins of Modernity*, ed. Julia Hell and Andreas Schönle, 169–192. Durham: Duke University Press.

Hell, Julia. 2019. *The Conquest of Ruins: The Third Reich and the Fall of Rome*. Chicago: University of Chicago Press.

Hodge, Joanna. 2003. Aesthetics and Politics: Between Adorno and Heidegger. In *The New Aestheticism*, ed. John J. Joughin and Simon Malpas, 218–236. Manchester: Manchester University Press.

Hui, Andrew. 2017. *The Poetics of Ruins in Renaissance Literature*. Oxford: Oxford University Press.

Huyssen, Andreas. 2010. Authentic Ruins: Products of Modernity. In *Ruins of Modernity*, ed. Julia Hell and Andreas Schönle, 17–28. Durham: Duke University Press.

James, Henry. 1994. *The American Scene*. New York: Penguin Books.

Keach, William. 2012. The Ruins of Empire and the Contradictions of Restoration: Barbauld, Byron, Hemans. In *Romanticism and Disaster*.

Romantic Circles Praxis Series. https://www.rc.umd.edu/praxis/disaster/ HTML/praxis.2012.keach.html. Accessed 3 Apr 2016.

Lacoue Labarthe, Philippe, and Jean-Luc Nancy. 1988. *The Literary Absolute: The Theory of Literature in German Romanticism.* New York: State University of New York.

Leask, Nigel. 2004. Byron and the Eastern Mediterranean. In *The Cambridge Companion to Byron,* ed. Drummond Bone. Cambridge: Cambridge University Press.

Macaulay, Rose. 1953. *Pleasure of Ruins.* New York: Walker and Company.

Malpas, Simon. 2003. Touching Art: Aesthetics, Fragmentation and Community. In *The New Aestheticism,* ed. John J. Joughin and Simon Malpas, 83–98. Manchester: Manchester University Press.

Masco, Joseph. 2008. "Survival Is Your Business": Engineering Ruins and Affect in Nuclear America. *Cultural Anthropology* 23 (2): 361–398.

McFarland, Thomas. 1981. *Romanticism and the Forms of Ruin: Wordsworth, Coleridge, and Modalities of Fragmentation.* Princeton: Princeton University Press.

Mellor, Leo. 2011. *Reading the Ruins: Modernism, Bombsites and British Culture.* Cambridge: Cambridge University Press.

Nochlin, Linda. 1994. *The Body in Pieces: The Fragment as a Metaphor of Modernity.* London: Thames and Hudson.

Orlando, Francesco. 2008. *Obsolete Objects in the Literary Imagination: Ruins, Relics, Rarities, Rubbish, Uninhabited Places, and Hidden Treasures.* New Haven: Yale University Press; first published in Italy in 1994.

Schönle, Andreas. 2010. Modernity as a "Destroyed Anthill": Tolstoy on History and the Aesthetics of Ruins. In *Ruins of Modernity,* ed. Julia Hell and Andreas Schönle, 89–103. Durham: Duke University Press.

Simmel, Georg. 1958. The Ruin, trans. David Kettler. *The Hudson Review* 11 (3): 379–385.

St. Clair, William. 1998. *Lord Elgin and the Marbles.* Oxford: Oxford University Press.

Tachibana, Reiko. 2009. The Japanese War. In *The Cambridge Companion to the Literature of World War II,* ed. Marina MacKay, 137–148. Cambridge: Cambridge University Press.

Thomas, Sophie. 2010. *Romanticism and Visuality.* London: Routledge.

Williams, Raymond. 1975. *The Country and the City.* New York: Oxford University Press.

Wood, Gillen d'Arcy. 2001. *The Shock of the Real: Romanticism and Visual Culture, 1760–1860.* New York: Palgrave.

Woodward, Christopher. 2001. *In Ruins.* London: Chatto & Windus.

Woolf, Virginia. 1924. *Mr. Bennett and Mrs. Brown.* London: Hogarth Press.

PART I

Allegory – Animation – Appropriation

CHAPTER 2

Amongst the Ruins of a European Gothic Phantasmagoria in Athens

Maria Vara

The Gothic has been thriving on ruins of abbeys and castles since its emergence in mid-eighteenth-century Britain as an architectural revival movement and a literary mode. Gothic ruins became an essential stage-set first of the landscape garden and later of Gothic fiction. The first Gothic novel, Horace Walpole's *The Castle of Otranto* (1764) with its castle of "long labyrinth of darkness" and rays of "moonshine, streaming through a cranny of the ruin" (Walpole 2008, 27, 30) established a taste for terror in ominous, moss-grown, crumbling settings which became a real mania at the end of the eighteenth century. This was the point in time when Gothic ruins left the page to become the actual setting of the phantasmagoria, a Gothic spectacle of optical illusion images projected by a magic lantern and popularized by Etienne Gaspar Robertson, who famously staged it in a ruinous Capuchin convent in Paris in the late 1790s. Drawing from the above, this essay sheds light on the ruins of a Capuchin monastery in the heart of Athens, which was destroyed in 1821 during the Greek Revolution, having accommodated, amongst many other visitors, Lord Byron for eight months (August 1810–April

M. Vara (✉)
Hellenic Air Force Academy, Attica, Greece

© The Author(s) 2019
E. Mitsi et al. (eds.), *Ruins in the Literary and Cultural Imagination,*
https://doi.org/10.1007/978-3-030-26905-0_2

1811), on his fashionable Grand Tour. The ruined convent of Athens, with its renowned "lantern of Diogenes," is here reintroduced as the key site of the city's Gothic phantasmagoria, whereby ghosts of residual cultural memory create intricate European kaleidoscopic patterns of history, literature and the visual arts.

AN IMAGINARY CITY

The urban network of Athens, renowned for the plethora of ancient Greek, Roman, Byzantine and Ottoman ruins, does not seem to invoke any Gothic spatialities. However, while the architectural designation of "Gothic Athens" was in the past given to Nuremberg (see Jameson 1893, 322), the Gothic, not so much as an architectural movement, or a literary mode, but as an aesthetic experience, has been inscribed on the city through a variety of texts and pictures—both real and of the imagination—which illustrate its mutability across Europe (Fig. 2.1).

Fig. 2.1 "Athene vel Minerva." In Schedel, Hartmann, *Liber Chronicarum*, 1493, fol. 27. Aikaterini Laskaridis Foundation, *Travelogues* website (http://eng.travelogues.gr/item.php?view=48193)

The first surviving images of Athens date back to the late fifteenth century and present a typical Gothic city of the imagination, with fortress-like character. The *Nuremberg Chronicle* (*Liber Chronicarum*, 1493), for example, one of the first illustrated books with views of cities, written in Latin by the physician and humanist Hartmann Schedel, includes an imaginary woodcut illustration of Athens as a medieval walled Gothic city with a cathedral, entitled "Athene vel Minerva," a plate used to illustrate many other cities, such as the ancient Greek Themiscyra, Alexandria and Pavia (Schedel 1493, fol. 27). Many similar invented views of Athens were published in Europe until the rise of the humanistic interest in classical antiquity during the Renaissance. Termed a "*Ruin-naissance*" by Andrew Hui, because "the ruin functions as a privileged cipher or a master topos that marks the rupture between the world of the humanists and the world of antiquity" (2016, 1, 2), this is the point in time when the Frenchman André Thevet, a Franciscan priest, explorer, cosmographer and writer, in his world geography entitled *Cosmographie Universelle* (1575), presented his own mental construction of Athens. Claiming that he had visited the city around 1550, Thevet describes it as a demolished place with scattered columns, an obelisk, arches and other traces of buildings once shaped like the Colosseum in Rome, but now lying in ruins (1575, bk. 18, 795–796) (Fig. 2.2).

Thevet's visit to Athens is disputed: the French archaeologist and traveller Léon de Laborde, for example, writing in 1854, attributes Thevet's knowledge of the city to "pure érudition" (1854, 49). Nevertheless, both Thevet's clearly imaginary description and the corresponding woodcut illustration that accompanies the text seem to encapsulate Petrarch's Renaissance humanist utopia of "my Rome, my Athens."[1] The woodcut image does justice to Thevet's narrative of a crumbling, imaginary city: this compilation of artificial ruins of a Roman building, an obelisk and other fragments of edifices are in technique and cultural connotations syncretistic, foreshadowing, in a sense, the eighteenth-century European fashion of fabricating ruins.

[1] The phrase appears in a letter written in 1353 by Petrarch during his stay in Vaucluse, where he claims to have established his utopian retreat (1966, 132).

Fig. 2.2 "The antiquities of Athens." In Thevet, André, *Cosmographie Universelle*, 1575, p. 795. Woodcut (13.5 × 15 cm). Collection of the Museum of the City of Athens-Vouros Eutaxias Foundation

CREATE YOUR OWN RUIN

In fact, when Thevet created his own ruin the city of Athens was under Ottoman occupation, hardly ever visited by foreign travellers, so all surviving depictions and descriptions from that epoch of the city lying in ruins are imaginary. At the same time in Britain, ruins had already become part of the landscape: the dissolution of over 800 Gothic monasteries—as alleged sites of Papal authority—under Henry VIII from 1535 to 1539 throughout the country during the Protestant reformation, had left behind ruins of Gothic architectural structures, such as mouldering vaulted arches, shattered flying buttresses and crypts, evocative architectural remains which gradually attracted visitors who contemplated on the emotional power of their mossy, dismembered skeletons. With many estates encompassing such suggestive remnants of crumbling monasteries, in the sixteenth and early seventeenth centuries ruins were reclaimed in garden and landscape architecture, either in their authentic form or in the form of fabricated dilapidation: gardens were frequently decorated with artificial fragments of building or "follies" (named so due to their high cost and lack of utility), made of plaster or stone, mostly in Gothic and ancient Greco-Roman style. By the late seventeenth century, the Gothic had become the main language of the ruin and the landscape garden had become a stage-set: no great estate was complete without its sham ruins, while garden designers of the time spread the idea to "create your own ruin" (Roth et al. 1997, 5).

The vogue of the folly contributed to the emergence of the so-called Gothic Revival in the final decades of the eighteenth century, concurrent with the emergence of the Gothic in literature. Horace Walpole converted a small, ordinary, seventeenth-century house into his Gothic fantasy Strawberry Hill House (constructed in various stages between 1749 and 1776), at Twickenham, London, which soon became a tourist attraction. "Replete with disproportionate towers, absurd plaster battlements, cloistered interiors and a plethora of pointed arches," Frederick S. Frank explains, "the Strawberry Hill project represented the first fulfilment of the Gothic imagination in artificial stone a decade well in advance of the composition of the novel" (2003, 12). In *The Castle of Otranto* (1764), when the homonymous castle self-destructs at the end, the power of the first Gothic ruin is introduced, amongst other spectacular forces, with its debris haunting the Gothic imagination and establishing a taste for terror in ominous settings of ruined abbeys, half-demolished castles and tombs ever since. Thus, Gothic ruins became an essential component of the novels written during the late eighteenth and early nineteenth centuries, their sway epitomized by Lucy, a character in Eliza Parsons's 1794 homonymous Gothic novel, who declares: "I dote on ruins, there is something sublime and awful in the sight of decayed grandeur, and large edifices tumbling to pieces" (1794, 233). At the turn of the century, the ruin-mania in Gothic fiction is evident in the flood of titles like *The Ruins of Avondale Priory* (1796, by Isabella Kelly), *Montrose, or the Gothic Ruin: A Novel* (1799, anonymous) or *The Ruins of Tivoli* (1804, by Francis Clifford), which provide a helpful shorthand language for the nature of the Gothic world at the time.

RUINS ESCAPING THE PAGE

The effect produced by the crumbling edifices of the stage-set design in landscape gardens must have been dramatic. Walpole fashioned a similar theatrical experience for the visitors of Strawberry Hill, which, according to Marion Harney, "is the first purpose-built antiquarian 'museum' interior, a sequence of theatrical spaces that played with scale, color and atmosphere, specifically designed to generate surprise and wonder in order to stimulate the imagination" (2016, 4). Walpole's Gothic Revival structure that juxtaposed "Classical artefacts with Gothic" (Harney 2016, 250) gradually became so popular that he had to issue rules, tours and free advance tickets (Warburton 1852, 548) for those who wished to experience the theatricality of his fictional castle and collection of oddities, including a Roman sarcophagus which contained the bones of a child (Katz 2007, 47). Actually, Walpole described his own collection as a "Gothic Vatican of Greece and Rome," borrowing the expression from *The Dunciad* by Alexander Pope (1784, iii).

Walpole's dramatic contribution to the Gothic paved the way for the theatricality of the phantasmagoria, the late 1790s Gothic entertainment of optical illusions, set, amongst other spaces, in the chill of a ruined Gothic convent and produced by a 1660s invention—probably by the Dutch scientist Christian Huygens (Vermeir 2005, 128)—the so-called magic lantern, an optical box with the ability to project frightening images (skeletons, spectres, phantoms, ghosts, etc.) painted on transparent slides. Coined from the ancient Greek words φάντασμα [phantasma] (apparition, reflection, image) and αγορά [agora] (assembly), the word "phantasmagoria" (or its French equivalent "fantasmagorie") at the time suggested a "gathering of ghosts."[2] The Paris-based Belgian scientist and showman Étienne-Gaspard Robert, known by the stage-name Robertson, presented himself as the inventor of the "Fantasmagorie," in the two volumes of his *Mémoires récréatifs, scientifiques et anecdotiques d'un physicien-aéronaute* (1831–1833). In reality, as Mannoni explains, "he did no more than borrow and exploit a method used by several

---

[2] Laurent Mannoni proposes an alternative etymology to "agora," that of "agoreuo," which means "I make a public speech," "an etymology which suggests a dialogue between the audience and the ghost called up by the magic lantern" (2000, 136). In fact, "agora" in ancient Greek denotes both "gathering" and "speaking in public," among other meanings.

Fig. 2.3 Frontispiece in Robertson's *Mémoires*, vol. 1, 1831, depicting his phantasmagoria show. Library of Congress (https://www.loc.gov/resource/rbc0001.2009houdini06148/)

others well before him, although he certainly did so with a great deal of skill" (2000, 137). By the turn of the century, due to Robertson, the phantasmagoria had become a fully-fledged multimedia Gothic spectacle in Paris soon to be exported to London, many other European cities, Russia and eventually America by travelling entertainers (Fig. 2.3).

Robertson famously staged his first Gothic horror show in January 1798 in post-revolutionary Paris in the aftermath of Terror, using a variety of projection devices, scientific techniques and a series of magic lantern glass slides to animate a repertoire of real horrors, connected to figures linked with historical events (Voltaire, Danton, Robespierre) and fictional horrors, plucked from mythology or the popular Gothic novels of the time—like "The Bleeding Nun" character from Matthew Lewis's *The Monk* (1796). Most notably, a year later, Robertson also appropriated the key setting of the Gothic novel of the time, situating his phantasmagoria within the grounds of a ruined 1688 Capuchin monastery (the Couvent des Capucines) near Place Vendôme, in Paris.

In order to enter the convent, one had to walk over broken tombstones piled up by the hundreds on the steps of the convent's courtyard, which, according to Robertson, increased the impression that the phantasmagoria apparitions "seemed to come out, so to speak, from real sepulchres, and wished to flutter around the mortal remains which they had animated and delivered to desecration" (1831, 276; my translation). Due to the gloomy atmosphere of the location, the mood of terror had already been established before the actual performance began, which comprised strange sound effects and smoke to enhance the visual and psychological effects of the ruined architecture, while the advanced mechanics of the hidden (often mobile) magic lantern allowed the projected images to give the impression of emerging suddenly out of darkness, as they moved and changed size on the screen. These extravaganzas, which according to an 1801 review included "tombs, caverns, and infernal dungeons" and actors dressed up as "spectres, ghosts, phantoms, goblins, and banchees" (*Morning Post* 1801, 2) thrilled the audience and wound up their fear to the highest pitch, causing faints or striking out with sticks against the seemingly supernatural apparitions, as the engraving above suggests. One of Robertson's favourite illusions, described in detailed in his *Mémoires*, was the spectral appearance of the Greek cynic philosopher "Diogenes with his lantern" seemingly moving up and down the rows between the spectators and causing fright (1831, 355).

Magic Lanterns Mushrooming

Indeed, Diogenes (c. 404–323 BCE) was best known for walking through the streets of ancient Athens holding a lantern to the faces of its citizens in search of an honest person, according to Diogenes Laertius's (third century CE) famous work, consisting of the biographies of ancient Greek philosophers (1915, 231). When Robertson's ghostly Diogenes and his lantern took Paris by storm, the actual "Lantern of Diogenes" was (and still is) standing in its original site, in the heart of Athens, a few steps from the hill of the Acropolis. This is how the ancient choragic Monument of Lysicrates was popularly known at the time, due to its lantern-like, round shape.[3] Erected in 335/34 BCE by the patron (*choregos*) Lysicrates to commemorate, as was the custom, winning

---

[3] Kampouroglou informs us that before the popularization of the name "lantern of Diogenes" the monument of Lysicrates was called "lantern of Demosthenes" (1890, 277). With Greece still under Ottoman occupation, the foreigners who referred to the monument in their publications used all of the above names, often interchangeably. For example,

Fig. 2.4 Choragic Monument of Lysicrates, Athens, September 2018. Courtesy of Yiannis Mitos

first prize in dithyramb (song and dance) competitions in honour of Dionysus at an ancient Greek dramatic festival (the Great or City Dionysia) in Athens, the small circular building is the only surviving example of the many erected in the area in antiquity. Resting on a tall square podium of poros stone, with an acanthus finial on its summit—that held the "tripod," the prize won by the *choregos*—it consists of six Corinthian columns alternating with panels of marble and is decorated with a continuous frieze carved with reliefs representing episodes from the myth of Dionysus with the Tyrrhenian pirates, whom the god transformed into dolphins (Fig. 2.4).

in a letter dated 9 August 1802 to Giovanni Battista Lusieri—the artist who helped Elgin remove the Parthenon Marbles—the notorious lord writes from Smyrna: "Continue your acquisitions, and add to my obligations – the lantern of Demosthenes!!! [The monument of Lysicrates]" (Smith 1916, 228). Fortunately, his plan was never realized.

To the English architects and artists James "Athenian" Stuart and Nicholas Revett, who visited Athens in 1751 on behalf of the Society of the Dilettanti (which subsidized scientific missions for the study of ancient Greek and Roman art) with a view to creating an exact recording of the city's monuments, is due the credit of being the first to recognize the story of Dionysus and the pirates told in the monument's reliefs, in their monumental four-volume *Antiquities of Athens*. The first volume, published in 1762, contains a whole chapter on the monument, with detailed architectural drawings and exquisite illustrations of the sculptural decoration of the frieze, which have rescued its visual narrative from the wear of time. Following the meticulous measurements of the choragic monument, Stuart designed a (surviving to date) replica in the late 1760s, the so-called Dark Lantern, installed in 1771 in the park of Shugborough, Staffordshire, and started a fashion (Noszlopy and Waterhouse 2005, 105).

Actually, Robertson's spectral lantern of Diogenes was not the only one in Paris during the final year of his phantasmagoria performances at the crumbling Capuchin convent. At the park of Saint-Cloud in Paris, which now contains the ruins of the Château de Saint-Cloud, "the Lantern of Diogenes" was erected in 1803 on the summit of an observatory atop of an obelisk, its design copied from the choragic Monument of Lysicrates (Wright and Allom 1845–1847, 62–63). Frequently lit to signal the presence of Napoleon Bonaparte in the premises, the monument was destroyed during the Franco-Prussian War in 1870, but its foundations in the grass are still discernible today.[4] Similar replicas of the Lysicrates monument sprang up everywhere over the next decades (in Edinburgh, London, Berlin, Philadelphia, Sydney, etc.) with many still standing at their original places. Although rooted in the implementation of the Greek Revival idea, these lanterns are also "magical": just like the ones held by the travelling entertainers, that projected scary images in the dark, these lanterns can project on the screen of memory the visual traces of their past, staging, as we shall see, a phantasmagoria of ghostly presences and scenes from myth and literature in a visionary swirl.

---

[4] The monument owed its presence there to Count Choiseul-Gouffier, French Ambassador to the Ottoman Empire in Constantinople, from 1784 to 1791, characterized by a profound interest for ancient Greek civilization (and a passion for looting and collecting antiquities) who, during a visit to Athens, made a cast of the whole Lysicrates monument and sent it to Paris (see Mauch 1910 [1845], n.p.).

The Phantasmagoria of a Visit

Stuart and Revett's seminal first volume of *The Antiquities of Athens*—the first scientific record of ancient Greek architecture—was preceded (by four years) by the publication of the French architect David Le Roy's *Les Ruines des plus beaux monuments de la Grèce* (1758), where, according to Bruce Redford "priority is not accurate documentation but subjective evocation" (2008, 53). This is evident in its inaccurate, though atmospheric, illustrations of the classical architecture of Athens, such as the distorted depiction of the Lysicrates monument, presented for the first time within its urban surroundings but with exaggerated proportions. A year later, in 1759, a highly unfaithful to the original, heavily abridged English version of Le Roy's *Les Ruines* appeared, entitled *Ruins of Athens, with Remains and Other Valuable Antiquities in Greece,* compiled by the English publisher Robert Sayer. The publication omitted Le Roy's text about the principles of classical architecture in Greece while it combined or superimposed upon each other most of the French edition's original plates, creating imaginary relationships between real monuments. Thus, once again, in 1759, Athens turns into an imaginary city, with the Lysicrates monument, for example, situated 8 kilometres away from its urban surroundings, near the sea, at Phalerum (or Phaleron), the ancient port of Athens, as the image below testifies (Fig. 2.5).

By combining two completely unrelated plates culled from Le Roy's *Les Ruines* (1758, plate 13 and plate 17) Sayer here "creates his own ruin," a picturesque, imaginary landscape with evocative power, while providing a glimpse of the actual building that surrounded the Lysicrates monument at the time. When in 1751 Stuart and Revett and in 1755 Le Roy first encountered the monument, it did not stand alone, as, since 1669 it had been immured in the Franciscan Capuchin monastery (a rectangular building with a hipped roof built in many stages) erected there (Fig. 2.6).[5]

The monument was preserved by the Franciscan Capuchin monks as a reading-room and library (after removing one marble panel to open an entrance), according to the account of the Irish archaeologist, painter

---

[5] The Capuchin monks, who first settled in Ottoman Athens in 1658, belonged to the third family of the First Franciscan Order and got their name from the long, pointed hood of their robes, called "cappucio" in Italian (see Roussos-Milidonis 1996, 464). In 1669 the monks bought a house adjoining the Lysicrates monument, so as to expand it into a

Fig. 2.5 Imaginary depiction of the monument of Lysicrates at Phalerum, the ancient port of Athens, in Sayer, Robert, *Ruins of Athens, with Remains and Other Valuable Antiquities in Greece*, 1759. Aikaterini Laskaridis Foundation, *Travelogues* website (http://eng.travelogues.gr/item.php?view=50621)

and writer Edward Dodwell in the first volume of his travelling chronicle *A Classical and Topographical Tour Through Greece During the Years 1801, 1805 and 1806*: "[t]he upper part of this monument is hollow, and contains a space of nearly six feet diameter, which is at present the library of the superior of the convent" (1819, 290–291). Dodwell's description is accompanied by the invaluable illustration shown below, by the Italian painter Simone Pomardi, Dodwell's companion while touring in Greece, which is the only surviving depiction of the monument as a study, with a monk in front of a library full of books (Fig. 2.7).

monastery, the ownership of which also included the monument (Dalezios 1964, 8). For information on the dispute over the monument's ownership and its subsequent settlement, see Pagonis (1993, 17).

Fig. 2.6 The monument of Lysicrates immured in the Athens Franciscan Capuchin monastery, in Stuart, James and Nicholas Revett, *The Antiquities of Athens*, vol. 1, 1762, n.p. Aikaterini Laskaridis Foundation, *Travelogues* website (http://eng.travelogues.gr/item.php?view=39923)

The convent soon became a busy hostelry and an important social and cultural centre of the city. According to the Scottish traveller W. R. Wilson, who was hosted there in 1819, it had been converted into "a kind of head-quarters for British travellers," something certified by "the crowd of names of Englishmen written and cut out on the walls" (1824, 375–376). Its most famous visitor, George Gordon, Lord Byron, lived there for eight months (August 1810–April 1811) when he first arrived in Greece at the age of 21, on his Grand Tour to the Eastern Mediterranean (September 1809–April 1811), with Athens a walled city of 12,000 people under Ottoman rule. For his life in the monastery Byron reported on 20 January 1811 in a letter to his friend Francis Hodgson: "I am living in the Capuchin Convent, Hymettus before me, the Acropolis behind, the Temple of Jove to my right, the Stadium in front, the town to the left; eh, Sir, there's a situation, there's your

Fig. 2.7 "Monument of Lysicrates" in Dodwell, Edward, *A Classical and Topographical Tour Through Greece*, vol. 1, 1819, p. 289. Aikaterini Laskaridis Foundation, *Travelogues* website (http://eng.travelogues.gr/item.php?view=47032)

picturesque! nothing like that, Sir, in Lunnun, no not even the Mansion House" (Murray 1922, 29–30).

Notably, the Irish clergyman and author Robert Walsh asserted that the poet "took pleasure in passing his time in the lantern" almost daily, either studying the books that existed there, or writing letters and poetry (1836, 129).[6] Having just finished the second canto of the semi-autobiographical *Childe Harold's Pilgrimage: A Romaunt* (comprising four cantos, 1812–1818) while staying elsewhere in Athens, Byron started the long poem *The Curse of Minerva* (1812) in the convent, a fact declared

---

[6] Just before its destruction, in 1821, Walsh visited the convent and met the prior who narrated to him details about Byron's stay there.

in the poem's heading: "Athens, Capuchin Convent, March 17, 1811" (Byron 1840, 453). He also composed the "Hints from Horace" there, dated "Athens, Capuchin Convent, March 12, 1811" as well as two long prose pieces included in the notes to *Childe Harold's Pilgrimage*, entitled "Franciscan Convent, Athens, January 23, 1811" and "Athens, Franciscan Convent, March 17, 1811," the latter being the same as in *The Curse of Minerva* (Byron 1840, 437, 764, 765). This repeated emphasis on the exact place and time of composition turns each piece into an irrefutable testimony of its period, allowing us to imagine Byron in the place of the monk studying in the monument (at Pomardi's earlier illustration), as he witnesses history in the making and captures the historical moment with his pen, when, for example, in the second canto of *Child Harold's Pilgrimage* the central character and narrator evokes Athens, urging us to "[l]ook on its broken arch, its ruin'd wall" (Byron 1840, 17).

"It was at Athens" Roderick Beaton contends, "that Byron found himself for the first time face to face with the ancient world in the form of monumental ruins," where "the ancient ruins still possessed the power to dominate the present-day landscape and the modern inhabitants" (2013, 11). This very power traverses through *Child Harold's Pilgrimage* and culminates in the fourth canto, with the narrator at the Colosseum demanding his wandering soul back "to meditate amongst decay and stand, A ruin amidst ruins" (Byron 1840, 44) in one of the most famous expressions of ruin sentiment in English literature.[7] The overnight success of *Child Harold's Pilgrimage* and Byron's untimely, sudden death in 1824, after arriving in Missolonghi to contribute to the Greek War of Independence, turned the poet into "the first European cultural celebrity of the modern age" (MacCarthy 2002, x). After Byron's death the convent of the Franciscan Capuchins, according to William Brockedon's account of 1833, became "a place of pilgrimage to all those travellers in Athens who have been aroused, subdued, or charmed by his power; and even those who are too obtuse to be impressed by the master-spell, go there for fashion to feel" (1833, n.p.). But what did the cultural visitors actually find there? The convent's buildings were burned down and abandoned in 1821, during the Greek Revolution, when Pasha Omer

---

[7] See also Michael Hollington, Chapter 3, on Byron's famous line.

Vrioni invaded Athens.[8] Thus, Byron's literary pilgrims in post-revolutionary Athens saw the monument of Lysicrates surrounded by monastic ruins, as evidenced by a vast number of images of the time, where artists often "created their own ruin" as regards debris positions and dimensions. For example, in the 1841 edition of *Childe Harold's Pilgrimage* the monument is depicted in the title page amongst unrealistic ruins. Also in an illustration of the area from the 1830s cited below, which accompanies G. N. Wright's text on "the Lantern of Diogenes" (1841, 40),[9] Konstantinos Pagonis spots a number of misrepresentations in the depiction of the ruins around the monument and also observes the existence of fictional spolia, compared to what one can see in the few surviving photographs of the area from the period (1993, 134) (Fig. 2.8).

The monastery lying in ruins with the broken tombstones of the monks or the foreigners buried there (see Kampouroglou 1922, 361; Filadelfefs 1921, 88) and the scattered columns that so much inspired all kinds of artists could have also evoked in the minds of the visitors of the time the familiar setting of the phantasmagoria. After all, according to David Jones, the poet's work was well connected by that time to the visual effects of the magic lantern: in 1818 a reviewer for *The Literary Gazette* noted that in *Childe Harold's Pilgrimage* "the transitions are so quickly performed, and there is so much of the magic lantern in the manner of whisking us from Venice to Rome, from Rome to Greece, from Greece to England, and back again to Venice … that our head is absolutely bewildered by the want of connexion" (qtd. in Jones 2014, 75).

---

[8] An account by an anonymous eyewitness testifies that in July 1821 "[e]ven the church of the Catholics in the hospice of the Capuchins was burnt down, and the beautiful monument of Lysicrates (called the Lantern) damaged by the fire" ("The Siege of the Acropolis of Athens, in the Years 1821–22 by an Eye-Witness" 1826, 197). Also, the American author Parker N. Willis, while visiting Athens during in his 1833 six-month Mediterranean cruise, observed the absence of the Capuchin convent and the existence of Byron's name on the surviving Lysicrates monument: "The poet's name is written with his own hand on a marble slab of the wall" (1853, 145).

[9] The exact date of the creation of the illustration is not given in the text, but an earlier similar watercolour painting by the same Swiss painter, J. J. Wolfenberger, dated 1834, can be found in Pushkin State Museum of Fine Arts in Moscow. For its reproduction, see the Greek edition of Vladimir Davidov's two-volume travelogue published in Russian in 1839–1840 (2004, 159).

Fig. 2.8 "The Lantern of Diogenes: or, Choragic Monument of Lysicrates" in Wright, George Newenham, *The Rhine, Italy, and Greece*, 1841, p. 40. Aikaterini Laskaridis Foundation, *Travelogues* website (http://eng.travelogues.gr/item.php?view=32624)

Notably, Jones contends, "Byron himself was well aware of the widespread association of his work with lantern shows" (2014, 76): "in different journals, English and foreign" the poet declared in 1821 "I have seen myself compared, personally or poetically, in English, French, German (*as* interpreted to me), Italian and Portuguese, within these nine years, to Rousseau, Goethe, Young, Aretine, Timon of Athens, Dante, Petrarch, 'an alabaster vase, lighted up within'… to the phantasmagoria" (Moore 1831, 537). The first three languages mentioned in the amusing list above bring to mind the multilingual nature of another phantasmagoria Byron knew well: during the legendary stormy night of 16 June 1816, at Villa Diodati, on the banks of Lake Geneva in Switzerland, he read with his famous English company (the Shelleys, Polidory and Clairmont) ghost stories from a collection entitled *Fantasmagoriana*, translated from the German into French.[10] A story in the anthology (translated in the abridged English edition as "The Death's Head") describes in detail the spectacle of the phantasmagoria: "The horror of the scene must be augmented by every possible means: for instance, we must hang the room with black; the lights must be extinguished; we must fix on midnight. It will be a species of phantasmagoria dessert after supper; an unexpected spectacle" (*Tales of the Dead* 1813, 102).

Actually, when, in the emerging age of tourism, Byron's literary pilgrims were visiting the monastic ruins in Athens, by then infused with the melancholic power of *Child Harold's Pilgrimage*, poet, monument and city had already become part of the magic lantern spectacle. In the nineteenth-century catalogue of a collection of magic lantern slides, belonging to the Society of the Promotion of Hellenic Studies, we find a vast number of entries referring to Athens maps and ancient monuments, such as the "Monument of Lysicrates" ("Front Matter" 1897, liv–lviii; Welford and Sturmey 1888, 245), while slide titles such as "Lord Byron—a poet of the first rate talent but of the most seductive and dangerous principles," "Byron's Bedroom," "Statue of Byron," "Portrait of Lord Byron" were also popular in lantern shows of the time (Crompton et al. 1990, 53). The poet was endlessly reborn as a ghostly image of magic lantern projections around Europe, in spectral performances infested with the language of the Gothic and the visuality of its ruinous settings, just as the poet's own oeuvre.

GRECIAN AND GOTHIC

If, for the nineteenth-century foreign visitors, the ruinous Athenian location was a three-dimensional Gothic *mise en scène* of the Byronic phantasmagoria, what is the effect of the site on contemporary spectators, now that the ancient monument stands alone, with all traces of the Capuchin convent long removed?[11] Ruins, "still with us after six centuries of obsession," as Brian Dillon succinctly puts it (2006, 8), are even now being invented, reconstructed and recuperated everywhere. On

---

[10]The collection's full French title, inspired by Robertson's phantasmagoria, is *Fantasmagoriana; ou Recueil d'histoires d'apparitions, de spectres, de revenans, fantômes*, etc. *Traduit de l'allemand, par un Amateur* (1812). The original German stories that compile the collection derive from many different sources (see Potter 2005, 77).

[11]The last traces of the convent disappeared in 1921 (Pagonis 1993, 36).

the whole, contemporary art manifests a ceaselessly renewed interest in urban ruin appropriation: ruin photography, for example, captures the image of disintegrating industrial sites, the contemporary equivalent of the evocative view of an ancient Greek or Roman ruin. In this light, today's spectators, immersed in the cultural fascination with (and appropriation of) ruins, could "create their own ruin" of the spectral, crumbling traces of the Capuchin monastery around the Lysicrates monument in Athens. With the name "lantern of Diogenes" still lingering on, the phantoms of the past are inscribed into the present city-space, offering a Gothic perspective on the world that shapes our sense of experience. In this "haunted" site, Byronic heroes, ancient Greek gods and pirates, controversial philosophers, Capuchin monks, cultural travellers and looters from a variety of epochs, hover, flicker and flutter in an ongoing phantasmagoria of intense cultural fusion, projected by the most extraordinary magic lantern.

Unlike Byron, we cannot enter the Lysicrates monument in Athens, as the removed marble panel has long been replaced, but we can enter a Belvedere "crowned with a cast-iron model of the Temple of Lysicrates at Athens" (Melville 1910, 324), in a location outside Bath, in Britain, infused with the power of the Gothic, that would have appealed to the poet. Standing amidst an old cemetery of over five thousand burials and many dilapidated graves in Classical and Gothic style, the eerie Lansdown Tower, also known as "Beckford's Tower," has on its roof an enthralling imitation of the Lysicrates monument, thus fusing the power and drama of a Gothic landscape with a classical form, much like Walpole's own sham castle that initiated the literary genre. The 47-metres tall extraordinary Lansdown Tower, which Byron did not survive to see, was built for the wealthy, eccentric author of Gothic fiction William Beckford, in 1827, as a study retreat, housing part of his art collection and library, after the collapse of his grandiose Gothic Revival Fonthill Abbey, in Wiltshire, an architectural peculiarity—of a partly ruinous and partly perfect convent—even more extravagant than Walpole's Strawberry Hill.[12] Beckford discussed with his architect Henry Edmund Goodridge the design of the Tower and of the lantern replica—a favourite theme for folly builders at the time—having probably consulted its key Greek sourcebook, the first volume of the *Antiquities*

---

[12] For more information on the tower see *Beckford's Tower and Museum*; "Beckford's Tower with Attached Wall and Railings"; Gibbes (1835, 65).

Fig. 2.9 Lantern of Lansdown Tower (Beckford's Tower), Bath (Courtesy of Tom Burrows. Tom Burrows Media/Beckford's Tower & Museum, Bath)

of Athens by Stuart and Revett, included in his vast collection of books, along two copies of Byron's satirical poem *English Bards and Scotch Reviewers* (1809) (Fig. 2.9).[13]

It is common knowledge that Beckford's orientalist Gothic fantasy *Vathek* (originally written in French in 1782, published in English in 1786 and in French in 1787), with the homonymous licentious caliph as its main character, influenced—the younger by 28 years—Byron heavily in the creation of *The Giaour* (1813), a poem replete with Gothic staples which is set in Greece in the 1770s. Thus, Byron might have liked to know that he had also shared with Beckford a similar aesthetic experience of a classical form that has become a popular tourist attraction. Contemporary visitors of Lansdown Tower—Beckford's own literary pilgrims—thrilled by the shadowy ruins of Fonthill Abbey, the fictional grandeur of caliph Vathek's immense observation tower, and the real,

[13] See *The Valuable Library of Books in Fonthill Abbey* (1823, 86, 356). Beckford's library was also very up to date with new books on classical architecture, as revealed by the existence of a copy of *An Examination of Grecian Architecture* by J. Gwilt, published in 1825, which contains a drawing of the Lysicrates monument and cites Stuart and Revett's book as a source. See Sotheby, Wilkinson, and Hodge, *Hamilton Palace Libraries sale of Beckford Library*.

gloomy surrounding cemetery that contains Beckford's own massive sarcophagus, share a spectacular experience chiefly in the language of the Gothic. Along this shadow play around the lantern at "Beckford's Tower," the lanterns in Shugborough, London, Liverpool, Edinburgh, Berlin, Philadelphia, Sydney and many other places, keep projecting a perpetual phantasmagoria of optical illusions first seen in Athens, amongst the ruins of its Capuchin convent, long-lost but endlessly recovered in the spectral patterns of history, literature and the visual arts.

References

Beaton, Roderick. 2013. *Byron's War: Romantic Rebellion, Greek Revolution.* Cambridge: Cambridge University Press.

Beckford's Tower and Museum. http://beckfordstower.org.uk/. Accessed 19 Aug 2018.

Beckford's Tower with Attached Wall and Railings. *Historic England.* https://historicengland.org.uk/listing/the-list/list-entry/1394133. Accessed 25 Aug 2018.

Brockedon, William. 1833. Franciscan Convent, Athens. In *Finden's Illustrations of the Life and Works of Lord Byron*, vol. 1. London: John Murray.

Byron, George Gordon, Lord. 1840. *The Works of Lord Byron: Complete in One Volume.* London: John Murray.

Crompton, Dennis, David Henry, and Stephen Herbert (eds.). 1990. A Magic Lantern Entertainment by Timothy Toddle. In *Magic Images: The Art of Hand-Painted and Photographic Lantern Slides*, 47–53. London: The Magic Lantern Society of Great Britain.

Dalezios, Eugenios. 1964. *Ereunai peri ton Latinikon Ekklision kai ton Monon ton Athinon epi Tourkokratias* [Research on the Latin Churches and Convents of Athens During the Ottoman Occupation]. Athens.

Davidov, Vladimir. 2004. *Taksidiotikes simiosis apo ta Ionia nisia, tin Ellada, ti Mikra Asia kai tin Tourkia sta 1835* [Travelling Notes from the Ionian Islands, Greece, Asia Minor and Turkey in 1835], trans. Oleg Tsimpenko. Athens: Commercial Bank of Greece.

Dillon, Brian. 2006. Fragments from a History of Ruin. *Cabinet* 20: 1–10.

Dodwell, Edward. 1819. *A Classical and Topographical Tour Through Greece During the Years 1801, 1805 and 1806*, vol. 1. London: Rodwell and Martin.

Filadelfefs, Alexandros. 1921. Anaskafi para to Lysikration Mnimion [Excavation Around the Lysicrates Monument]. *Archaiologiki Efimeris* [Archaiological Newspaper]: 83–97.

Frank, Frederic S. 2003. Introduction. In *The Castle of Otranto and the Mysterious Mother*, ed. Frederick S. Frank, 11–34. Peterborough, ON: Broadview.

Front Matter. 1897. *The Journal of Hellenic Studies* 17: i–lxxvii.

Gibbes, George Smith. 1835. *The Historical and Local New Bath Guide*. Bath: C. Duffield.

Harney, Marion. 2016. *Place-Making for the Imagination: Horace Walpole and Strawberry Hill*. London: Routledge.

Hui, Andrew. 2016. *The Poetics of Ruins in Renaissance Literature*. New York: Fordham University Press.

Jameson, Anna. 1893. *Sketches of Art, Literature and Character*. Boston: Houghton Mifflin and Company.

Jones, David J. 2014. *Sexuality and the Gothic Magic Lantern: Desire, Eroticism and Literary Visibilities from Byron to Bram Stoker*. Basingstoke: Palgrave Macmillan.

Kampouroglou, Demetrios. 1890. *Istoria ton Atheneon, Tourkokratia: Periodos Proti 1458–1687* [History of the Athenians, Ottoman Occupation: First Period 1458–1687]. Athens: Papageorgiou.

Kampouroglou, Demetrios. 1922. *Ai Palaiai Athenai* [The Old Athens]. Athens: Vivliopoleion Georgiou I. Vasileiou.

Katz, Sarah R. 2007. *Strawberry Hill: A Landscape Study with Recommendations for Restoration*. University of Pennsylvania. http://www.conlab.org/IndividRepSH/KatzSHLandscape.pdf. Accessed 2 Sept 2018.

Laborde, Léon Emmanuel S.J. de, Marquis. 1854. *Athènes aux XVe, XVIe et XVIIe siècles, Tome Premier*. Paris: Jules Renouard.

Laertius, Diogenes. 1915. *The Lives and Opinions of Eminent Philosophers*, trans. C.D. Yonge. London: G. Bell and Sons.

Le Roy, David. 1758. *Les Ruines des plus beaux monuments de la Grèce*. Paris: H. L. Guerin & Delatour.

MacCarthy, Fiona. 2002. *Byron, Life and Legend*. London: Faber and Faber.

Mannoni, Laurent. 2000. *The Great Art of Light and Shadow: Archaeology of the Cinema*, ed. and trans. Richard Crangle. Exeter: University of Exeter Press.

Mauch, J.M. 1910 [1845]. *The Greek and Roman Orders: Architectural Reprint Edition*, ed. W.B. Olmsted, trans. E.R.A. Litzau. Washington, DC: The Reprint Co.

Morning Post. 1801. Madame Bonaparte, August 18.

Melville, Lewis. 1910. *The Life and Letters of William Beckford of Fonthill*. London: William Heinemann.

Moore, Thomas. 1831. *Letters and Journals of Lord Byron: With Notices of His Life*, vol. 2. New York: J. and J. Harper.

Murray, John (ed.). 1922. *Lord Byron's Correspondence*, vol. 1. London: John Murray.

Noszlopy, George Thomas, and Fiona Waterhouse. 2005. *Public Sculpture of Staffordshire and the Black Country, Public Sculpture of Britain*. Liverpool: Liverpool University Press.

Pagonis, Konstantinos G. 1993. *To Ktiriako Sygkrotima tis Monis ton Kapoukinon stin Athina kai e Periochi tou* [The Convent of the Capuchin Order in Athens and Its Surroundings]. Doctoral Dissertation, National Technical University of Athens. https://www.didaktorika.gr/eadd/handle/10442/2623. Accessed 12 Aug 2018.

Parsons, Eliza. 1794. *Lucy*, 3 vols., vol. 1. London: William Lane.

Petrarch. 1966. *Letters from Petrarch*, trans. Morris Bishop. Bloomington: Indiana University Press.

Potter, Franz J. 2005. *The History of Gothic Publishing, 1800–1835: Exhuming the Trade*. Basingstoke: Palgrave Macmillan.

Redford, Bruce. 2008. *Dilettanti: The Antic and the Antique in Eighteenth-Century England*. Los Angeles, CA: Getty Publications.

Robertson, E.G. 1831. *Mémoires récréatifs, scientifiques et anecdotiques d'un physicien-aéronaute*, vol. 1. Paris: Chez l'auteur.

Roth, Michael S., Claire Lyons, and Charles Merewether. 1997. *Irresistible Decay: Ruins Reclaimed*. Los Angeles: Getty Research Institute for the History of Art and the Humanities.

Roussos-Milidonis, Markos. 1996. *Franciskani Kapoukinoi. 400 chronia prosfora stous Ellines 1585–1995 (Franciscan Capuchins. 400 Years of Offer to the Greeks 1585–1995)*. Athens: Holy Community of the Capuchins of Greece.

Sayer, Robert. 1759. *Ruins of Athens, with Remains and Other Valuable Antiquities in Greece*. London: Robert Sayer.

Schedel, Hartmann. 1493. *Liber Chronicarium*. Nuremberg.

Smith, A.H. 1916. Lord Elgin and His Collection. *Journal of Hellenic Studies* 36: 163–372.

Sotheby, Wilkinson, and Hodge. 1882. *Hamilton Palace Libraries Sale of Beckford Library, in Three Portions from 30th June 1882, 1st Portion, 7th Days Sale, Lot 1789*. Bath: Beckford's Tower & Museum.

Stuart, James, and Nicholas Revett. 1762. *The Antiquities of Athens Measured and Delineated by James Stuart F.R.S. and F.S.A. and Nicholas Revett, Painters and Architects*, vol. 1. London: John Haberkorn.

Tales of the Dead Principally translated from the French. 1813. Translated by Sarah Elizabeth Brown Utterson, Mrs. London: White, Cochrane and Co.

The Siege of the Acropolis of Athens, in the Years 1821–22 by an Eye-Witness. 1826. *The London Magazine* 4: 193–208.

The Valuable Library of Books in Fonthill Abbey. A Catalogue of the Magnificent, Rare and Valuable Library (of 20,000 volumes) [...] Which Will Be Sold by Auction, by Mr. Phillips. 1823. London: Smith & Nephew (s.n.).

Thevet, André. 1575. *Cosmographie Universelle. Tome Second*. Paris: Guillaume Chaudière.

Vermeir, Koen. 2005. The Magic of the Magic Lantern (1660–1700): On Analogical Demonstration and the Visualization of the Invisible. *The British Journal for the History of Science* 38 (2): 127–159.

Walpole, Horace. 1784. *A Description of the Villa of Mr. Horace Walpole, Youngest Son of Sir Robert Walpole Earl of Oxford, at Strawberry Hill Near Twickenham, Middlesex.* Strawberry-Hill.

Walpole, Horace. 2008. *The Castle of Otranto: A Gothic Story,* ed. W.S. Lewis. Oxford: Oxford University Press.

Walsh, Robert. 1836. *A Residence at Constantinople During a Period Including the Commencement, Progress and Termination of the Greek and Turkish Revolutions,* vol. 1. London: F. Westley and A. H. Davies.

Warburton, Eliot (ed.). 1852. *Memoirs of Horace Walpole and His Contemporaries; Including Numerous Original Letters Chiefly from Strawberry Hill: In Two Volumes,* vol. 2. London: Colburn and Co.

Welford, Walter D., and Henry Sturmey (eds.). 1888. *The "Indispensable Handbook" to the Optical Lantern: A Complete Cyclopaedia on the Subject of Optical Lanterns, Slides, and Accessory Apparatus.* London: Iliffe and Son.

Willis, Parker N. 1853. *Summer Cruise in the Mediterranean on Board an American Frigate.* London: T. Bosworth.

Wilson, William Rae. 1824. *Travels in Egypt and The Holy Land,* 2nd ed. London: Printed for Longman et al.

Wright, George Newenham. 1841. *The Rhine, Italy, and Greece. In a Series of Drawings from Nature…with Historical and Legendary Descriptions by the Rev. G. N. Wright,* vol. 1. London: Fisher, Son & Co.

Wright, George Newenham, and Thomas Allom. 1845–1847. *France Illustrated: Exhibiting Its Landscape Scenery, Antiquities, Military and Ecclesiastical Architecture, & c.,* vol. 2. London: Fisher, Son & Co.

CHAPTER 3

Dickens's Animate Ruins

Michael Hollington

After a childhood in Chatham and Rochester spent amongst "the nooks of ruin where the old monks had once had their refectories and gardens" (Dickens 1998, 418), it is not surprising that from an early stage of his career Dickens's observant eye was arrested by the non-monastic ruins he saw about him in the streets of London. "Shops and their Tenants" in *Sketches by Boz* is a major exhibit of this, especially if we respond fully to its opening exclamation—"what inexhaustible food for speculation, do the streets of London afford!" (Dickens 1995, 80)—as a statement of quasi-philosophical intent. The sketch probes nineteenth-century capitalism and consumerism to uncover in its manner of functioning built-in principles of obsolescence that inevitably throw up ruined buildings, the husks of enterprises that fail outright or are unable to adapt to the never-ending process of change and upheaval that characterizes it.

Here, anticipating *Bleak House*, Boz identifies the legal system of nineteenth-century Britain as a major additional cause of these urban ruins by fastening his eye on one that "was originally a substantial, good-looking private house enough; the landlord got into difficulties, the house got into Chancery, the tenant went away, and the house went to ruin...the paint was all worn off; the windows were broken, the area

M. Hollington (✉)
University of Kent, Canterbury, UK

© The Author(s) 2019
E. Mitsi et al. (eds.), *Ruins in the Literary and Cultural Imagination*,
https://doi.org/10.1007/978-3-030-26905-0_3

was green with neglect and the overflowings of the water-butt; the butt itself was without a lid, and the street-door was the very picture of misery" (Dickens 1995, 81). Yet on his next visit Boz is surprised to find a complete transformation: the house has become a draper's shop, with gold lettering to announce the name of its proprietor "and Co." But there is in fact no "Co.", and the shop soon gets into difficulties. The signs of ruin return—"the shop became dirty, broken panes of glass remained unmended, and the stock disappeared piecemeal"—and the proprietor commits suicide, to be followed by a "fancy stationer" who survives for a while in more modest style but likewise goes under, his family sunk into poverty, his eldest daughter dying of consumption. In a third phase, the cycle of rise and fall is doubly confirmed. The small shop is divided into two yet smaller establishments, which change hands with ever-increasing speed until now "the occupiers of the shops have gradually given up room after room, until they have only reserved the little parlour for themselves." But even letting out rooms fails to stop the house's inexorable descent into ruin, for "when we last passed it, a 'dairy' was established in the area, and a party of melancholy-looking fowls were amusing themselves by running in at the front door, and out at the back one" (84).

There is no need here to chart the development of this fascination with ruins in any detail in novels like *Barnaby Rudge* or *Old Curiosity Shop*, where it is prominent, but a quick glance at the "ruinous" slum Tom-all-Alone's in *Bleak House* (a "desirable property…in Chancery, of course"—[Dickens 1977a, 198]) is essential for my purposes. Here one of the great features of Dickens's ruins is decidedly on view—that ruins often display the characteristics of humans, and humans are often like ruins. The point is established through detailed comparison: "as, on the ruined human wretch, vermin parasites appear, so these ruined shelters have bred a crowd of foul existence that crawls in and out of gaps in walls and boards" (Dickens 1977a, 197); that is to say, the building is subject to putrefaction, as if it were a rotting human corpse.

Nonetheless, I provide here a few further examples of what is no more than a specific instance of a broader principle in Dickens: the wholesale deliberate confusion of the animate and the inanimate. In "The City of the Absent," for instance, one of the papers included in *The Uncommercial Traveller* of 1860, itself clearly linked to *Bleak House*, there are anthropomorphic chimneys gazing down upon pestilential graveyards in urban slum areas, illustrating the "contagion of slow ruin" that infects such places: "old crazy stacks of chimneys seem to look down as they overhang, dubiously calculating how far they will have to fall" (Dickens 2015, 228). And in several other novels, the same mysterious "crash and cloud of dust" occurs, as at Tom-all-Alone's, to announce the fall of one of the ruins, as if it were possessed of secret judgemental volition. This occurs metaphorically at the end of *Nicholas Nickleby*, where Ralph realizes that the game is up—"his plot with Gride overset at the very moment of triumph, his after-schemes discovered, himself in danger, the object of his persecution and Nicholas's love, his own wretched boy; everything crumbled and fallen upon him, and he beaten down beneath the ruins and grovelling in the dust" (Dickens 1990, 804)—and hangs himself, and literally at a similar strategic point at the end of *Little Dorrit*, in the fall of the House of Clennam, where the chimneys finally get to play their part in a moment of apocalypse: "the great pile of chimneys, which was then alone left standing like a tower in a whirlwind, rocked, broke, and hailed itself down upon the heap of ruin, as if every tumbling fragment were intent on burying the crushed wretch deeper" (Dickens 1999, 776). The principle of Dickens's favourite childhood reading, *The Terrific Register*,[1] that crime will always come out because of a lurking urge to expose and revenge that lies in the surroundings where it takes place, is on view here and elsewhere in his work.

But what I particularly want to do here is to link these frequent references to ruined or ruinous contemporary urban constructions, the product of a feverish preoccupation with progress and change driven by money-greed (continuing right up until the last completed novel, *Our Mutual Friend*, with its satire of unplanned urban growth, exemplified in "another unfinished street already in ruins" [Dickens 1963, 218]), with Dickens's reactions to the classic ruins in Rome that he encountered during his year in Italy in early 1845. These are related in their turn to a tradition of writing represented most immediately in accounts of Grand Tours, but in fact stretching back to antiquity. They belong at least in part to the category of what Francesco Orlando terms "solemn-admonitory" writing about ruins (2005, 67–69 and 85–91); that is to say, they seek to draw from their contemplation a moral about the transience of all human endeavour. And, of course, the message about the ruins of grand classical architecture and about the hasty

---

[1] For an account of the impact of this publication on Dickens's mind and imagination, see McMaster (1981, 37–53).

ephemerality of its contemporary London equivalent is at one level essentially the same, for both are equally subject to the power of time.

As for many other commentators, it was the Colosseum that struck Dickens as "the great sensation ... I never *can* forget it" (Dickens 1977b, 258n). To John Forster, he wrote that he had never been "so moved and overcome by any sight as by that of the Coliseum, except perhaps by the first contemplation of the Falls of Niagara" (Forster 1928, 369)—and at Niagara, both in 1842 and 1868, he thought of death. Adapting these words, he writes, again, in the account of his visit in January 1845 in *Pictures from* Italy, of any visitor to the Colosseum, that "never in his life, perhaps, will he be so moved and overcome by any sight, not immediately connected with his own affections and afflictions" (Dickens 1996, 366). What was it that so moved Dickens at the Colosseum? The answer, I suggest, is to be sought in a kind of dual perspective contained, first, in the oxymoron "softened sorrow" and the list of four adjectives he uses to characterize it—a group of three: "solemn, grand, majestic," followed by the contrasting "mournful" (Dickens 1996, 366). There is dualism too in the simultaneous urge to project the imagination into the reality of the past, "with thousands of eager faces staring down into the arena, and such a whirl of strife and blood and dust," and to condemn, seeing traces of that world in contemporary Roman physiognomies, where the beauty of Italian faces "becomes devilish" (Dickens 1996, 368). It is, "GOD be thanked: a ruin!" (Dickens 1996, 368), and Dickens's fascination with it combines, in Rose Macaulay's phrase, "the pleasure of ruins" with relief that they are indeed ruins.

There may be traces here of a special, positive view of ruins prevalent in the period of Romanticism, connected in particular with Volney's *Ruins* (1791), a text of significance for the French Revolution, which saw them as welcome signs that all tyrannies must end, and as incitements to revolt. The monster in Mary Shelley's *Frankenstein*, indeed, learns about the course of human history by eavesdropping on Felix reading Volney aloud to his sister (Shelley 1996, 82). From such a perspective, Dickens looking at ruins in Italy can be seen again to be contemplating what he saw as the inevitable decline and fall of empires with a degree of evident satisfaction. He became an ardent supporter, partly through friendship with Giuseppe Mazzini and other exiled Italian patriots, of the cause of Italian unity espoused by the multiple elements of the Italian Risorgimento; he worked actively with them to bring about the downfall of the rule of foreign powers like Austria and Spain—not to mention the Papal states which were under the control of the Catholic Church—the consequence of which was wholesale backwardness and social neglect in most parts of the fragmented peninsula. Arriving in Albaro in the summer of 1844, he speaks of a depression caused by the contemplation of "so much ruin and neglect" about him (Dickens 1996, 284).

But he was also, as Sally Ledger (2007) and others have shown, an ardent supporter of progress and modernization, so that in November 1853 he could announce gleefully in a letter to Emile de la Rue that "the Electric Telegraph shoots through the Colosseum like a sun-beam—in at one ruined arch, and out at another" (Dickens 1993, 193). Thus, although I can smile at Rose Macaulay's ironic view of Dickens's "macabre pleasure" at Pompeii (Macaulay 1984, 296), as he describes how even corpses in tombs were turned out of their resting-places and showered with lava ("the mouths, and eyes, and skulls of all the skeletons, were stuffed with this terrible hail" [Dickens 1996, 417]), I don't think she gets the entire point about Dickens's characterization of Vesuvius as "the doom and destiny of this beautiful country, biding its time" (Dickens 1996, 418). Her comment—that "no one would have been more pleased than he, had Vesuvius spouted forth again" (Macaulay 1984, 296)—doesn't take into account, perhaps, the Risorgimento context, with its destructive longing for the sweeping away of the old order and the creation of new and thoroughly welcome ruins—ruins to "thank God for" again; for Dickens visited Italy at a time when revolutionary change was indeed "biding its time."

But a third discussion of Roman ruins in *Pictures from Italy* is perhaps the most interesting and important as an index of Dickens's imaginative response to them. It is the description of an excursion along the Appian Way, worth quoting at some length:

> For twelve miles we went climbing on, over an unbroken succession of mounds, and heaps, and hills of ruin. Tombs and temples, overthrown and prostrate; small fragments of columns, friezes, pediments; great blocks of granite and marble; mouldering arches, grass-grown and decayed; ruin enough to build a spacious city from; lay strewn about us. Sometimes, loose walls, built up from these fragments by the shepherds, came across our path; sometimes, a ditch between two mounds of broken stones, obstructed our progress; sometimes, the fragments themselves, rolling

from beneath our feet, made it a toilsome matter to advance, but it was always ruin. Now we tracked a piece of the old road, above the ground; now traced it, underneath a grassy covering, as if that were its grave; but all the way was ruin. Now in the distance, ruined aqueducts went stalking on their giant course along the plain; and every breath of wind that swept towards us, stirred early flowers, and grasses, springing up, spontaneously, on miles of ruin. The unseen larks above us, who alone disturbed the awful silence, had their nests in ruin; and the fierce herdsmen, clad in sheepskins, who now and then scowled out upon us from their sleeping nooks, were housed in ruin. The aspect of the desolate Campagna in one direction, where it was most level, reminded me of an American prairie; but what is the solitude of a region where men have never dwelt, to that of a Desert, where a mighty race have left their footprints in the earth from which they have vanished; where the resting-places of their Dead, have fallen like their Dead; and the broken hour-glass of Time is but a heap of idle dust! Returning by the road, at sunset! and looking, from the distance, on the course we had taken in the morning, I almost feel (as I had felt when I first saw it at that hour) as if the sun would never rise again, but looked its last, that night, upon a ruined world. (Dickens 1996, 396–397)

Here, Dickens writes a kind of prose poem, in which ruins become decidedly allegorical. His favourite allegory, Bunyan's *Pilgrim's Progress*, may be at the back of his mind, judging by the presence of words like "progress" itself, and "advance." The ruins figure as symbolic obstructions to the progress of the walkers, and as such readily stand for the ubiquitous obstacles to advancement witnessed during Dickens's tour of Italy. The repetitive prose rhythms of the passage, structured through anaphora, ending regularly with the word "ruin," register a mood of gloom and depression, as does the pervasive intensifying metaphoric doubling: the burying of corpses and then of their tombs; the marking of time by the symbolic hour-glass which itself later turns to dust. And despite moments of relief and renewal—flowers and grass grow, birds nest in the ruins—we end with an apocalyptic vision of the end of the world.

That this is not just a vision of the "doom and destiny" of that "beautiful country" Italy alone can be seen in the way it foreshadows an apocalyptic moment at the beginning of *Bleak House*, where the flakes of soot produced by industrial London that flutter down from smoky chimneys in the fog are compared to snow-flakes "gone into mourning, one might imagine, for the death of the sun" (Dickens 1977a, 5).

In that novel too, "ruin" functions allegorically—not only, as we have seen, in Tom-all-Alone's, but in the names of Miss Flite's birds, which include "Dust, Ashes, Waste, Want, Ruin, Despair, Madness, [and] Death" (Dickens 1977a, 180). The allegorical figure of allegory itself on Mr Tulkinghorn's neoclassical ceiling is "for ever toppling out of the clouds and pointing," even if, symbolically, "it is too dark to see much of allegory over-head" (Dickens 1977a, 517). The Chancery fog may blur but cannot completely conceal the numerous warning signs of conflagration or indeed Vesuvian eruption "biding its time" in the hopelessly flawed and broken society depicted in the novel.

Yet the passage that links ruins with allegory that interests me most of all occurs in another of Dickens's mature masterpieces, *Little Dorrit*. The novelist's own meditations in Rome are echoed and amplified by those of Dorrit herself, whose deeply thoughtful response to the ruins is a world apart from those of Mrs. General, derived from the stale facts she finds in the Catholic writer Eustace's guidebook. Dorrit sees in them a reflection of her own life:

> Little Dorrit would often ride out in a hired carriage that was left them, and alight alone and wander among the ruins of old Rome. The ruins of the vast old Amphitheatre, of the old Temples, of the old commemorative Arches, of the old trodden highways, of the old tombs, besides being what they were, to her were ruins of the old Marshalsea—ruins of her own old life—ruins of the faces and forms that of old peopled it—ruins of its loves, hopes, cares, and joys. Two ruined spheres of action and suffering were before the solitary girl often sitting on some broken fragment; and in the lonely place, under the blue sky, she saw them both together. (Dickens 1999, 601)[2]

To be fully understood and appreciated, this passage needs to be placed in the context of earlier Romantic writing about ruins, notably the brilliant lines in Byron's *Childe Harold's Pilgrimage* Canto 4, where the poet contemplates the meaning of the ruins of Rome and likewise uncovers a duality:

---

[2] See Chapter 5, where Chryssa Marinou analyses Isabel Archer's similar contemplation of the Roman ruins in Henry James's *The Portrait of a Lady*.

But my soul wanders; I demand it back
To meditate amongst decay, and stand
A ruin amidst ruins; there to track
Fall'n states and buried greatness. (Byron 2009, 194)

These lines were widely admired and imitated, both in England, amongst the Shelleys, for example, and abroad in other parts of Europe and beyond.[3] And if one looks to abroad—to Heinrich Heine, writing back from Bagni di Lucca to Eduard von Schenk in Munich in September 1828—we encounter a clear echo of Byron that brings us remarkably close to the mood of this passage in *Little Dorrit*. "Bin ich doch selbst eine Ruine, die unter Ruinen wandelt"/"I myself am a ruin wandering among ruins" (Heine 1971, 339).

Earlier in the same letter Heine has more to say about his experiences, and, again, these are remarkably Dickensian. He laments not being able to speak Italian, and thus, to converse with the inhabitants he meets. But he stresses that he is not without some form of communication with the stones and fragments of antiquity, because "Auch sie scheinen tief zu fühlen, was ich denke. So eine abgebrochene Säule aus der Römerzeit, so ein zerbröckelter Longobardenthurm, so ein verwittertes gothische Pfeilerstück versteht mich recht gut."/"They seem to have deep feeling for what I am thinking. A broken off column from Roman times, a crumbling tower of the Langobards, a weathered gothic arrow fragment, these understand me perfectly well" (Heine 1971, 339).[4] Heine explores here in dialogue with ruins in Italy a thoroughly modern sense of his own personality as fragmentary and multiple rather than single and unitary that finds remarkable echo in Dorrit herself—not usually thought of as a modern girl, but perhaps in the process of becoming one through a properly felt response to her new surroundings. Dorrit is able to progress—to grow into the woman who will marry Arthur Clennam—because she refuses to blot out and reject her Marshalsea past, which the other members of her family (with the exception of her uncle Fred) wish to do. She is able to hold in her mind two superimposed images—that which pertains to the history of Rome and that which pertains to the

[3] On Byron's view of the power of Greek ruins to affect the present landscape, a power that is imaginatively evoked in *Childe Harold's Pilgrimage*, see also Chapter 2 by Maria Vara.

[4] The translations of the Heine text are mine.

history of her own life—in a manner that enables her to uncover effective functional meaning in the ruins that both surround her body and condition her psyche, and thus to make progress in her life.

One last comment about a related, heavily ironic passage earlier in the same chapter, which is principally devoted to the marriage of Dorrit's sister Fanny to the doltish heir to the supposed Merdle fortune, Edward Sparkler. It reflects on historic change, that turning wheel that brings about a present in which the English, once provincial barbarians from the point of view of ancient Rome, now rule the roost in this city of ruined echoes of the past. And it imagines those ruins as animate, sprung to life again from the fragments strewn about in the present:

> The day came, and the She-Wolf in the Capitol might have snarled with envy to see how the Island Savages contrived these things now-a-days. The murderous-headed statues of the wicked Emperors of the Soldiery, whom sculptors had not been able to flatter out of their villainous hideousness, might have come off their pedestals to run away with the Bride. The choked old fountain, where erst the gladiators washed, might have leaped into life again to honour the ceremony. The Temple of Vesta might have sprung up anew from its ruins, expressly to lend its countenance to the occasion. Might have done; but did not. Like sentient things—even like the lords and ladies of creation sometimes—might have done much, but did nothing. (Dickens 1999, 597)

The irony is again double. "GOD be thanked!"; the "murderous-headed statues" of "wicked Emperors" do not return to tyrannize once more. But in their inertia they echo the complacent "Nobody's Fault" philosophy of contemporary "lords and ladies of creation" amongst contemporary British islanders, who remain savages. The pointing figure of allegory warns again: act so that things may change, or you will become animate ruins too.

REFERENCES

Byron, Lord George. 2009. *Childe Harold's Pilgrimage*. Newcastle-upon-Tyne: Cambridge Scholars Press.

Dickens, Charles. 1963 [1952]. *Our Mutual Friend*, introd. E. Salter Davies. London: Oxford University Press (The New Oxford Illustrated Dickens).

Dickens, Charles. 1977a. *Bleak House*, ed. George Ford and Sylvère Monod. New York: W. W. Norton (Norton Critical Editions).

Dickens, Charles. 1977b. *Letters*, vol IV, ed. Kathleen Tillotson. Oxford: Clarendon Press (Pilgrim Edition).

Dickens, Charles. 1990. *Nicholas Nickleby*, ed. Paul Schlicke. Oxford: Oxford University Press.

Dickens, Charles. 1993. *Letters*, vol VII, ed. Graham Storey, Kathleen Tillotson, and Angus Easson. Oxford: Clarendon Press (Pilgrim Edition).

Dickens, Charles. 1995. *Sketches by Boz*, ed. Dennis Walder. London: Penguin Books.

Dickens, Charles. 1996 [1957]. *Pictures from Italy*. In *American Notes and Pictures from Italy*, introd. Sacheverell Sitwell. London: Oxford University Press (The New Oxford Illustrated Dickens).

Dickens, Charles. 1998. *Great Expectations*, ed. Graham Law and Adrian Pinnington. Peterborough, ON: Broadview Press.

Dickens, Charles. 1999. *Little Dorrit*, ed. Harvey P. Sucksmith. Oxford: Oxford University Press (Oxford World Classics).

Dickens, Charles. 2015. *The Uncommercial Traveller*, ed. Daniel Tyler. London: Oxford University Press.

Forster, John. 1928. *The Life of Charles Dickens*, ed. J.W.T. Ley. London: Cecil Palmer.

Heine, Heinrich. 1971. *Säkularausgabe XX: Briefe I 1815–31*, ed. Fritz H. Eisner. Berlin: Walter de Gruyter.

Ledger, Sally. 2007. *Dickens and the Popular Radical Imagination*. Cambridge: Cambridge University Press.

Macaulay, Rose. 1984 [1953]. *Pleasure of Ruins*. London: Thames and Hudson.

McMaster, Rowland. 1981. Dickens and the Horrific. In *The Novel from Sterne to James: Essays on the Relation of Literature to Life*, ed. Juliet McMaster and Rowland McMaster, 37–53. London: Macmillan.

Orlando, Francesco. 2005. *Obsolete Objects in the Literary Imagination*. New Haven, CT: Yale University Press.

Shelley, Mary. 1996. *Frankenstein*, ed. J. Paul Hunter. New York: Norton (Norton Critical Editions).

CHAPTER 4

The Indifference of Fragments: Untimely Ruin in *Tess of the d'Urbervilles*

Claire Potter

> *… Poor wounded name! My bosom as a bed.*
> Shall lodge thee.—W. Shakespeare

Introduction

To begin at the heart of matters, as suggested by the Shakespearian epigraph to *Tess of the d'Urbervilles*, is perhaps also to start at the edge where, like exposed ripple marks in a text, the cumulative effect of Tess's execution is most poignantly felt in the image of a black flag waving silently in the breeze.[1] This last remaining fragment of Tess,

---

[1] It was customary in Victorian times to raise a black flag after an execution. Letters addressed to Queen Victoria describe how a "large crowd gathered and waited for the hoisting of the Black flag" (Buckle 2014, 423). Not all shared in the Queen's 1887 Jubilee celebrations: in Ireland, a prominent black flag was raised by Republican movement in the name of starved, mistreated and evicted Irish people, leading us to speculate on Hardy's poignant use of the black flag in *Tess*. My thanks to Jaya Savige for discussions on vexillology.

C. Potter (✉)
Architectural Association, London, UK

© The Author(s) 2019
E. Mitsi et al. (eds.), *Ruins in the Literary and Cultural Imagination*,
https://doi.org/10.1007/978-3-030-26905-0_4

indelibly embedded within the moral and physical landscape of the novel, signals the acme of the bleak ruin and tragedy that besets the narrative. However, almost to counterweigh—and indeed foreground—the pathos and sentimentality of this final gesture, a strange indifference exists in the way the flag is depicted; its solitary wave not only personifies the inanimate object, but reminds us in a deadpan fashion of Hardy's intention to signal the falsity of "Justice" having been done as well as the untimely ruin of Tess's becoming. An antithesis to surrender, the black flag stands in contrast to the white dress synonymous with Tess, illustrating the notion that while the flag signifies a wider context of ruin in the novel, it also encapsulates something defiant in the text. Here, the fragment of flag—in a negative capacity much like the character of Tess herself— works *against* the whole it claims to represent, defying ruin, as I hope to illustrate, with possibility and chance.

Like a geologist discerning matter layer by layer, Hardy fastidiously structures the last paragraphs of *Tess* in accordance with a concentric pattern that leads the reader's eye incrementally towards the final image of the novel: "In the valley *beneath* lay the city … *Behind* the city swept the rotund upland … further off, landscape *beyond* landscape … viewed from this spot … one blot on the city's beauty … something moved slowly up the staff … It was a black flag" (Hardy 2008, 419–420; my italics). Here the scene of Tess's untimely ruin—her death—is described as a "blot" phonetically as well as spatially linked to a distant viewing "spot."[2] This aural bracketing of the terminus and distance of death suggests a return to a pre-linguistic stage that remains untranslatable: between the "spot" and the "blot" reverberates an echo that cannot be put into words since it accounts only for pure sound, a kind of knowledge that is undecipherable. Thus, *before* we encounter the "black flag," Hardy takes his reader *beneath, behind* and then *beyond*—"landscape *beyond* landscape"—into an accordion-like logic that sets the scene for a pluralistic and unrepresentable moment of crisis both bracketed by time and without heed to time. Between the flag and the hills, we find images of repetition that support the Nietzschean notion that time is recurrent and that time disturbs the horizon of inherited meaning by overlapping different cycles of meaning, for example the geographical

---

[2] In the original 1892 manuscript held at the British Library, the flag "shot" up the staff, adding a discarded third rhyme to the phrase, *blot, spot* and *shot*. The removal of the word "shot" brings a sense of the timelessness to the last pages.

(spot) with the literary (blot), disrupting, as Nietzsche observes, the view of history as one long teleological progression.[3]

To tentatively approach a theory of ruins, I would like to follow this thread from *Tess*—landscape *beyond* landscape—in order to move beyond the temporal cycle of birth and decay and instead explore how literature is already an act of giving way to the literary fragment that both negates and sustains it. In other words, we only arrive at the *spot* of the *blot*—at the fragment of black flag *beyond* the ruin—indirectly and by not-saying; that is, by a *poetical* signalling that expresses the impossible—Mallarmé's flower "absent from every bouquet," the ruin absent from every ruin (1982, 76). Unencumbered by actual space and time, literary space captures the unsettling, ambiguous and symbolic back-and-forth movement between meaning and writing Blanchot described as analogous to a void, a nowhere (1999, 391). In this way, Tess's untimely death is abstracted into an untimely flag and nothing else. This *nothing else* is a strange measure—a pausing or a waiting, if you will, that attends to the weight of history by way of a gesture: the waving black flag.[4] Following the *poiesis* of Hardy's text in this way, and seeking a theory from writing and a fragment from ruin, and not the other way around, this is how my essay hopes to proceed.

Un/Timeliness

Perhaps one of the most powerful elements in Hardy's writing is the tension between context and character which is left unclosed, or rather, as I have come to explore more widely for this essay, it is the tension between ruin and fragment that is left unclosed and complicated by the suggestion that a fragment is simply a left-over or remnant of ruin. More so than his characters, it can be argued that it is Hardy's contexts that are ruined or ruinous: surfaces layered with the "un"—the undone and the undoing, the unconscious and the unknowing—nature as foreboding and indifferent. We think of this visually through the Romantic lens of Caspar David Friedrich whose tiny figures roam within a wild landscape,

---

[3]The relevant Nietzsche essay here is the third meditation in *Untimely Meditations* (2005), entitled "On the Uses and Disadvantages of History for Life."

[4]This stepping backwards in order to go forwards will characterize the theoretical path of my paper and was inspired by Steve Connor's proposition that "A ruin is a temporal conundrum ... it is a distempering of times, that puts time out of joint" (2006).

and yet unlike a Byronic hero enmeshed in nature, Hardy's characters are often set anachronistically *against* a more ancient landscape of ruin—and I use the word *against* in an artistic sense as if his characters were superimposed and painted at variance to their surface or societal purview.

This word "against" features often in the Hardyean lexicon: the tower in which Tess is imprisoned at the end of the novel rises "*Against …* far stretches of country," "*against* the east horizon" and lastly "*against* the light" (2008, 420). Recounting Martha Browne's public hanging in 1856, Hardy remembers "what a fine figure she showed *against* the sky as she hung in the misty rain, and how the tight black silk gown set off her shape as she wheeled half-round and back," all this being suggestive of how Hardy draws a fragment from a setting of ruin so as to create the distance he requires to move beyond, behind and beneath ruin in order to graft the literary fragment onto a new writing surface (Millgate 1982, 62–63). Yet inescapably, Hardy's fragment carries the trace of ruin as well and for this reason works as an untimely counterweight against ruin—the fragment exists in a *third mode* that Nietzsche describes in the *Untimely Meditations* as a *critical* mode, "If he is to live, man must possess and from time to time employ the strength to break up and dissolve a part of the past: he does this by bringing it before the tribunal, scrupulously examining it and finally by condemning it; every past, however, is worthy to be condemned" (2005, 75–76). Here the word "condemn" in Nietzsche functions in a similar way to the word "against" in Hardy; judgement is pronounced against a *part of the past* simultaneously recognized as being worthy of condemning. Embodying a conundrum, the fragment of flag in *Tess* both condemns and is condemning, working against the context of ruin it represents by not looking backwards: in many ways, the fragment of flag narrates not an outcome of ruin, but an unambiguous fault line already within literature.

In the paragraph alluding to Tess's execution, an untimeliness disrupts the precision of the clock: "A few minutes after the hour had struck something moved slowly up the staff …" (2008, 420). As if deliberately confronting the forgetfulness that Nietzsche ascribes to living without the past, the definition of what moved up the staff is given *after* the words *something moved*: "It was a black flag" (2008, 420). The significance of *after* brings us to the notion of an eternally incomplete action rather than a completed one, or at least an action completed retrospectively. The fragment here works according to its own time, moving languidly up the staff, signalling a degree of blindness in the text—Tess's execution is not depicted—and in the reader for whom the moment is not described. However, as Nietzsche explains apropos of a child who "plays in blissful blindness between hedges of past and future," this blindness does not last long: as soon as the words "it was" are learnt, existence is put forward "only as an uninterrupted has-been," in other words, "an imperfect tense that can never become a perfect one" (2005, 61).

Like her confession-wish to have "never been born" mirrored at times in the frustratingly slow pace by which she often moves—unconsciously, half-asleep—Tess embodies the contradictory speed of a freefalling fragment in slow motion, a name brought into being in order to end its being (2008, 88).

THE FALLENNESS OF LANGUAGE

In literary space, with the imperatives of gravity and geography held at bay, the reader is taken on a psychical voyage into language akin the journey taken by the early psychoanalytic work that Freud likened to the "clearing away ... material layer by layer ... we liked to compare it with the technique of excavating a buried city" (2001, 139). Literary language, unlike everyday language, as Blanchot explains in "Literature and the Right to Death," is not only made up of contradictions, but of uneasiness: it is the radical representation not only of "nonexistence," but of "nonexistence made *word*" (1999, 382).[5] Etymologically stemming from the sense to fall or collapse—the act of giving way—the word *ruin* is profoundly implicated, as Derrida suggests in *Memoirs of the Blind*, in its own temporal duality. Ruins belong as well as fall upon their own time: "a ruin ... does not come *after* the work but remains produced, *already from the origin*, by the advent and the structure of the work. In the beginning, at the origin, there was ruin" (Derrida 1993, 65). The nature of the literary fragment—detached, chaotic and supposedly posterior to ruin and origin—then, neither refers to nor desires restoration; if the manuscript of *Tess* illustrates nothing else, it is how, from the first draft of writing, a fragment, such as a name, can carry traces of ruin, but itself also be held responsible for ruin.

In the penultimate chapter of *Tess*, in a scene of evasion and repose, Angel Clare and Tess take shelter within a "place [that] was all doors

---

[5] See Chapter 8 where David Tucker deals with Beckett's textual ruins.

and pillars" (2008, 415). A few lines later their "pavilion of the night" is revealed as Stonehenge, a name linked, in Christopher Chippindale's *Stonehenge Complete*, to the Old English words *stan*, meaning rock, and *henge*, meaning hinge or hanging gallows (1987, 20). Described in Chippindale as "erected in the manner of a doorway, so that doorway appears to have been raised on doorway," Stonehenge as a site and a structure appears as pure form in the text, and Angel is only able to divine the nature of the structure by touch. However, Angel's first instinct is not to misrecognize their surroundings, locating himself and Tess within a "very Temple of the Winds" (Chippindale 1987, 11; Hardy 2008, 415).[6] The veracity of *very* here proves to be false, and yet, as a doorway raised upon doorway, the text analogously draws the two archaeological sites together as if there were a common ground between them that Angel blindly perceives. Hardy's personification of "wind playing upon the edifice," weaving "among the pillars" until "the night wind died out," references the Waterclock's frieze of eight *Anemoi* or wind gods who encircle the orthogonal tower; the personification of the wind playing and weaving through Stonehenge is suggestive of a spectral third who likewise moves between ancient Greece and the Salisbury Plain (Hardy 2008, 415–417).

This uneasy movement between is as much psychical as it is architectural, and the shared template of time-keeping and doorways across both structures is encapsulated in the word *temple* so pertinent to both Stonehenge and the Waterclock; as Steve Connor elucidates, "Ruins are always a kind of mental architecture. The word *contemplate*, the primary meaning of which is to mark out or survey a *templum*, a consecrated site for augury. Contemplation … is already an architectural act" (2006). The nocturnal contemplation afforded to Tess and Angel within the temple/template of Stonehenge is vulnerable and roofless; however, it soon becomes apparent that the state of reverie, namely contemplation itself, is what sets impassable and sacred lines of trespass. Different to a sundial that only counts time during daylight hours, the Waterclock or *clepsydra* measures the passage of time but also during the night. Stemming from the Greek words *clephtis* meaning thief and *hydor* relating to water,

---

[6] The Temple of the Winds known also as the *Waterclock of Andronikos of Kyrrhos* can be found in Athens, at the site of the Roman Agora; it was built in around 50 BC. The Athenian Waterclock or *clepsydra* was one of the first ancient devices for keeping time, and like Stonehenge today, it stands in ruins.

clepsydra depicts a sense of a water-stealer, someone stealing from the flow of time, suggesting time is not being measured "on site" but elsewhere. By linking Stonehenge with its chthonic counterpart—the Temple of the Winds—Tess stirs only when Stonehenge, as a sundial, gives her away: "Soon the light was strong, and a ray shone upon her unconscious form, peering under her eyelids and waking her" (2008, 418). Furthermore, the soldiers encircling Tess's sleeping form are likewise held at bay: they "stood watching her, as still as the pillars around"; it is only when darkness subsides that Tess crosses the threshold, telling the soldiers, in a quiet clock-worthy manner, "I am ready" (2008, 418).

Here Tess's "I am ready" complicates the outcome not only of the arrest, but of the capture of a criminal. Evoking Sophocles's Antigone whose "I" walks towards fate as her only way out, Tess reads and delivers her sentence to the letter, knowing without naivety that its evasion could not last. Desiring a proper burial for her illegitimate child, respecting "not the civil law" (Hardy 2008, 108), murdering her abusive husband and telling Angel Clare, when the soldiers come for her, that "It is as it should be! ... I am almost glad—yes, glad!" (2008, 418), Tess, for all the passivity that Hardy confers upon her character, defies the moral code of her context both by her actions and by articulating, in the third person, that her arrest is "as it should be," as if she is at once Chorus and agent (2008, 418). Like Antigone, Tess thinks her way out of the bind by declaring fearlessly, and therefore ruinously, that she will *give way* to fate, a declaration that causes unease in the reader because it foregrounds literature's capacity to not only illustrate negation, but put it into words. In Reginald Gibbons and Charles Segal's translation of *Antigone*, the Greek word for "the worst of fates," *atê*, is translated throughout the play as "ruin," with Gibbons arguing that "the *cause* of ruin effectively implicates human decisions ... *atê* also suggests the emotional state, the mistaken impulse ... that leads someone to ruin" (Sophocles 2003, 41). For Lacan, Antigone's actions are not simply led by a state of affairs; instead, her trajectory is one that plays out on limits of the law, by crossing ultimately beyond the limit of *atê*. Examining the Chorus's key address (lines 611–614 and 620–625), Lacan concentrates on two spatial qualifications of the word *atê*, one signifying "an outside or what happens once the limit of *atê* has been crossed" (*Ektos atas*) and the other describing man as "going towards ... *atê*" (*pros atan*) (1992, 270). Both Gibbons-Segal's and Lacan's readings underscore a compulsion towards ruin that seems to accumulate from a chain of events that pushes the characters over the limit. It is in this way that Derrida describes ruin as neither a "monumental fragment" nor a "theme," but an experience akin to "memory like an open eye … that lets you see without showing you anything at all" (1993, 69).

Mise en Abyme

That the event Hardy witnessed in 1856 at Dorchester Goal, as a sixteen-year-old, left him traumatized would be an understatement. Hardy's subsequent effort to metabolize Martha Browne's public hanging and make sense of his reaction to it would not only play itself out in *Tess* thirty-five years later, but also in subsequent letters, poems and stories recounted to friends.[7] What is important about the event is not the veracity of facts, corroborated yet retold differently by Hardy, but how an event—a story of ruin—proliferates, as J. H. Miller describes, into "… a repetition or a representation of history, the copy of a copy, writing about another writing" (1970, xiv).

It is perhaps for these reasons that we find on the original manuscript of *Tess*, the paternalistic title, "A Daughter of the D'Urbervilles," half effaced with the name "Tess" written above the words, "A Daughter." This alteration from common noun (A Daughter), to proper noun (Tess), signifies the importance Hardy accorded to the name and more specifically to naming. This is perhaps further exemplified by Hardy's choice of epigraph from Shakespeare's *Two Gentlemen of Verona*: "Poor wounded name, my bosom as a bed / Shall lodge thee" (2008). In many ways, *Tess* can be read as a book about the iterations of a name, as well as the complications and crises endemic to naming itself—"Be calm, good wind, blow not a word away / Till I have found each letter in the letter," Julia says (Shakespeare 1973, 30).[8] Reminiscent of Julia's regret for her rash deed which induces reparation, Hardy's rescue and embedding of a name within a name indicates a tension already at work in the text—in representation—that circles an origin of ruin without locating it.

---

[7] In *The Madder Stain* Annie Ramel, asking if Hardy as a newborn emitted a cry while his mother was being saved, cogently traces the literary effects not of biographical material, but of biographical material—such as "Hardy's particular relation to silence and to the voice"—made into word (2015, 163).

[8] See Chapter 6, where Sheila Teahan also discusses the relation between name and ruin/fragment.

As Melanie Klein illustrates in *Love, Guilt and Reparation*, the very early "wishes to bite up and to tear up ... [the] mother" are overcome by what Klein calls "imaginative thinking" that morphs into imagination: the child may "build up phantasies that he is putting the bits together again and repairing her" (1998, 308).[9]

Mirroring the discord between the two gentlemen of Verona and the Angel/Alec characters, Hardy divides himself between author and fictional author in *Tess* as illustrated in the novel's dramatic, authorial sub-title, "Faithfully presented by Thomas Hardy." This gesture captures an uneasy literary tension inherent in the legitimacy—or in Blanchot's terms *non-existence*—of naming and writing by using the experience itself of writing, of being an author, as an embodiment of discord between truth and fiction.[10] The theme of legitimacy is of course prolific in *Tess*; however, alongside pressing questions concerning genealogy in the text—does Tess descend from an aristocratic bloodline?—lie subtle linguistic and therefore ontological questions concerning naming that Hardy raises from the very first page of the novel. The meeting of Jack Durbeyfield, a self-professed "haggler," and the parson, who impulsively addresses him as "Sir John," brings to light the currency—the double-edged value and ruin—that a name carries: *Tess* begins with a fault line that divides Tess's family from the start—existence is bisected into two paths because of a name. As Tess conveys in the fifth chapter, "Our names are worn away to Durbeyfield: but we have ... an old seal, marked with a ramping lion on a shield and a castle over him. And we have a very old silver spoon ..." (2008, 46). Here the double-edged nature of naming in *Tess*—names are valuable and worn away in the manner of an ancestral shield or spoon—echoes what Mallarmé attempted to convey as "mobility in the letter," an act of naming that gives way to a "nameless system of relationships which will embrace and strengthen fiction" (1982, 82). Hardy's choice of shield and old spoon, two reflective

---

[9]As Steve Connor notes, "the instinct for reparation which Melanie Klein thought lay behind all artistic work" captures not only the sense of destruction—and guilt—Hardy must have felt witnessing Martha Browne's hanging, but also his debt to that event for the impetus to create *Tess* (2006).

[10]The sense of imbrication of author and subject was very much on the minds of many writers at the *fin de siècle*. In the work of Proust, Freud and Mallarmé, we find examples of this textual self-referencing. A poignant example is that of Gustav Mahler, who in 1900 confessed to a friend that "It becomes clearer and clearer to me that one does not compose; one is composed" (qtd. in Johnston 2009, 47).

objects, brings to mind a sense of ruin—as a copy of a copy—that permeates context as well as sets forth value. As the Chorus in *Antigone* almost paradoxically reminds us, "Nothing great ... lies / Beyond the reach of ruin," and yet the tension between what stays and what escapes—what is different in a name and what is *in*different—is mirrored in all the unnameable moments in *Tess* where language comes up against the limits of *atê* and what lies beyond it (2003, 81).

Looking at the distance between faithfulness and fiction, event and narrative, we return to Tess's name as a wound, a thing to be repaired—like an errant fragment—by being rehomed within the bosom-book of Hardy's heart. And yet like the multiple hearts that feature in *Tess*, the wound is itself like a roving fragment, lodging and repeating itself almost parasitically again, elsewhere. The wounded name is reminiscent of Tess's wish never to be born and its fragmentary, broken nature echoes a defiance against the whole, evoking the notion, like the Latin etymology of the word *frangere* suggests, of "a piece broken off."[11] Like the epistolary fragments Julia laments having torn up in *Two Gentlemen of Verona*, the wounded name stands in as a metonym for the missing corpus or body, thus exposing the gap not only between name and thing, but the threat of a letter that killeth.[12] The reparative, tomb-like setting of a bosom in which a name is placed is suggestive of reprieve and stillness, and yet the name of Tess, like its character, traverses the novel as a roving existence without reprieve. When Tess finally assumes the authority of her voice—at the moment of textual reversal where Alex becomes the victim and not Tess—an image of the heart again comes into focus, and unsurprisingly, it is a tiny fragment that has dislodged it: "The wound was small, but the point of the blade had touched the heart of the victim" (2008, 405). Here, as Blanchot writes, literature can be grasped in all its ambiguities when it "*begins* with the *end*," when language assumes the position of both revealing the end and endings by being "the *life that endures death and maintains itself in it*" (1999, 341; italics in original). In some

---

[11] *Online Etymology Dictionary*: fragment (n.) early 15c., "small piece or part," from Latin *fragmentum* "a fragment, remnant," literally "a piece broken off," from base of *frangere* "to break."

[12] A genealogy from *The Two Gentlemen from Verona* to Martha Browne's hanging and to *Tess* can to some degree be traced in Hardy's poem "The Torn Letter." For a feminist reading of the reparative elements of this poem, see my essay, "A Love Letter from Beyond the Grave: Irigaray, Nothingness, and *La femme n'existe pas*" (2013).

sense, Alec's small wound and the point of Tess's knife are sufficient to maim the whole being by virtue of being fragmentary; broken off from the whole, they reiterate the incapacity of language to round meaning into closure and ensure, in Blanchot's words, that "when we speak we are leaning on a tomb" (1999, 391). Each of the four major instances of death in *Tess*—when Prince dies, Sorrow dies, the partridges and Alec dies—reverberate by posing a question not only of the reader, but of the text itself: what does it mean to endure an ending that does not end? As we find in the ominous scene of Prince's death where the horse's blood "was … falling with a hiss," the chapter's last lines perform an unfinished echo, "… the children cried anew. All except Tess. Her face was dry and pale as though she regarded herself in the light of a murderess" (2008, 38, 40).

FOUNDATIONS

There is a mythical and epic quality that imbues all of Hardy's work with the behest that literature must hold "an ear for the 'still sad music of humanity'" (Wordsworth, qtd. in Hardy 1966, 137).[13] Like distance that underwrites the parameters of proximity, the ear attuned to the melancholy of the human condition, for Hardy and Wordsworth, reconstructs that melancholy into a sum greater than its parts, into a literary language that relies upon aesthetic distance in order to come, albeit negatively, into being.

Extending this notion, Sally Ledger evokes Foucault's assertion that "discourse can be both an instrument and an effect of power, but also a hindrance, a stumbling-block, a point of resistance and a starting point for an opposing strategy"; she argues that "the hostile dominant discourse *on* the New Woman made possible 'the formation of a "reverse" discourse': the New Woman began to speak on her own behalf" (1987, 10; my italics). In this vein, the foundational position given to ruin in *Tess* sets up a literary architecture that from the very first page of the narrative is purposefully discombobulated and discombobulating.

---

[13] Hardy quotes this line from Wordsworth's "Tintern Abbey" in his article, "The Science of Fiction" (1891), an essay he published while writing *Tess*. It is not difficult to read a sense of mourning for the inexactitudes and fictions of literary endeavour felt to be at odds with a period in history being catapulted into a new scientific and quantitative millennium.

While the parameters of time are given—"an evening in the latter part of May"—within a few lines, they are reversed, and Jack Durbeyfield halts his crooked gait that "inclined him somewhat left of a straight line," finding himself confronted with information that takes him metaphorically back in time: "... you are the lineal representative of the ancient and knightly family of the d'Urbervilles" (2008, 13). Here the figurative text carries and bears the weight of ruin by itself being bent: not only is Durbeyfield's name dislocated from the present and bisected into two versions, but his crooked gait and the forked genealogy of his family's abode—Blackmore or Blakemoor—suggest forms of disturbance from the very beginning. Fragments of place and time from the outset work against the patriarchal discourse such that an undercurrent of a "reverse discourse" inheres throughout the text; Tess, in the latter half of the novel, deliberately takes up the oblique trajectory set in motion by her lineage, not simply to live out its fate, but move against it.

This *reverse discourse* is untimely insofar as it makes use of what Annie Ramel describes as a "deficiency of the paternal function"; parodying the hands of a clock, Tess follows the motions of time in order to exist on, and make known, a different plane to the clock-face itself (2015, 24). Yet we find discord between the particular and the general. Hardy wants to put forward that "a field woman is a portion of the field; [that] she has somehow lost her own margin"; however, he somewhat involuntarily draws the reader's eye from a wide-screen purview to a close-up of Tess's ruin set within a very specific horizon: "This morning the eye returns involuntarily to the girl in the pink cotton jacket ... Her binding proceeds with clock-like monotony ... her naked arm ... becomes scarified by the stubble, and bleeds" (2008, 101). The great care Hardy takes in depictions of idyllic portions of field and ambiguous margins gives way to a grid of urbanization that scarifies surfaces and people, and yet this economy allows him, in Nietzsche's words, to subtly "organise the chaos," by bringing forth his subject to "become human again" (2005, 122). This shift takes Hardy's character beyond the mere feminine qualities conferred on a field, and vice versa; instead, Tess is unmeshed from her naturalistic horizon even if that removal causes suffering and ruin.

Examples of environmental, moral, linguistic and social ruin thus draw the reader's eye back and forward from ruin to fragment and from the resolutely temporal—ruin and its proximal decay—to the resolutely atemporal—the fragment and its distinct free-play. Since language for Hardy is the structural tool closest to hand, it is the grating—as well as the overlap—of fragment against ruin and small against big, that in the text's visual paradigm, reveals the distinct morphological patterns that emerge and recur throughout the novel. *Tess* thus begins with the lines: "On an evening in the latter part of May a middle-aged man was walking homeward from Shaston to the village of Marlott, in the adjoining Vale of Blakemore or Blackmoor" (2008, 13). Here the disarray of context and name hinges on the verb "walking" as if his footsteps were already wearing away history upon the surface of earth. Furthermore, the temporal words "evening ... latter ... May ... middle-aged" are undone by the ambivalence of the spatial: place could be Blakemore *or* Blackmoor, names are eroded and set in motion, and the frenetic wish, embodied by Tess's father, is to recuperate a rightful name—d'Urberville—albeit "worn away" (2008, 46). Working for and against Jack Durbeyfield's wish to bring past and present into unison is the word, "or," as in the homophones Blakemore *or* Blackmoor, the synophones Durbeyfield *or* d'Urberville, that on one level holds the words (worlds) apart, but on another more ambivalent level, phonetically embed the homonymous hinge even further in the names themselves. Here writing and language for Hardy are indicative of ruin that cannot stay contained. In *Tess*, and one could argue his oeuvre, Hardy conducts ruins—social and architectural—like dormant, negative, centrifugal centres that on the one hand lie static and fallen and, on the other, send out haunting ripples in accordance with the weight of their time: these letter-fragments morph, change and symbolize; the settings of his ruins do not.

By way of contrast, Tess's dialect, erring from the one the narrator describes as taught at the "village school," holds a common ground between ruins and fragments. As Hardy suggests,

> The dialect was on her tongue to some extent, despite the village school; the characteristic intonation for that dialect, for this district, being the voice approximately rendered by the syllable UR, probably as rich an utterance as any found in human speech. (2008, 21)

Hardy specifies that Tess's speech is rendered "on her tongue" and specifically in a phonetic fragment of dialect, "the syllable UR." This morpheme or syllable references paradoxically both the UR prefix in German meaning original or earliest version of a text—something pristine—as well as the UR in the Durbeyfield/d'Urberville name—something old and worn away. Furthermore, the more recent name,

Durbeyfield, suggests a field, the other—grammatically more elevated by the apostrophe and the French—suggests "of a city" and, by the temporal comparison *qua* conundrum, suggests a city worn back to a field: a *ville* worn back to a *field*. Although Tess easily pronounces the native syllable UR belonging to her district, her pronunciation both reveals and conceals a different name: her ancestor's city three-syllable name *d'Urberville* and her father's three-syllable country name *Durbeyfield* are indistinguishable in the first two syllables—it is only the last syllable which gives away difference. Like a kind of Ur-writing or, in Derridean terms, an arch-writing, Hardy here is describing a language that predates Tess inasmuch as spoken language—dialect—is fragmented, malleable and moveable; however, the erosion of her family name can only be *seen* in writing by the consonants F and V. We do not necessarily hear the difference and the erosion of the name from *ville* to *field* in speech; however, we perceive its decay in writing. The commonality shared thus between ruins and fragments is precisely one of translation and dialect: what breaks off from an original language will bear the indelible, yet fragmented, trace of that breakthrough time. Like Hardy's own hand that returned to patinate the manuscript—he edited dialect back into *Tess's* dialogue—the vice versa of ruin and fragment, of antecedents and consequents, is one of both translation and transposition.

In Tess's name, we hear the word *tesserae*, small blocks of stone, tile or pieces of glass used in the construction of a mosaic. In Hardy's *Tess*, however, the name Tess also works in the opposite way: rather than being a fragment *contributing* to a mosaic—a literary picture or truth— Tess as a singular name, and character, evades both the Durby*field* and d'Urber*ville* setting laid out for her and from very early on, chides and moves against the static milieu she is written as inescapably part of. It is in this sense that the setting, by the end of the novel, is what stagnantly remains ruined, while the weight of the tragedy—via language—is passed from the novel into the context of reading, that is onto the reader; *Tess of the d'Urbervilles* becomes known, and not simply abbreviated, as *Tess*.

Repair

The character of Tess is often introduced to the reader as a-part, spatially, aesthetically and psychologically: she is "a *mere* vessel" (2008, 21; my italics), suggesting, by the etymology of the word "mere," that Tess is absolute and complete in herself in that moment. Following the line of Hardy's textual fabric, our first introduction to Tess is, in cinematic language, off-camera; her father hears the sound of a brass band accompanying the women's club-walking of which his "da'ter is one o' the members" (2008, 17). Then, as the text moves closer via "a votive of sisterhood," an "every woman and girl" (2008, 17–19)—from universal to particular—in Chapter II Tess is revealed in close-up, in fragments of herself: in order, her head, mouth, eyes, red ribbon, tongue, lip, cheek, until she is gathered into a whole white form: "one of the white company" (2008, 20). To again borrow from cinematic language, this textual reveal of Tess on the move in the women's club-walking at Marlott mirrors the dimensions by which Hardy presents her, firstly as part of a "whole body" and then as a moving fragment tessellated in moments of time: "Phases of her childhood lurked in her aspect still. As she walked along you could sometimes see her twelfth year in her cheek ... her ninth sparkling from her eyes ... even her fifth would flit ..." (2008, 21). This serialized, fragmentary description of Tess paints an untroubled vista that safely brackets time into the limited sequence Hardy chooses to depict; however, the close narrative observations take a different turn and start to slowly reveal a subject out of step not only with her dance, but her looks: "she wore a red ribbon in her hair, and was the only one" (2008, 20). Like Sophocles's early demarcation and separation of Antigone's position from her sister's, Hardy ensures, from the moment of introduction, that Tess's path differs from those around her: like Antigone, Tess is bracketed by context, but the limits of that context are precisely what she moves beyond and against. As Helen Vendler writes, this attempt on the part of the poet "to obscure ... constructive invention, and to appear merely transcriptive," contains "the anxiety attendant on Zeno's paradox—the fact that time is infinitely divisible" (2004, 67). For Hardy the predilection to over-describe Tess, spatially and physically—he counts the street under Tess's foot in "inches of land"—starts to come undone and his textual viewfinder blurs and recedes as he passes the gaze to another. Seen through the eyes of her husband to be, Angel Clare, Tess by the end of the chapter morphs into a "white shape" standing "apart by the hedge all alone"; as a subject she is "dismissed ... from his mind" (2008, 24, 30), suggesting, as Vendler notes, the change from "inch-by-inch" descriptive writing to ambiguity "over the termination of a sequence" (2004, 67).

Returning to the overlap of the geographical and the literary, Tess tolerates the "imprint" of Alec's farewell kiss upon her cheek, by turning herself into a statue "like a marble term," as Hardy describes her, "term" being not only indicative of a period of time, but the archaic word for "a statue or bust ... representing [only] the upper part of the body, sometimes without the arms, and terminating below in a pillar" (2008, 90, 425–426n). This petrification is further described by the observation that "Her eyes vaguely rested on the remotest trees in the lane while the kiss was given, as though she were nearly unconscious of what he did" (2008, 90). While the text produces and in many ways itself enacts evidence of a kind of reductive and capitalistic use of Tess's body, it is crucial to note that it is neither Alec's kiss nor his pending violation that alter Tess's agency belonging to the scene. Conversely, it is Tess who in both cases escapes presence by bracketing time and turning herself into a copy (of herself), thus accomplishing the geographical feat of standing in for herself despite psychically being miles away. By aestheticizing herself superficially, Tess facilitates an interiority of escape, thus putting into question the rapport between interior and exterior, hard and soft, skin and marble and masculine and feminine.

However, Tess's experience of both Alec's violation and his kiss forewarns the expectation that an imprint will wash away when converted into writing. As we find subsequently, the confessional letter Tess writes to her husband remains unread and therefore unreadable, inferring that Tess's writing does not find expression in terms of patriarchal logocentrism belonging either to her husband, her patrilineal family, or Alec d'Urberville. Tess's recourse to action via Hardy's thought into image is with a stylo-like object, that is the mute violence that over-writes Alec, turning him into a pictorial fragment, a hieroglyph on the ceiling—a "gigantic [red] ace of hearts" (2008, 404)—that ominously depicts not simply what has taken place in the present, but in the past.[14] That there can be any doubt about the homophonous link between the colour red and its symbolism of being "read" as writing, is dispelled by the landlady whose

---

[14]In Chapter 11, the scene of Tess's rape, Tess is seen by Alec only in pictorial terms; while "Everything else was blackness alike," Tess is firstly as "invisible" and then "absolutely nothing but a pale nebulousness at his feet" (2008, 81–82). Silent transformations, at key moments, of characters into colours halt the reader's ability to read and go forward

eyes glanced casually over the ceiling, till they were arrested by a spot in the middle of its white surface ... it speedily grew as large as the palm of her hand and then she could perceive that it was red. The oblong white ceiling, with this scarlet blot in the midst ... She got upon the table, and touched the spot ... with her fingers. It was damp, and she fancied that it was a blood-stain. (2008, 404)

The distance from "spot" to "blot" is one of translation. Once the spot turns red, it becomes a "blot"; again once the "spot" is touched, it becomes a "blood-stain," thus creating a word-play between "red" and "read" and "reading," and as we have already seen between the untranslatable sounds of "spot" and "blot."

In her essay on *Far from the Madding Crowd*, Isabelle Gadoin reads the white space of Bathsheba's blank card as "the fantasmastic white space of the letter—the symptom of shattered or rather impossible communication" (2017, 22). In the mute, "scarlet blot" delivered and read on the "oblong white ceiling" in *Tess*, we find the effects of an envelope being read "from the wrong side ... showing not the address but the seal," and this anomaly, Gadoin argues, shifts the scene from the "textual to the visual ... from the readable to the invisible or the unseen" (2017, 24). In this sense, the textual reversal (*peripeteia*) that depicts change in character and event is complicated by two further levels of reversal, namely architectural and poetic: the scarlet blot in *Tess* develops on the opposite side of the murder scene—on its underside—and the text not only makes use of the hotel's structure to unfold and layer events, but is itself structured like a building. In this key chapter of Alec's murder, the moment of reversal and fragmentation serves to destructure the wider logic of the textural architecture: keyholes and thin walls are narrative doorways into the different rooms where "fragments of ... conversation" are revealed like tiny stanzas (rooms) in themselves (2008, 402). Likewise, it is the blood-stained ceiling that vocalizes events on the first floor, creating a moment where time both looks backwards and stands still; the seal on the envelope is read before the address, suggesting that it is often through the formal elements that the pictorial via the poetic is brought to stand where language otherwise falls short.

in the plot. Instead, reading becomes enmeshed in a fragmentary moment that is detached from time and sensory rather than legible.

It is in this vein that the dimensional nature of reading and legibility comes to the fore and everything, as Gadoin notes, "seems strangely reversed" and two-sided as it does in *Tess* (2017, 24). Here the role of language in the text changes from communicative readability and instead a visual and poetic inflection is brought to the surface, moving us from the legible to the experiential: a *blot* enlarges into a homophonous *spot*, and the visual representation of this ruinous event is mirrored in a fragmentary three-syllable plosive—*Drip, drip, drip*—whose recourse to action is to widen by recurrence (2008, 404).

The repair of ambivalence—like the repair of a ruin—is bridged by a syntactical music that echoes and reverberates a different rhythm throughout the text as if by means of a different linguistic register entirely composed by reading. Yet, it is a manner of reading that translates loss for another loss, albeit in a different measure. The proliferation of loss, then, into an aesthetic, poetic-sensory substitute, turns out to be a going beyond the ruin that brings fragments of meaning to the surface of language. As the Chorus notes in *Antigone* apropos of Creon, "Only a short / Time does he stay / Beyond the reach of ruin" (2003, 81). The literary distances between nodal rhymes, colours and words that Hardy creates throughout *Tess*, on the one hand, serve as fragments that, in a negative and indifferent capacity, reference a greater whole, but, on the other hand, function as letters-in-bottles, invitations sent out to our own sensibilities, as readers, to intermingle in the story within ourselves. The *poiesis* in the work—that which *makes* poetry—creates stepping-stones throughout *Tess* that mark the fallenness of language as well as offer the flawed possibility of literature in its place.

CONCLUSION

In the original manuscript of *Tess*, a paragraph from the last chapter is effaced, one that lays open one of Hardy's fears in writing *Tess*, and perhaps, his guilt of having retained Martha Browne's hanging so violently. Hardy avers, "[g]ladly sometimes would surely anyone lie for dear curiosity's sake, but for the ever-haunting afterthought, 'This work was not honest and may do harm'" (1966, 523). My essay has focused on two aspects of ruin—un/timeliness and writing—in order to suggest that a pivotal tension in *Tess* is the disjunction between ruin and fragment insofar as the aesthetic or the poetic—the fragmentary—moves against a more classical category of ruin, whereby a decaying temporal order is haunted by what becomes "broken off": in Shakespeare, time is out of joint; in Hardy, time has already vacated its joint.

As Hardy summarizes in *Tess*, "Beauty ... lay not in the thing, but in what the thing symbolised" (2008, 316). Ruin, permeating as the architectural landscape, determines the horizon for nearly all Hardy's literary settings. Yet his settings contain characters and elements that are anything but temporal and contained; instead, ruinous contexts are fragmented, superstitious, anachronistic and volatile; as gravitational centres, they propel characters to the limits of their fate. It is the alignment, or misalignment, of these two planes—the thing and what the thing symbolizes—that ruptures and distempers the Hardyean oeuvre, but equally at work is the profound undercurrent of *poiesis*—the poetical—that ensures these fissures have literary weight; as Virginia Woolf notes, it was precisely these "inequalities ... on the margin of the unexpressed" that in Hardy's writing produced "the most profound sense of satisfaction" (1986, 247). In Hardy, the antidote of artistic creation overlaps primary experience with aesthetic experience, lived experience with the profoundly moving reading experience. This is neither a derivative of *ruinenwert* or ruin-value nor a reassertion of history, but the expression of unresolved ambivalence inherent to the writer who knows that there is nothing beyond the ruin, as the sentiment of Byron's poem reminds us: "But my soul wanders; I demand it back / To ... stand / A ruin amidst ruins" (1846, Canto IV, 209). To return to the beginning of this essay, it is as if, through the final fragment of black flag embedded within the ruinology of *Tess*, Hardy offers his reader an obscured yet contiguous image of a silk black dress hanging so unjustly in the rain that he, as a young boy, was unable to read.

References

Blanchot, Maurice. 1999. *The Station Hill Reader: Fiction and Literary Essays*, ed. George Quasha, trans. Lydia Davis, Paul Auster, and Robert Lamberton. Barrytown: Station Hill Press.

Buckle, George. 2014. *The Letters of Queen Victoria Volume 6: 1879–1885*. Cambridge: Cambridge University Press.

Byron, Lord. 1846. *Childe Harold's Pilgrimage*. London: John Murray.

Chippindale, Christopher. 1987. *Stonehenge Complete*. London: Thames and Hudson.

Connor, Steve. 2006. Sufficiently Decayed. Talk given at the Frieze Art Fair Regent's Park, London, October 15.

Derrida, Jacques. 1993. *Memoirs of the Blind: The Self-Portrait and Other Ruins*, trans. Pascale-Anne Brault and Michael Naas. Chicago: University of Chicago Press.

Fragment. *Online Etymology Dictionary*. https://www.etymonline.com/word/fragment#etymonline_v_11859. Accessed 19 Feb 2019.

Freud, Sigmund. 2001. *Studies on Hysteria: Volume II (1893–2895)*. London: Vintage.

Gadoin, Isabelle. 2017. Blank Letters and Ensnared Eyes in *Far from the Maddening Crowd*, ed. Rosemary Morgan. *The Hardy Review* 19 (2): 18–30.

Hardy, Thomas. 1889–1891. *Tess of the D'Urbervilles*, original autograph MS, British Library, Add MS 38182.

Hardy, Thomas. 1966. The Science of Fiction. In *Thomas Hardy's Personal Writings*, ed. Harold Orel. Lawrence: The University of Kansas Press.

Hardy, Thomas. 2008. *Tess of the D'Urbervilles*, ed. Juliet Grindle and Simon Gatrell. Oxford: Oxford University Press.

Johnston, Julian. 2009. *Mahler's Voices: Expression and Irony in the Songs and Symphonies*. Oxford: Oxford University Press.

Klein, Melanie. 1998. *Love, Guilt and Reparation, and Other Works 1921–1945*. London: Vintage.

Lacan, Jacques. 1992. *The Ethics of Psychoanalysis Book VII (1959–1960)*, ed. Jacques-Alain Miller, trans. Dennis Porter. New York: W. W. Norton.

Ledger, Sally. 1987. *The New Woman: Fiction and Feminism at the fin de siècle*. Manchester: Manchester University Press.

Mallarmé, Stéphane. 1982. *Selected Poetry and Prose*, ed. Mary Anne Caws. New York: New Directions Books.

Miller, J.H. 1970. *Thomas Hardy: Distance and Desire*. London: Oxford University Press.

Millgate, Michael. 1982. *Thomas Hardy: A Biography*. New York: Random.

Nietzsche, Friedrich. 2005. *Untimely Meditations*, ed. Daniel Breazeale, trans. R.J. Hollingdale. Cambridge: Cambridge University Press.

Potter, Claire. 2013. A Love Letter from Beyond the Grave: Irigaray, Nothingness, and *La femme n'existe pas*. In *Engaging the World: Thinking After Irigaray*, ed. Mary C. Rawlinson, 91–114. Albany: State University of New York Press.

Ramel, Annie. 2015. *The Madder Stain: A Psychoanalytic Reading of Thomas Hardy*. Leiden: Brill.

Shakespeare, William. 1973. *Complete Works of Shakespeare*, ed. Peter Alexander. London: Collins.

Sophocles. 2003. *Antigone*, trans. Reginald Gibbons and Charles Segal. Oxford: Oxford University Press.

Vendler, Helen. 2004. *Poets Thinking*. Cambridge, MA: Harvard University Press.

Woolf, Virginia. 1986. *The Second Common Reader*, ed. Andrew McNeillie. London: Harcourt Inc.

CHAPTER 5

Rising from Ruins: Isabel Archer at the Roman Campagna

Chryssa Marinou

History decays into images, not into stories.
Walter Benjamin (1999, 476)

"[I]n a world of ruins the ruin of her happiness seemed a less unnatural catastrophe."[1] Isabel Archer's thoughts, near the closing of Henry James's *The Portrait of a Lady*, are the outcome of a long process of illumination accomplished due to her reception of social, cultural and spatial stimuli abundantly offered throughout her trajectory from the New to the Old World. Her "venture capital" (Adams 1999, 485), provided by her cousin Ralph Touchett, effectively eases her way into the marriage market and attracts Gilbert Osmond's interest in her, as well as in the

---

[1] My essay has greatly benefited from the thorough editing of Mina Karavanta, who took the time not just to critically read the piece, but to engage in an intellectual dialogue with all that I struggled to articulate. Without her help and comments, this would undoubtedly be poorer work. I also remain indebted to Anna Despotopoulou, Efterpi Mitsi, Michael Hollington and Miriam Piedade Mansur Andrade for their generosity and critical feedback.

C. Marinou (✉)
Department of English Language & Literature, National and Kapodistrian University of Athens, Athens, Greece

© The Author(s) 2019
E. Mitsi et al. (eds.), *Ruins in the Literary and Cultural Imagination*,
https://doi.org/10.1007/978-3-030-26905-0_5

79

property and wealth she embodies.[2] Osmond collects Isabel as the rarest commodity and exceptional work of art and their married life, for the most part at least, portrays the story of Isabel's commodification. Her long afternoon visit to the Roman ruins may well be viewed as the realization of this process, which marks a scene of epiphany: Isabel's gaze at the ruins affords a view of the site that enables her to reconfigure her personal misfortune with the Roman historically burdened environs, a reconfiguration that reveals what Walter Benjamin terms as the moment when "history has physically merged into the setting" (2009, 177–178). Isabel's experience of the monumental architectural ruins triggers her understanding of her own ruins of unrealized possibilities in a dialectical image where the historical enfolds the personal.

Drawing on Benjamin's discussion of ruins in his *Origin of the German Tragic Drama*, I will examine Isabel's experience of ruins, the ruins of monuments that symptomatically reveal the ruins of her unfulfilled life to argue that the site of ruins becomes an image-as-text, an image to be read, which alludes to Benjamin's dialectical image. For Benjamin, the image entails reframing effects, namely *profane illumination* and *awakening*, and invariably emerges to be read in "the now of recognisability" (1999, 462). I trace this moment of recognizability in James's narrative to demonstrate how Isabel's awakening to the harsh realities of her life, signifies the effort that she makes to read her present as part of a larger present time made of multiple sedimented historical tenses. In Benjamin's *oeuvre*, ruins are part of a quadripartite schema that brings together thoughts, things, allegories and ruins: "[a]llegories are, in the realm of thoughts, what ruins are in the realm of things" (Benjamin 2009, 178). The sentence attempts to clarify the notions of allegory and ruin contextualizing them within the realms of thoughts and things respectively. Allegories and ruins can then be read as the rubble, the debris or the "X-ray"—as Benjamin would have it—of thoughts and things. Ruins are entities divested of superfluous or unnecessary details and rather lay bare, while much as allegory is representational of the reflective realm, the ruin is representational of the "realm of things."

To reverse the schema, ruins have also been viewed as allegories wherein the ruin, like an index finger, points to an absence in

---

[2] As Donatella Izzo argues, "[b]y enfranchising Isabel from material need, her uncle's bequest sets her 'free,' literally from everything *but* her imagination" (Izzo 2008, 359; emphasis in the original).

"the here and now" (Benjamin 1996, 103). If ruins are "allegories of thinking itself" (Benjamin 2009, 177–178), they remain valuable since they are not just read as objects, but rather as processes that bring history to the fore. Benjamin defines allegory as that which "means precisely the non-existence of what it presents" (2009, 233). In the course of her reflection of the ruins, Isabel becomes the allegorist of cultural-historical ruins. What is visibly before her both triggers her dialectical thinking and is swallowed by it. The visual and optical nature of the allegory remains, yet it constitutes a visuality that merges the seen with the unseen, the visitable with the inaccessible and the actuality of experience with the remembrance of things past.

Isabel's active seeing of the site ruins generates her reading of her past—her failed loveless marriage to the cruel aesthete Gilbert Osmond, her being deceived and trapped by Madame Merle and Osmond, and her unfulfilled potential—through the actuality of her present. My analysis here of the heroine's new-found profane illumination draws heavily on Mina Karavanta's term of *reconstellation* as a cultural and political practice that brings together "discrepant histories," enabling "the 'complete consort' of incommensurable forces 'dancing together contrapuntally'" (Said 1994, 332; Karavanta 2015, 121). Following Theodor W. Adorno, Karavanta is attentive to the Benjaminian genealogy of *constellation* and coins *reconstellation* as an "always already double" engagement, which entwines concept with object; it is a "new act of interpretation and repetition" that "both engages previously untried affiliations and relations and unavoidably returns to the previously set contexts from which concepts and objects are wrenched" (Karavanta and Morgan 2008, 18–19). Latent in Isabel's sightseeing is the wish to encounter the phantasmagoria of the Old World, the spectral images of European history which the sight of historical ruins has the potential of awakening. Isabel forcefully decides to engage this power of the ruins in all its dialectics of both enlightening and obliterating effects.

As Eduardo Cadava argues in his essay "Lapsus Imaginis," "[t]here can be no image that is not about destruction and survival, and this is especially the case in the image of ruin" (2001, 35). For Cadava, the image of ruin "bears witness to the enigmatic relation between death and survival, loss and life, destruction and preservation, mourning and memory" (2001, 35). In much the same way that Benjamin's arcade as a dream space allows the activation of the phantasmagoria of the commodity, the Roman monuments and ruins bear the trace of a living continental past that Isabel, the American expatriate, is to embrace. Benjamin notes that "[t]he trace is appearance of a nearness, however far removed the thing that left it behind may be. ... In the trace, we gain *possession* of the thing" (1999, 447, emphasis mine). In her epiphanic moment, Isabel possesses and is possessed by the sight of ruins; the images she sees endow her simultaneously with historical perception and an understanding of her own story and history. Reflecting on her misfortune she observes: "Small it was, in the large Roman *record*, and her haunting sense of the continuity of the human lot easily carried her *from the less to the greater*" (James 1996, 511; emphasis mine). The excerpt bespeaks her effort to contextualize her pain within the historical suffering that has become embedded in the site, while the word "record" points to an archivization of suffering and alludes to the practice of historical documentation. The image of ruins triggers the process of self-awakening that involves the recognition of the ruins of her life; the image of ruins becomes the text that enables the "recognizability" of the past at the specific moment of the present. The function of the dialectical image can be used to describe the way in which Isabel converges the long and discontinuous trajectory of history immanent in the ruins with her own trajectory, or otherwise put, her act of conflating the fate of the ruins with her personal fate.

In this context of concurring filiations, elective affinities and intertwining paths, I read Isabel's train of thought as reconstellating the personal with the historical past, reconfiguring active seeing with reflective processes in the present and eventually perceiving the ruin as the Benjaminian "remnant" (2009, 178) that persists as the highly significant manifestation which enables the dialectical movement between the extremes of subject (Isabel) and history. The gravitational pull of ruins to which Isabel is drawn is perhaps this petrified and frozen element of civilization that has been fossilized in time and is now assuming the form of both the "flow of thoughts" and their "arrest" (Benjamin 2009, 178) through Isabel's reading. The image of ruins she is able to read, that is the image in the now of its recognizability, "bears ... the imprint of the perilous critical moment on which all reading is founded" (1999, 463). Commenting on Benjamin's formulation, Cadava agrees that "there can be no reading of an image that does not expose us to a danger" and emphasizes that the reading of the image-as-text always carries the potential of demonstrating "the non-contemporaneity of the present, the absence of linearity in the representation of historical time, and therefore the fugacity of the past and the present" (2001, 42). Isabel's critical moment thus relies on the act of reading her own story through the illuminating lens of the ruin. It is a reading through seeing "that emerges suddenly, in a flash" (Benjamin 1999, 473). The overwhelming suddenness of this flash is evident in Chapter 49, when Isabel "seemed to wake from a long pernicious dream" (James 1996, 508) and realizes what has happened to her: "she fell back, covering her face with her hands. It had come over her like a high-surging wave that Mrs. Touchett was right. Madame Merle had married her" (James 1996, 511). This moment of realization that she has been ensnared in her marriage with Osmond, understanding that Madame Merle has "made a convenience of [her]" (James 1996, 564), is the prologue to her epiphanic reading of the ruin scene.

Quite appropriately, Isabel is early on described as "bookish": "Her reputation of reading a great deal hung about her like the cloudy envelope of a goddess in an epic" (James 1996, 47). Isabel hates "to be thought bookish" (James 1996, 47), yet it is her reading skills that perhaps lead to the legibility of the dialectical image. In understanding her past, Isabel is actualizing her present since the function of the dialectical image is "not that what is past casts its light on what is present, or what is present its light on the past; rather, image is that wherein /what has been comes together in a flash with the now to form a constellation" (Benjamin 1999, 462). As Cadava notes, when Benjamin refers to the image's "historical index," he does not mean that the image belongs to a specific time, but rather refers to the moment in time when the image enters into legibility (2001, 38). The time of legibility, Isabel's moment of reading, is the time when the ruin-site becomes a sight, or else an image that is rendered legible. The space that was previously part of the ancient Roman landmarks now resonates with Isabel's dismay. This moment of epiphany is strategically placed in James's text, prefacing the closing of *The Portrait of a Lady*. Isabel's commodification within the confines of her marriage has come full circle at this point; so has the accumulation of her Grand Tour educational travel experience. From Isabel's earlier visit to St. Peter's, we know that her "conception of greatness rose and dizzily rose. After this it never lacked space to soar. She gazed and wondered like a child or a peasant, she paid her silent tribute to the seated sublime" (James 1996, 296). Rome then becomes for Isabel what Chloe Chard terms in her *Pleasure and Guilt on the Grand Tour* an "imaginative geography" (1999, 10), that is, a privileged malleable space that accommodates the memory, will and aspirations of the subject, in this case, of Isabel. The legibility of the ruins appropriately comes to light amidst the specific Roman setting, which stands in the novel as an emblematic centre of the Old World, Europe and certainly as the centre of the Roman Empire.

Foretelling his heroine's trials and tribulations with history, James makes special reference to the historical load of the Roman ruins. In the Preface to the *Portrait*, he seems preoccupied that perhaps the richness in life of such places, the grand narrative may rob his smaller narrative of attention. In his own words, "romantic and historic sites, such as the land of Italy abounds in, … are too rich in their own life and too charged with their own meanings … they draw him away from his small questions to their own greater one" (James 1996, 3). Perhaps then in foregrounding the smaller narrative, the text makes a point about the reception of the grand narrative, whose significance it shifts in a gesture of reconfiguring it in the minor (hi)story of a woman. Early in the novel, Ralph's explanation of the relation of Rome to one's experience of the inner world is proleptic of Isabel's epiphany: "Rome, as Ralph said, confessed to the psychological moment" (James 1996, 312). The eternal city in *The Portrait of a Lady* is the epitome of the Old World in that while it embodies high culture, a sense of history and the potentiality of "endless knowledge" (James 1996, 197), at the same time it attests to a loss of innocence, as it is here that Isabel, the independent, strong-minded American, painfully reaps the benefits of experience. The intertwining of the personal and the public is characteristic of James's "persistent interest in transatlantic and pan-European crossings," which according to Anna Despotopoulou, sheds light on the "Rome scene" as "one of the many in which James explores the melding of the local and the global, the personal and the universal" (2014, 142, 150).

The beginning of Chapter 50 reintroduces Isabel's initial relation to the ruins in a seemingly innocent and almost superficial context, which nevertheless reveals Isabel's serious engagement in active seeing:

> Isabel, however, was not a severe cicerone; she used to visit the ruins chiefly because they offered an excuse for talking about other matters than the love affairs of the ladies of Florence, as to which her companion [Countess Gemini] was never weary of offering information. (James 1996, 519)

Both Ralph's comment and the seeing of ruins as Isabel's strategy employed for avoiding gossip offer two aspects of the experience of ruins that have in the meantime been unsettled in the novel. I argue that contrary to Ralph's description, the Roman space does not simply attest to or speak of Isabel's mood and condition, but rather constitutes the setting where she becomes awakened to her self-knowledge; in other words, it is the specific site that engenders the possibilities for Isabel's epiphany. Isabel's awakening from her dream of herself—the "long pernicious dream" (James 1996, 508) that has allowed her to believe she has chosen her husband and planned her life trajectory—owes much to her seeing of ruins; in the end, Rome as a synecdoche of the Old World stands as the dialectical other end of America and Isabel's epiphany entails the acknowledgement of her movement, in leaps and bounds, between these two polar opposites. In a similar manner, the above excerpt attests to the fact that Isabel's reluctance to hear of the love affairs of Florentine ladies has already been turned into her recognition of the disturbing truths about her own life with Osmond. Madame Merle has successfully procured Isabel for Osmond, the father of her child, and together they have destroyed Isabel's life. The text's characterization of Isabel as "not a severe cicerone" means she bears no resemblance to the touristy sort of sightseer, since she seizes and uses her visit of the ruins as an opportunity to talk about grave matters and eschew Countess Gemini's gossip.

Isabel's epiphany at the site of ruins is worth reading along with Benjamin's elaboration of the dialectical image as a convergence of immobility and movement: "To thinking belongs the movement as well as the arrest of thoughts. Where thinking comes to a standstill in a constellation saturated with tensions—there the dialectical image appears" (Benjamin 1999, 475). The two dialectical extremes of "movement" and "arrest" mark the moment of great tension, the moment of the apparition of the dialectical image and therefore the moment of its readability. Isabel is both overwhelmed by the sight she encounters and engaged in an effort to process it. Although her impression of Rome is initially that of "a land of promise, a land in which a love of the beautiful might be comforted by endless knowledge," when she leaves Rome, after her encounter with Madame Merle, she has become indifferent and detached, taking "little pleasure in the countries she traversed" (James 1996, 197, 474). Her perception radically changes accompanied by the full realization of what has happened to her; the following passage bespeaks this cognitive and emotional shift:

She had long before this taken old Rome into her confidence, for in a
world of *ruins* the ruin of her happiness seemed a less unnatural catastrophe. She rested her weariness upon *things* that had crumbled for centuries
and yet still were upright; she dropped her secret sadness into the silence
of lonely places, where its very *modern* quality detached itself and grew
objective, so that as she sat in a sun-warmed angle on a winter's day, or
stood in a mouldy church to which no one came, she could almost smile
at it and think of its smallness. Small it was, in the large Roman *record*,
and her haunting sense of the continuity of the human lot easily carried
her *from the less to the greater*. She had become *deeply, tenderly* acquainted
with Rome; it interfused and moderated her passion. But she had grown
to think of it chiefly as the place where people had suffered. (James 1996,
511; emphases mine)

Isabel's train of thought reveals an engagement with the landscape
that assumes more than one form. She witnesses the passage of time
which is accumulated and legible in the site and its "things" and which
renders ruins as bearers not solely of the past, but rather of a present
filled with encoded past knowledge. As Bill Brown avers, things are a
privileged term in James's lexicon (2003, 294); the excerpt of Isabel's
thoughts reaffirms the Benjaminian schema not just because "her intimacy with the inanimate object world proves self-sustaining" as Brown
claims (2003, 295), but also due to the text's interchangeability of the
terms "ruins" and "things that had crumbled for centuries" (James
1996, 551). The Roman ruins are not just the ruins of monuments and
works of art that Isabel's venture capital has brought to her attention,
but rather the ruins of the entire "realm of things" of the *Portrait of
a Lady*: Isabel's new-found wealth, Osmond's art collection, the small
cup on Madame Merle's chimney mantel that "already has a small crack"
(James 1996, 483), Ned Rosier's enamels and his chimney piece which
is "better draped than the high shoulders of many a duchess" (James
1996, 220) are only a few of the material objects that parade the pages of
the novel. Isabel expresses the feeling of knowledgeable experience and
historical burden, while the expression "Roman record" alludes to her
felt knowledge of the history that lies in the ruins. Having been com-
modified—"[Madame Merle] made a convenience of me" (James 1996,
564)—Isabel demonstrates an empathy with the ruin/object. Rather
than passively take in her surroundings, she actively reads them in a
gesture that conjoins the personal to the historical, the animate to the

inanimate and dialectically positions her lived experience in conjunction with a larger social and historical framework.

Multifarious meanings reveal themselves during Isabel's encounter with the ruin; in Max Pensky's phrasing, the ruin is "rune: a cipher or mark" that warns us about "the omnipresence of guaranteed oblivion" (2011, 68). In her moment of recognizability, Isabel is warned of this oblivion and her active, reflective sightseeing becomes a form of practical memory[3] that commemorates and contextualizes her suffering ("the less") as part of "the Roman record" ("the greater"). In the phrase of Rose Macaulay, whose 1953 *Pleasure of Ruins* more or less inaugurated the exploration of ruins in literary criticism, ruins are "the ghosts of dead ages sleeping together" (1966, 127). The image of phantasms of dead ages sleeping together, the phantasmagoria of disparate tenses that are summoned and awakened is also the cohabitation of the "very modern" quality of Isabel's individual sadness with the collective ancient Roman record. Cadava insists that "while the relation of the present to the past is a purely temporal, continuous one, the relation of the Then to the Now is dialectical: not temporal in nature but imagistic" (2001, 38). The cohabitation of the individual and the collective attests precisely to this convergence when temporalities cohabit the time of the now and the dialectical is always/already an image-as-text.

Such contextualization of Isabel's specific experience in the entirety of the Roman record, the positioning of the part within the whole, offers more when compared to Benjamin's exploration of the notion of space. Discussing how the flâneur becomes intoxicated with space in the course of his urban peregrinations, Benjamin notes that it "allows him to be affected even by the knowledge of dead dates as something experienced and lived," a "felt knowledge" (1999, 1052–1054). Isabel's knowledge is felt as the adjectives "deeply" and "tenderly," used to describe the extent and profoundness of her "acquaintance" with Rome, indicate. She has developed an empathy with this man-made landscape composed of ruins/things.[4] *Stricto sensu*, Isabel is no flâneuse—accepting inheritances and marrying

---

[3] In Convolute H, The Collector of *The Arcades Project*, Benjamin discusses the practice of collection as "a form of practical memory" and argues that "of all the profane manifestations of 'nearness' it is the most binding" (1999, 205).

[4] Discussing the empathy felt by the flâneur, Benjamin cites an excerpt from Gustave Flaubert that exemplifies the idea of concurring tenses:

> I see myself at different moments of history, very clearly.... I was boatman on the Nile, *leno* (procurer) in Rome at the time of the Punic wars, then Greek

the sophisticated yet shady art collector, she is too involved in the market to be able to distance herself from it. Nevertheless, she is certainly a traveller following the tradition of women travellers who take the Grand Tour as part of complementing their education. In Isabel's case, education also entails emotional development and self-knowledge that amounts to the emergence of her "dialectics of seeing"—to borrow here Susan Buck-Morss's compelling term (1991)—and despite her early declaration of wishing to avoid "the cup of experience" (James 1996, 159), by the end of the novel, she has accumulated all the experience she can handle.

Early in the novel, talking with her friend Henrietta Stackpole about her potential marriage prospects to the American industrialist Caspar Goodwood, Henrietta, the demanding American correspondent, asks Isabel: "Do you know where you're drifting?" (James 1996, 174). Isabel's quick response is typical of her initial innocence and optimism: "No, I haven't the least idea, and I find it very pleasant not to know. A swift carriage, of a dark night, rattling with four horses over roads that one can't see—that's my idea of happiness" (James 1996, 174). The carriage image that Isabel has originally imagined taking her to an unforeseen future resurfaces in the text in this late scene set at the Roman ruins. It is the carriage in which she takes "a drive alone that afternoon; she wished to be far away, under the sky, where she could descend from the carriage and tread upon the daisies" (James 1996, 511). As much else in the novel, the connotations of the carriage have altered according to the heroine's perception. The promising darkness of the night and the invisibility of the roads of the first excerpt give way to the wish to descend from the carriage and experience the site in the latter.

rhetorician in Suburra, where I was devoured by bed-bugs. I died, during the Crusades, from eating too many grapes on the beach in Syria. I was pirate and monk, mountebank and coachman—perhaps Emperor of the East, who knows? (Flaubert 1982, 89, qtd. in Benjamin 1999, 449)

The passage, taken from Flaubert's September 29, 1866, letter to George Sand is intriguing for both its reference to "different moments of history" and for its array of mostly marginal figures. Flaubert here exemplifies his "*real* genealogy" and insists that "[his] present self is the result of all his vanished selves" (Flaubert 1982, 89). The boatman, the unfortunate rhetorician, the victim of grapes—rather than of the Crusades—the pirate, the monk, the mountebank and the coachman may all be read as a parade of the defeated in Flaubert's imagination. The only figure of grandeur, the Emperor is saved for last and undermined by the uncertainty of "perhaps" that precedes it.

Not seeing is substituted with seeing, night-time with afternoon, riding with treading, all in the process of Isabel's path towards encountering the dialectical image.

At the moment of Isabel's awakening, her sadness is small "in the large Roman record" and the prevailing feeling of "continuity of the human lot" transfers her "from the less to the greater." Critics such as Jonathan Freedman have discussed the change in Isabel's perception of Rome and have argued about a turn in her aesthetic education; from Osmond's reifying "aestheticizing vision" (Freedman 1990, 152), she gradually progresses to a more "ethical" mode of seeing. Freedman argues that acknowledging the commonality of suffering, "Isabel asserts her own aestheticizing vision that grants her an 'embeddedness in historical process, her own participation in the human community'" (Freedman 1990, 162, qtd. in Jottkandt 2004, 69). Her perception does not repeat or in any way reproduce the male gaze on things. It constitutes taking a distance both from Osmond's aesthetics and from Ralph's psychological vision. In an early scene of the novel, Isabel asks Ralph whether Gardencourt is haunted by a ghost, a "castle-spectre, *a thing that appears*" (James 1996, 59; emphasis mine) to which Ralph insightfully responds that even if it were, Isabel would be unable to see it since ghosts are visible only to those who have "suffered greatly, have gained some miserable knowledge" (1996, 60).[5] In Isabel's conflation of her individual experience and the trace of the historical condition, the common denominator of individual and collective experience is suffering. The "thing that appears" is made visible to Isabel after having suffered and upon her encounter with the ruins.

In a later scene in the novel, when Isabel returns to Gardencourt to visit the dying Ralph, she again revisits her epiphanic ruin-moment and, this time on a second level of reflection, resorts to the memory of the dialectical image that has produced her felt knowledge. Drawing on what she had previously seen and cannot see, but solely remember at the given moment, she offers an alternative image of herself in an attempt of self-narrative: "She sat in her corner, so motionless, so passive, simply with the sense of being carried, so detached from hope and regret, that she recalled to herself one of those Etruscan figures couched upon the receptacle of their ashes" (James 1996, 553). If the ruin has

---

[5] Kristin Boudreau (2011) also offers a relevant reading of this scene.

hitherto performed the task of towering over the realm of things, this is the moment when Isabel's explicit perception of herself as the Etruscan figure, the work of art that stands for an ancient, mythical and mystical Italy, transforms the ruins into an allegory of herself. It is certainly an allegory which towers over the realm of her thoughts and perhaps a gesture in which Benjamin's differentiated counterpart notions of ruin and allegory meet. As Benjamin puts it, allegory "holds fast to ruins; it offers the image of petrified unrest" (1999, 329). The Etruscan figure, as the surviving trace of a civilization that was completely obliterated by the Romans, may be read as Benjamin's "highly significant fragment, the remnant," in other words his definition of the ruin in *The Origin of German Tragic Drama* (2009, 178).

Having reflected upon the general, the monumental ruins she has roamed, Isabel pinpoints the particular, the Etruscan figure. As Goethe states, "whoever grasps the particular in all its vitality also grasps the general, without being aware of it, or only becoming aware of it at a late stage" (qtd. in Benjamin 2009, 161). Apart from their obvious essence as remainders of ancient Roman buildings, the ruins that Isabel visits also symbolize the world as dismantled into shards, fragments and pieces; they stand as the telltale signs of destruction, of a discarded past, but also of the tenacity and resilience in the face of catastrophe. In the spectacle of ruins, the frozen time of destruction brings forth a "time-space which becomes separated from the continuous idea of history" (Lindroos 1998, 231–232). If the closing of the novel is interpreted as a resistance to complete the frame of Isabel's portrait (Freedman 1990, 165), then there is something ruinous and yet redemptive to be read in the text's ending—what Despotopoulou graphically describes as characteristic of James's "female protagonists in mid-air, about to make their most decided leap toward an unrepresentable future" (2014, 154). Isabel's transient and contingent experience of seeing the ruins and reading their image-as-text brings to the fore a reading of a confluent past and present that opens a literary space for her new way of seeing. The relics of what has been continue to haunt the "now" and allow for a constant retelling of the bygone, which triggers the revelation of the hidden connections between the personal and the collective and results in a shift in the social and political paradigms that frame women in modernity.

REFERENCES

Adams, Richard. 1999. Heir of Propriety: Inheritance, "The Impressions of a Cousin," and the Proprietary Vision of Henry James. *American Literature* 71 (3): 463–491. *JSTOR*. https://muse.jhu.edu/.

Benjamin, Walter. 1996. *Selected Writings*, vol. 3, ed. Marcus Bullock and Michael W. Jennings. Cambridge: Belknap.

Benjamin, Walter. 1999. *The Arcades Project*, ed. Rolf Tiedemann. Cambridge, MA: Harvard University Press.

Benjamin, Walter. 2009. *The Origin of German Tragic Drama*, trans. John Osborne. London: Verso.

Boudreau, Kristin. 2011. Immensities of Perception and Yearning: The Haunting of Henry James's Heroes. In *Henry James and the Supernatural*, ed. Anna Despotopoulou and Kimberly C. Reed, 35–57. New York: Palgrave Macmillan.

Brown, Bill. 2003. *A Sense of Things: The Object Matter of American Literature.* Chicago: University of Chicago Press.

Buck-Morss, Susan. 1991. *The Dialectics of Seeing: Walter Benjamin and the Arcades Project.* Studies in Contemporary German Social Thought. Boston: MIT Press.

Cadava, Eduardo. 2001. "Lapsus Imaginis": The Image in Ruins. *October* 96: 35–60. http://www.jstor.org/stable/779116.

Chard, Chloe. 1999. *Pleasure and Guilt on the Grand Tour: Travel Writing and Imaginative Geography, 1600–1830.* Manchester: Manchester University Press.

Despotopoulou, Anna. 2014. "No Natural Place Anywhere": Women's Precarious Mobility and Cosmopolitanism in James's Novels. *The Henry James Review* 35: 141–156. https://doi.org/10.1353/hjr.2014.0015.

Flaubert, Gustave. 1982. *The Letters of Gustave Flaubert, 1857–1880*, trans. Francis Steegmuller. Cambridge, MA: Harvard University Press.

Freedman, Jonathan. 1990. *Professions of Taste: Henry James, British Aestheticism, and Commodity Culture.* Stanford: Stanford University Press.

Izzo, Donatella. 2008. Nothing Personal: Women Characters, Gender Ideology, and Literary Representation. In *A Companion to Henry James*, ed. Greg W. Zacharias, 343–359. Malden: Wiley-Blackwell.

James, Henry. 1996. *The Portrait of a Lady.* Hertfordshire: Wordsworth Editions Limited.

Jottkandt, Sigi. 2004. Portrait of an Act: Aesthetics and Ethics in the Portrait of a Lady. *The Henry James Review* 25 (1): 67–86. https://doi.org/10.1353/hjr.2004.0007.

Karavanta, Mina. 2015. William V. Spanos's Ontopolitical Criticism: Risky A-filiations and the Call of the *Kore's Meidiama*. *Boundary 2* 42 (1): 115–138. https://doi.org/10.1215/01903659-2828290.

Karavanta, Mina, and Nina Morgan (eds.). 2008. *Edward Said and Jacques Derrida: Reconstellating Humanism and the Global Hybrid.* Newcastle: Cambridge Scholars Publishing.

Lindroos, Kia. 1998. *Now-Time/Image-Space: Temporalization of Politics in Walter Benjamin's Philosophy of History and Art.* Jyvaskyla: SoPhi, University of Jyvaskyla.

Macaulay, Rose. 1966 [1953]. *Pleasure of Ruins.* New York: Walker and Company.

Pensky, Max. 2011. Three Kinds of Ruin: Heidegger, Benjamin, Sebald. *Poligrafi* (no iss. no): 65–89. http://www2.binghamton.edu/philosophy/people/docs/pensky-kinds-of-ruin.pdf.

Said, Edward. 1994. *Culture and Imperialism.* New York: Vintage.

CHAPTER 6

Untimely Returns: Shoring Fragments Against Ruins in Daphne du Maurier's *Rebecca*

Sheila Teahan

The closing lines of T. S. Eliot's *The Waste Land* contain an enigmatic image linking the key figure of the conceptualization of the present essay collection, the ruin, to the fragment: "These fragments I have shored against my ruins" (1934, 67). Among other angles of approach, this volume offers a suggestive distinction between the historical and aesthetic status of these two figures. On this view, as the book's Introduction states, the ruin "predominantly recalls a classical or distant past" as a "silent yet privileged ground for [the] reconstruction" of the past, whereas the fragment signifies "a metonymy of nostalgic wholeness." In "The Waste Land," Eliot's speaker posits the fragment and the ruin as not only contrastive but antithetical by suggesting that fragmentation offers an antidote to the condition of ruination. Can one shore fragments against ruins, and if so, what would it mean to do so? In its thematic and tropological preoccupation with fragmentation and ruination alike, Daphne du Maurier's *Rebecca* thinks through this question,

S. Teahan (✉)
Michigan State University, East Lansing, MI, USA

© The Author(s) 2019
E. Mitsi et al. (eds.), *Ruins in the Literary and Cultural Imagination*,
https://doi.org/10.1007/978-3-030-26905-0_6

especially as dramatized by the narrator's tortuous relation to the spaces, places and objects associated with her predecessor Rebecca, the first Mrs. de Winter. In what follows, I propose to consider how the narrator's double and contradictory relation to Rebecca entails the attempted (re) construction of the imagined and imaginary whole denoted by the trope of the "symbol"—a keyword in the novel.

In its analysis of many of the occulted spaces also explored in *Rebecca*, Gaston Bachelard's *Poetics of Space* offers a rich theoretical intertext for the consideration of fragmentary and ruined spaces in the novel. Bachelard describes the temporal dynamic of the concealment and escape of a being in hiding—a dynamic that speaks to the plot of *Rebecca*, which is a story of emergence from an occulted space of repression, disavowal and hidden knowledge.

> A creature that hides and "withdraws into its shell," is preparing a "way out." This is true of the entire scale of metaphors, from the resurrection of a man in his grave, to the sudden outburst of one who has long been silent. If we remain at the heart of the image under consideration, we have the impression that, by staying in the motionlessness of its shell, the creature is preparing temporal explosions, not to say whirlwinds, of being. The most dynamic escape takes place in cases of repressed being, and not in the flabby laziness of the lazy creature whose only desire is to go and be lazy elsewhere. If we experience the imaginary paradox of a vigorous mollusk ... we attain to the most decisive type of aggressiveness, which is postponed aggressiveness, aggressiveness that bides its time. (Bachelard 1994, 111–112)

Whether the space from which the creature or man emerges is a shell, a grave or a long silence ripe for an "outburst"—all tropes that figure in *Rebecca*—the temporal dynamic is the same. It is structured by an inverse relation between, on the one hand, the extremity of the subject's withdrawal, its motionlessness and silence, its temporal delay, and on the other the violence and suddenness of its emergence. Bachelard's analysis is powerfully suggestive for du Maurier's *Rebecca*, whose (un)dead eponymous protagonist stages a spectacular resurrection from the grave a year after her murder by her husband Maxim de Winter, a return announced by the name of the boat that bears her body: "Je Reviens." When de Winter confesses to his second wife, the novel's narrator, that he had murdered her predecessor, she remarks that "for no reason the stupid proverb of my school-days ran through my mind, 'Time and Tide wait for no man'" (du Maurier 2006, 271). Like Bachelard's mollusc, Rebecca bides her time, and the tide facilitates her staging of a spectacular return by water—a key figure for temporality in the novel—of the repressed and disavowed. Rebecca haunts the narrator, who feels herself a mere shadow of the first Mrs. de Winter, an interloper and intruder who can neither rival or recover what she imagines to have been Rebecca's matchless and glamorous mode of being.

In his exploration of "the poetics of the house," Bachelard humanizes the metaphor of the shell, imagining human spaces as repositories of a past that resists forgetting: "how can secret rooms, rooms that have disappeared, become abodes for an unforgettable past?" (Bachelard 1994, xxxvi). This is a fair plot summary of *Rebecca*, in which the occulted spaces of Rebecca's bedroom, morning room, and the cottage and boathouse associated with her promiscuous double life become sites of what Nicholas Abraham and Maria Torok have theorized as "the phantom," the "unknowing awareness of another's secret" or "a haunting by the secret of another" (Smith 1992, 291, 292). As distinct from repression, the phantom is a formation of the unconscious that was never conscious in the first place. In positing that "characters in literary texts may be construed as cryptic poetic entities whose words and actions can be heard to tell the secret history generating their existence" (Esther Rashkin, qtd. in Smith 1992, 291–292), Abraham describes Rebecca's own secret history as revealed (and constructed) by the double movement of the narrator's simultaneous pursuit of and flight from knowledge of the first Mrs. de Winter and by her contradictory and impossible effort to summon and eradicate her phantasmal presence.

As reflected in its preoccupation with letters, both epistolary and alphabetical, *Rebecca* is concerned with language as an agent of repression, concealment and violent release. Bachelard proposes that "words are little houses, each with its cellar and garret" (1994, 147), spaces redolent of the oneiric and the rational, respectively. I would add that in *Rebecca*, names are houses, too. Citing Nicholas Rand's "Translator's Introduction" to Abraham and Torok's *The Wolf Man's Magic Word: A Cryptonomy*, Allan Lloyd Smith similarly suggests that words, "as carriers of veiled lexical relationships, can be 'cryptonyms,' words that hide" (Smith 1992, 293). *Rebecca* may be understood as a narrativization of the cryptonymic properties of Rebecca's name.[1] Smith comments on the implications of the recursive prefix—re; he observes that Rebecca "includes the suggestion of a revenant: Rebecca, who comes again, who *beckons* again." By contrast, the narrator's name is never revealed, and the novel goes to comically hyperbolic lengths to emphasize its occlusion, as when Mrs. Van Hopper "mumbles" her name when introducing her to de Winter, when de Winter comments on her "very lovely and unusual name," and sends her a note with "my name … on the envelope, and spelt correctly, an unusual thing," or "murmur[s] my name" when he tells her for the first time, just after he has confessed to Rebecca's murder, that he loves her (du Maurier 2006, 14, 24, 20, 272). The envelope is a key trope in a text preoccupied with receptacles: envelopes, shells, pockets, drawers, wardrobes, rooms and crypts.

The narrator first encounters the ruined and ruinous house of Manderley in a picture postcard, purchased as a child and "lost long ago in some forgotten book" (du Maurier 2006, 23), as she recalls when de Winter proposes to her. Bracketed by the ironic statement that "I considered my name" and by the incantatory triple repetition of the gratifying anticipation that "I would be Mrs. de Winter," the narrator recalls: "He wanted to show me Manderley … I knew now why I had bought that picture post-card as a child, it was a premonition, a blank step into the future" (du Maurier 2006, 54). She reads their arrival at Manderley after their honeymoon as the retrospectively figured prolepsis of the postcard.

> I leant back in my chair, glancing about the room, trying to instil into myself some measure of confidence, some genuine realisation that I was here, at Manderley, the house of the picture post-card, the Manderley that was famous. I had to teach myself that all this was mine now, mine as much as his, the deep chair I was sitting in, that mass of books stretching to the ceiling, the pictures on the walls, the gardens, the woods, the Manderley I had read about, all of this was mine now because I was married to Maxim. (du Maurier 2006, 70)

Despite her ironized assertions of presence and plenitude ("I was here," "all this was mine now"), the postcard seems—as reflected in the ambiguous genitive in "the house of the picture post-card"—to enjoy temporal

---

[1] In Chapter 4, Claire Potter also ponders on the significance of the name in Hardy's *Tess of the d'Urbervilles*, seeing Tess's name as a wound.

and ontological priority over the house it represents. The narrator's arrival at Manderley is mediated and pre-empted by its pictorial representation, and the original is experienced as a copy of its own reproduction. Like Rebecca, Manderley is a revenant, belated in relation to its textual representations. Like a ghost, it can only return without ever having been present in the first place. The postcard is an apt figure for the causal and narrative mechanism that affects Rebecca's return despite de Winter's best effort to dispatch forever his murdered wife, whose motto might well be: return to sender.

Bachelard's notion of the "oneiric house, a house of dream-memory, that is lost in the shadow of a beyond of the real past" (1994, 15) is suggestive for the dream sequence of the first chapter. Its opening words, "Last night I dreamt I went to Manderley again," establish the recursive character of the narrative, which is structured around the trope of return (du Maurier 2006, 1). The "again" is ambiguous (Did she dream again, or dream that she went to Manderley again?), as is the temporal status of the dream. How many times has the narrator dreamed this dream, and what is its temporal relation either to the fire that destroys Manderley or to the diminished and valedictory account in Chapter 2 of the de Winters' pursuit in an unidentified locale sometime after the fire of taking tea and perusing English sporting magazines?[2] The opening of Chapter 2 declares: "We can never go back again" (du Maurier 2006, 5), but this is just what the narrator does in her dream, in which she is doubly barred from entering the estate by an "iron gate" and a "padlock" (du Maurier 2006, 5). Bachelard notes that the lock represents a "psychological threshold" (1994, 81), and although the narrator passes "like a spirit through the barrier before me" (du Maurier 2006, 1), she does not enter the house, which figures the unconscious content of the narrative that follows. As Bachelard observes, "the unconscious is housed," and the house is an image of a "psychic state" (1994, 10, 72). The narrator similarly declares: "The house was a sepulchre, our fear and suffering lay buried in the ruins. There would be no resurrection" (du Maurier 2006, 3). Yet the novel's trajectory, figured by the narratological tropes of the path, ribbon, thread and labyrinth, works towards the resurrectional return of Rebecca from her grave. With its feminized prosopopoeia, the landscape is heavily psychologized and allegorical, rife with

---

[2] As Light observes, the narrator "ends, as she began, as a paid companion" (1984, 20).

imagery alluding to Rebecca's promiscuous and incestuous sexuality: to take only a few examples, images of monstrosity and parasitism, the "strange embrace" of branches, the "alien marriage" of rhododendrons and shrubs (a possible double allusion to de Winter's two marriages) and the oxymoronic "unnatural growth" that figures Rebecca's false claim of being pregnant with an illegitimate heir to Manderley (du Maurier 2006, 1, 2). The narrator concludes that "I would not tell my dream," a performative contradiction that belies this ironized locus amoenus of Manderley's "lost garden," the ironically dubbed "Happy Valley" (du Maurier 2006, 4, 2, 110). With its dense prolepsis, this dream sequence is the coiled spring from which the entire novel unfolds.

Rebecca haunts the narrator even before her arrival at Manderley. On the drive that initiates their courtship, Maxim takes her to the place where he had once stifled a murderous impulse to throw Rebecca over the precipice after her heretofore withheld "outburst," in Bachelardian terms, revealing her contempt for de Winter and their marriage. Feeling "sick and giddy," the narrator senses that their presence at the summit is a repetition: "'Do you know this place?' I asked. 'Have you been here before?' … 'Then you have been here before?'" (du Maurier 2006, 30, 29–30). She feels for her gloves in the car's "pocket," a carefully chosen word that anticipates her later discovery in the pocket of Rebecca's raincoat. In addition to the gloves, she finds in the car's glove box a book "whose slim covers told of poetry … I was glad, and held it tightly with my gloves. I felt I wanted some possession of his" (du Maurier 2006, 32). But what she imagines to be a metonym for her possession of Maxim and Manderley turns out to be the very "symbol" of Rebecca (du Maurier 2006, 44). The book's dedication page is literally and figuratively marked by Rebecca's dedication ("Max—from Rebecca") and by her "black and strong" signature, "the tall and sloping R dwarfing the other letters" (du Maurier 2006, 33). This towering R undermines de Winter's figuration of his marriage proposal as an erasure and forgetting of his past: "Something happened a year ago that altered my whole life, and I want to forget every phase of my existence up to that time. Those days are finished. They are blotted out … You have blotted out the past for me" (du Maurier 2006, 40). But the R, bold and tall like Rebecca herself, testifies otherwise, as does the "blob of ink"[3] that mars

---

[3] See also Potter's discussion of the "blot" in Hardy (Chapter 4).

"the white page opposite," as though the materiality of Rebecca's letter, fantastically enlarged by the narrator's perception, has metastasized onto the facing page in an anamorphic inscription of Rebecca's uncanny power.[4] This textual trace of Rebecca's presence and power attains a fetishized and eroticized status for the narrator: she harbours it underneath her pillow and dwells upon "that bold, slanting hand, stabbing the white paper, the symbol of herself, so certain, so assured" (du Maurier 2006, 44). When de Winter later reveals to the narrator the chronic promiscuity that led him to murder Rebecca after she falsely boasts that she is pregnant with an illegitimate baby who will inherit Manderley, we realize that Rebecca's habitual abbreviation of "Maxim" to "Max" is a linguistic and tropological castration in keeping with this taunting unmanning of her husband.[5]

So threatened is the narrator by the textual evidence of Rebecca's endurance that she attempts to destroy it.

> I cut the page right out of the book. I left no jagged edges, and the book looked white and clean when the page was gone. A new book, that had not been touched. I tore the page up in many little fragments and threw them into the wastepaper basket. Then I went and sat on the window seat again. But I kept thinking of the torn scraps in the basket, and after a moment I had to get up and look in the basket once more. Even now the ink stood up on the fragments thick and black, the writing was not destroyed. I took a box of matches and set fire to the fragments. The flame had a lovely light, staining the paper, curling the edges, making the slanting writing impossible to distinguish. The fragments to grey ashes. The letter R was the last to go, it twisted in the flame, it curled outwards for a moment, becoming larger than ever. Then it crumpled too; the flame destroyed it. It was not ashes even, it was feathery dust … I went and washed my hands in the basin. I felt better, much better. I had the clean, new feeling that one has when the calendar is hung on the wall at the beginning of the year. (du Maurier 2006, 58–59)

---

[4] Smith links "the sloping 'R' of Rebecca's signature" to the phenomenon of the phantom, citing it as a sign of the narrator's "unconscious participation in Max's secret" (Smith 1992, 303).

[5] Hovey argues that Maxim "covers over the memory of his sexual rejection and castration at his first wife's hands"; he further "represses his part in her murder, as well as his role in the similarly national murders of others on the battlefields of the First World War" (2001, 161).

In a cutting that repeats rather than undoes Rebecca's stabbing motion, this extraordinary enactment of magical thinking dramatizes the impossibility of eradicating her presence. The narrator's attempt is fourfold: she cuts the dedication page out of the book, tears it into fragments, throws the fragments away and finally burns them (in a prolepsis of the burning of Manderley). But her tearing of the page into fragments has the ironic effect of proliferating the text of the dedication page. Through another effect of anamorphosis, her burning of the fragments of the offending R makes it "larger than ever." Even this triple ritualistic purgation does not suffice, since it is followed by a supplementary hand-washing that is bathetically and retrospectively defeated by Mrs. Van Hopper's dismissal after de Winter informs her of their engagement: "I wash my hands of the whole affair" (du Maurier 2006, 59). Smith argues that Rebecca's initial is "linked hermeneutically with the obsessive ideas of trace, sign and clue which underlie the narrative," such that "fragmentation is not enough; the word [Rebecca's name] must be consumed by fire in a *mise en abyme* of the novel's larger movement" (Smith 1992, 302). But whereas Smith concludes that the burning of the paper signifies that Rebecca's signature "has be to completely obliterated for this reason: not the narrator's understandable jealousy, but her unconscious participation in Max's secret" (1992, 303), I contend that it multiplies the textual fragments it seeks to destroy. In a progression from fragment to ashes to dust, the ashes are further disseminated into a fine, "feathery" dust that broadcasts Rebecca's presence like seed in space and time. The narrator believes that her action will obliterate the past: "A new confidence had been born in me when I burnt that page and scattered the fragments ... The past had blown away like the ashes in the wastepaper basket" (du Maurier 2006, 61). But the image of dust recurs when, after the discovery of Rebecca's body on the boat, she reflects: "It was not Rebecca who was lying in that coffin in the crypt, it was dust. Only dust" (du Maurier 2006, 326). The dust is disseminated spatially and temporally in ways that defeat her complacency, since the coffin in the crypt turns out not to contain Rebecca's body at all. One thinks here of Patricia Parker's work on the trope of dilation: "'Dilate' comes to us from the same Latin root as Derrida's différance and involves ... that term's curious combination of difference and deferral, dilation, expansion, or dispersal in space but also postponement in time" (1987, 9). Like Rebecca's boat, the narrator's strategy runs aground, since her deferred and disavowed knowledge, which initially obeys the logic of the phantom, succumbs to the uncanny return of what ought to have remained secret and hidden.

The fragments of the dedication page reappear in the pigeonholes of Rebecca's writing desk, reconstituted and organized in docketed compartments—letters answered, household, estate, addresses, miscellaneous and so on, "each ticket written in the same scrawling pointed hand that I knew already. And it shocked me, even startled me, to recognize it again, for I had not seen it since I had destroyed the page from the book of poems, and I had not thought to see it again" (du Maurier 2006, 86). The fragments reproduce themselves into innumerable "little notes." When Rebecca's body is discovered in the boat and the narrator urges de Winter to claim that "it's the body of someone you don't know. Someone you've never seen before," de Winter points out that she will be identifiable by her "things" (du Maurier 2006, 287). *Rebecca* is preoccupied with things and their interanimation. In his analysis of what might be termed the phenomenology of housekeeping, Bachelard notes that "consciousness rejuvenates everything, giving a quality of beginning to the most everyday actions. It even dominates memory ... A house that shines from the care it receives appears to have been rebuilt from the inside ... what a great life it would be if, every morning, every object in the house could be made anew by our hands, could 'issue' from our hands" (1994, 67, 68, 69). This is the ontological purification that the narrator seeks. In an early encounter with Rebecca's "things," de Winter, in his eagerness to depart for a walk, rejects the narrator's wish to fetch her own coat, insisting that Robert bring one from the flower room. The raincoat Robert brings is, of course, Rebecca's, and it is "too big, of course, and too long" (du Maurier 2006, 108); as this emblematic detail announces almost too loudly, the narrator doesn't measure up. In the coat pocket, the narrator finds a handkerchief, a text triply marked by Rebecca's lipstick, by the scent of azaleas aligned with the toxic fallen garden of the dream sequence and by the ineluctable monogram, here ironically "interlaced" with de Winter's own initials (du Maurier 2006, 120).

The narrator's alienation from the Rebecca object world is brilliantly dramatized in the vignette involving the four volumes about the history of painting, a wedding gift from de Winter's sister Beatrice. She is confounded as to how to integrate these large and unwieldy volumes into the morning room, itself a metonymic receptacle of Rebecca's refined and delicate elegance.

> I had a sudden, stupid desire to cry. I gathered up the heavy volumes and looked round the morning-room for somewhere to put them. They were out of place in that fragile delicate room. Never mind, it was my room now, after all. I arranged them in a row on the top of the desk. They swayed dangerously, leaning one against the other. I stood back a bit, to watch the effect. Perhaps I moved too quickly, and it disturbed them. At any rate the foremost one fell, and the others slid after it. They upset a little china cupid who had hitherto stood alone on the desk except for the candlesticks. He fell to the ground, hitting the wastepaper basket as he did so, and broke into fragments. I glanced hurriedly at the door, like a guilty child. I knelt on the floor and swept up the pieces into my hand. I found an envelope to put them in. I hid the envelope at the back of one of the drawers in the desk. Then I took the books off to the library and found room for them on the shelves. (du Maurier 2006, 141–142)

The passive tonality and self-infantilizing penchant of her narration belie its aggressive agency. As if in a spirit of neutral curiosity, she experimentally arranges the books and stands back to witness the results (her retrospective claim that her sudden movement away may have disturbed them is fantastical). Her unstable stacking of the volumes creates a cascading effect that upsets each volume in turn, smashing the ironically emblematic cupid figurine, whose fragments, like those of the dedication page, end up in the wastepaper basket. As Harriet Kramer Linkin observes: the "intentional destruction of the Cupid ostensibly represents an assault on Rebecca and her ways, but it also initiates a symbolic attack on Maxim as a Psyche-inhibiting Cupid" (2016, 236). Her attack on the Cupid, which de Winter identifies after the fact as a wedding present to Rebecca, leaves another pile of fragments associated with Rebecca that must be disposed of. She fashions them into a kind of epistolary text, depositing them in an envelope and burying it in the desk drawer. As Bachelard says, "an empty drawer is *unimaginable*" (1994, xxxvii), and the narrator accordingly fills this one with an epistle that she both does and does not mean de Winter to receive. The drawer is another occulted receptacle: "Wardrobes with their shelves, desks with their drawers, and closets with their false bottoms are veritable organs of the secret psychological life" (Bachelard 1994, 78). But this recessive space, like the pigeonholes in the desk, is always already Rebecca's. Hence, the narrator's missive is returned when Mrs. Danvers's accusation that the servant Robert has broken the missing ornament and concealed its missing fragments impels her humiliating confession of the truth. The narrator makes explicit her agency in the breakage of the cupid when she assumes de Winter must think "how strange it was that a wedding present to me should have been the cause of destroying a wedding present to Rebecca" (du Maurier 2006, 150–151). Like the postcard that retrospectively prefigures her tenuous marriage and stewardship of Manderley, the Cupid is a miniature. Bachelard contends that miniaturization is an attempted exercise of emotional and phenomenological power in which "[r]epresentation is dominated by Imagination ... The cleverer I am at miniaturizing the world, the better I possess it" (1994, 150). The narrator's preoccupation with the cupid and dedication page reflects her exercise of power in the miniature and miniaturized field of agency available to her.[6]

Although Maxim credits her with having "blotted out" his past (du Maurier 2006, 40), the narrator introduces an antithetical trope that speaks to the power of unrepression:

> "If only there could be an invention," I said impulsively, "that bottled up a memory, like a scent. And it never faded, and it never got stale. And then, when one wanted it, the bottle could be uncorked, and it would be like living the moment all over again." (du Maurier 2006, 37)

The figure of uncorking speaks to the structure of the phantom as articulated by Abraham and Torok: the haunting by the secret of another. In "Notes on the Phantom," Abraham postulates that we see ghosts or phantoms because "the dead were shamed during their lifetime or ... took unspeakable secrets to the grave" (1994, 171). Such secrets leave a gap or crypt in the unconscious, "the gap produced in us by the concealment of some part of a loved object's life ... what haunts us are not the dead, but the gaps left within us by the secrets of others" (Abraham 1994, 171).[7] Like the scent of azaleas that lingers on Rebecca's handkerchief, the bottled "memory" of Maxim's past awaits its uncorking, although the tonality of the narrator's formulation here is idealized and appears ironized only in retrospect. More, the figure of the phantom appears in the narrator's own lexicon. When Mrs. Van Hopper recalls that Rebecca was "very lovely. Exquisitely turned out, and brilliant in

---

[6]Linkin argues that the narrator employs paralipsis, omission, underreporting and misreporting to "exonerate her actions in Monte Carlo, in Manderley, and in exile" (Linkin 2016, 224).

[7]Abraham and Torok's phantom effect is also discussed in Chapter 11 by Jeffrey Spear.

every way," the narrator reports that "I was following a phantom in my mind, whose shadowy form had taken shape at last. Her features were blurred, her colouring indistinct, the setting of her eyes and the texture of her hair were still uncertain, still to be revealed" (du Maurier 2006, 43, 44). The truth about Rebecca's life and death constitute the phantom that the narrator follows with her mind until Maxim's explosive revelation after the costume ball. "I—I don't know … I don't mean anything," she defensively responds to Maxim's alarmed and indignant reaction to her suggestion that he married her because "there would never be any gossip about me": she has no access to the content of the secret knowledge she both seeks and disavows (du Maurier 2006, 147). "Dear God, I did not want to think about Rebecca" (du Maurier 2006, 140): the narrator's injunctions to herself (and from others) not to think or remember resonate through the novel, in an impossible imperative that enlists memory in the cause of forgetting. *Rebecca* may be regarded as an extended occultation (Latin "concealment; insinuation; suggestion"), also termed paralepsis or praeteritio, the figure of speech that "emphasiz[es] something by pointedly seeming to pass over it" (Lanham 1991, 104). Praeteritio is the trope that declares, I am not going to talk about (or think about) X.

After the episode of the Cupid figurine, Maxim leaves to conduct business in London for two days, and his absence facilitates the narrator's exploration of two spaces associated with Rebecca: the cottage that turns out to be the site of her erotic assignations, and her bedroom in the mysteriously abandoned west wing of the house. In accord with Bachelard's notion of the "dream geometry" of houses (1994, 48), the east and west wings of Manderley are antithetical spaces, associated, respectively, with the elegant veneer of Maxim's life after Rebecca and with Rebecca's turbulent life and death. His departure from Manderley prompts a fantasy that the narrator entertains in detail:

> When I saw the car disappear round the sweep in the drive I felt exactly as though it were to be a final parting and I should never see him again. There would be an accident of course and later on in the afternoon, when I came back from my walk, I should find Frith white and frightened waiting for me with a message. The doctor would have rung up from some cottage hospital. "You must be very brave," he would say, "I am afraid you must be prepared for a great shock" … I went through the whole thing as I was sitting at lunch. I could see the crowd of local people clustering

around round the churchyard at the funeral ... It was so real to me that I could scarcely eat my lunch, and I kept straining my ears to hear the telephone should it ring. (du Maurier 2006, 152)

The intensity and detail of this fantasy are remarkable, and its quality of wish fulfilment is strongly reminiscent of Kate Chopin's 1894 "The Story of an Hour," in which a businessman's wife experiences a liberating sense of rebirth upon being mistakenly informed that her husband has been killed in a train accident. When he walks through the door, she dies of a heart attack, felled by what Chopin ironically couches the "joy that kills" (2016, 672). The narrator's ambivalent rumination about Maxim ("Maxim was in London. How lovely it was to be alone again. No, I did not mean that. It was disloyal, wicked. It was not what I meant. Maxim was my life and my world" [du Maurier 2006, 54]) activates her determination to seek out Rebecca's traces. Following the dog Jasper to the cove even while "pretending to myself I did not want to go to the other beach," she encounters there the buoy bearing the proleptic name of the boat that will return Rebecca's body: "Je Reviens." She judges that "it [the name 'Je Reviens'] had not been right for that particular boat which would never come back again," return though it will (du Maurier 2006, 154, 155). Outside the cottage, the "idiot" savant Ben (who provides the text's first unmystified glimpse into Rebecca's true nature) presents the narrator with a shell, a detail that echoes the narrator's contradictory figures for the ruined Manderley, in the opening dream sequence, first as "not an empty shell" and then as "a desolate shell" (du Maurier 2006, 3). Bachelard again provides an apt intertext in his metaphor of the loved spaces of "our night dreams. These retreats have the value of a shell," such as the shell from which the hidden creature prepares its way out (Bachelard 1994, 10, 111). In sum, Ben presents the narrator with an emblem not only of Manderley itself but also, in Bachelardian terms, of the novel's plot of aggressive return.

When the narrator then explores Rebecca's bedroom in the mysterious west wing, the display of Rebecca's things produces a sense of temporal dislocation, of "seeing back into Time"; she imagines Rebecca entering the room and studying her reflection in the mirror (du Maurier 2006, 167, 168). Annamarie Jagose identifies this passage as "the novel's most concentrated remembering of that primal scene which spooks the narrative all the more efficiently for being nowhere spoken: the first and second Mrs. de Winters in their bedroom, at last, alone"

(1998, 359). Even as the narrator (inaccurately) reassures herself that Rebecca is "buried in the crypt of the church," she feels "a guest again. An uninvited guest" (du Maurier 2006, 168). The passage bears out Bachelard's contention that "both room and house are psychological diagrams," that indeed we "read" and "write" rooms and houses (1994, 38, 14). Rebecca has written her bedroom, and Danvers preserves its text for the narrator to read. Her scrutiny of its contents is reprised by Danvers, who catches her there and offers her own prurient and sexualized commentary, confirming the narrator's intuition that the nightdress has not been washed "since she wore it for the last time" (du Maurier 2006, 171). Danvers appears "startlingly familiar" (du Maurier 2006, 170), an oxymoron that plays on "familiar" in the sense of ghost and identifies her with Rebecca, whom she images as a perverse Venus de Milo dismembered into fragmentary "bits" ("rocks had battered her to bits, you know … her beautiful face unrecognizable, and both arms gone," du Maurier 2006, 173). Danvers's obsessive maintenance of the room preserves Rebecca's absent presence by staging her death again and again.

The climactic ball episode is prompted by a guest's query: "Is there any chance of you reviving the Manderley fancy dress ball?" (du Maurier 2006, 195). At Mrs. Danvers's urging, the narrator dresses as the portrait of Lady Caroline de Winter in the gallery, and her determination to keep the costume a "dead secret"—an oxymoron in the lexicon of a novel in which secrets bide their time, but possess considerable narrative agency and inevitably emerge from their hiding places—anticipates her "revival" of Rebecca. In her costume, the narrator appears "[n]ot me at all. Someone much more interesting, more vivid and alive," echoing her admiration of Rebecca's "vividly alive" morning room (du Maurier 2006, 204, 85), as if Rebecca is more alive than she is. In impersonating Caroline de Winter, she (whether knowingly or not seems undecidable) repeats Rebecca's impersonation of the portrait the previous year, becoming an inadvertent representation of a representation, and so arguably distancing herself still further from her lost phantasmatic presence.[8] As Beatrice says: "You stood there on the stairs, and for

---

[8] Most critics assume that the narrator is unaware that Rebecca had worn the Caroline de Winter costume the previous year. But see Linkin, who contends that she "likely had ample opportunity to glimpse the masquerade costume and perhaps even read about it in the society pages" (2016, 237).

one ghastly moment I thought…": what she leaves unsaid is "that you were Rebecca" (du Maurier 2006, 220). When the narrator discovers her grotesque error, the portrait "facing me in the gallery" is invested with a ghastly prosopopoeic animism, as if Caroline de Winter, too, has returned from the grave (du Maurier 2006, 226).

The narrator's inadvertent (or not) doubling of Rebecca in the tableau vivant scene is profoundly connected to the novel's play with the trope of the symbol. Etymologically, the symbol signifies a throwing or putting together of signs or tokens. It signifies a restoration and conjoining of previously disjoined fragments or missing halves. Citing Abraham and Torok's work on trauma, Smith observes that symbols may be understood as "fragments or broken halves of a missing whole which need to be reconnected to their absent complements" (1992, 292). We have seen that the narrator identifies the collection of poetry she retrieves from Maxim's glove compartment as the quintessential "symbol" of Rebecca. As reflected by the darkly comic moment when the narrator answers Mrs. Danvers's phone call by reporting that "Mrs. de Winter has been dead for over a year" (du Maurier 2006, 86), the narrator both is and is not Mrs. de Winter. This is precisely the trouble. But if her obsession with Rebecca is driven by a desire to achieve wholeness through reunion with a lost self or other, this drive is condemned to failure, as reflected by the novel's preoccupation with images of fragmentation and splitting. The silence that follows Danvers's proposal that the narrator jump to her death is "shattered" by the sound of the rockets marking the return of the boat (du Maurier 2006, 251). And although the discovery of Rebecca's body and Maxim's subsequent revelations about her appear initially to signify the narrator's psychic reintegration and self-coincidence ("these two selves merged and became one again" [du Maurier 2006, 289]), the novel's final section is dominated by images of splitting, breaking, fragmentation, disjunction and cracking, as in the cracking of the boat's planks and the splitting in half of its mast as recounted in de Winter's narrative of his attempt to dispose of her body (du Maurier 2006, 285). Although the narrator twice uses the trope of jigsaw pieces to characterize her alleged new sense of psychic wholeness (du Maurier 2006, 276, 280), her claim to have been reunited with the pieces of a lost or alternative self, as with the missing half of the symbol, is overridden by the counterforce of the incompatible images. The novel would seem to have it that the enterprise of shoring fragments against ruins concludes in a ruinous proliferation of fragments.

The revival of Rebecca in the tableau vivant episode appears causally to summon and produce her body. When the narrator confronts Mrs. Danvers about her agency in the selection of the costume, Danvers unleashes an abusive tirade that ventriloquizes the narrator's own convictions: "Nobody wanted you at Manderley. We were all right until you came. Why did you not stay where you were out in France? … You tried to take Mrs. de Winter's place … the real Mrs. de Winter [is] lying dead and cold and forgotten in the church crypt … She's still mistress here, even if she's dead. She's the real Mrs. de Winter, not you. It's you that's the shadow and the ghost … It's you that ought to be lying there in the church crypt, not her" (du Maurier 2006, 245, 246, 250). Danvers channels the narrator's self-hatred as mere copy to Rebecca's original and finally urges her to jump from the window (a homage to Bertha's jump in *Jane Eyre*). The narrator entertains the prospect, feeling the thick mist as "an anaesthetic," but just as she "relax[es]" into acquiescence, the mist is "shattered" by the explosion of rockets announcing a ship gone ashore (du Maurier 2006, 251, 268). She is saved from this potential suicidal jump by Rebecca's timely return. This return from the "stillness of the black water, and the unknown things that lay beneath" actualizes the narrator's abiding sense that "I was like a guest, biding my time, waiting for the return of the hostess" (du Maurier 2006, 268, 140). The narrator bides her time, and she is rewarded for her waiting game by winning Maxim and Manderley from Rebecca at last.[9] She gets the last word: the note proffered by Paul Favell as evidence against Rebecca's alleged suicide, a note that seems to contradict the narrator's assertion that Rebecca "can't speak, she can't bear witness," is a mere placeholder for an utterance that is anticipated but never occurs ("*I've got something to tell you,*" she informs Favell [du Maurier 2006, 286, 331]). Bachelard writes of the casket as a "dwelling-place in which a house is hidden" (1994, 86); Rebecca not only declines to remain in "her" crypt but never occupied it in the first place. The narrator's belated pronouncement that "Rebecca was dead" (du Maurier 2006, 380) exposes the compensatory status of this bathetic echo of her early self-reassurance: "She was dead"

---

[9] Joan Copjec argues that the discovery of Rebecca's body releases the narrator from her psychic vise: because the dead-without knowing-it Rebecca refuses to relinquish her place, [the narrator] is unable to enter the symbolic network of the household. What releases the younger woman, finally, is the *exteriorization* of her battle with the excess body, the double (2015, 132).

(du Maurier 2006, 38). Rebecca's "second" death raises an obvious question: How many times, exactly, need Rebecca die?

Perhaps Rebecca, or *Rebecca*, cannot die. The novel's recursive structure of (un)timely returns traced here is strikingly and hyperbolically replicated in *Rebecca*'s textual history. Mirroring the narrator's obsessive preoccupation with Rebecca's texts, du Maurier seems to have been unable to let the novel go. Her revisionary labours on *Rebecca* continued over years. She displaced the novel's original epilogue to the dream vision of the opening chapter, composed a second epilogue ("The Rebecca Epilogue") that was ultimately incorporated into the text of the novel, added an "Author's Note" recounting the novel's composition some forty years after the fact and wrote the autobiographical essay "The House of Secrets," which describes her relation to Mandebilly, the estate on which Manderley is based. Perhaps needless to say, the title "House of Secrets" is a pleonasm, like the haunted house. Is there an unhaunted house or a house without secrets? In "The House of Secrets," du Maurier follows in the narrator's footsteps as a belated trespasser who repeats the narrator's own repetition of Rebecca's trajectory. More, du Maurier's assertion that "we are one, the house and I" (du Maurier 2006, 400) repeats the narrator's fantasy of (re)union with Manderley in a manner that recalls Bachelard's comments on the image of the fusion of being with a lost house. The essay is exemplary of the endless recursiveness of the novel it supplements, both pointing to a putative lack in the novel and generating further discursive production. The interminability of Rebecca's and *Rebecca*'s narrative reflected by this proliferation of fragmentary paratexts speaks of the ghostly nature of the literary itself, whose business is forever unfinished. Like Rebecca, *Rebecca* refuses to stay put.

References

Abraham, Nicholas. 1994. Notes on the Phantom: A Complement to Freud's Metapsychology. In *The Shell and the Kernel: Renewals of Psychoanalysis*, by Nicholas Abraham and Maria Torok, 171–176. Chicago: Chicago University Press.

Bachelard, Gaston. 1994. *The Poetics of Space*, trans. Maria Jolas. Boston: Beacon Press.

Chopin, Kate. 2016. The Story of an Hour. In *The Norton Introduction to Literature*, 12th ed., ed. Kelly Mays, 671–672. New York: W. W. Norton.

Copjec, Joan. 2015. *Read My Desire: Lacan Against the Historicists*. London: Verso.

du Maurier, Daphne. 2006. *Rebecca*. New York: HarperCollins.

Eliot, T.S. 1934. *Selected Poems*. New York: Harcourt, Brace & World.

Hovey, Jaime. 2001. In Rebecca's Shoes. In *Footnotes: On Shoes*, ed. Shari Benstock and Suzanne Ferris, 156–176. New Brunswick: Rutgers University Press.

Jagose, Annamarie. 1998. First Wife, Second Wife: Sexual Perversion and the Problem of Precedence in Rebecca. *Intimacy* 24 (2): 352–377.

Lanham, Richard A. 1991. *A Handlist of Rhetorical Terms*, 2nd ed. Berkeley: University of California Press.

Light, Alison. 1984. "Returning to Manderley": Romance Fiction, Female Sexuality and Class. *Feminist Review* 16: 7–25.

Linkin, Harriet. 2016. The Deceptively Strategic Narrator of *Rebecca*. *Journal of Narrative Theory* 46 (2): 223–253.

Parker, Partricia. 1987. *Literary Fat Ladies: Rhetoric, Gender, Property*. London and New York: Methuen.

Smith, Allan Lloyd. 1992. The Phantoms of Drood and Manderley: The Uncanny Reencountered Through Abraham and Torok's "Cryptonomy." *Poetics Today* 13 (2): 285–308.

CHAPTER 7

"There Must Be No Ruins": Ruinophobia and Urban Morphology in Turn-of-the-Century New York

Theodora Tsimpouki

In 1951, Heidegger delivered a lecture entitled "Building, Dwelling, Thinking."[1] In it, Heidegger offered a philosophical exploration of the essence of building in a modern, technological age—ideas that were perhaps inevitably shaped by the carpet-bombed German landscape in which the philosopher found himself. Its audience was those architects who had undertaken the task of solving the "housing shortage" faced by Germany's urban centres following the war (Heidegger 1971, 144). In his essay, Heidegger downplayed the historical reasons for this shortage and the dire need for urban reconstruction, emphasizing instead

---

[1] Heidegger's lecture on "Bauen Wohnen Denken" was published in the form of an essay in 1954 and in English in 1971.

I borrow this phrase from Max Pensky's essay "Three Kinds of Ruin: Heidegger, Benjamin, Sebald" where he argues that "implicit in [Heidegger's] pastoralism is the principle that *there must be no ruins*" (Pensky 2011, 73).

T. Tsimpouki (✉)
National and Kapodistrian University of Athens, Athens, Greece

© The Author(s) 2019   111
E. Mitsi et al. (eds.), *Ruins in the Literary and Cultural Imagination*,
https://doi.org/10.1007/978-3-030-26905-0_7

dwelling as a mode of being. In his words: "To be a human being means to be on the earth as a mortal. It means to dwell" (145). He associated the modern "plight of dwelling" with the human failure to "learn to dwell" properly (159), without ever explicitly referring to the external circumstances of this plight. Indeed, one might argue, that his suggestion of a pastoral mode of dwelling and being in the world was an attempt to effectively erase the memory of the destruction. In other words, we may interpret Heidegger's "groundedness" (his retreat to the Black Forest farmhouse), and the conspicuous absence of any mention of urban ruins, as a form of manipulation, a reconfiguring of urban memory so that "the ruin cannot be registered at all" (Pensky 2011, 73).

Heidegger's "willed blindness" (Pensky 2011, 74) vis-à-vis these rubble piles and stacks of blasted brick can also be seen as an expression of his antipathy to the Americanized residential architecture that dominated Western German reconstruction as cities emerged from their ruins. This kind of modernist architecture, marked by its aspiration "to create universal, clean, pure, ordered and rational forms and spaces" (Capobianco 2010, 126) was incompatible with Heidegger's thought. For him, if ruins were to be replaced with functional, mass-produced buildings, it was far better to pretend ruins did not exist. The newness and uniformity of the housing construction, the ahistorical recovery from the ruins by rebuilding the demolished sites could not, in Heidegger's view, be justified by historical necessity.

In what follows, however, I do not propose a response to why Heidegger so abhorred modern urban American-style architecture to the extent that he wilfully suppressed the omnipresence of urban ruins. Instead, risking anachronism, I use Heidegger's "Building Dwelling Thinking" to explore an earlier version of the ruinophobic gaze, on the other side of the Atlantic. The fear of ruins, I contend, characterizes American urban modernity in the decades preceding and immediately following the turn of the twentieth century. Unlike the wartime ruins whose reality Heidegger refused to acknowledge, nineteenth-century American ruins—both real and imagined—generated scepticism and concern about America's self-fashioning as a young nation oriented towards social progress and unfettered material pursuit. I argue that both the physical presence of ruined buildings and the feelings of nostalgia they could potentially generate were perceived as a threat to the Progressive era's project of modernization. The very sight of ruins threatened the uninterrupted linear narrative of progress, championed by the era's dominant political class and the architects tasked with redesigning the cities. The relationship between building, urban development and the formation of American national identity is important for framing a series of questions concerning the ruin. I examine this in the work of a select few canonical American authors of the late nineteenth century. While there exists a wealth of scholarship examining the depiction of urban renewal in Walt Whitman, Henry James and Edith Wharton's literary works, the significance of this subject in their essays and other nonfiction has remained largely ignored. Moreover, considering that New York City was the preeminent American city, the premier American metropolis which has become a template for the twentieth-century American and global city, my examples centre around the New York experience as, I, too, regard it as paradigmatic.

Ruins are ambiguous sites. The burden of their meaning, in other words the way in which ruins are interpreted by the viewer, is a matter of historical perspective and memory of the past. But, according to the French sociologist Maurice Halbwachs, it is not just temporal but spatial factors that are co-constitutive in the social construction of memory. Halbwachs believed, that "place and group have each received the imprint of the other" (1980, 130), thus underscoring the role of spatial variables in establishing collective memory. To the extent that national collective memory "unfolds in a spatial framework" (Halbwachs 1980, 140), then, when it comes to myths of American exceptionalism and national identity formation in the American collective memory, spatial variables tenaciously excluded places of urban decay and ruin.

Ruins are undesirable, seen as "matter out of place" (Douglas 2002, 44). They embody anxieties, commemorating failed national and cultural endeavours. Dependent on what they do not have—"completeness, full form, order" (Cairns and Jacobs 2014, 168)—ruins are antithetical to progressive temporality. Ruins are defined both against time and utility, marked by a suspension of their function, making materially apparent a time of non-performance and unproductivity (Viney 2014, 129). Ruins are visible emblems of modernity's decline and of modernity's failure to sustain its utopic visions. The American nation, self-confident and optimistic, unencumbered by tradition and by the past, and drawing strength from its vital energy and dynamism, focused on the singular national narrative of development and progress, based on the premise of the "Great Story" into which all voices, documents and artefacts were woven

(Berkhofer 1989, 590).[2] For it is "in America and nowhere else," as Baudrillard stated in his book *America*, "that modernity is original," and "all the myths of modernity are American" (1988, 81). "Safely sheltered from the vicissitudes of history" (90), America "allowed itself to imagine it could create an ideal world from nothing" (77)—and surely not on traces of destruction and ruins of the past.

Before I am also accused of "willed blindness," let me clarify that I do not deny the existence of ruins in both the physical world and the cultural imagination of the period. In his *Untimely Ruins*, Nick Yablon has demonstrated persuasively the reality of, what he calls, "day-old" ruins, that is ruins that have not yet acquired the patina of age, as well as the cultural manifestations of fantasy ruination in nineteenth-century America. While acknowledging Yablon's reading of ruins as concurrent with American modernity and urbanity, this essay expounds on American culture's time-honoured intolerance towards ruins and the simultaneous fascination with architecture's generative performance, its propensity towards newness, innovation, transformation and reconstruction. Nor do I underestimate the economic benefits and profitability entailed in sweeping away architectural ruins in order to replace them with ultra-modern and ultra-functional high-rise buildings. Not only did the growth of vertical architecture in turn-of-the-century urban America come to symbolize power, progress and modernity but it successfully accommodated the intensified demand of buildable urban land. Indeed, the materiality of architecture as a result of the rapid pace of construction physically demonstrated American culture's predilection towards a positivist ideology of automatic historical progress.

Cultural observers since Charles Baudelaire have defined urban experience as quintessentially modern, but, in the United States, modernity and urbanity became inextricably intertwined. At the turn of the nineteenth century, American cities witnessed a building frenzy that altered their urban morphology, as illustrated in the skyscrapers, bridges, railway terminals, warehouses and world fairs that attest to the impressive scale and sheer dynamism of urban growth. For this reason, to the extent that urban forms are artefacts of ideological reasons as well as

---

[2] In *Beyond the Great Story: History as Text and Discourse* (1995), Berkhofer argues in favour of a voice, a viewpoint and a practice of history that is reflexive, plural and challenging. Nevertheless, the narrativization of the past as history, following the nineteenth-century model of narrative, meant organizing historical content into a single coherent story.

the culture and economy that produced them, an elucidation of the physical form of cities would provide "a powerful lens through which to examine the workings of society at large." "By knowing the form of its cities, one learns a great deal about a society" (Conzen 1980, 119). The frenetic rhythm in which material urban space changed as a result of population growth, the dominance of economic motives, applications of technological prowess, individualism and laissez-faire government, cultivated cultural assumptions of America's future greatness and left no physical room for ruins or the nostalgic reflection of the past. This distinctly American dynamic and forward-looking perspective materialized into spatial forms through "creative destruction" strategies that dominated turn-of-the-century urban politics. Although this phrase was coined by Austrian economist Joseph Schumpeter to characterize the incessant mutation of capitalist economy,[3] policymakers, reformers and realtors alike saw destruction, elimination and demolition as the "ultimate creative act" when applied to urban morphology (Page 1999, 70). Indeed, in *The Creative Destruction of Manhattan 1900–1940*, Max Page has portrayed with accuracy New York's urban transformation and growth, the constant destructions and reconstructions at the heart of the city. But, while Page describes the specific moment of New York's capitalist urbanization, he does not probe the causes of aversion and apprehension that abandoned structures evoked, which, in turn, provoked an acceleration of rebuilding and reshaping of the physical environment. Turn-of-the-century American ruinophobia, I submit, derived the bulk of its power to frighten and repel from the national aspiration to break clean with tradition and be modern. This endless process of destruction and rebuilding, reinforced by the anxiety of the official closing of the frontier in 1890,[4] contributed to the preservation of an exalted American national identity. Indeed, one way to respond to the post-frontier anxiety while remaining attached to the idea of

---

[3] As Schumpeter characteristically wrote, trying to understand capitalist economy without entrepreneurial innovation that brings about *"gales of creative destruction"* is "like *Hamlet* without the Danish prince" (emphasis in the original 1976, 86).

[4] In 1890, the superintendent of the US Census announced that rapid western settlement meant that "there can hardly be said to be a frontier line" ("Closing the Western Frontier").

American exceptionalism was by way of urban land expansion with an emphasis on entrepreneurship for economic growth.[5]

In *All That Is Solid Melts into Air*, Marshall Berman provided a Marxist reading of "creative destruction" as he saw it implemented paradigmatically in New York from the 1880s onwards. He argued:

> The pathos of all bourgeois monuments is that their material strength and solidity actually count for nothing and carry no weight at all, that they are blown away like frail reeds by the very forces of capitalist development that they celebrate. Even the most beautiful and impressive bourgeois buildings and public works are disposable, capitalized for fast depreciation and planned to be obsolete, closer in their social functions to tents and encampments than to "Egyptian pyramids, Roman aqueducts, Gothic cathedrals." (1982, 99)

America's urban vigour, Berman contended, would not be undermined by the slow process of ruination. Demolition rather than restoration, destruction rather than preservation reflected better the phantasmagoric visions of American capitalist economy. Moreover, the incredible construction boom contributed to the ascendancy of national pride and patriotic aspirations, and buttressed the nation state.

Without intending to short-circuit the multifaceted and open-ended theoretical discourse on the "urban phenomenon" (Lefebvre 1970), the remainder of this essay presents a series of critical and creative representations of metropolitan growth and spatial transformation, in order to elucidate the cultural dimensions of turn-of-the-century American urban ruinophobia. My contention is that America's response to worries about the nation's future and fear of failure was to embrace both innovation and renewal as well as the inevitability of social and economic progress based on the liberal tradition. In the context of the built environment, this attitude translated into "incessantly destroying the old one, incessantly creating a new one," to borrow Schumpeter's words (1976, 83). Nevertheless, not all contemporary writers and thinkers, as we shall

---

[5] In his path-breaking essay "The Significance of the Frontier in American History," Frederick Jackson Turner assigned transformative powers to the frontier. Not only did urbanization in the United States occur alongside westward expansion, but the cultural forces necessary to frontier life were readjusted to accommodate the needs and energy of late nineteenth-century urban growth. Urbanization undoubtedly played a crucial role in sustaining American exceptionalism.

see, adopted a positive approach towards the dynamic change of the American urban environment in the late nineteenth century.

As "America's first great poetic celebrant of metropolitan life," Walt Whitman documents the "splendor and modernity and ferment" of urban life (Bauerlein 1998, 121). In his glorification of the American city however, he was also among the first to introduce the rhetoric of urban renewal to aging and distressed neighbourhoods. His journalistic work, spanning from the 1830s to the 1860s, accurately records New York City's dilapidated places and crumbling buildings that stand as witnesses to the fracturing discourse of American faith in progress and reform. "Tear down and build over again," was his admonition as early as 1845. "Let us level to the earth all the houses that were not built within the last ten years; let us raise the devil and break things" (Whitman 1845, 536). Whitman was not alone in documenting the city's eagerness to eradicate old buildings and assert its authority over the past. In the same year, but lacking the enthusiasm, Philip Hone, former mayor of New York, wrote in his diary: "Overturn, overturn, overturn! is the maxim of New York. The very bones of our ancestors are not permitted to lie quiet a quarter of a century, and one generation of men seem studious to remove all relics of those who precede them" (Hone 1889, 246). Whitman's entrepreneurial discourse was based on the assumption that urban redevelopment improved both civil society and the state. "[W]e would have all dilapidated buildings, as well as all ruinous laws and customs, carefully levelled to the ground, forthwith and better ones put in their places." He adds: "No friend are we to the rotten structures of the past, either of architecture or of government" (538), even though he recognized the social cost of the process of displacement and the rhetoric of loss and decay generated by the old buildings' "crumbling walls" (536). According to Peter J. L. Riley, Whitman's active involvement in property speculation made him complicit in an urban restlessness of the mid-nineteenth century, rendering it difficult to distance Whitman "the real estate developer from Whitman the poet" (Riley 2011, 170). In this respect, it is extremely suggestive to speak of the development of *Leaves of Grass* "in the terms of a restless process of building up and demolishing, of reshaping and remodeling" (Riley 2011,176).

Creative destruction was also essential for slum clearance and urban renewal in late nineteenth-century Manhattan. Intended largely for poor immigrants, hundreds of tenements were built in the 1860s and 1870s. But, by the late nineteenth century, housing conditions were so squalid that no tenement house law could adequately improve them without obliging builders to tear down old structures in order to utilize larger land sites.[6] According to Max Page, for many progressive urban reformers slums encapsulated "the menace of great cities" and their demolition would allow for the rapid and drastic physical transformation of the city as well as for social and political stability (1999, 80). Indeed, slum ruins were considered undesirable and an aberration to the linear,[7] orderly movement towards progress, exposing the nation's dominant narratives to doubt and suspicion. America's progress was measured by the steps taken to move away from the spectral legacies of segregation and poverty lurking in "toxic" ruins. As a matter of fact, slum ruination was conceived as contagious and contaminative, it threatened to impact the urban body, infecting its surroundings with crime, violence, death and despair, and, according to Lawrence Veiller, secretary of the 1901 Tenement House Commission, "send[ing] forth its evil influences to pollute the stream of our civic life" (Page 1999, 76). In the battle against the slums, one name stands apart, that of Jacob Riis, whose photojournalistic work contributed to the demolition of "Mulberry Bend," known as one of New York's worst slums, or according to Riis, "the wickedest of American slums" (Riis 1902, Chapter 2). When Riis exposed with his pictures the squalid conditions of the slums and wrote that "[n]othing short of entire demolition will ever prove of radical benefit" (Riis 1890, Chapter 6), he expressed the aspiration of urban reformers to implement strategies of rationality and improvement by applying the creatively destructive cycle of urban development to slums. More enthusiastic with modernity's process of accelerated renewal, progressive urban reformers like Riis firmly believed in the reconstruction of the tenement neighbourhoods because they provided to the city both an impulse for social development and poverty reduction as well as a response to the urban housing problem.[8]

[6]The first Tenement House Act passed in 1867 was followed by the "Old Law" Tenement Act in 1879 which produced what is known as "dumbbell tenements." However, it was the New York State Tenement House Act of 1901 that met the broader concerns of urban planning.

[7]On slum ruins see also Chapter 3, "Dickens's Animate Ruins," where Michael Hollington discusses Dickens's response to London's ruinous slums.

[8]The creative impulse that dominated the late nineteenth century greatly continued to affect urban development politics and public policy strategies for the next hundred years. In the 1930s, the New Deal institutionalized large-scale programmes of slum clearance.

Creative destruction was not limited to slums but involved large segments of the city centre as part of their rejuvenation and urban economic development. For example, in a 1914 report, the Tenement House Department of New York noted that "it is not an unusual sight to see a business building, erected only a decade ago, being torn down to give place to a new structure in keeping with modern demands" (Page 1999, 93). As an emblematic capitalist city and the epicentre of urban transition, New York was often described as "a city continuously in its making, in which comparatively young buildings [were] ruthlessly destroyed to make way for others of great height and more modern equipment."[9] The short life of buildings, quickly built and prone to replacement, has been a salient characteristic of the morphology of the American city (Conzen 1980, 120). Ironically, the unprecedented growth of downtown Manhattan as early as the mid-nineteenth century led to an "abbreviated rate of architectural obsolescence," turning the city into a site of "untimely" ruination (Yablon 2009, 123) as more buildings were turned into ruins before becoming enfolded by the patina of age.[10] The "universal newness" and uncontrolled "habit of change" that had eliminated all physical evidence of the past led Harvard Professor Charles Eliot Norton to regret, in 1889, that "a large part of New York is as fresh as Kansas City" (Norton 1889, 639). Moreover, prior to the National Historic Preservation Act (NHPA) of 1966, intended to preserve landmarks of historic significance, the conservation of architectural landmarks depended more often than not on the economics of real estate and the value of urban land, as evinced in the tumultuous process of speculation, construction and demolition.

The theme of New York City's fast-paced destruction of the old and creation of the new also featured in Edith Wharton's autobiography, *A Backward Glance* (1934), and is woven into the tapestry of many of her

During the 1950s in New York, Robert Moses led the largest slum clearance programme in the United States.

[9]James Ford, *Slums and Housing* (Cambridge: Harvard University Press, 1936), qtd. in Page (1999, 96).

[10]Yablon also speaks of unfinished or abandoned constructions: "New York's ruination appears to precede the completion of its buildings, or indeed the very commencement of their construction" (2009, 124).

novels.[11] Such was the rapidity of urban transformation in fin-de-siècle New York that Edith Wharton wrote late in her life that the metropolis of her youth had been destined to become "as much a vanished city as Atlantis or the lowest level of Schliemann's Troy" (1934, 55). Yet, like Whitman and the social reformers before her, Edith Wharton did not feel nostalgic about the past. Even though she admitted that "[n]othing but the Atlantis-fate of old New York" (1934, 55) made her put her childhood memories into words, in her autobiography she was not attempting to reclaim her lost past or aestheticize her memories of it. If Jean Starobinski is right about the conflation of desired place and desired past generating nostalgia, then, surely, neither Wharton nor Whitman or Riis share the cultural fantasy of preserving the city's history by locating it in particular buildings or spaces (Starobinski 1966, 87). "One of the most depressing impressions of my childhood is my recollection of the intolerable ugliness of New York," wrote Wharton, expressing her disdain about her hometown's architecture "cursed with its universal chocolate-coloured coating of the most hideous stone ever quarried, this cramped horizontal gridiron of a town without towers, porticoes, fountains or perspectives, hide-bound in its deadly uniformity of mean ugliness" (Wharton 1934, 55). Clearly, she despised new New York's built forms, the lack of beauty and deadly uniformity of its architectural structures. With her own work on architectural design and decoration, particularly *The Decoration of Houses* (1897), she attempted to intervene and potentially improve late nineteenth-century American architecture. With that in mind, she adamantly denounced end-of-the-century architecture and decoration in America as being a "veritable labyrinth of dubious eclecticism" (Wharton 1897, 2). Instead, she favoured as "especially suited to modern [American] life" those buildings erected "in Italy after the beginning of the sixteenth century, and in other European countries after the full assimilation of the Italian influence" (2). Obviously, she did not wholeheartedly embrace her homeland's fascination with architectural modernity and its endless affirmation of the ever-new, but searched out a negotiation between tradition and progress, seeking to adapt the comforting elements of the past into the present as a way of making the transition into modernity easier.

---

[11] "Old New York" in Wharton's novels, both as an actual place and a symbolic landscape has been extensively analysed, and therefore, it will not be further discussed in this essay.

More complicated and ambivalent was Henry James's response to the urban transformation of his homeland, as articulated in the essay "New York Revisited"[12] first published in Harper's *Monthly Magazine* in 1906, and later incorporated in *The American Scene* (1907). The book is a creative account of James's reminiscences of his return to the United States, in 1904, after a self-imposed exile of a quarter of a century. In "New York Revisited," the narrative point of view is divided between the narrator ("I") and himself as a character in the narrative ("he"). Thus, James claims for himself the "oxymoronic identity" (Posnock 1987, 36) of a "restless analyst" and a "reinstated absentee" (James 1907, 182, 266), both distanced and emotionally engaged, someone who seeks to establish his past familiarity with the city of his childhood but who finds this difficult due to New York's "restless renewal" (James 1907, 111). Like Edith Wharton, James was horrified by the "ravage" (1907, 162) of the American scene which had included architectural constructions of diverse and impressive styles, all combined to create the unique visual character of the New York of his childhood, but which had rapidly receded due to the tidal wave of growth and progress. Evidently, he detested this "strange vertiginous" city with its new skyscrapers, which he deemed "grossly tall and grossly ugly" (88) and "extravagant pins in a cushion already overplanted, and stuck in as in the dark, anywhere and anyhow" (77). He particularly disliked the novelty of these "tall buildings" which he saw as a common characteristic of "so many other terrible things in America" (77). He was equally disturbed by "the fury of the sound" of construction (109), the deafening noise of the city streets, "the bigness and bravery and insolence, [e]specially, of everything that rushed and shrieked" (75). Like Whitman before him, James deplored the short life of the city's buildings, "[c]rowned not only with no history, but with no credible possibility of time for history, and consecrated by no uses save the commercial at any cost" (78). Elsewhere, New York's built space is perceived as the embodiment of the natural and technological sublime, as a "loose nosegay of architectural flowers" waiting to be sliced apart by sheers (77). On visiting his birthplace in Washington Place, James realizes that the building and the adjacent university edifices have "vanished

<hr/>

[12] James's most eloquent fictional account of his relationship to the city of his birth is his short story "The Jolly Corner." This "profoundly autobiographical tale" (Edel 1972, 322), which discloses much of James's complex reaction to the changes of New York, has been extensively analysed and therefore it will not be further discussed.

from the earth" (71). This cruel annihilation of his past makes him feel "amputated of half [his] history" (71). He complains about the uniformity of the grid, claiming that "thanks to this consistency, the city is, of all great cities, the least endowed with any blest item of stately square or goodly garden, with any happy accident or surprise, any fortunate nook or casual corner, any deviation, in fine, into the liberal or the charming" (101). And yet, despite his distress "at the readiness of his fellow Americans to abolish the past" (Haviland 2004, 286), James is also perplexed by the capacity of the city to elude definition, to defy the simplistic explanations of the observer. New York's "perpetually provisional" status reinforces its undecipherability (James 1907, 300). His references to "cold change," "the dreadful chill of change" (172), "the harshness of change" (169) combined with his qualification of the city's ceaseless transformation as "positive ravage" (162), all indicate James's attempt to reconcile with his native land and reassert a sense of national belonging. "New York Revisited" voices James's discomfort of modern New York as a landscape of flux, change and endless mutations. Yet, reading the memoir reveals that even if James deplored the anti-historical stance of American capitalism motivated by a "perpetual passionate pecuniary purpose" (111), he regarded it as inevitable, as part and parcel of a national identity in continuous formation.

A few years after James had published *The American Scene*, in 1911, George Santayana delivered his well-known address, "The Genteel Tradition in American Philosophy." In his lecture, Santayana proposed the thesis that America was "a country with two mentalities," one that was rooted in the traditions of Old Europe and another that expressed the country's vitality, dynamism, optimism and creativity. He conceptualized this division of "a young country with an old mentality" (Santayana 1967, 39) in a symbolic architectural metaphor. In his words, "a neat reproduction of the colonial mansions—with some modern comforts introduced surreptitiously—stands beside the skyscraper. The American Will inhabits the skyscraper; the American Intellect inhabits the colonial mansion ... The one is all aggressive enterprise; the other is all genteel tradition" (39–40). Though perhaps Henry James, as well as his brother, William, were "tightly swaddled in the genteel tradition" (54), they undermined it through confrontation and analysis. In particular, Henry, according to Santayana, managed to overcome it by "turning the genteel American tradition, as he turns everything else, into a subject-matter for analysis" (54), by exploring and trying to understand the richness and variety of American experience.

In addition, architectural historian Anthony Vidler contends that James's Unheimlich experience, his sense of uncanny strangeness, has been seen as endemic to urban modernity, linked to perpetual urban renewal, in terms of both its spatial and social transformation (Vidler 1996). Thus, in James's travelogue, the narrator seems overwhelmed by the drastic changes in the material urban space he observes, yet he recognizes the tremendous creative drive of American capitalism. The city as a place of perpetual novelty, with its dauntless power and "insolence," made him both uneasy and "oddly thrilled" (Toibin 2009, 254). More than the city, the whole nation was experienced by James as undergoing a tumultuous process of ceaseless transformations, as is evident in his address to America in the last pages of *The American Scene*:

> You are not final ... you are not even definite ... you are as yet but an installment, a current number, like that of the morning paper, a specimen of a type in course of serialization—like the hero of the magazine novel, by the highly successful author, the climax of which is still far off. (1907, 300)

By way of conclusion, I shall reiterate that New York's fundamental process of urbanization that took place at the turn of the twentieth century was based on creative destruction, on a perpetual demolishing and rebuilding. The city in perpetual motion, manifested in the architectural renewal of the urban fabric, is what gave meaning to the city's present. Moreover, belief in the narrative of transformation and change and above all in the discourse of the nation's future progress was appropriated symbolically on the architectural, spatial and landscaping frame of the city.

More than a century later, on September 11, 2001, the collapse of the two main towers of the World Trade Center caused massive damage to the rest of the complex and nearby buildings transforming their unbearably painful ruins into repositories of memory. As a result, beyond the challenge of reconstructing the landscape of Ground Zero, the September 11 tragedy has provided an occasion for rethinking and reworking national identity. Despite the conflicts involved between the competing parties and the endless delay they have produced, the dual objective of rebuilding and remembrance was pursued from the start. Without underestimating the complicated and contentious process of Ground Zero redevelopment caused by the competing interests (public vs private, the claim of the victims' families, the consensus among the public), institutional and professional constituencies on this massive-scale project in the heart of Manhattan was to rebuild the WTC site and reintegrate it into the fabric of the city.[13] "[T]he blank space was embarrassing," says the head of Amy Waldman's fictional appointed jury to select the appropriate memorial design at Ground Zero (Waldman 2012, 10).[14] "The longer that space [WTC] stayed clear, the more it became a symbol of defeat, of surrender, something for 'them,' whoever they were to mock" (10).

The collective wish to fill "the void," the "deep hole," the "graveyard" as soon as the 1.5 million tons of debris were removed reflects the American cultural predilection for not dwelling on the past. The district's renewal, the city's revival and the nation's defiance depended upon actively eliminating the negative space of the Twin Towers that once existed and vigorously eradicating absences present in the material remains which were destroyed. In his essay written shortly after the attacks, James E. Young invokes America's time-honoured discourse on ruinophobia to argue against the preservation of ruins of the World Trade Center: "Americans have never made ruins their home or allowed ruins to define—and thereby shape—their future" (Young 2003, 217). Erasing the ruins and rebuilding the site would best deploy and exemplify "our modernity, our tolerance, our diversity, our egalitarianism," Young writes (221–222). In a sense, Young was articulating the nation's dominant anti-ruination discursive tradition from its founding to the present, as we have seen it unfolding in turn-of-the-century New York.

---

[13]See Lynne B. Sagalyn (2016) for a detailed account of the controversies between the multiple forces underlying the decision-making in the world's most visible redevelopment project.

[14]Waldman's *The Submission* follows the memorial design competition as it actually took place—the forums and meetings of different constituent groups, the confidentiality of the jurors, the anonymous selection of the finalists.

REFERENCES

Baudrillard, Jean. 1988. *America*, trans. Chris Turner. New York and London: Verso.

Bauerlein, Mark. 1998. Whitman and the City. In *The Routledge Encyclopedia of Walt Whitman*, ed. J.R. LeMaster and Donald D. Kummings, 121–124. London: Routledge.

Berkhofer, Robert F., Jr. 1989. A New Context for a New American Studies? *American Quarterly* 41 (4): 588–613.

Berkhofer, Robert F., Jr. 1995. *Beyond the Great Story: History as Text and Discourse*. Cambridge: Belknap Press of Harvard University Press.

Berman, Marshall. 1982. *All That Is Solid Melts into Air: The Experience of Modernity*. New York: Penguin.

Cairns, Stephen, and Jane M. Jacobs. 2014. *Buildings Must Die: A Perverse View of Architecture*. Cambridge, MA: MIT Press.

Capobianco, Richard. 2010. *Engaging Heidegger*. Toronto: University of Toronto Press.

"Closing the Western Frontier." *Digital History*. www.digitalhistory.uh.edu. Accessed 29 Jan 2019.

Conzen, Michael P. 1980. The Morphology of Nineteenth-Century Cities in the United States. *Urban History Review*, 119–141. https://doi.org/10.7202/1020702ar. Accessed 5 Jan 2019.

Douglas, Mary. 2002 [1966]. *Purity and Danger: An Analysis of Concepts of Pollution and Taboo*. London: Routledge Classics.

Edel, Leon. 1972. *Henry James: The Master 1901–1916*. Philadelphia: Lippincott.

Halbwachs, Maurice. 1980. *The Collective Memory*, trans. J. Francis and Vida Yazdi Ditter. New York: Harper & Row.

Haviland, Beverly. 2004. Henry James @ Ground Zero: Remembering the Future. *The Henry James Review* 25 (3): 285–295.

Heidegger, Martin. 1971. Building Dwelling Thinking. *Poetry, Language, Thought*, trans. Albert Hofstadter. New York: Harper & Row.

Hone, Philip. 1889. *The Diary of Philip Hone 1828–1851*. The Internet Archive. http://www.archive.org/details/diaryofphiliphon01honeuoft. Accessed 5 Jan 2019.

James, Henry. 1907. *The American Scene*. London: Chapman and Hall, Ltd. https://archive.org/details/americanscene00jame/page/n3. Accessed 5 Jan 2019.

Lefebvre, Henri. 2003 [1970]. *The Urban Revolution*, trans. Robert Bononno. Minneapolis, MN: University of Minnesota Press.

Norton, Charles Eliot. 1889. The Lack of Old Homes in America. *Scribner's Magazine* 5: 636–640.

Page, Max. 1999. *The Creative Destruction of Manhattan, 1900–1940*. Chicago: University of Chicago Press.

Pensky, Max. 2011. Three Kinds of Ruin: Heidegger, Benjamin, Sebald. *Poligrafi* 16: 65–89.

Posnock, Ross. 1987. Henry James, Veblen and Adorno: The Crisis of the Modern Self. *Journal of American Studies* 21 (1): 31–54.

Riis, Jacob. 1890. *How the Other Half Lives: Studies Among the Tenements of New York*. New York: Charles Scribner's Sons. https://www.historyonthenet.com/authentichistory/1898-1913/2-progressivism/2-riis. Accessed 5 Jan 2019.

Riis, Jacob. 1902. *The Battle with the Slum*. New York: The Macmillan Company. http://www.gutenberg.org/files/28228/28228-h/28228-h.htm. Accessed 5 Jan 2019.

Riley, Peter J.L. 2011. Leaves of Grass and Real Estate. *Walt Whitman Quarterly Review* 28 (4): 163–187.

Sagalyn, Lynne B. 2016. *Power at Ground Zero: Politics, Money, and the Remaking of Lower Manhattan*. Oxford: Oxford University Press.

Santayana, George. 1967. *The Genteel Tradition*, ed. Douglas L. Wilson. Cambridge, MA: Harvard University Press.

Schumpeter, Joseph. 1976 [1942]. *Capitalism, Socialism and Democracy*. New York: Harper & Row.

Starobinski, Jean, and William S. Kemp. 1966. The Idea of Nostalgia. *Diogenes* 54: 81–103.

Toibin, Colm. 2009. Henry James's New York. *The Henry James Review* 30 (3): 244–259.

Turner, Frederick Jackson. 1894. *The Significance of the Frontier in American History*. Madison: State Historical Society of Wisconsin.

Vidler, Anthony. 1996. *The Architectural Uncanny: Essays in the Modern Unhomely*. Cambridge, MA and London: MIT.

Viney, William. 2014. *Waste: A Philosophy of Things*. London: Bloomsbury.

Waldman, Amy. 2012. *The Submission*. New York: Farrar, Straus & Giroux.

Wharton, Edith. 1934. *A Backward Glance*. New York and London: D. Appleton-Century Co.

Wharton, Edith. 1978 [1897]. *The Decoration of Houses*. New York: Norton.

Whitman, Walt. 1845. Tear Down and Build Over Again. *The American Review: A Whig Journal of Politics, Literature, Art, and Science*, vol. 2, ed. George Hooker Colton and James Davenport Whelpley, 536–538. New York: Wiley and Putnam. https://en.wikisource.org/wiki/Index:The_American_Review_Volume_02.djvu. Accessed 13 Feb 2019.

Yablon, Nick. 2009. *Untimely Ruins: An Archaeology of American Urban Modernity, 1819–1919*. Chicago: University of Chicago Press.

Young, James E. 2003. Remember Life with Life: The New World Trade Center. In *Trauma at Home—After 9/11*, ed. Judith Greenberg, 216–222. Lincoln: University of Nebraska Press.

PART II

Re-collection – Trauma – Aftermath

CHAPTER 8

"Ruins True Refuge": Beckett and Pinter

David Tucker

This essay is about literary lineage, the ways in which the contours of one author's presence might be traced through the work of another. Specifically, I want to propose that aspects of how Samuel Beckett was an important figure for Harold Pinter might be thought in terms of the former's work instancing a particularly *textual,* as distinct from a *dramatic,* mode of ruin. I have looked elsewhere at how Pinter might be partly indebted to Beckett with regard to a kind of radical onstage presence, that is, the presentation of a character without realist context, and onto whom Pinter projects his own rarefied sense of realism. I have also argued for certain ways in which Beckett's and Pinter's interests in prose coalesced around Proust in Pinter's writing his still un-filmed screenplay *À la recherché du temps perdu* (see Tucker 2016). Here, however, I want to explore more broadly the possibility of a debt that is rooted in a self-reflexively ruinous language, a language which itself has the capacity to ruin itself. Pinter rightly considered his sometime mentor and always idol Beckett to be more than solely a dramatist—he was a *writer*—and I want to test the argument that the present volume's topic of the ruin can enable certain textual, writerly aspects of this literary–historical relationship to come to the fore.

D. Tucker (✉)
Goldsmiths, University of London, London, UK

E. Mitsi et al. (eds.), *Ruins in the Literary and Cultural Imagination,*
https://doi.org/10.1007/978-3-030-26905-0_8

The early stages of such an argument are straightforward; it is uncontroversial to point out that Beckett's works abound in ruin. Molloy in the novel of his name recounts travelling through winter snow: "I forged my way through it, towards what I would have called my ruin if I could have conceived what I had left to be ruined" (2009b, 173). In the same novel, Beckett also alludes to the philosophical metaphor usually attributed to Leibniz of the universe as a pair of synchronized clocks when Molloy describes a "Watch wound and buried by the watchmaker, before he died, whose ruined works will one day speak of God, to the worms" (2009b, 34).

The later novel *How It Is* similarly describes transit but also refuge in relation to ruins, for instance when the narrator recalls going "out by day no by night less light a little less hid by day a hole a ruin land strewn with ruins" (2009a, 74). The narrator of the 1946s *The End* "can't tell between dens and ruins" (1996b, 62), thereby asserting an ambivalence resolved by the time of 1969s *Lessness*, where the binary collapses as ruins become den, the text opening with "Ruins true refuge long last towards which so many false time out of mind" (1996c, 197).

Rough for Theatre I takes place on a "*Street corner. Ruins*" (2006a, 227). *The Old Tune* speaks of a "place ruinated, even the weather" (2006c, 339), while *That Time* calls back to the muddy recollections of *How It Is* to ask "was the ruin still there where you hid as a child" (2006b, 391).[1] We also have the one instance of journalistic reportage Beckett produced in his lifetime, "The Capital of the Ruins," a piece intended for French radio but never recorded, about Beckett's experiences at the end of the Second World War in the French town of Saint-Lô. Beckett writes of how those who like him toiled in the rubble of the town might depart the place with "a vision and sense of a time-honoured conception of humanity in ruins" (1996a, 278).

It might also be noted that there are ruined locations, objects and bodies throughout Beckett's works that are not explicitly described as ruined: the busted-shelter skull-space and the damaged bodies of the *Endgame* stage, for example, or the once despotic space of Moran's house in *Molloy* as he returns to it after his pseudo-quest only to find the farmyard creatures previously of his dominion are now all dead, his once

---

[1] Eoin O'Brien discusses possible real-life counterparts of such fictionalized, memorialized ruins in *The Beckett Country*, such as one on the slopes of Prince William's Seat in the Wicklow mountains outside Dublin (1986, 63).

wondrous bees and their infinite, mysterious dance reduced to "A little dust of annulets and wings" (2009b, 183). In turn, we might also think of such desiccated landscapes, stage sets and physical bodies as reflecting the shattered psychological interiors speaking or narrating within or of them, as instanced by Lucky's speech in *Waiting for Godot* where the once purportedly great thinker is now a thinking ruin. As Lucky literally struggles to physically carry various weights of baggage, similarly his maddened monologue on the condition of humanity only partially manages to balance concepts of progress, health and aspiration with a creeping sense of deathly entropy as he reaches a babbling, *ruined*, crescendo with "tennis the skull alas the stones" (2006d, 43).

Such depictions of ruin, however, even when they themselves signpost or manifest an internal psychological mode, might be seen as merely the surface ripples of a deeper, abiding concern Beckett had with ruin, that is a concern with *ruining* as distinct from only describing ruin. Much as Lucky speaks his madness rather than speaks of it, so too Beckett was concerned with bringing about ruin as an aesthetic—even also partly an ethical—priority and obligation beyond mere evocative depictions of the ruined, and it is this more thoroughgoing, at once performative and self-reflexive mode of ruination, which seeks a degradation of language through language, that I propose can provide an interesting way of thinking about Beckett's legacy with regard to Pinter.

In 1949, Beckett famously wrote in an elliptical critical essay which was partially based on written correspondence between himself and the art critic and editor Georges Duthuit that, wearying of an art which merely tinkered upon what Beckett called "the plane of the feasible," he preferred instead the admittedly logically impossible "expression that there is nothing to express, nothing with which to express, nothing from which to express, no power to express, no desire to express, together with the obligation to express" (1984b, 139). Beckett was specifically writing of contemporaneous visual artists such as Henri Matisse (who was Duthuit's father-in-law) as well as the ostensible subjects of the *Three Dialogues with Georges Duthuit* themselves—Pierre Tal-Coat, André Masson and Bram van Velde—but unsurprisingly critics have also read Beckett's lamenting and self-lacerating critical text alongside, or as a way into, his own fictional and dramatic texts. However, perhaps one of the more interesting yet less extensively discussed aspects of this now well-worn quote about the "expression that there is nothing to express" is that the quote can point us towards Beckett having a place within a lineage of so-called language scepticism, a lineage that goes back to authors such as Maurice Blanchot and Franz Kafka and extends to the turn of the twentieth century with Fritz Mauthner. We might go further even and bring the concept of the ruin to bear on this history in order to advance parallels between Beckett's "plane of the feasible" and his depictions of ruin, and between the "expression that there is nothing to express" and his bringing about ruin itself.

To bolster this possibility of situating Beckett's elliptical statements in such a broader history, it is worth noting that in the introduction to a collection of his essays *Faux pas*, of 1943, six years prior to Beckett's *Three Dialogues*, Blanchot wrote the following:

> the writer finds himself in the increasingly ludicrous condition of having nothing to write, of having no means with which to write it, and of being constrained by the utter necessity of always writing it. (2001, 3)

As has been pointed out by critics such as Shane Weller, Blanchot's statement is strikingly similar to Beckett's (Weller 2008, 87–88), and it is in part a tradition of language scepticism, that is, a scepticism constituted by thinking of written literature as both necessary and, by this point in the mid-twentieth century, in a certain sense, impossible (and which, in practice, tends to produce or prioritize texts pushed to a purported aesthetic limit-point) that allows us to locate the ruin as important to the literary aesthetics Beckett would bequeath subsequent authors.

In an also often-cited letter to a friend written over a decade earlier in 1937, Beckett wrote of how

> more and more my own language appears to me like a veil that must be torn apart in order to get at the things (or the Nothingness) behind it. To bore one hole after another in it, until what lurks behind it—be it something or nothing—begins to seep through; I cannot imagine a higher goal for a writer today. (1984a, 171–172)

The "expression that there is nothing to express" articulated twelve years later, as I want to claim, can be read as a development of this earlier more viscerally expressed desire to wreck and ruin the surfaces of language. If by 1949, the vocabulary expressing this had changed to become one informed, to some extent, by Blanchot—even though Beckett was not minded to do the scholarly thing and cite that origin—we can at least now partly historicize how and why that change in vocabulary might have taken place.[2] But we can also move on from it to follow the lineages of ruin that are important to Beckett's middle-and later-period aesthetics.[3] Fundamentally, that is, I want to claim that ruin-ation was integral to Beckett's early aesthetics but it is also vital to his middle and later work, with a through-line traceable via his non-fiction prose.

The arguments add some historicizing impetuses to discussions of the 1980s and 1990s that interpreted Beckett via then-current forms of criti-cal theory. Taking a genetic approach to the issues, S. E. Gontarski wrote of Beckett's redrafting method as being one characterized by the impe-tus to "Vaguen" (a term deriving from a note to self on the manuscript of *Happy Days*): "Revision is often toward a patterned disconnection, as motifs are organized not by causality but by some form of recurrence and (near) symmetry. This process often entails the conscious destruc-tion of logical relations, the abandonment of linear argument, and the substitution of more abstract patterns of numbers, music, and so forth, to shape a work" (1985, 4). Gontarski's "destruction" bears comparison with the notion of the "ruin," as do Steven Connor's conceptions of rep-etition in Beckett's prose, which Connor understood in part as modes of sundering connections between word and world. Situating the debate in the context of postmodern theories of the time, Connor drew on Derrida and Deleuze in order to argue that it is "repetition, more than any other trope, that draws the attention of the reader to the medium of language" (1985, 17), and it is specifically language's relation to the world that repetition points us to: "The abstraction of language from the world which it names, and its capacity for repetition, are … aspects of the same thing" (18). Vaguening, repeating, sundering, all bear compar-ison with the notion of ruining, and a question might abide, following this, of how subsequent authors have taken up these aspects of Beckett's

---

[2]With personal correspondence now available it is possible to note that Beckett did indeed discuss Blanchot during the six-year period between Blanchot publishing *Faux pas* and Beckett writing the *Three Dialogues*. Duthuit sent articles by Blanchot to Beckett, at least one of which—likely an essay on Sade—was sent in order that Beckett would translate it. In 1951 Beckett mentions *Faux pas* explicitly when advising Duthuit on how to present the text for publication in Duthuit's journal *Transition*.

[3]For an excellent introduction to reading Beckett in relation to broader traditions of lan-guage/linguistic scepticism, see Dirk van Hulle's essay in *Beckett/Philosophy* (2015).

work. In order to address this question, I want to parallel the approach to Beckett taken above and build from statements Pinter made in correspondence and in interviews.

In August 1955, Pinter responded to a letter from his friend Mick Goldstein about *Waiting for Godot*, which Goldstein had seen and clearly had reservations about. Pinter had neither seen nor read Beckett's play by this point, but nevertheless he responded to Goldstein's accusation that Beckett used (what Goldstein called) unspecified "tricks." Saying that he felt obliged to describe Beckett's art not as what he called a question posed (i.e. what might this mean?) but as a necessity, Pinter states: "The necessity to what? The necessity to say. To say what? Whatever's to be said. What is to be said? Nothing is to be said, all is to be said."[4] It is a statement that tallies with both Beckett's and Blanchot's literary impetus towards impossibility, specifically in a collapsing of the all-encompassing and its counter factor, nothingness, into one another. However, Pinter is discussing Beckett's work, not his own, here, so the clipped phrasing might be seen as indebted to that of Beckett for that very reason. Yet much as Beckett's statements about painters have been employed as ways of refracting his own other writing, so I want to make a comparable manoeuvre with regard to Pinter, reading Pinter's statement as both exemplary of what he saw in Beckett but at the same time as expressive of an aspect of Pinter's broader aesthetic affinity with the older author.

We can better see these literary–historical currents flowing through aspects of Pinter's own quasi-realist drama if we consider statements made in a radio interview of October 1969, where he responded to a question that bluntly described his characters as not communicating with one another. The interviewer was positing that in Pinter's works to date there is dialogue and back and forth, call and response, certainly, but not what the interviewer thought of as substantive communication. It is a relatively vague mode of interpretation, and seeking to sharpen the focus Pinter responded (perhaps with one eye on the actual situation in front of him) with the following: "Communication itself, between people, is so frightening that, rather than do that, there is a continual cross-talk between people, a continual talking, about other things rather than what

[4]Harold Pinter, letter to Mick Goldstein, August 1955, reprinted in Pinter (2009, 17–18).

is at the root of their relationship, what is on the table between them."[5] I propose interpreting this semi-domestic description of a "relationship," one ostensibly conducted, i.e. mediated, via a "table," as also in a sense radically undomesticated, in terms of how Gerald Bruns has described Blanchot's conception of writing, the act of authoring, as being of a piece with language-sceptical descriptions of literature as that which is both necessary yet impossible, but in particular via what Bruns calls "an experience of subjection to the material autonomy of words" (2015, 79). According to such a reading, the "cross-talk" Pinter points to then appears as more than mere sublimation of a character's psychological and personal drives of sex, power and social class, the ever-threatening "real" subjects of a dialogue, even while Pinter was undoubtedly concerned with such earthly matters. Such "cross-talk" can also be heard as Bruns's, Blanchot's and by extension Beckett's "subjection to the material auton-omy of words," and as such it articulates Pinter's otherwise on-the-face-of-it contrary impulses of realism and the metaphysical, where "the root of a relationship" is analogous to language scepticism's limit points of language in being that which can be approached but never reached.

It might be objected at this stage that we do not necessarily need to go to the trouble of arguing through language scepticism and unrav-elling Beckett's circuitous statements on aesthetics in order to connect Beckett's and Pinter's language. There are more straightforward ways in which Pinter can be read as writing in Beckett's wake, even in the wake of Beckett as writer as distinct from dramatist. In *The Dumb Waiter* (1957), for example, two men wait for a man called Wilson who might never arrive but who sends envelopes, all of which could easily put an audience in mind of the boy delivering messages in lieu of the ever-de-ferred arrival of his master in *Waiting for Godot*, or indeed of the many other instances of messengers and waiting across Beckett's oeuvre:

Ben: You'll have to wait.
Gus: What for?
Ben: For Wilson.
Gus: He might not come. He might just send a message. He doesn't always come. (Pinter 1996a, 128)

---

[5] Martin Esslin Collection, Keble College, Oxford, AD 65/HP/2/83.

As critics such as Ruby Cohn noted as early as 1965, there are a range of similarities between the two plays. For the most part, Cohn focuses on the physical action of the play and the set, though she also refers to the "rhythms of *Godot* [as being] sometimes reflected" (Cohn 1965, 237). The phrasing is also strikingly similar to that most iconic of Beckett's dialogue, from a moment which is itself repeated with slight variation some six times across the play:

> *Estragon*: ... Let's go.
> *Vladimir*: We can't.
> *Estragon*: Why not?
> *Vladimir*: We're waiting for Godot.
> *Estragon*: [*Despairingly.*] Ah! [*Pause.*] You're sure it was here?
> *Vladimir*: What?
> *Estragon*: That we were to wait.
> *Vladimir*: He said by the tree. (2006d, 15)

There are numerous other instances of such surface-level textual comparison to be made across the two writers' oeuvres. However, to paraphrase Beckett's Malone, "I have that feeling" (2010, 3) that a way is needed to delve further inside Pinter's language in order to uncover the Beckett there, or, perhaps better, to trace contours of traditions of which both Beckett and Pinter take part. After all, it is well known that it was Beckett's prose which first made an impression on the young Pinter, with his reading the early novels *Murphy* and *Watt* and enthusing to friends in written correspondence of how, upon his encountering the great novels of the trilogy, "Molloy and Malone have knocked me from here to yesterday,"[6] and that "Beckett is the most important writer of this decade."[7] Indeed, when Pinter praises Goldstein's own writing he frames the admiration in terms of Beckett's *Malone Meurt*, saying "some of the writing reminds me of yours."[8] That is, Pinter's early fascination with Beckett was with language, with words flat on a page, before such words were animated in staged drama.

Yet I would want to claim, as Blanchot also believed, that whereas Beckett takes part in a history of language and literature that pushes

---

[6] Harold Pinter, letter to Mick Goldstein, BL Add MS 89083/1/1/2, letter 12.

[7] Harold Pinter, letter to Mick Goldstein, BL Add MS 89083/1/1/2, letter 8.

[8] Harold Pinter, letter to Mick Goldstein, BL Add MS 89083/1/1/3, letter 8.

both to places entirely new, producing, as Blanchot described it with regard to *L'Innomable*, an "experiment without results" (1979, 128), Pinter does not provide so novel a development, even while he finds a place within this history. An example of the sort of text where these issues might be focused can be found in 1968s *Night School*, in which Milly and Annie produce some of that "cross-talk" Pinter mentioned, but which also calls us back to the material surfaces of Beckett's more explicitly experimental serial prose works:

> *Milly*: I don't want the milk hot, I want it cold.
> *Annie*: It is cold.
> *Milly*: I thought you warmed it up.
> *Annie*: I did. The time I got up here it's gone cold.
> *Milly*: You should have kept it in the pan. If you'd brought it up in the pan it would have still been hot.
> *Annie*: I thought you said you didn't want it hot.
> *Milly*: I don't want it hot.
> *Annie*: Well, that's why I'm saying it's cold.
> *Milly*: I know that. But if I had wanted it hot. That's all I'm saying. (*She sips the milk*.) It could be colder.
> *Annie*: Do you want a piece of anchovy or a doughnut.
> *Milly*: I'll have the anchovy. What are you going to have?
> *Annie*: I'm going downstairs, to have a doughnut.
> *Milly*: You can have this one.
> *Annie*: No, I've got one downstairs. You can have it after the anchovy.
> *Milly*: Why don't you have the anchovy? (Pinter 1996b, 204)

Such dialogue comes, in a number of senses, after Beckett's *Watt*, one of the texts that made an early impression on Pinter. In this novel, a maid, Mary,

> settled herself firmly in a comfortable semi-upright posture before the task to be performed and remained there quietly eating onions and peppermints turn and turn about, I mean first an onion, then a peppermint, then another onion, then another peppermint, then another onion, then another peppermint, then another onion, then another peppermint, then another onion, then another peppermint, then another onion, then another peppermint, then another onion, then another peppermint, then another onion, then another peppermint, then another onion, then another peppermint, and so on, while little by little the reason for her presence in that place faded from her mind, as with the dawn the figments of

the id, and the duster, whose burden up till now she had so bravely born, fell from her fingers, to the dust, where having at once assumed the colour (grey) of its surroundings it disappeared until the following Spring. (Beckett 2009c, 42)

Similarly, in *The Hothouse* of 1958, two characters debate education:

Lush.
I mean, not only are you a scientist, but you have literary ability, musical ability, knowledge of most schools of philosophy, philology, photography, anthropology, cosmology, theology, phytology, phytonomy, phytotomy

Roote.
Oh, no, no, not phytotomy. (Pinter 1996c, 261)

Which might put us in mind of *Molloy*:

Yes, I once took an interest in astronomy, I don't deny it. Then it was geology that killed a few years for me. The next pain in the balls was anthropology and the other disciplines, such as psychiatry …
Oh I've tried everything. In the end it was magic that had the honour of my ruins. (2009b, 38)

In order to bring some of these issues into sharper relief, it might help to focus on a particular period, the mid-1960s to early 1970s, a period which affords a view of a number of intriguing works and connections. Pinter's *Silence*, for instance, first staged in 1969, is a text that has long been recognized for its Beckettian resonances; a review in the *Observer* published four days after its premiere described the play as "worryingly close to Beckett."[9] The following is a previously unpublished extract from a working draft of the play, which Pinter cut. It survives in the Martin Esslin archive at Keble College, Oxford, and it seems worth at least speculating, might have been cut partly because Pinter at times also worried that he was getting overly close to his mentor:

[9] Review of *Silence* and *Landscape* at The Aldwych Theatre, London in *The Observer* July 6, 1969.

A long way a long way a long way over the hills I can see lights far far away. Far far into the distance over the hills which are black the sky just less black and lights far far away a long long way away over the hills which are black.

From where I am I can see lights far away in the distance.

As his face bends I look up over his shoulder and see them.

As my eyes close I see last of lights far over black across black under my eyes far away lights over hills closing.[10]

Beckett's *How It Is* (his own translation of *Comment C'est*) had been published a few years earlier in 1964, a period during which Pinter was not writing very much. Mark Taylor-Batty describes the mid- to late 1960s as a transitional period for Pinter, one in which "convergence of an increasing artistic interest in the potency of an unverifiable past with an older concern in the impossibility of defining truth ... runs in tandem with his shift towards greater attention to domestic sexual relationships" (2011, n.p.). While this multifaceted weaving together of various concerns might sound like a description of the sex and power games of works such as *The Homecoming*, *Old Times* or *Betrayal*, it also applies to the formally more unusual *Landscape* and *Silence*. The following is a section from part one of *How It Is*, a text in which fleeting emotive memories erupt into the narrative, inflicting various kinds of pain before dissipating, thereby paralleling the physical action of the serial punishments inflicted upon the bodies of the novel's characters. Here, the narrator recalls a pastoral picnic with a lover:

suddenly we are eating sandwiches alternate bites I mine she hers and exchanging endearments my sweet girl I bite she swallows my sweet boy she bites I swallow we don't yet coo with our bills full

my darling girl I bite she swallows my darling boy she bites I swallow brief black and there we are again dwindling again across the pastures hand in hand swinging heads high towards the heights smaller and smaller out of sight first the dog then us the scene is shut of us

some animals still the sheep like granite outcrops a horse I hadn't seen standing motionless back bent head sunk animals know

---

[10] Martin Esslin Collection, Keble College, Oxford, AD 65/HP/2.

blue and white of sky a moment still April morning in the mud it's over it's done I've had the image the scene is empty a few animals still then goes out no more blue I stay there. (2009a, 24–25)

It is clear that by the late 1960s Pinter had picked up a number of stylistic tropes from Beckett, not least the specifics of omitting definite articles and commas, with repetition and distillation working cumulatively, all of which are found in *How It Is*. It also seems fair to state that Beckett's text is one of multifarious ruin, depicting and manifesting ruination at one and the same time as the narrator disavows such "scenes" and "images" as belonging to or deriving from himself as memories. They are, the narrator insists, separate to, or now separated from, himself, as interior and exterior have not only been ruined independently but even such boundaries that once demarcated the two have themselves also been ruined. "I've had the image," the narrator says, elsewhere even disavowing the possibility that such is any kind of positivist achievement, "I pissed and shat another image in my crib" (2009a, 5), which states the two facts that the narrator recalls doing these acts in his crib but also that this remembering is itself an act akin to those of pissing and shitting.

Finally, we might consider a prose text of Beckett's which Pinter performed a reading of for BBC radio in 1971, and from which the present essay takes its title, *Lessness*. *Lessness* is an anomaly in the Beckett canon in that it is "the only text in which Beckett ever approached anything like the aleatory methods of the Burroughs cut-up," as Connor has described (2010, n.p.); which is to say, Beckett writes 60 sentences, and then organizes these sentences into six themed groups and numbers the sentences one to ten within these groups. As C. J. Ackerley and Gontarski describe, Beckett's compositional method then involved drawing the sentences "from a container one at a time, recording the result. He repeated the process so that the second set emerged in a different aleatory sequence, and paragraph structure was developed likewise" (2006, 318). But perhaps rather than seeing this method as only of a piece with the sorts of cutups William Burroughs was producing in the 1950s and 1960s, we might see it as part of the history of Beckett's language scepticism, where the compositional process is simultaneously one of decomposition, a narrative of ruins that is itself ruined.

In the radio broadcast of *Lessness* in which Pinter read, Martin Esslin as producer introduced the reading by saying "We are in a landscape of ruins." Esslin was referring to the literal ruins of the text's setting.

But we are also in a "word-scape" of ruins, a language of ruination. We might even make an analogous formulation alongside Deleuze's description of the various stages of "exhaustion" he tracks across Beckett's oeuvre, that there are simultaneously tracks of ruination, stages that are in turn reflected in Pinter's own changing approaches to dramatic language. Much as how Deleuze's stages of linguistic exhaustion are ones of progression from description to enactment, grounded on a distinction between tiredness and exhaustion, so too a distinction I am arguing for the importance of here is one between depiction and production. If we recall Beckett's essay on the French town of St Lô, we might note that the quote above from that text was a little truncated, and as the sentence runs on, this sense of ruin becomes not only an end point for Beckett but also one proffered as a source of potential when he writes of "a vision and sense of a time-honoured conception of humanity in ruins, and perhaps even an inkling of the terms in which our condition is to be thought again" (1996a, 278).

Beckett, then, as Pinter himself admitted on numerous occasions, is in the reading offered here the primary author, chronologically and aesthetically. As Pinter said, "his achievements … are so far beyond my own." Yet Pinter went on to say that because of this disparity, "I don't see where I relate to him at all" (Pinter qtd. in Gussow 1996, 30), which seems worth arguing against. Pinter was perhaps less aesthetically minded than Beckett, less wilfully given to theorizing than even Beckett, and so, in order to read Pinter in a history of language scepticism, we are in fact obliged to turn, as Pinter did, back to Beckett. I want to claim that not only did Pinter indeed see multifarious ways to weave new lineages from Beckett's staged dramatics, he also found a way to burrow inside the earlier author's language and thereby locate his own work in a history of language scepticism and its attendant literary impetuses, of self-conscious language pushed to a limit.

References

Ackerley, C.J., and S.E. Gontarski. 2006. *The Faber Companion to Samuel Beckett*. London: Faber & Faber.

Beckett, Samuel. 1984a. *Letter to Axel Kaun*. Reprinted in *Disjecta*. New York: Grove Press.

Beckett, Samuel. 1984b. *Three Dialogues with Georges Duthuit in Disjecta*. New York: Grove Press.

Beckett, Samuel. 1996a. *The Capital of the Ruins: The Complete Short Prose, 1929–1989*. New York: Grove Press.

Beckett, Samuel. 1996b. *The End: The Complete Short Prose, 1929–1989*. New York: Grove Press.

Beckett, Samuel. 1996c. *Lessness: The Complete Short Prose, 1929–1989*. New York: Grove Press.

Beckett, Samuel. 2006a. *Rough for Theatre I: The Complete Dramatic Works*. London: Faber & Faber.

Beckett, Samuel. 2006b. *That Time: The Complete Dramatic Works*. London: Faber & Faber.

Beckett, Samuel. 2006c. *The Old Tune: The Complete Dramatic Works*. London: Faber & Faber.

Beckett, Samuel. 2006d. *Waiting for Godot: The Complete Dramatic Works*. London: Faber & Faber.

Beckett, Samuel. 2009a. *How It Is*. London: Faber & Faber.

Beckett, Samuel. 2009b. *Molloy*. London: Faber & Faber.

Beckett, Samuel. 2009c. *Watt*. London: Faber & Faber.

Beckett, Samuel. 2010. *Malone Dies*. London: Faber & Faber.

Blanchot, Maurice. 1979. Review of *The Unnamable* in *Nouvelle Revue Française*, October 1953. In *Samuel Beckett: The Critical Heritage*, ed. L. Graver and R. Federman, 128–132. London and New York: Routledge.

Blanchot, Maurice. 2001. *Faux Pas*. Stanford: Stanford University Press.

Bruns, Gerald. 2015. The Impossible Experience of Words: Blanchot, Beckett, and the Materiality of Language. *Modern Language Quarterly* 76 (1): 79–95.

Cohn, Ruby. 1965. The Absurdly Absurd: Avatars of Godot. *Comparative Literature Studies* 2 (3): 233–240.

Connor, Steven. 2010. Looping the Loop: Tape-Time in Burroughs and Beckett. www.stevenconnor.com/looping. Accessed 27 Apr 2018.

Deleuze, Gilles, and Anthony Uhlmann. 1995. The Exhausted. *SubStance* 24 (3/78): 3–28.

Gontarski, S.E. 1985. *The Intent of Undoing in Samuel Beckett's Dramatic Texts*. Bloomington: Indiana University Press.

Gussow, Mel. 1996. *Conversations with Pinter*. New York: Grove Press.

Harold Pinter Collection at the British Library, BL Add MS 89083/1/1/2, and BL Add MS 89083/1/1/3.

Martin Esslin Collection, Keble College, Oxford, AD 65/HP.

O'Brien, Eoin. 1986. *The Beckett Country: Samuel Beckett's Ireland*. Dublin: Black Cat Press.

Pinter, Harold. 1996a. *The Dumb Waiter in Plays 1*. London: Faber & Faber.

Pinter, Harold. 1996b. *Night School in Plays 2*. London: Faber & Faber.

Pinter, Harold. 1996c. *The Hothouse in Plays 1*. London: Faber & Faber.

Pinter, Harold. 2009. Letter to Mick Goldstein. *Various Voices: Sixty Years of Prose, Poetry Politics, 1948–2008*, 17–19. London: Faber & Faber.

Taylor-Batty, Mark. 2011. Joyce's Bridge to Late Twentieth-Century British Theater: Harold Pinter's Dialogues with *Exiles*. In *A Companion to James Joyce*, ed. Richard Brown. London: Blackwell, Epub edition.

Tucker, David. 2016. "That First Last Look in the Shadows": Beckett's Legacies for Harold Pinter. In *Staging Beckett in Great Britain*, ed. David Tucker and Trish McTighe, 193–208. London: Methuen.

Van Hulle, Dirk. 2015. "Eff It": Beckett and Linguistic Skepticism. In *Beckett/Philosophy*, ed. Matthew Feldmann and Karim Mamdani, 279–297. Stuttgart: Ibidem.

Weller, Shane. 2008. *Literature, Philosophy, Nihilism: The Uncanniest of Guests*. Basingstoke: Palgrave.

CHAPTER 9

Out of the Ruins of Dresden: Destructive Plasticity in Kurt Vonnegut's *Slaughterhouse-Five*

Giorgos Giannakopoulos

Kurt Vonnegut's celebrated novel *Slaughterhouse-Five* stages the author's idiosyncratic literary response to the traumatic experience of the Second World War. Vonnegut fought in Europe as an American soldier, was captured by the Germans, and was transported to Dresden as a Prisoner of War. He survived the 1945 destruction of Dresden by British and American air forces, taking shelter in the underground meat cellar of the titular slaughterhouse. Published in 1969, at the height of the Vietnam War, the novel follows Vonnegut's fictional alter-ego named Billy Pilgrim in the same course through the war in Europe, narrated in parallel with his later life in America in the late 1960s. It is a generic hybrid of the war novel and science fiction, in which Vonnegut makes extensive use of metafictional devices and violates a number of literary conventions by blending autobiography and political satire with literary fiction and blurring the boundary separating author, narrator and character. In what follows, the novel's fragmented structure will be read through the lens

G. Giannakopoulos (✉)
National and Kapodistrian University of Athens, Athens, Greece

© The Author(s) 2019
E. Mitsi et al. (eds.), *Ruins in the Literary and Cultural Imagination*,
https://doi.org/10.1007/978-3-030-26905-0_9

145

of Catherine Malabou's theorization of trauma, so as to shed light on Vonnegut's literary treatment of the issue of trauma and draw connections between text, psyche and city. The ruins of the destroyed German city, only briefly referred to towards the end of *Slaughterhouse-Five*, find a textual analogy in the fragmented form of the novel and, simultaneously, are reflected in the image of the shattered subjectivity conveyed in its pages.

Slaughterhouse-Five opens with an autobiographical chapter that provides a self-reflexive account of how the novel came to be written. Vonnegut describes his failed attempts to write his "war book" over a period of twenty-three years and the difficulties and contradictions he had to face, mainly due to the absence of memories of the Dresden bombing: "I think of how useless the Dresden part of my memory has been, and yet how tempting Dresden has been to write about" (Vonnegut 1971, 2). The traumatic events he experienced during the war had lasting effects on him, as he explains, including the complete erasure of the memory of Dresden. He composed a complex outline for a realistic war novel, narrated in linear fashion, that he never managed to follow, as the blank spot in his memory had deprived his novel of the material necessary for its climax. The impasse was finally surmounted by the employment of a narrative technique involving the organization of small narrative fragments around the central traumatic scene of the slaughterhouse basement, which is largely absent from the novel. As Peter Freese points out, "it is Vonnegut's survivor's guilt and his need to suppress the unbearable horror that offer biographical reasons for the fact that the thematic center of his novel is endlessly circumnavigated but never fully encountered and that only a few gory details … are briefly referred to" (Freese 2009, 30). Psychological necessity led Vonnegut to invent a complex narrative structure of bits and pieces of Billy Pilgrim's life story scattered around the central absence of the Dresden firestorm. The trauma of Dresden phantasmatically repeats itself not only in the psyche but also on the terrain of politics and the scene of history. Dresden and Vietnam become two historical and psychic events that converge and overlap as the author attempts to overcome the limitations imposed by the traumatic memory loss and articulate his trauma in its manifestations in the present historical moment. In effect, the fragmented form of the novel, its protagonist's shattered psyche, and the ruined landscape of the catastrophe mirror each other. Recent developments in trauma theory, namely Malabou's work on destructive plasticity, can shed light on the above-mentioned analogies and address the meaning and significance of Billy's affliction in ways that, as I intend to show, considerably renew the insights offered by previous approaches.

In a 1980 interview with Robert K. Musil for *The Nation*, entitled "There Must Be More to Love than Death: A Conversation with Kurt Vonnegut," Vonnegut comments on his loss of the memory of the Dresden bombing as a symptom of trauma and his ensuing attempts at recovery as follows:

> it took me a long time and it was painful. The most difficult thing about it was that I had forgotten about it. And I learned about catastrophes ... that there is some device in our brain which switches off and prevents us from remembering catastrophes above a certain scale. I don't know whether it is just a limitation of our nervous system, or whether it's actually a gadget which protects us in some way. But I, in fact, remembered nothing about the bombing of Dresden although I had been there, and did everything short of hiring a hypnotist to recover the information. (qtd. in Gibbs 2014, 57)

Vonnegut attempts an explanation for his suffering apparently drawn from the then-emerging field of trauma theory, as 1980 was marked by the inclusion of Post-Traumatic Stress Disorder in the publication of *DSM-III* (the third edition of the *Diagnostic and Statistical Manual of Mental Disorders*). His interpretation anticipates analyses of his famous novel undertaken by a number of literary critics who read the novel as a paradigmatic literary response to trauma, and as containing the specific symptomatology typically exhibited by trauma patients.[1] In terms of genre, Alan Gibbs notes that it is "a classic example of historiographic metafiction or a prototypical one of traumatic metafiction" (2014, 62). The critic has also noted the political relevance of Vonnegut's staging of the traumatic experience, as the novel "ably critiques political ideologies that would support warfare, while simultaneously dramatizing the acute damage wrought by traumatic experience" (Gibbs 2014, 63).

---

[1] Alberto Cacicedo notes that "the repressed memory of the bombing of Dresden produces in Vonnegut a 'disease' ... [which reproduces] the dynamic of trauma," and views the writing of the novel as a therapeutic process aiming toward the recovery of the lost memory (2009, 129). Vees-Gulani argues that Billy exhibits a series of symptoms typically associated with PTSD (2003, 162–170).

Overall, the large body of critical work focusing on *Slaughterhouse-Five* has predominantly relied on biographical and psychological interpretations.

The second chapter of *Slaughterhouse-Five*, opening the novel proper, begins with the introduction of Billy Pilgrim, an optometrist living in Ilium, New York, whose involuntary time-travels serve as the vehicle for the novel's complex narrative development:

> Listen:
> Billy Pilgrim has come unstuck in time.
> Billy has gone to sleep a senile widower and awakened on his wedding day. He has walked through a door in 1955 and come out another one in 1941. He has gone back through that door to find himself in 1963. He has seen his birth and death many times, he says, and pays random visits to all the events in between. (1971, 23)

The novel follows Billy's time travels, which begin in December 1944, in Europe, when the traumatic experience of war originally brought about his becoming "unstuck in time." The destruction of Dresden two months later functions as the gravitational centre which the narrative fragments incessantly circle. Vonnegut gradually approaches this elusive centre in the scenes describing Billy's wartime experiences and abruptly retreats away from it by way of temporal leaps in Billy's past or future life. Billy's repeated back-and-forth movement, noticeably resembling a Freudian *fort/da* game, predominantly takes place between the two historical instances designated in the novel by the proper names Dresden and Vietnam, wartime Europe and 1960s America, the European battlefields of 1945 and the civil rights protests of 1967. A human spool in the hands of the author, he goes back and forth as if enacting an invincible repetition compulsion by bringing the war and its horrors into view before he is violently pulled back into safety each time danger is lurking.

Throughout the novel, Vonnegut draws numerous parallels and connections between the war fragments and those referring to Billy's life after the war, thus stressing the fact that the memory of the war imposes a constant and tormenting presence upon Billy. References to the combination of the colours ivory and blue are scattered at various points in the text, first referring to the "corpses with bare feet that were blue and ivory," that Billy saw during the war (1971, 65). The smell of "mustard gas and roses" also appears at several points, before we are informed, towards the end of the novel, that the bodies of the victims of the

Dresden air raids "rotted and liquefied, and the stink was like roses and mustard gas" (1971, 214). The secure American setting often evokes the race riots of the 1960s and reminds Billy of the devastated German city: "[Ilium's black ghetto] looked like Dresden after it was fire-bombed—like the surface of the moon" (1971, 59). His apparently normal life in America is disturbed by painful memories that surface unexpectedly and indicate the fact that he has never managed to leave the Second World War and Dresden behind. The trauma of war returns in times of apparent peace to distort and reshape the experience of the present and violently impose a new form and a new meaning onto it.

Malabou's important work on trauma is marked by her effort to reshape the discourses of Freudian psychoanalysis with the aid of recent developments in neuroscience. The concept of plasticity, originally identified and explored philosophically in Hegel's writings, is central in her endeavour. Plasticity, as Malabou points out, can bear both positive and negative connotations. It can designate the capacity of certain materials like clay to receive form, the power to give form as in sculpting or plastic surgery and the possibility of explosion of form. The third, negative sense of plasticity derives from the use of the word in phrases such as plastic explosive, or the French word *plastiquage*, meaning, interestingly, bombing. Plasticity, therefore, is associated with both the creation or acquisition of form and the destruction of form (Malabou 2012a, 17). Negative plasticity does not oppose or contradict positive plasticity. On the contrary, it acquires a position of anteriority in relation to its positive counterpart and must be understood as the condition of its possibility. Malabou identified the destructive work of negative plasticity in cases when the psychic apparatus is violently attacked by the shock of a devastating accident, a serious disease or an overwhelming natural or political catastrophe. The study of a variety of case histories of patients suffering from Alzheimer's disease, severe depression, PTSD and various forms of brain damage led Malabou to observe that both organic trauma and war trauma often have similar effects involving the disruption of the continuity of psychic life and the ensuing formation of a radical alterity that emerges so as to take the place of the self. Destructive plasticity, according to Malabou, is at work in phenomena of psychic transformation that take place when a total change of identity occurs as an immediate response to trauma.

Vonnegut's novel includes such a striking instance of transformation associated with the experience of trauma. Towards the end of the opening chapter of *Slaughterhouse-Five*, Vonnegut employs a biblical allusion to the destruction of Sodom when he refers to his admiration for Lot's wife who turned her gaze back to the burning city, so as to be immediately transformed into a pillar of salt. Vonnegut identifies with the mythical female figure: "I've finished my war book now. The next one I write is going to be fun. This one is a failure, and had to be, since it was written by a pillar of salt" (Vonnegut 1971, 22). Looking back to the catastrophe, Vonnegut finds himself, like Lot's wife, transformed. The author's metamorphosis can be understood as a telling metaphor for the destructive effect of the traumatic event upon the psychic apparatus. In *Ontology of the Accident: An Essay on Destructive Plasticity*, Malabou elucidates the idea of negative plasticity by drawing on famous works of literature and philosophy. In addition, she refers to the fact that transformation is a very common motif in classical mythology. She relates the story of Daphne who turns into a tree when she is chased by Phoebus and finds herself unable to run fast enough and escape. Malabou identifies in the myth an instance exemplifying the plastic destruction that occurs when one is encountered with an insoluble impasse and the impossibility of flight when flight appears as the only possible solution. As Malabou argues, "We must allow for the impossibility of flight in situations in which an extreme tension, a pain or malaise push a person towards an outside that does not exist" (Malabou 2012b, 10). Sodom and Dresden, the divine or natural destruction of biblical times and the political catastrophe of the recent historical past, are placed side by side as two proper names of the event of an incurable wound and the radical ineffability of trauma. Looking back to his Dresden experience in order to write his book, Vonnegut seems to suggest, involved an immediate destructive process of transformation. It froze him into a still image resembling a sculpture, silent and immobile, unable to utter a word about the event itself. "Destruction, too, is formative," Malabou argues. "A smashed-up face is still a face, a stump a limb, a traumatized psyche remains a psyche. Destruction has its own sculpting tools" (2012b, 4). The destruction of Dresden appears to have a plastic effect on Vonnegut, bringing about its destructive work of negativity by depriving the author of the ability to write and bear witness to the traumatic experience itself. Both Dresden and Sodom serve as metaphors for the irreversible damage inflicted upon both the author and his protagonist due to the traumatic experience of war.

Malabou's work on trauma has foregrounded the historical and political relevance of psychic phenomena.[2] In *The New Wounded: From Neurosis to Brain Damage*, she explores the extent to which "sociopolitical trauma," a generic term she employs to refer to "all damage caused by extreme relational violence," can be examined along the lines of the effects of organic trauma (2012a, 11). More specifically, Malabou argues that *"the determination of psychic disturbances … is always contemporaneous with a certain state or a certain age of war"* (2012a, xvi; italics in original). The similarities of behaviours of patients suffering from war trauma and those with brain lesions led her to conclude that it is impossible to separate *"the effects of political trauma from the effects of organic trauma"* (2012a, xviii; italics in original). Vonnegut's novel can be read as foreshadowing Malabou's approach, as we will see shortly, by articulating together the political trauma of war and the organic trauma of brain damage. From the war neuroses of Freudian psychoanalysis, first diagnosed in soldiers returning home from the trenches of the First World War, to the psychiatric category of PTSD, originally devised for Vietnam veterans, and then to the contemporary globalized forms of trauma, often relating to terrorism and the "war on terror," Malabou stresses the fact that different types of trauma must always be situated historically and understood in relation to their political implications. She emphasizes the timely necessity for cerebral and psychic trauma to form one general category and, consequently, for the introduction of concepts and discoveries drawn from the work of contemporary neuroscientists into the discourses of psychoanalysis. Malabou questions Freud's concept of neurosis as a category capable of addressing the issue of trauma today. In addition, she opposes the analyst's reluctance to take the brain into consideration as an organ whose physiology plays a vital part in the function of the psychic apparatus and the workings of the unconscious and thus turns her attention to the cerebral side of the human psyche.

In order to formulate what she calls a "general theory of trauma," Malabou coins a neologism, introducing the concept of cerebrality and its corresponding hypothesis of a cerebral unconscious (2012a, 10). Cerebrality allows Malabou to locate in the brain the existence

---

[2] For a detailed discussion of Malabou's work on trauma and its political ramifications, especially in her book *The New Wounded*, see Kellogg (2015, 111–132). For an account of Malabou's work on plasticity in relation to neuroscience and a critical reading of *The New Wounded*, see Watkin (2016, 93–109).

of a causality of psychic events functioning independently of the sexual aetiology of Freudian psychoanalysis. Announcing a new regime of events, cerebrality, as opposed to sexuality, embraces the possibility of the creation of new forms out of the total annihilation of form, the unexpected explosion and destruction of the psyche as a result of trauma. According to the Freudian concept of the unconscious, by contrast, psychic events are always of a sexual nature and have their source in pre-existing occurrences in the subject's prehistory that the unconscious mind has preserved as ineffaceable inscriptions or traces. As Malabou notes, the psyche according to Freud is plastic only in the positive sense. Its plasticity refers, on the one hand, to the capacity of the libido to change its object and, on the other, to the indestructible nature of psychic life. Within the psyche nothing is forgotten, deleted or effaced. Traces can be deformed, distorted, condensed or displaced but they persist. The cerebral unconscious, by contrast, mortal and destructible, reveals itself in moments of extreme tension when cerebral auto-affection is disrupted and a new form or a new identity emerges unexpectedly. Malabou conceives the psychic event as an accident or an unexpected catastrophe that causes a radical break between what came before and what comes after. According to Malabou,

> The specificity of the traumatic event … inheres in its *metamorphic power*. The traumatic event, in a certain sense, invents its subject. The past of the traumatized individual changes, becomes *another past* when it is not pure and simply destroyed or consigned to oblivion. Accordingly, a *new subject* enters the scene in order to assume this past that never took place. (2012a, 152)

According to Malabou, the subject is inescapably haunted by the negativity of destructive plasticity. In effect, subjectivity is conceived as a fragile and precarious terrain that is always exposed to the threat of being totally destroyed and annihilated so as to be replaced by a new subjectivity—one with which it shares no common past or history.

The protagonist of *Slaughterhouse-Five* goes through two instances of trauma that are accompanied by two radical changes in his personality. The first trauma takes place in late 1944, as is noted above, during the war in Europe, and is followed by Billy's being "unstuck in time." The resulting condition tellingly exemplifies the plasticity of trauma and the plastic potential of the human psyche. The experience of becoming "spastic in time" (Vonnegut 1971, 23), which can also be understood, in Malabou's meaning of the term, as becoming *plastic* in time, occurs unexpectedly, immediately, as Billy leans against the trunk of a tree in the wartime German countryside (43). The continuity of Billy's history and psychic life is from then on disrupted and shattered. The fragmented subjectivity of the traumatized self is literalized in his convulsive and paroxysmal back-and-forth travels in time. Billy moves through his life as if wandering inside a frozen and static monument, a convoluted labyrinth or a kaleidoscopic space of spatiotemporal fragmentation and ruin. At certain points, Billy appears to live simultaneously in two different periods of his life: "he was simultaneously on foot in Germany in 1944 and riding in his Cadillac in 1967" (58). Billy becomes an indefinable portrayal of a "Protean man" (Lundquist 1977, 79), a dissonant combination of different personalities existing at once, outside the linearity of temporal experience. His involuntary time travels take place on a broken line surrounding the event of Dresden without allowing access to it. At the core of Billy's subjectivity lies a central absence, a defining violent moment of loss that has displaced the memory of Dresden. The continuity of his psychic life explodes and opens before the reader destroyed like the landscape of the bombed city of Dresden.[3]

The second trauma occurs in early 1968, when Billy survives a plane crash. He comes out of the accident with a fractured skull and undergoes a three-hour operation by a brain surgeon (Vonnegut 1971, 157). The event is accompanied by his kidnapping by a flying saucer and subsequent trip to the planet Tralfamadore. Billy assumes the invented past of an other, parallel self that lives happily in the simulated Earth environment of a Tralfamadorian zoo and shares his extraterrestrial habitat with a female movie star, also kidnapped from Earth. With the plane crash, a cerebral trauma is added to the preceding psychic trauma of war. Vonnegut creates a portrait of the traumatized subject that takes into consideration both the psychic and the physical aspects of trauma as producing similar destructive effects involving the irrevocable loss of the sense of temporal and spatial coherence and the emergence of a new self. The novel thus demonstrates the self-destructive potential of the psyche, understood in Malabou's terms as a cerebral psyche, and presents the

---

[3]In a similar vein, Adam Beardsworth in Chapter 10 discusses how the destruction wrought by the atom bomb and the fear of nuclear annihilation impacts on psychic life in Cold War America.

unconscious mind as being incessantly exposed to the threat of annihilation, irreversible damage, ashes and ruins.

Billy's responses to trauma produce a plastic effect on the formal aspects of the novel, radically transforming the initial linear narrative of the outline referred to in the novel's first chapter. Billy's time travels become a plastic (in the negative sense) literary device that causes an explosion within the linear development of the novel. As a result, the novel assumes a highly fragmented form of successive small narrative units. Vonnegut makes use of a number of transitional devices that enable him to pass smoothly from one scene to the next and suture his fragments together in a manner that is "more properly associated with film editing techniques than literary ones" (Boon 2011, 54). Through these cinematic "form cuts" (also called in cinematic terminology "plastic cuts"), Vonnegut reorganizes his material into a new, plastic form (in the positive sense) that gives the impression of simultaneity. Vonnegut implicitly offers a description of the form that the novel acquires in the scene of Billy's discussion with the aliens about Tralfamadorian books:

> We Tralfamadorians read them all at once, not one after the other. There isn't any particular relationship between all the messages, except that the author has chosen them carefully, so that, when seen all at once, they produce an image of life that is beautiful and surprising and deep. There is no beginning, no middle, no end, no suspense, no moral, no causes, no effects. What we love in our books are the depths of many marvelous moments seen all at one time. (1971, 88)

Slaughterhouse-Five, like the books read by the aliens, breaks with the typical temporal development of literary works and their teleological structures of causality. Unexpected and apparently non-causal relations between the narrated events emerge, and Vonnegut manages to reshape the historical narrative and "create a new narrative in which World War II flows directly into Vietnam" (Jarvis 2011, 85). The two traumas that Billy experiences introduce two typical science fiction themes to *Slaughterhouse-Five*, namely time travel and space travel. Thus, the war novel Vonnegut initially intended to write is transformed into an extravagant science fiction parable. The destruction of the narrative line into the fragmented plot can be viewed as a result of the violent breach caused by the impact of the traumatic events upon the sense of historical and narrative continuity, coherence of form and stability of meaning.

In *Slaughterhouse-Five*, the work of the author emerges as the shattering and rearrangement of the temporal and spatial continuum of his narrative into a totally new and meaningful whole and involves what Malabou calls "the plastic art of destruction" (2012b, 4).

Apart from being a textual manifestation of the plasticity of the traumatized psyche, the novel's distinctive fragmentation also appears to suggest the haunting image of a city in ruins. The formal structure of the novel reflects Billy's fractured skull, the disrupted the continuity of psychic history, and the moonscape of the bombed city of Dresden. However, Dresden is not the only destroyed city referred to in the novel. Including brief references and allusions to Ilium (another name for Troy), Sodom, Hanoi and other cities of North Vietnam (Vonnegut 1971, 60) and Hiroshima (185), Vonnegut becomes a cartographer of ruined cities, drawing an imaginary map that defies temporal and spatial limitations, and crosses historical and mythological boundaries. In his 1990 novel *Hocus Pocus*, presented in an equally fragmented narrative, Vonnegut focuses once again on the destruction of a city. The narrator, a Vietnam veteran, survives the destruction of the town Scipio (an implicit allusion to the destruction of Carthage by Roman General Scipio Africanus) and the spectre of Vietnam returns to haunt him as the trauma of Dresden haunts the protagonist of *Slaughterhouse-Five*. Vonnegut's new record of ruined cities is extended with passing references to Hiroshima (Vonnegut 1990, 218–219) and Pompeii (140). Freud himself, fascinated by the archaeological discoveries of his time, frequently employs what has become known as "the archaeological metaphor"[4] for the work of the analyst by way of references to ancient cities which, invariably, function as metaphors for the unconscious mind and as figurative sites of repression. A comparison of the metaphorical use of cities in the work of Freud and Vonnegut would reveal two different conceptions of the unconscious mind. In his 1907 essay *Delusions and Dreams in Jensen's* Gradiva, Freud uses the destruction of Pompeii as a metaphor for repression: "there was a perfect similarity between the burial of Pompeii—the disappearance of the past combined with its preservation—and repression" (Freud 1959, 51).[5] For Freud, destruction, when considered in terms of the psychic life, is always accompanied

---

[4] On Freud's archaeological metaphor, see Khanna (2003, 38–46).

[5] See also Chapter 14 on Benjamin's reading of the ruination of Pompeii.

by the preservation of indestructible traces, that is, remnants of a buried past that can be read and interpreted by the analyst and disclose that which has been repressed. In *The New Wounded*, Malabou refers to another city metaphor drawn from Freud's work. In the opening chapter of *Civilization and Its Discontents*, the analyst famously compares the unconscious to Rome, the Eternal City, so as to stress the fact that the psyche is an ahistorical terrain, eternal and immortal. However, Freud does not fail to recognize the imperfection of his metaphor because Rome's architectural past is destroyed and survives in the present only in ruins. For Freud, as Malabou notes, "[t]he total preservation of the past, without destruction, alteration, or ruins, is only possible for the psyche" (2012a, 178). Vonnegut's obsession with ruined cities and cities destroyed by fire and war, if viewed as a metaphor for the traumatized psyche, attests to another conception of the unconscious mind, differing radically for Freud's: it conveys an image of the psyche in ruins, destructible, fragile, exposed to history and its events, and subject to the unforeseeable economy of the accident. In other words, it provides a metaphorical literary depiction of Malabou's hypothesis of the cerebral unconscious, that is, a conception of the psyche as a site always exposed to the possibility of irrevocable destruction and ruin.

In *The New Wounded*, Malabou identifies an early trace of the idea of destructive plasticity in Freud's conception of the death drive. She places *Beyond the Pleasure Principle*, the seminal work of psychoanalytic literature that focuses on the issue of trauma, under the scrutiny of her critical reading so as to look into Freud's handling of the issue of negativity and destruction in the psychic life of the traumatized subject. Freud examines the possibility of a destructive force operating within the psyche in opposition to the authority of the pleasure principle. As Malabou points out, despite his detours and hesitations, Freud ultimately answers the question about the "beyond" of the pleasure principle in the negative. Ultimately, the pleasure principle remains unchallenged and the death drive remains structureless and formless, without representative figures, and its plastic potential remains unexplored. Malabou examines in detail Freud's reluctance to recognize the possibility that the death drive opens so as to bring to light the destruction and annihilation at work in cases that do not fall into the known category of neurosis and, therefore, lie beyond his powers of healing and therapy. These cases, "living figures of death" or the "new wounded" of our time, have only recently appeared on the scene (Malabou 2012a, 209). Malabou's work points towards the urgent necessity to see these figures, victims of extreme violence, terrorism and all kinds of natural and political catastrophes as expressing "a *posttraumatic condition* that reigns everywhere today and demands to be thought" (Malabou 2012a, 17).

Returning to Vonnegut, we can, perhaps, revisit the complex fragmentation of his trauma narrative and read the novel as one that embodies the plasticity of trauma in its structure, its metaphors and its central character. With his repetitive back-and-forth movement in space and time, his complex *fort/da* game, Billy Pilgrim provides more than mere evidence or symptoms of the death drive. As a survivor of war and its horrors, with his fractured skull, fragmented subjectivity and the permanent erasure of parts of his memory, he emerges out of the ruins of Dresden as a representative figure of the death drive and an early literary portrayal of a traumatized subject that anticipates those figures that Malabou would, much later, identify as the spectral constituency of "the new wounded."

References

Boon, Kevin Alexander. 2011. Temporal Cohesion and Disorientation in *Slaughterhouse-Five*: A Chronicle of Form Cuts and Transitional Devices in the Novel. In *Slaughterhouse-Five by Kurt Vonnegut: Critical Insights*, ed. Leonard Mustazza, 36–63. Pasadena and Hackensack: Salem Press.

Cacicedo, Alberto. 2009. "You Must Remember This": Trauma and Memory in *Catch-22* and *Slaughterhouse-Five*. In *Kurt Vonnegut's* Slaughterhouse-Five, ed. Harold Bloom, 125–138. New York: Infobase. Originally Published in *Critique* 46.4 (2005): 357–368.

Freese, Peter. 2009. Kurt Vonnegut's *Slaughterhouse-Five* or, How to Storify an Atrocity. In *Kurt Vonnegut's* Slaughterhouse-Five, ed. Harold Bloom, 17–32. New York: Infobase. Originally Published in 1994. *Historiographic Metafiction in Modern American and Canadian Literature*, ed. Bernd Engler and Kurt Müller, 209–222. Paderborn: Schoningh.

Freud, Sigmund. 1959. Delusions and Dreams in Jensen's *Gradiva*. In *The Standard Edition of the Complete Psychological Works of Sigmund Freud*, vol. 9, trans. and ed. James Strachey, 3–95. London: Hogarth Press.

Gibbs, Alan. 2014. *Contemporary American Trauma Narratives*. Edinburgh: Edinburgh University Press.

Jarvis, Christina. 2011. The Vietnamization of World War II in *Slaughterhouse-Five* and *Gravity's Rainbow*. In Slaughterhouse-Five *by Kurt Vonnegut: Critical Insights*, ed. Leonard Mustazza, 80–108. Pasadena and Hackensack:

Salem Press. Originally Published in 2003. *War, Literature, and the Arts* 15 (1–2): 95–117.

Kellogg, Catherine. 2015. Plasticity and the Cerebral Unconscious: New Wounds, New Violences, New Politics. In *Plastic Materialities: Politics, Legality, and Metamorphosis in the work of Catherine Malabou*, ed. Brenna Bhandar and Jonathan Goldberg-Hiller, 111–132. Durham and London: Duke University Press.

Khanna, Ranjana. 2003. *Dark Continents: Psychoanalysis and Colonialism*. Durham: Duke University Press.

Lundquist, James. 1977. *Kurt Vonnegut*. New York: Frederick Ungar Publishing.

Malabou, Catherine. 2012a. *The New Wounded: From Neurosis to Brain Damage*, trans. Steven Miller. New York: Fordham University Press.

Malabou, Catherine. 2012b. *Ontology of the Accident: An Essay on Destructive Plasticity*, trans. Carolyn Shread. Cambridge: Polity.

Vees-Gulani, Susanne. 2003. *Trauma and Guilt: Literature of Wartime Bombing in Germany*. Berlin and New York: Walter de Gruyter.

Vonnegut, Kurt. 1971. *Slaughterhouse-Five*. New York: Dell.

Vonnegut, Kurt. 1990. *Hocus Pocus*. New York: Putnam.

Watkin, Christopher. 2016. *French Philosophy Today: New Figures of the Human in Badiou, Meillassoux, Malabou, Serres and Latour*. Edinburgh: Edinburgh University Press.

CHAPTER 10

Melancholia and the Bomb: Robert Lowell, Anne Sexton and the Fragmented Atomic Psyche

Adam Beardsworth

In the years immediately following the United States's atomic bombing of Hiroshima and Nagasaki, a *hibakusha*, or survivor of the atomic bomb, was asked what sort of monument he felt should be built to honour the victims. His response conveys the difficulty of symbolizing the ruin wrought by the bomb: "[w]e should figure out the exact hypocenter—and possibly put some small artistic monument on it—or better still, leave it devoid of anything at all.... Such a weapon has the power to make everything into nothing, and I think this should be symbolized" (Lifton and Mitchell 1995, 218). This essay examines how atomic destruction led to traumatic psychological fragmentation not just for those who experienced the bomb directly, but also for those living in the era of nuclear threat. While that threat is global, this essay specifically examines how the ideological interests of the early Cold War United States exploited the fear of nuclear ruin in order to build a culture of consensus that would support abusive foreign and domestic policies.

A. Beardsworth (✉)
Grenfell Campus, Memorial University of Newfoundland,
Corner Brook, NL, Canada

© The Author(s) 2019
E. Mitsi et al. (eds.), *Ruins in the Literary and Cultural Imagination*,
https://doi.org/10.1007/978-3-030-26905-0_10

The first detonation of atomic bombs opened a fissure in the American psyche. Rather than attempt to heal that wound, US political interests sought to contain, naturalize and exploit the anxiety that it created. The cultural Cold War worked tirelessly to justify nuclear proliferation in the name of maintaining sovereignty against the communist other, naturalized atomic culture by propagating the technological and commercial potential of nuclear futures and appeased anxiety through the emergence of powerful psychological, biopolitical and technological institutions. As Joseph Masco argues, "rather than offering citizens an image of safety or of a war that could end in victory, the early Cold War state sought instead to calibrate everyday American life to the minute-to-minute possibility of nuclear warfare" (2008, 366). By stoking fear as a matter of policy, the Cold War apparatus waged an affective war, one predicated upon using both the threat of catastrophe and the rewards of conformity as forces aimed at regulating the everyday lives of American subjects.

Coinciding with the Cold War management of affect was the so-called confessional turn in lyric poetry. Exemplars of the movement such as Robert Lowell and Anne Sexton turned inward to find material for their poetry, often exploring personal subjects previously considered taboo. Central among these issues was mental illness; both writers suffered numerous breakdowns, and their poetry frequently explores the toll illness took on their private lives. Given the anxious historical moment in which they lived, it is not surprising that their work often reveals psychic turmoil. Their autobiographic voices suggest that feelings of anxiety and persecution were not symptomatic of a failure to thrive as self-determined Americans; rather, they were propelled by powerful institutional forces trading on the terror of imminent catastrophe, and selling the optimistic rewards promised by the cultural status quo of American domesticity. The poetry of Lowell and Sexton therefore posits an unlikely form of aesthetic resistance: by focusing on the anxiety, illness and fear generated in the aftermath of atomic ruins, they reveal the psychological toll that the nuclear rhetoric of the Cold War had on US citizens. Turning inward to explore the ruins of fragmented selves, Lowell and Sexton identify how the political logic of fear suppresses, disenfranchises and disempowers both individual and collective responses to political repression. Both writers consider psychological suffering as symptomatic of the epistemological incertitude that was delivered on the backs of atomic weapons. However, their work also positions mental illness as an adverse reaction to the political ontology of threat that exploited nuclear fear for political gain, a tactic that benefited political interests by wearing down voices of dissent. Their autobiographical poetics therefore responds to the ways in which Cold War ideology sought to manage, and transform, psychological responses to the nuclear age. By examining the impact of this psychological intervention, their poetry reveals how Cold War politics informed, created and exploited personal suffering in order to achieve ideological goals.

In "Fall 1961," a poem composed around the time of the Berlin Wall Crisis, Robert Lowell describes the implicit anxiety of living during a period of nuclear brinksmanship:

> All autumn, the chafe and jar
> of nuclear war;
> we have talked our extinction to death.
> I swim like a minnow
> behind my studio window. (Lowell 2003, 329)

The poem conveys a feeling of existential helplessness that corresponds with life in the early Cold War era, a time when a rash political decision could have meant civilization's ruin. As a private citizen, Lowell is contained within his studio, meek and ineffectual as a minnow waiting to be preyed upon. Indeed, he expresses similar feelings of frustration in letters written during the same period, which at once convey the anxiety created by living with the prospect of nuclear war, and the sense of futility grounded in knowing that there is little he can do, as an individual, to improve the situation. In a 1961 letter to Randall Jarrell, for instance, Lowell writes "The world is very much under my skin and really seems like a murderous nightmare when one looks outward. I am sick of nations armed to the teeth. It can't be true we must raise a finger or a whisper" (qtd. in Hamilton 1982, 295). Later that year, Lowell conveyed similar feelings in a letter to his cousin Harriet Winslow: "The world's really strange isn't it? I mean the world of the news and the nations and the bomb testings ... Under a certain calm, there seems to be a question that must be answered. If one could think of the question" (qtd. in Hamilton 1982, 294). In each of these letters, Lowell reveals his anxiety about living in the bomb's shadow, as well as his confusion about what his precise role is in this apocalyptic scenario, or what "question must be answered."

Anne Sexton, who first met Lowell while enrolled in the Boston University writing workshop he taught in 1958, expressed similar sentiments of uncertainty about the relationship between her personal life and the Cold War political apparatus. Although Sexton's poems rarely venture into overtly political terrain, they frequently express her frustration with—and even contempt for—a Cold War ideology that conflates domestic security with domesticity and exalts the role of the submissive and subservient housewife. In poems such as "The Road Back," published in her 1960 book *To Bedlam and Part Way Back*, Sexton employs a nuclear metaphor to describe the sense of foreboding that accompanies the experience of middle-class family life:

> There is no word for time.
> Today we will
> not think to number another summer
> or watch its white bird into the ground.
> Today, all cars,
> all fathers, all mothers, all
> children and lovers will
> have to forget
> about that thing in the sky,
> going around
> like a persistent rumor
> that will get us yet. (Sexton 1999, 31)

The "thing in the sky" Sexton alludes to, but refuses to name, invokes a bomber, its payload lingering in the consciousness of post-war Americans like a "persistent rumor." As Sexton recognized, the bomb's persistent presence helped license a political ideology that advocated—both culturally and politically—for the virtues of a contained (and quiet) domestic femininity. The fact that the passing plane evokes nuclear ruination indicates how the anxiety of nuclear ruination was, for those living in the early Cold War era, a part of everyday life. While the spectre of atomic destruction impacted the personal lives of Lowell and Sexton differently (certainly Lowell, as a privileged white man, was not expected to live according to the repressive gender codes that Sexton contended with), each poet struggled to find the appropriate means of responding to a culture that was at once confronted by the possibility of destruction and targeted by ideological interests invested in containing anxiety and restoring a complacent, politically disinterested, domestic sphere. These means often led them to explore the psychic, rather than physical, ruins of the early atomic age.[1]

For both Lowell and Sexton, as for countless Americans during the early Cold War period, the possibility of nuclear warfare represented a powerful, if confusing, new form of political life. The ever-present possibility of a catastrophic nuclear event impacted (and continues to impact) the American psyche on both latent and manifest levels. As Robert J. Lifton and Greg Mitchell observe in *Hiroshima in America*, their study of the psychological impact of the nuclear age on American citizens,

> Since Hiroshima, we have been captives of nuclear weapons. We rely on them and we flaunt them, but psychologically and politically they have imprisoned us. In exploding atomic bombs over Hiroshima and Nagasaki we frightened no one more than ourselves. Ever since, we have struggled to overcome our own terror and re-establish lost "security" by means of embracing the objects of that terror and attaching ourselves to their ultimate power, their omnipotence. At the same time our insistent need to justify the atomic bombings has required us to view nuclear devices as potentially usable weapons. (Lifton and Mitchell 1995, 392)

Lifton and Mitchell here frame the American relationship to atomic weapons in terms that reflect the classic Freudian model of melancholia, wherein, as Julia Kristeva explains,

> mourning conceals an aggressiveness toward the lost object, thus revealing the ambivalence of the depressed person with respect to the object of mourning. "I love that object," is what that person seems to say about the lost object, "but even more so I hate it; because I love it, and in order not to lose it, I imbed it in myself; but because I hate it, that other within myself is a bad self, I am bad, I am non-existent, I shall kill myself." (Kristeva 1989, 11)

Thus, in the relationship with nuclear weapons, the bomb takes the place of the lost object—that which is at once loved (as a signifier of geopolitical security) and hated (as a signifier of mass death and destruction).

---

[1] For an exploration of the psychic ruin in the wake of World War II, see Giannakopoulos's discussion of the traumatized subject in Kurt Vonnegut's *Slaughterhouse Five* in Chapter 9.

Attachment to the bomb is particularly destructive when considered in relation to the *hibakusha*'s notion that it signifies nothingness. Embracing the bomb as lost object is therefore a paradoxical gesture: as an object of annihilation, its perfected state is nothingness. Knowing that the bomb represents nothingness, those who try, in Lifton's terms, to "embrace the objects of power," are theoretically also embracing the nothingness that the bomb represents. To internalize that nothingness as the object of both love and hate is to keep oneself in contact with the knowledge of the profound, irretrievable absence—or the psychic ruins—that the bomb both signifies and literally creates. For many Americans, this complex, depressive relationship to the atomic threat was a profound source of both psychological anxiety and epistemological angst.

In the United States of the 1950s, reminders of nuclear threat drifted throughout popular and political culture like the fallout that drifted across the country from Nevada test sites. Forgetting the bomb was, in other words, difficult to do. As Paul Boyer argues,

> "fallout" from the nuclear arms race, with its endless rounds of nuclear tests, was clearly not limited to strontium 90 and other deadly substances; it also worked its way into the mental and imaginative world of an entire generation, adults and children alike, producing not only nightmares, worried conversations, and activist campaigns, but also a diverse array of cultural artifacts, ranging from poems, novels, and paintings to popular songs, slang, movies, advertisements, radio shows, and television specials. (Boyer 1998, xii–xiv)

Containment of the psychological fallout set adrift by the nuclear era was, paradoxically, contingent upon maintaining a permanent state of anxiety. For the ideological interests of the Cold War United States, the anxiety, fear and melancholia created by this fallout presented a unique political opportunity. The myriad ways in which Cold War culture feared, fetishized and fantasized about atomic catastrophes and communist contagion suggest that the era was ideologically driven by a politics that both produced and embraced fear, just as the depressive both internalizes and tries to expel the lost Other.

The ideological use of anxiety as a means of social control constitutes what Brian Massumi has labelled the political ontology of threat. For Massumi, the threat of potential disaster has a prolonged impact on both psychological and felt realities. According to Massumi, insofar as threat is experienced as an affective reality, it "legitimates preemptive action, once and for all. Any action taken to pre-empt a threat from emerging into a clear and present danger is legitimated by the affective fact of fear, actual facts aside" (2009, 54). When fear becomes an affective reality, ever-present and independent of specific moments of catastrophe, it fractures social solidarity and encourages individuals to guard themselves, their families and their property against lurking, and often invisible, dangers. Each new catastrophe, however hyper-mediated, reproduces the anxiety that justifies the political ontology of threat, and corroborates that threat's status as "a *felt quality* independent of any particular instance of itself" (Massumi 2009, 62).

The paradoxical combination of containment tactics aimed at naturalizing the atomic age, and the politics of threat aimed at exploiting future catastrophes, meant that the possibility of nuclear ruin was a constant presence for US citizens of the Cold War. For poets living in the nuclear shadow, the task became one of finding ways to represent the absurd fact that humans now live with the technological capacity for self-annihilation. Although representing the relationship to the nuclear hypocentre is a difficult task, many poets have, since the dawn of the nuclear age, sought ways of expressing this paradoxical position. As John Gery argues,

> [b]y exposing how we have come to picture ourselves in the nuclear age, the best poets express what is needed to outlive it—an articulation and critique of our current paradoxical situation. So although it is not wrong to say that nuclear age poetry unites in resistance against annihilation, it also serves the more reconstructive function of portraying "ways of nothingness" by which ... we can carry on a meaningful existence. (Gery 1996, 11)

For poets such as Lowell and Sexton, portraying "ways of nothingness" meant exploring the relationship between fractured, pathological selves and the social, political and psychological entities that sought to rebuild those selves in the image of compliant, docile subjects. While their poems frequently allude to the spectre of nothingness, the traumatic epicentre of post-war culture, their focus tends to be more on personal struggle and grief. Implicit in this grief is a desire to come to terms with a profound, and irretrievable, sense of loss connected either explicitly or implicitly to the fractured selfhood detonated by the bomb and its insidious psychological fallout.[2]

In Lowell's *Life Studies*, this loss is bound to a feeling that old hierarchies and orders have fallen into symbolic ruins in the wake of World War II, a feeling that is particularly evident in poems such as "Beyond the Alps," which transgresses personal and political terrain. In the poem, Lowell describes how in the post-war world

> Life changed to landscape. Much against my will
> I left the City of God where it belongs
> There the skirt-mad Mussolini unfurled
> the eagle of Caesar. (Lowell 2003, 113)

The idea of life as "landscape" suggests a levelling of political hierarchies. The speaker's departure from the City of God in the wake of Mussolini's fascist politics implies the problematic nature of abiding by orthodoxies erected in the service of violent, totalitarian agendas. At the same time, the loss of old orthodoxies exposes an absence at the centre of post-war politics. As Lowell's train descends the Alps, he muses, metaphorically, that "[t]here were no tickets for that altitude"; rather, in this post-hierarchical era he is left confounded, contemplating "the miscarriage of the brain" (Lowell 2003, 117), or his own psychological confusion in a post-hierarchical era.

Other poems in *Life Studies*, including "Inauguration Day: January 1953," which laments the inauguration of Dwight D. Eisenhower, extend this loss of political hierarchy to Cold War America. The poem describes post-war Americans as "lack-land atoms, split apart," invoking a nuclear metaphor to suggest a shared psychic fragmentation that has, as its source, a reckless Cold War politics. For Lowell, this fragmentation explains why "the Republic summons Ike, / the mausoleum in her heart" (2003, 117). Eisenhower, with his aggressive anti-communist agenda and commitment to nuclear brinksmanship, is seen as an agent of containment; the politics of both threat and containment that he stood for, in Lowell's view, aimed to cover up the "mausoleum," or trauma, in

---

[2] See also Chapter 11, where Spear discusses the ways in which the historical trauma of the Holocaust impacted on the depressive, fractured psyche that Leonard Cohen dramatized in his lyrics.

the hearts of post-war citizens, implying a link between political ideology and the biopolitical management of American lives.

While poems such as "Beyond the Alps" and "Inauguration Day: January 1953" express a tangible connection between politics and psychic fragmentation, it is in his overtly pathological poems that Lowell most explicitly conveys both the personal and psychological impact of nuclear politics. Poems such as "Home After Three Months Away," for example, describe the speaker's feelings of sadness and alienation upon returning to the daily domestic routines of home after several weeks in a psychiatric institution. The poem, however, does not directly express the anguish of the atomic ruin. Rather, it expresses frustration at the way in which his personality has been subjected to the conformist principles aimed at concealing the psychological impact of that ruin. On the surface, the poem does little more than describe the subtle ways in which things at home have changed—and have remained the same—during his institutionalization. In the second stanza, for instance, Lowell muses on these subtle changes:

> they tell me nothing's gone.
> Though I am forty-one,
> not forty now, the time I put away
> was child's-play. After thirteen weeks
> my child still dabs her cheeks
> to start me shaving. When
> we dress her in her sky-blue corduroy,
> she changes to a boy,
> and floats my shaving brush
> and washcloth in the flush...
> Dearest, I cannot loiter here
> in lather like a polar bear. (Lowell 2003, 185)

In these poignant scenes of a bathing routine, Lowell makes the personal impact of his institutionalization felt. Although the autobiographical speaker is told that "nothing's gone," or nothing has changed during his time away (and although his daughter picks up on their routine as though he'd never left), he cannot help but feel the personal anguish of lost time. He makes this sentiment apparent in his assertion that he's "forty-one, / not forty, now." In the stanza's concluding lines, however, the tone shifts slightly from the poignant to the ominous. Although the image of Lowell being left by his daughter to "loiter here / in lather like a polar bear" is playful and suggests a strong father/daughter bond, it also implies a frustration with being contained by domestic routine. Lowell is loitering, aimless and bored; the image of the polar bear indicates the presence of a powerful, even violent, force neutralized by his daily routines.

However, as the next stanza indicates, the cause of this frustration with domestic life is not the family itself, or his own personal circumstances. Rather, it is the larger social and biopolitical situation that has sought to normalize and administrate post-war existence. This becomes apparent in the poem's third stanza, which begins

> Recuperating, I neither spin nor toil.
> Three stories down below,
> a choreman tends our coffin's length of soil,
> and seven horizontal tulips blow.
> Just twelve months ago,
> these flowers were pedigreed
> imported Dutchmen; now no one need
> distinguish them from weed.
> Bushed by the late spring snow,
> they cannot meet
> another year's snowballing enervation. (Lowell 2003, 186)

In this stanza, Lowell uses an extended gardening metaphor to suggest the implications of the biopolitical management of his psychological suffering. From his stable, recuperative position in which, as he says, "I neither spin nor toil," he looks down at the "choreman" who is taking care of the property on the garden. The image recalls "Fall 1961," where Lowell expresses similar feelings of being helplessly contained inside the glass of his home as he awaits a nuclear attack. The "choreman" tends tulips that, under his management, have gone from their distinguished status as "pedigreed / imported Dutchmen," to plants that can no longer be distinguished "from weed" only a year later. For Lowell, the gardener's tending of the flowers is conflated with a feeling of "snowballing enervation" or heightened anxiety. Indeed, it is precisely the mixture of personal enervation and management by the gardener that seems responsible for reducing the once "pedigreed" tulips to weeds. As a metaphor for his psychological state, Lowell's garden imagery extends beyond the suggestion that his suffering is merely the result of his illness. Rather, that illness, and the state of enervation that it leads to, is heightened by the intervention of a third party. For Lowell, this third party may be the psychological institution or the more insidious ideological imperatives that seek to contain both anxiety and dissent in the nuclear age (or, indeed, an amalgam of both). This feeling of being managed into a position of complacency and indifference leads to the poem's emphatic, if paradoxical, conclusion: "I keep no rank nor station. / Cured, I am frizzled, stale and small" (Lowell 2003, 84). Far from being an endorsement of the turmoil caused by mental illness, these lines call into question the legitimacy of the "cure" rather than suggesting, from a Romantic perspective, a link between madness and creativity. For Lowell, the "cure" is coextensive with a conformist and domestic existence wherein he keeps "no rank nor station," suggesting that wellness in the post-war era is contingent upon relinquishing individuality. Lowell's ironic suggestion that when cured he is "frizzled, stale, and small" demonstrates the toll that the "enervation" of both psychological management and living within an era of anxiety has on his system. It is ultimately this cure, rather than the destructive illness that led to his institutionalization, that Lowell posits as a form of psychic ruin. While the poem does not endorse psychic turmoil as a source of creativity, it does condemn the psychiatric treatment Lowell experienced, indicating that its emphasis on discipline and conformity levelled the psychic landscape from which he drew inspiration. Writing from his "cured" position within this psychic ruin, Lowell feels as though his experience in the institution worked to diminish, or at least contain, his affective responses to the social and political environment. The psychic ruin the institution helped create was therefore politically expedient insofar as it helped construct a more manageable Cold War subject, even if it was destructive for Lowell's creative psyche.

The poem's sociological dimension thus implies a correlation between the psychiatric institution and biopolitical management, one that, in Lowell's gardening metaphor, is responsible for cultivating a country of conformist and "stale" individuals. For Lowell, this conformist state is the psychic ruin: it tends, and even weeds out, aesthetic responses to both culture and politics. As Nikolas Rose argues, the growth of biopolitics in the mid-century United States was coextensive with the rise of psychiatric paradigms. For Rose, psychiatric technologies have enabled both political authorities and individuals to reinterpret the mundane elements of everyday life-conduct—shopping, working, cooking—as dimensions of "life-style choice": activities *in which* people invest themselves and *through which* they both express and manifest their worth and value as selves. In these and other locales, the ethical technologies in which psychology participates, and within which psychological expertise is so deeply enmeshed, provide a means for shaping, sustaining, and managing human beings not in opposition to their personal identity but precisely in order to produce such an identity: a necessary reciprocal element of the political valorization of freedom. (Rose 1996, 98)

For women such as Anne Sexton, who came of age in an era that valorized "life-style" activities such as shopping, cooking and child-rearing as the apotheosis of feminine life in post-war liberal democracy, failing to find value in those choices manifested itself as a failure of self-actualization and/or as a sign of psychological illness. The fact that Sexton struggled to conform to the domestic expectations placed upon young women in the 1950s has been well documented. Diane Wood Middlebrook's controversial inclusion of transcripts from Sexton's psychological counselling sessions with Dr. Martin Orne clearly indicates the degree to which she struggled, as a young woman, to find valorization as a wife and mother. For example, in a 1955 session with Dr. Orne that precedes her career as a poet, Sexton writes

> I am so alone—nothing seems worth while—I walk from room to room trying to think of something to do—for a while I will do something, make cookies or clean the bathroom—make beds—answer the telephone—but all along I have this almost terrible energy in me and nothing seems to help … I sit in a chair and try to read a magazine and I twirl my hair until it is a mass [of] snarls—then as I pass a mirror I see myself and comb it again … Then I walk up and down the room—back and forth—and I feel like a caged tiger. (Middlebrook 1991, 36)

Like Lowell in "Home After Three Months Away," Sexton here feels "stale and small," reduced to her domestic function at the expense of her "terrible" creative energy. Indeed, the domestic situation she describes resembles the sort of "cruel optimism" that Lauren Berlant argues is a pivotal component of neoliberal democracies. According to Berlant, "A relation of cruel optimism exists when something you desire is actually an obstacle to your flourishing … These kinds of optimistic relations are not inherently cruel. They become cruel only when the object that draws your attachment actively impedes the aim that brought you to it initially" (Berlant 2011, 1). The imperative for middle-class women of the 1950s to find happiness within a restrictive domestic scenario was, at least in Sexton's case, the precise obstacle to her flourishing. The difficulty was understanding why (and how) the domestic life failed to provide the sense of fulfilment that it promised. This, as Berlant explains, is due to the affective structure of the optimistic scenario: "[w]hatever the *experience* of optimism is in particular, then, the *affective structure* of an optimistic attachment involves a sustaining inclination to return to the scene of fantasy that enables you to expect that *this* time, nearness to *this* thing will help you or a world to become different in just the right way" (Berlant 2011, 2). From the perspective of Cold War biopolitics, this affective structure functions much like the political ontology of threat: it keeps individuals attached to an object—in one case an optimistic one, in the other case an anxious one—that ultimately prevents flourishing. On one level, these affective structures help to sustain ideological interests, such as those of the Cold War United States, predicated upon repressing dissent and political engagement on the domestic front. On the level of the individual, however, they structure the phantasmatic psychic ruin that poets such as Sexton were confronted by. With the possibility of literal nuclear ruin always looming, Sexton is simultaneously faced with daily injunctions to enjoy her domestic lifestyle. However, as the transcript of her session with Dr. Orne indicates, Sexton was sensitive to the logic of cruel optimism that governed such injunctions. She found herself both implicitly aware of the fact that her agency as a woman in the Cold War era was being managed, and incapable of overcoming the ideological conditions that fixed her containment, leaving her feeling like a "caged tiger." Indeed, it was Sexton's very inability to enjoy domestic life that exacerbated her pathologies and made her feel as though her unhappiness in the post-war domestic scenario revealed deep psychological flaws. It simply made no sense, within the context of a post-war era that promised endless possibilities for domestic women, that she should be unhappy. However, as Sexton came to recognize, the political valorization of domestic lifestyle, a valorization linked to the management of affect in an era of nuclear anxiety, constituted its own form of psychic ruin. It left her feeling as though she had no option other than to concede her agency as an individual and creative thinker, and to enjoy her confinement within a cultural landscape that demanded she conforms to dominant discourses of feminine domesticity, or risk ostracism, depression and even institutionalization.

This logic of cruel optimism, therefore, was in part responsible for Sexton's fractured psychological state. While such affect management strategies sought to conceal and contain the anxiety and epistemological uncertainty at the core of the nuclear age, they also worked to rehabilitate individuals by asking them to buy into the emergent neoliberal ethos. For Sexton, however, conforming to such rehabilitative strategies meant buying into what she perceived as a post-war culture that confined women to a space of domestic—and psychic—ruins. In poems such as "Home After Three Months Away," Lowell expresses a sense of weariness about being "cultivated" by the biopolitical resources of his era. Sexton expresses a similar weariness in poems such as "You, Doctor Martin."

Written about one of several stays at a psychiatric institution, "You, Dr. Martin," which opens Sexton's first book *To Bedlam and Part Way Back*, is addressed directly to her long-time psychologist Dr. Martin Orne. The poem's first stanza includes Sexton's description of the asylum, "where the moving dead still talk / of pushing their bones against the thrust / of cure." Within this space, Sexton envisages herself as "queen of this summer hotel / or the laughing bee on a stalk / of death" (Sexton 1999, 3). Her description of the asylum is replete with images of a carefully manicured and managed existence:

> We stand in broken
> lines and wait while they unlock
> the door and count as at the frozen gates
> of dinner. The shibboleth is spoken
> and we move to gravy in our smock
> of smiles. We chew in rows, our plates
> scratch and whine like chalk
>
> in school. There are no knives
> for cutting your throat. I make
> moccasins all morning. (Sexton 1999, 3)

Sexton's description positions the patients as a uniform, obedient mass, chewing their institutional food behind their "smock of smiles." The fact that the knives have been removed suggests they have been figuratively de-clawed; no longer are they a threat to themselves or to each other. Instead, they are reduced to pure function, making "moccasins all morning" or performing rudimentary tasks. The image of the patients making moccasins conjures the remedial tasks of domestic life such as darning socks and mending clothes. The fact that these are activities meant, presumably, to help keep patients occupied and to give them a source of accomplishment within the institution, also implies that they are being taught to conform to a redundant and uniform existence outside of the asylum, one in which vitality, signified by the knives, is all but removed. The implication is that rehabilitation is coextensive with a sanctioned, institutionally managed, fragmentation of identity. The patients are taught to discipline their actions according to the institution's rules, rules that prepare them to be obedient subjects once their rehabilitation has been completed. As Sexton implies in the poem, the patients are "[b]roken"; they are taught to line up, to obey and to conform. However, these injunctions are not overtly repressive; rather, they work on the level of the individual psyche. Within the institutional setting, the patients are offered correctives that will help them mitigate the epistemological ruin of early Cold War culture, and the anxiety that it spawns, once they are released from institutional life. In other words, by being taught to conform to a disciplined domestic existence, they are given the tools necessary for living within a Cold War culture pitted between cruel optimism and the political ontology of threat. From Sexton's perspective, her psychological treatment is less focused on healing psychic wounds, and more focused on the management of affect. Its fundamental goal is not to cure; rather, it is to break patients who are otherwise incapable of conforming to the containment strategies of the early Cold War. The patients in Sexton's poem are therefore the victims of an insidious ideological apparatus aimed at fragmenting psychic selves in order to produce docile subjects.

By addressing the poem to Dr. Orne, Sexton implies that he—as a symbol of institutional authority—is responsible for helping to engineer such lives of quiet conformity and discipline. This is perhaps most evident in the poem's final two stanzas:

> What large children we are
> here. All over I grow most tall
> in the best ward. Your business is people,
> you call at the madhouse, an oracular

eye in our nest. Out in the hall
the intercom pages you. You twist in the pull
of the foxy children who fall

like floods of life in frost.
And we are magic talking to itself,
noisy and alone. I am queen of all my sins
forgotten. Am I still lost?
Once I was beautiful. Now I am myself,
counting this row and that row of moccasins
waiting on the silent shelf. (Sexton 1999, 4)

Here, Sexton positions the patients as "children," and Orne as the adult responsible for shaping them. He is described as a powerful patriarch with an "oracular eye / in our nest," conveying at once the authority that his knowledge brings, and the power of surveillance that he wields over them. The fact that he is paged on the "intercom" implies that he is at once important, and that he exists as part of the institutional apparatus, outside of the lives of the "foxy children" that he twists to get away from. His job, therefore, is to utilize his psychiatric expertise to produce compliant subjects. By calling the patients "foxy," with its connotations of wildness, Sexton implies that they must be broken by Orne so that they can then be domesticated and returned to society as docile beings. In other words, Orne stands in the poem as a figure of discipline who is bent on fragmenting psyches to the point of submission and obedience rather than healing psychic wounds.

Sexton, like Lowell in "Home After Three Months Away," therefore challenges the logic of institutionally administered discipline. The poem's final lines reflect Lowell's poem by questioning whether or not she is better off now that she has been rehabilitated according to psychiatric paradigms. As she writes, "Once I was beautiful. Now I am myself." For Sexton, the psychologically managed self is an institutional construct, something that has been liquidated of its "beautiful" qualities in favour of the neoliberal virtues of discipline and conformity. Sexton's new self is a regulated one, doing the work of "counting this row and that row of moccasins / waiting on the shelf." Like the moccasins, Sexton feels that she too has been reduced to her bare function in the world. In the institution, she is now "on the shelf," waiting to be released back into the world as a useful and productive, if less beautiful and volatile, citizen. In this regard, she is more psychologically fragmented, more broken, than when she entered the institution. As a victim of Cold War biopower, she is therefore more prepared to accept the psychic ruin of a domestic life governed by the stifling logic of cruel optimism and the epistemological uncertainty of nuclear brinksmanship.

While there is little doubt that Sexton did suffer from serious psychological ailments, her criticism in this poem is therefore not of diagnostic or even analytical paradigms; rather, it is levelled at the rehabilitative structures that conflate recovery with domesticity, conformity and productivity in an emergent neoliberal era. From this perspective, Sexton's poetry about mental illness, like Lowell's, examines what emerges from the psychic ruins of anxiety and illness in the nuclear era. For both poets, the political ontology of threat and the logic of cruel optimism help institutions—psychiatric and otherwise—administrate a more compliant consensus culture. By turning inward, their "confessional" poetics demonstrates the impact that the ideological apparatus of the American Cold War had on the everyday lives of its subjects. By using their poetry to probe the epistemological uncertainty generated by the atomic ruin, their poetry exposes the manner in which the political exploits the fear of the atomic ruin in order to construct compliant Cold War subjects.

References

Berlant, Lauren. 2011. *Cruel Optimism*. Durham, NC: Duke University Press.

Boyer, Paul. 1998. *Fallout*. Columbus, OH: Ohio State University Press.

Gery, John. 1996. *Ways of Nothingness*. Gainesville: University of Florida Press.

Hamilton, Ian. 1982. *Robert Lowell*. New York: Random House.

Kristeva. Julia. 1989. *Black Sun: Depression and Melancholia*. New York: Columbia University Press.

Lifton, Robert J., and Greg Mitchell. 1995. *Hiroshima in America*. New York: Putnam.

Lowell, Robert. 2003. *Collected Poems*, ed. Frank Bidart. New York: Farrar, Strauss & Giroux.

Masco, Joseph. 2008. Survival Is Your Business: Engineering Ruins and Affect in Nuclear America. *Cultural Anthropology* 23 (2): 361–398.

Massumi, Brian. 2009. The Future Birth of the Affective Fact: The Political Ontology of Threat. In *The Affect Theory Reader*, ed. Melissa Gregg and Gregory J. Seighworth, 52–70. Durham, NC: Duke University Press.

Middlebrook, Diane Wood. 1991. *Anne Sexton: A Biography*. Boston: Houghton Mifflin.

Rose, Nikolas. 1996. *Inventing Our Selves*. London: Cambridge University Press.

Sexton, Anne. 1999. *The Complete Poems*. Boston: Mariner Books.

CHAPTER 11

The Fractured World of Leonard Cohen

Jeffrey L. Spear

That's where we are—we're on Boogie Street. We're in Babylon.

Interview with Brett Grainger 2001. (Burger 2014)

Thinking about Cohen's life in text, biographies, interviews and manuscripts in relation to fragment and ruin, three traumas stand out that seem to haunt his work: the death of his father when Leonard was nine, his struggle with depression and the aftermath of the Holocaust.[1] This haunting in theme and style calls to mind the

---

[1] Biographies by Ira B. Nadel (1996), reprinted with an Afterword (2007), and Sylvie Simmons (2012) were written with Cohen's permission and the cooperation of people important his life. The biography by L. S. Dorman and C. L. Rawlins (1990) is still valuable and Liel Leibovitz (2014) has lively summaries of key moments in Cohen's career. There are many unreprinted interviews. I am grateful to the staff of the Thomas Fischer Rare Book Room, University of Toronto, for permission and kind assistance while consulting the Leonard Cohen Archive, and to the Cohen estate and the Wylie Agency for permission to quote from Cohen's lyrics and poetry.

J. L. Spear (✉)
New York University, New York, NY, USA

© The Author(s) 2019
E. Mitsi et al. (eds.), *Ruins in the Literary and Cultural Imagination*,
https://doi.org/10.1007/978-3-030-26905-0_11

work of Nicolas Abraham and Maria Torok on mourning and transgen-erational trauma (Abraham and Torok 1994).[2]

In Abraham and Torok's theory, the stages of development have no fixed content. If there are complexes, fixations and the like that cause blockages or distortions in self-fashioning they come from culture as mediated initially by the family. The first section of this essay looks at these three traumas in terms of what Abraham and Torok call the psychic crypt and the phantom effect. Crypt and phantom provide a way to link Cohen's struggle with conflicting inner voices to his spiritual quest and the fragmentary images and references in his work. Such images often work as reversible metaphors for inner and outer conflict. The second section deals briefly with non-musical influences on Cohen, particularly his debt to Romanticism and the role of visual arts as a model for the juxtaposition of disparate images: "I've had to scrape [my songs] out of my heart. They come to me in pieces at a time and in showers at a time and in showers and fragments."[3] The final section looks at the social side of Cohen's lyrics, the hybrid voice of, in Aubrey Glazer's terms, a post-secular, Zen-*Tzaddik*, or bringer of light (Glazer 2017, 72–80). To situate that voice, we will be following a winding road from Montreal to Babylon.

Trauma and Text

Cohen was proud of his father's WWI service as a Lieutenant in a com-bat engineering unit, but Nathan returned with a chronic, debilitating medical condition—unlike his younger brother Horace who received a battlefield promotion to Captain and came home unscathed. Nathan, the nattily dressed older brother became the public face of Freedman Company clothiers, but the business was actually managed by Horace, a displacement, Ira Nadel notes, that Nathan resented (1996, 150). Despite Nathan's obvious decline, the adults assured Leonard his father would recover, so his death was at once expected and a shock. The boy who would later weep over the death of his dog could not cry at his father's funeral, substituting his own, private memorial service. He slit one of his father's bow ties, inserted words of his own, dug through the

---

[2] Esther Rashkin (1992) explicates the differences between Abraham and Torok's theory and other schools of psychoanalysis.

[3] Interview with Billy Walker (Burger 2014, 26).

snow and buried the tie in the backyard never to be seen again. Whether literally or figuratively, Cohen considered those interred words to be the beginning of his writing career. "Everybody knows that the boat is leaking / Everybody knows that the captain lied / Everybody got this broken feeling / Like their father or their dog just died."[4]

Looking back as an adult, Leonard faced the facts of his father's death in a tone more aggrieved than grieving for the man who "lay on a blood-sopped pillow, / his heart half rotted / and his throat dry with regret" (Cohen 1956, 19). The inner consequence of Cohen's substitute burial and the failure to go through the process of mourning would be what Abraham and Torok call a psychic crypt: "Inexpressible mourning erects a secret tomb inside the subject. Reconstituted from the memories of words, scenes and affects, the objectal correlative of the loss is buried alive in the crypt as a full-fledged person" (Abraham and Torok 1994, 130). It is not surprising that despite what others might see, Cohen could look in the mirror and see his father: "In the world I alone / wear his face / And here I am in places / he never would have travelled / among men who / think I am myself" (Nadel 1996, 18). His formal dress, "the costume / That I wore," was a paternal homage ("Going Home" 2012).

Anointed the new man of the family before the ritual transition of Bar Mitzvah, Leonard demanded the pistol Nathan had brought back from the war, the talisman of a strong father, the officer he never knew and the disciplinarian of earliest memory. Military imagery and references run through Cohen's work in almost any context, even the erotic and romantic. If the walls of the crypt, so to speak, were generated by Leonard's need to deny Nathan's weakness and preserve a positive image of the father whose place he was prematurely assuming, the haunting would come from denial and secrets, things sensed but unspoken—at the minimum Nathan's feeling of having been displaced, betrayed by his younger brother, while maintaining a false front as declining health turned him into an impotent figurehead—let alone whatever unspoken trauma he carried back from the war.

"Crypts are only constructed when the shameful secret is the love object's doing and when that object also functions as an ego ideal"

---

[4] "Everybody Knows," *I'm Your Man*. London: Sony/ATV UK, 1988. Hereafter Cohen's songs will be cited in the text by title and release date. There is a key at the end of the References.

(Abraham and Torok 1994, 131). Mourning that works through grief referentially, what Abraham and Torok term "introjection," allows loss to be taken in and gradually accepted, prompting a new stage of personal development. The incorporated figure in the crypt arrests that aspect of development. Traces of what has been denied by the creation of the crypt, emotions, secrets, things the love object revealed but never stated, are experienced as haunting by a phantom that threatens to expose the "concealed and unspoken parental fear" (Abraham and Torok 1994, 181). Looking back, Cohen recalled a home where everyone led a secret personal life ("la vie personnelle secrète que chacun menait," Fevret 1991). Because the phantom effect breaks the link between signifier and signified regarding the transgenerational secrets of the crypt and their attendant emotions ("preservative repression"), it makes its presence known through a kind of poetics: linguistic deflections, distortions, detours, substitution and figures of speech that both conceal and implicitly reveal what cannot be directly spoken ("the captain lied"). The phantom disrupts logical sequences and narrative coherence. "Cryptonymy" entails "reading a life-long poem and, at first, envisioning life as the creation of a readable poem" (Abraham and Torok 1986, lvi, 79–83). It is no surprise that so many Cohen lyrics occasioned by a personal experience fuse or arrange imagistic fragments.

The bedtime ritual of Nathan leading Leonard up the stairs to bed is perfectly assimilated into the story of a nine-year-old Isaac being led up the mountain by his father. The Binding of Isaac would be seamlessly transformed into a powerful anti-war statement were it not for these reversible lines in the last stanza: "I will kill you if I must, / I will help you if I can … / I will help you if I must, / I will kill you if I can" ("Story of Issac" 1969). Is this an implicit dialogue with "You who build these altars now/to sacrifice these children," or a split self?

The splitting between the conventional meaning of words and symbols, which remain available in a dictionary sense, and their encrypted affect is experienced as self-division, the feeling of hosting an alien, a wound, a blindness that can split the ego into different voices and give rise to inexplicable feelings. Although the epistolary song "Famous Blue Raincoat" is signed "sincerely L. Cohen," the singer has been cuckolded by a fictional twin, a doppelgänger. It was L. Cohen himself who owned the Burberry and contemplated "going clear."[5]

---

[5] "I said this can't be me / Must be my double," "I Can't Forget" 1988; there is a symposium on "Raincoat" in Scobie (2000, 100–117).

Cohen's depression manifested itself, as Abraham and Torok would predict, as "a mental violence of conflicting voices," so that when he wrote he had to penetrate the "meaningless debate that is occupying most of my attention, I have to come up with something that really speaks to my deepest interest" (Interview with Paul Zollo in Burger 2014, 265). His notoriously long creative process was a working through or refining until he arrived at a voice or voices that felt true, not obviously contingent upon an incident of origin, transmuting, for example, the base metal of a specific memory, "Your hair was flung in squalls/ upon your wide white shoulders," into "Your hair upon the pillow like a sleepy golden storm" ("Hey, That's No Way To Say Goodbye" 1967).[6] But his long struggle with lyrics that sometimes engaged his whole body as if he were wrestling with an angel or a demon also suggests that the process involved an attempt to work through in a psychological as well as aesthetic sense: "I followed the course / from chaos to art / desire the horse / depression the cart" (Cohen 2006, 1) (Fig. 11.1).

A prime Cohen characteristic comes out of this multivocal inner struggle: in his work and even in interviews, the same voice expresses alternative or even opposing perspectives. In "Is This What You Wanted" (1974), the singer's body is "a house that is haunted / by the ghost of you and me." A whole series of projected contrasts resolve into "me," as the interior, unwrinkled seventeen-year-old, and "you," the body housing this conflict as "old and wrinkled"—a description more appropriate to the paternal phantom than the twenty-nine-year-old Cohen. In the world outside the self, Cohen could imagine himself on both sides of most oppositions, even victim and oppressor. One constant, however, was a distrust of governmental and other forms of institutionalized power that was confirmed when he went to Cuba in 1961 to witness a revolution only to see families waiting outside the new regime's secret police headquarters for news of their loved ones, just as other families had under the old. The true believers from the USA and Canada threatened to turn him in when Cohen dared question the righteousness of the new regime (Nadel 1996, 91–98).

---

[6]Notebook, Box 8A, Leonard Cohen Collection, Thomas Fisher Rare Book Library, University of Toronto. Ms of "Hey, That's No Way to Say Goodbye" (New York: Sony USA, 1967). Permission to access and quote given by Robert Kory, trustee of the Leonard Cohen Estate.

Fig. 11.1 Leonard Cohen "the background singers" (2012) © The Wylie agency LLC and Leonard Cohen

Cohen came of age when Nazi mass murder was still referred to as the Final Solution in North America. The Shoah did not become the Holocaust, a proper noun, until the 1960s. As Cohen grew up his family went on with their ordinary lives, attended synagogue and paid little heed to the events in Europe. Cohen's draft dedication to *Flowers for Hitler* (1964) was not directed to the outer world, but to Jews of his parents' generation whose attention to material advancement seemed morally oblivious just as their religion lacked fervour: it begins, "With scorn, love, nausea, and above all, / a paralysing sense of community" (Simmons 2012, 119). Like many Jews of his generation, the Holocaust blocked Cohen's sense of Jewish communal continuity embodied in the traditional liturgy, leading him to Zen, Jewish mysticism and other spiritual practices both to find himself and to connect with the Jewish past.

Like my father's family, Cohen's mother emigrated from the Jewish Pale during the civil war that followed the Bolshevik Revolution. His links to the Yiddish speaking Ashkenazi culture of Eastern Europe that the Nazis murdered, leaving the future to the minority that wanted to revive spoken Hebrew and return to the Holy Land, came through songs his mother sang and his beloved maternal grandfather Rabbi Solomon Klinitsky-Klein with whom he studied the Book of Isaiah. He lost no immediate family, but Cohen felt compelled to be a secondary witness to the Shoah, one who saw in the safe community of Montreal a refusal to comprehend that "Jews must survive in their loneliness as witnesses" (Nadel 1996, 126). That means taking in horror you did not personally see. "I learn nothing because my mind is stuffed with bodies: / blurred parades, hosts of soft lead wings, / tragic heaped holes of the starved, / the tangled closer than snakes" (Cohen 1964, 19).

Cohen's long struggle with depression mysteriously ended in 1999 while he was studying with Ramesh Balsekar. He was wary of attributing what he experienced as a gift of grace to any single cause, but what Ramesh taught was sublime indifference. Nothing that comes from the inside matters; everything comes to us. "God is everywhere … you don't keep meditating your way to God" (Simmons 2012, 421). Not surprisingly, there is a Kabbalistic parallel: "No vessel can contain God, unless you think of yourself as Nothing" (Ariel 2006, 210). What positive memory Cohen did have of his early experience in the synagogue his family helped found came from the music, but with his depression lifted he found meaning in the liturgy that had once seemed empty. Cohen's final recording *You Like It Darker* (2016) features the choir from Shaar Hashomayim.

As Cohen's attempt to deal with inner voices by getting high gave way in middle age, his work took a more spiritual turn. He attained a perspective that expresses the social aspect of preservative repression that Kristen Gwyer attributes to second-generation Holocaust fiction[7]: "it haunts secondarily traumatized individuals as the spectral absent presence of an incident not repressed but never known," generating fictional worlds that are "without centre, periphery, or exit, boundless in space and through time" (Gwyer 2014, 97). "Behold the gates of mercy in arbitrary space," writes Cohen in "Come Healing" of 2012. A key transitional lyric is the original 1984 version of Cohen's best-known song, "Hallelujah."

[7]For a discussion of the "un-assimilability" of the memory of the Holocaust "in the absence of ruins," see Chapter 13.

The original "Hallelujah" was largely ignored. Cohen wrote what amounted to a new song around the chorus in 1988 that removed King David and linked ecstatic sex with the holy dove in a Pentecostal orgasm before "it all went wrong" (*Live in Concert* 1994). John Cale put the Davidic head on the orgasmic body, and with some variations that is how the song has been covered ever since—including by Cohen himself on his later tours. It is the unsettling, forward-looking original that matters here.[8]

Like Marc Chagall's two-faced David of *David and Bathsheba* (1956) and the Sufi poets he admired, Cohen decontextualizes David. Cohen replaces the Lord of Hosts, who condemns David through the prophet Nathan, namesake of his disciplinary father, with the Lord of Song who can be pleased by a lyric born of a failed proof of faith. A pleasing "secret chord" suggests that strain of Kabbalistic Judaism that sought to transform evil from within, so that "certain actions which are in reality pure and holy, must bear the outward appearance of sin" (Scholem 1954, 318). Unlike the esoteric David, the biblical king was never baffled. He was self-assured to the point of rashness, which is how Nathan caught him out with a parable. In the second verse, the "event" that gave rise to the secret chord of the first is a surreal montage that conflates space and time in a manner at once intense, comic and uniquely Cohen. David enraptured by Bathsheba in the moonlight morphs into Samson tied to the torture chair of thriller films (e.g. the Bondage scene in *You Only Live Twice*), to the broken throne, Samson's hair and the eroticized hallelujah.

In the post-Cale song, the references to a "you" who was once a lover feedback to the beginning and Cohen's earlier songs. But in the 1984 original each verse addresses a different "you." The final one, "I didn't come to fool you," is in both versions and addressed to the audience. The second "you," who claims "I took the name in vain," thinks only the conventional, imperative, hallelujah legitimate; the broken one blasphemous. But according to the Kabbalistic Breaking of the Vessels the same holy spark that can rationalize intercourse with the alien woman by the just man is also there to be released in every (albeit Hebrew) letter, so "There's a blaze of light / In every word / It doesn't matter which you heard / The holy or the broken hallelujah" (Idel 2013, 218;

---

[8]For a history of the versions of "Hallelujah," see Light (2012). For a feminist history of gender and performance of the song, see Babich (2013).

Wolfson 2006, 127). Cohen later said that if he had a creed it came from the Breaking of the Vessels: "Ring the bells that still can ring / Forget your perfect offering / There is a crack, a crack in everything / That's how the light gets in" ("Anthem" 1992).

The reference of the first, accusatory you ("You don't really care for music, do ya"), seems as secret as the chord. It could accuse those who declare only one kind of music or one message acceptable, but the context of Psalms suggests a more esoteric possibility. The conventional hallelujah of Psalms is an imperative to praise the Lord, but there is an exception, Psalm 137. There is no Jewish Lord of Song, but "by the rivers of Babylon" the exiles ask "How shall we sing the Lord's song in a strange land?" They refer to a mocking demand by their Babylonian captors: "they that wasted us required of us in mirth, saying, 'Sing us one of the songs of Zion,'" implying that, with the temple destroyed, the song would be meaningless entertainment. Ancient Babylon was not just the place of exiles yearning to return to Jerusalem, it was also the holy place where diasporic Judaism was born.[9]

As Elliot Wolfson points out, in the Chasidic tradition Cohen draws upon "Psalms were personal, composed by King David from a broken heart" (2006, 128). The secret chord comes from the broken heart of a post-Holocaust, Jewish Canadian exile akin emotionally to the Jews dispersed after the destruction of the first temple, creators of the "oral Torah" that became the Babylonian Talmud. Mystical sexuality revivifies fragments of the ancient tradition when customary practice seems unresponsive in the face of catastrophe. "Even though it all went wrong," when Cohen imagines David seeing Bathsheba, he is looking through a Kabbalistic lens that makes his hallelujah possible. "HE gives her the beauty and the complexion. Thus, the source of her beauty is the divine power. Why, then, should I be drawn to the partial when I can unite with the source of the entire universe" (*Sefer Tzeva'at ha-Rivash*, Ariel 2006, 195). By this reading, Cohen would see fans who want to be part of the "scene," who value the charisma of the singer over the spirit of the song, as latter-day Babylonians: "you don't really care for music, do ya."

The "remorse and rumination [that] arise at the libidinal spring of prohibited sexual desire" (Abraham and Torok 1994, 121) would be totally

---

[9] See Boyarin (2015) for historical detail. "By the Rivers Dark" (2001) "was inspired by Psalm 137." Interview with Brett Grainger in Berger (2014). For more on the "intime poético-mystique" behind Cohen's lyrics, see Pleshoyano (2014).

subsumed or rationalized in the light of the Kabbalah in "Hallelujah" were it not for two lines in both of Cohen's versions of the song that won't link up, a fragment that in fifteen words all but sums up the illness of mourning: "I did my best, it wasn't much / I couldn't feel, so I tried to touch." Aubrey Glazer concludes his account of Cohen as a Jewish artist by noting that "melancholic wisdom centers on the discernment that wholeness can be restored only in the fragment, the sacrifice of the aggregate to the suffering of the part" (Glazer 2017, 250).

THE WORKER IN SONG

Although Cohen first came to notice as a singer songwriter during the protest era of the late 1960s and early 1970s, he was a generation older than Bob Dylan and most of the Woodstock cohort. Before his first album appeared in 1967 he had published two novels and three volumes of poetry in Canada where he remains a major literary figure. In addition to Irving Layton and the older generation of Canadian poets, his formative intellectual horizon came from the period of the Beats, archetypal criticism, California Zen, Existentialism, androcentric sexual liberation and pre-French Freud.[10] A belated Romantic, he not only draws on his personal life, he repurposes conventional symbols, mythologizes his relationships with women, creates dramatic monologues and dislocated allegories—poems and songs structured as allegory without invoking the frame of reference conventional allegory relies on for intelligibility. It is not the echoes of the lyrical Keats and Shelley as in "The Nightingale" (2004) that matter here; rather that aspect of the Romantic tradition that creates imaginative links to distant pasts that bridge historical ruptures, particularly the work of Cohen's Irish "master," W. B. Yeats, who turned Troy, Bethlehem and Byzantium into nodal points in an esoteric system of historical cycles (Yeats 1938). Whereas the Romantic tradition focused on the antecedents of modern European civilization, Cohen applied the tradition to his Jewish roots writing as a Romantic Jew, rather than, *pace* Glazer, a "Jewish artist." For Cohen, the Romantic, experiencing the poet's raw material, means both immersion in life and immersion in text, particularly biblical text: "That biblical landscape is our urgent invitation, and we have to be there ... Now what *is* the biblical landscape? It is the

---

[10]For essays elaborating these references, see Scobie (2000), Holt (2014), Ringuet and Rabinovitch (2016), Billingham (2017).

victory of experience. That's what the Bible celebrates" (Interview with Arthur Kurzweil 1994, in Burger 2014, 387). "Babylon-as-ruin is the foundational image for western depictions of lost cities, dead and belated civilizations" (Scheil 2016, 198), but for Cohen, Babylon is at once a ruined place and a situation, a metonymy for exile. The spiritual substratum for Cohen is not a ruin, not even the Wailing Wall, it is the first promise, the contested land from which he sings his own psalm drawing from an eve of Yom Kippur prayer: "From this broken hill / All your praises they shall ring / If it be your will / To let me sing" ("If It Be Your Will" 1984).

Both the Kabbalah and the mystical traditions that fed into the Romantic tradition have a root in Neoplatonism. Many of these features are at work in "Different Sides" (2012) in which Cohen, as only he can, recasts the conflict between the written and oral law foreshadowed in "Hallelujah" as a lover's quarrel between vividly personified abstractions.

> We find ourselves on different sides
> Of a line nobody drew
> Though it all may be one in the higher eye
> Down here where we live, it is two.
> ….
> Both of us say there are laws to obey
> But frankly I don't like your tone
> ….
> You want to live where the suffering is
> I want to get out of town
> C'mon baby, give me a kiss
> Stop writing everything down.

When Cohen said we are living on Boogie Street and in Babylon he implicitly invoked a Blakean double vision, material and spiritual in the same site of writing. Many songs from *The Future* (1992) to his final album switch focus between Boogie Street and Babylon. Boogie Street is not just Los Angeles, it is the modern, materialistic world from its most benign aspects to the most brutal with a spiritual or moral infusion. The songs of the spiritual Babylon are visionary and move towards transcendence, but always carry traces of Boogie Street.

In addition to the influence of spiritual guides, writers and musicians, visual artists and filmmakers were always part of Cohen's circle.

The sculptor Morton Rosengarten was a youthful companion and life-long friend. There is more to the Chelsea Hotel period than Janis Joplin, the Warhol Factory, Lou Reed and Nico of the Velvet Underground. At the Chelsea, he met the artist, folklorist and experimental filmmaker Harry Everett Smith, whose associates included the collage artist couple Claude Pélieu and Mary Beach. The hip Village crowd frequenting Andy Warhol's Dom and Max's Kansas City included painters as well as musicians and writers (Simmons 2012, 155–168).

Only a few Cohen songs developed organically from an original idea to a coherent composition. Most often he wrote verse after verse and then moved them around like pieces of a puzzle or a collage. Collage often juxtaposes decontextualized images turning them into visual floating signifiers, leaving it to the viewer to assemble meaning (Fig. 11.2).

Cohen uses both decontextualized images and floating signifiers in the cultural studies sense of a common term without a stable signified. Both types are used together in the refrain line "There's a Law, there's an Arm, there's a Hand" ("The Law" 1984), for example. He often eases the listener in by providing a familiar frame for his enigmatic phrases and images. "There Is a War" (1974) contains a paradigm of this device in four lines: "There is a war between the rich and poor [class warfare] / a war between the man and the woman [battle of the sexes] / There is a war between the ones who say there is a war/and the ones say there isn't." Because they express familiar concepts the first two lines can be understood passively, but lines three and four are a Cohen *kaon* with no obvious referent and so demand active interpretation.

Sometimes Cohen sequences images like cinematic montage before freezing into collage:

> The rain falls down on last year's man,
> that's a jew's harp on the table, that is a crayon in his hand.
> And the corners of the blueprint are ruined since they rolled
> far past the stems of thumbtacks
> that throw shadows on the wood.
> And the skylight is like a skin for a drum I'll never mend
> and all the rain falls down amen
> on the works of last year's man.
> ("Last Year's Man" 1974)

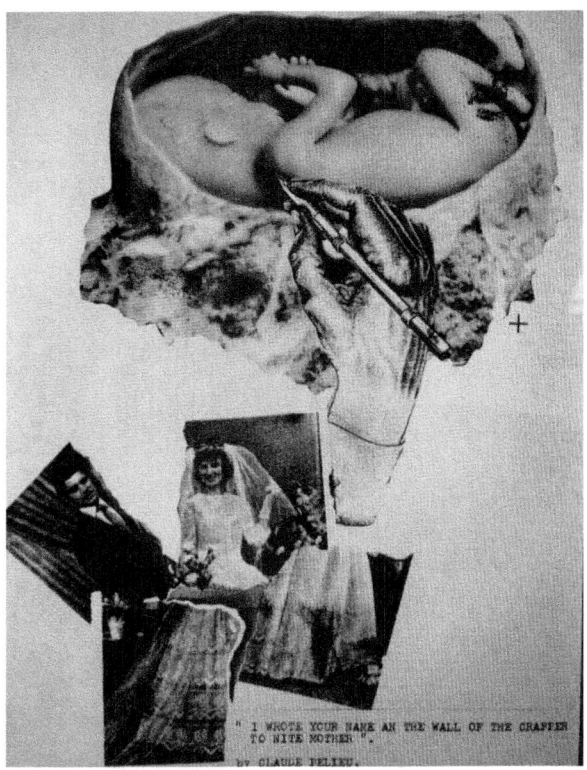

Fig. 11.2 Claude Pélieu, "collage from *Bulletin from Nothing 2*" (1965) © Claude Pélieu estate, 2019

Occasionally there are direct visual/verbal parallels (Fig. 11.3).

"You'll see your woman hanging upside down / Her features covered by her fallen gown."[11]

---

[11] *Relaxed* was displayed at the Centre Pompidou and on a catalogue cover in 1982 when Cohen was often in Paris.

Fig. 11.3   Toyen,
Relâche (Relaxed), 1943
© 2019 artists rights
society (ARS), New
York/ADAGP, Paris

THE ZEN-*TZADIK* KOHAN ON REMORSE
AND THE CONDITION OF THE HEART

The image of the inverted woman comes from "The Future" (1992), which begins with an angry/sadistic/fascistic voice that wants "absolute control / over every living soul … Give me crack and anal sex / Take the only tree that's left / and stuff it up the hole / in your culture. / Give me back the Berlin Wall / give me Stalin and St Paul / I've seen the future brother: / it is murder." It is no surprise that this voice wonders what they meant "When they said, REPENT, REPENT." Then, the "little jew [sic] / who wrote the Bible" seizes the inner microphone singing: "I've seen the nations rise and fall / I've heard the stories heard, them all / but love's the only engine of survival." True, but for this voice too, the future is murder. Finally, the voice of prophecy is heard: "There'll be the breaking of the ancient / western code / Your private life will suddenly explode." "Phantoms and fires on the road" echo Stoker's *Dracula* setting up the uncanny image of "the white man 'dancin.'" It ends with a yearning for certainty of any kind—"give me Christ or give me Hiroshima." Without acknowledging the need to be forgiven, repentance is an empty word.

But the murderous absolute of "The Future" is not Cohen's final statement. His lyric "I," that once took listeners on erotic quests down Boogie Street becomes increasingly spiritual, and the "you" that once implied a woman who might be, and sometimes could be, identified, take on one or another characteristic of an eternal feminine–muse, lover, wife, or remain an indefinite "you." On the male side, instead of a master, teacher or lover, the "I" turns to the root of ancient Jewish difference—the idea of a god whose name cannot be uttered, whose being is beyond representation, and of a Jew aspiring to the role of cross-cultural everyman "dressed as Arab / dressed as Jew ("There for You" 2004). Cohen did not go back to religion, but through secularism becoming, as Aubrey Glazer contends, a "prophet calling for a post-secular age" (Glazer 2017, 214). His response to the accusation of taking "the name in vain" in "Hallelujah" was "I don't even know the name." By the time he wrote "Born in Chains" (2014) he believed that the wish to know the Name (*Hashem*) or act in the name of the Name was a false pursuit that wounded the Name. But Cohen did not give up paradox: "In the Grip of Sensual Illusion / A sweet unknowing / Unified the Name."

Solitary passage out of a mental Egypt, "out of Pharaoh's dream," like the hallelujah of the erotically tormented David, comes through a functional illusion, an ecstasy that opens the way for the Name to be written on the heart by the black on white fire of the divine Torah where it can be felt, but not read. In the collective story of the *Haggadah* only the Wise Son, the Simple Son and the Son Who Knows Not How to Ask would have been saved, but these waters parted for the Wicked Son who questioned the ritual tradition. It is a story from Cohen's Babylon.

In so far as Cohen had a politics in the root sense, it was implied by his epigraph to *Flowers for Hitler* (1964) from Primo Levi: "Take care not to suffer in your own homes what is inflicted on us here." Starting at the level of individuals, that which brings us together—love in the broadest sense—promotes an organically cohesive society. Cruelty, segregation, Othering totalled up becomes "Egypt"—a heartless "cruel and dark regime." Remorse, or in stark Anglo-Saxon, agenbite, to be bitten again as in Agenbite of Inwit, the re/morse of conscience, is the moral key to overcoming difference in the interest of commonwealth, to make a mutual one out of our divisive many.

The anticipated response to repentance looks forward, it is forgiveness, grace, but Cohen's is not a Protestant usage: "I know that I'm forgiven, / But I don't know how I know/ I don't trust my inner feelings / Inner feelings come and go" ("That Don't Make It Junk" 2001). Remorse is historical; it looks back to the transgression. The anticipated response is compensatory, atonement, reparation. That is why remorse has a place in the law when considering sentencing and parole. The song in question is one of purification:

> Tell me again
> When the victims are singing
> And the Laws of Remorse are restored …
> Tell me again
> When the filth of the butcher
> Is washed in the blood of the lamb
> Tell me again
> When the rest of the culture
> Has passed thru' the Eye of the Camp.
> ("Amen" 2012)

The "Eye of the Camp" is another Cohen floating image, evocative but without a clear referent. I read it as a double reference to the entrance to the camp (cf. the eye of a needle) and the "hole in the world," the malign last judgment at the Birkenau railhead under the eye of Dr. Mengele who pointed the way to death and to such life as might survive hard labour or his experiments. Cohen implies that Western culture is itself a Holocaust survivor, and we should all see ourselves and our societies in that light.

If there is a *law* of remorse, it is universal. How is it that the USA has so many sites of Holocaust remembrance, and so few dealing with slavery? Surely, we should be searching our own hearts about our own transgenerational historical traumas.[12] That would mean absorbing, so far as Americans not of African lineage can, the experience of slavery and its transgenerational effects. Remorse was the promise of forty acres and a mule, broken at once and still owed. Remorse would compensate for the Trail of Tears, reservations, the decimation of Native American cultures, our domestic colonial and post-colonial narrative, and so on. Only then might the USA create one nation, as the Pledge of Allegiance declares, out of a multitudinous state. This is the implicit message of "Democracy" (1992).

The future tense assertion that "democracy is coming to the USA" directly challenges the national ideology by insisting that genuine democracy has not arrived, that it requires inclusion of Others, a message more urgent today than when the song was written. The mighty Ship of State must get to the "Shores of Need" past "the Reefs of Greed / through the Squalls of Hate"; take in the homeless, reckon with the "ashes of the gay"; struggle with the assertion in the Sermon on the Mount that the meek shall inherit the earth, that the persecuted and those who mourn shall be saved; find renewal in the meeting of the races, from the breaking of the patriarchal family and reordering of power between men and women—"the heart must open in a fundamental way." What Kierkegaard said about remorse can apply to nations as well as individuals: "… if … a person wishes to bluster out of, to defy, or to slink away from remorse, alas, which is indeed the most terrible thing to say of him, that he failed, or—that he succeeded?" (1956, 39).

---

[12] On how the trauma of historical catastrophe and the ensuing psychic ruin is probed in postwar American fiction and poetry, see Chapters 9 and 10.

Coda: "Invincible Defeat"

Walter Benjamin asked me once in Paris...whether there were really enough torturers back there to carry out the orders of the Nazis. There were enough.

"Education after Auschwitz," Theodor Adorno. (1998)

From first to last, the condition of the heart was Cohen's central motif. The Unified Heart colophon (entwined hearts, yin and yang, Star of David) symbolizes the hopeful side of his life and work, but hearts have to be tortured, twisted or cut to be joined together. The heart can be betrayed by institutions that preach love. "The blood, the soil, the faith / O love, aren't you tired yet? / A cross on every hill / A star, a minaret / So many graves to fill" ("The Faith" 2004). If any established institutions should have as their purpose the empathic education that Adorno hoped (against hope) would deprive future tyrants of their torturers, they are the religions of the cross, the star, the minaret—symbols Cohen pointedly links to the Nazi slogan *Blut und Boden*.

In an age when mass media can bring the whole world's catastrophes crashing into the living room with the immediacy of a local event, we can be overwhelmed with "compassion fatigue," a euphemism Cohen calls out with one of his boldest inversions. "Almost Like the Blues" (2014) inverts "almost." The blues transform individual and collective pain into song, but instead of referring to things that do not measure up, "almost" here references horrors that are excessive, that cannot be encompassed by art. Cohen's "almost" expresses a gap between signifier and signified that must not be bridged—a necessary and disquieting failure. Inevitably on Boogie Street, mundane concerns displace the immediate impact of distant horror. "There's torture and there's killing / And there's all my bad reviews." It stirs up what may be Cohen's oldest and deepest fear. "I let my heart get frozen / To keep away the rot." But the song about the limits of song is a song: "Almost Like a Blues" is a blues.

In a final message from the Babylon of the spirit, Cohen steers his heart towards eternity ("Steer Your Way" 2016). "Steer your way through the ruins / Of the altar and the mall ... Steer your heart past the truth / You believed in yesterday." Although reduced to a whisper, the voice of the abiding biblical landscape shames the faith of Boogie Street and its Ba'al, the Lord of the Market.

They whisper still, the ancient stones
The blunted mountains weep
As he died to make men holy
Let us die to make things cheap
And say the Mea Culpa which you've probably forgot
Year by Year
Month by month
Day by day
Thought by thought.
("Steer Your Way" 2016)

REFERENCES

Abraham, Nicolas, and Maria Torok. 1986. *The Wolf Man's Magic Word: A Cryptonymy*, trans. Nicholas Rand. Forward by Jacques Derrida. Minneapolis: University of Minnesota Press.

Abraham, Nicolas, and Maria Torok. 1994. *The Shell and the Kernel*, ed. and trans. Nicholas T. Rand. Chicago: University of Chicago Press.

Adorno, Theodor. 1998. Education After Auschwitz. In *Critical Models: Interventions and Catchwords*, trans. Henry W. Pickford. New York: Columbia University Press.

Ariel, David. 2006. *Kabbalah: The Mystic Quest in Judaism*. New York: Rowman & Littlefield.

Babich, Babbette. 2013. *The Hallelujah Effect*. Burlington, VT: Ashgate.

Billingham, Peter (ed.). 2017. *Spirituality and Desire in Leonard Cohen's Songs and Poems*. Newcastle upon Tyne: Cambridge Scholars.

Boyarin, Daniel. 2015. *A Traveling Homeland: The Babylonian Talmud as Diaspora*. Philadelphia: University of Pennsylvania Press.

Burger, Jeff (ed.). 2014. Interviews with Billy Walker, Paul Zollo, Arthur Kurzweil, and Brett Graiger. *Leonard Cohen on Leonard Cohen* 26: 261–291; 369–393; 386–392. Chicago: Chicago Review Press.

Cohen, Leonard. 1956. *Let Us Compare Mythologies*. Toronto: Contact Press.

Cohen, Leonard. 1964. *Flowers for Hitler*. Toronto: McClelland & Stewart.

Cohen, Leonard. 1967. Draft Verses of "Hey, That's No Way to Say Goodbye" in Mss Notebook, Box 8A, Leonard Cohen Collection, Thomas Fisher Rare Book Library, University of Toronto.

Cohen, Leonard. 2006. *The Book of Longing*. Toronto: McClelland & Stewart.

Dorman, Loranne S., and Clive L. Rawlins. 1990. *Leonard Cohen: Prophet of the Heart*. New York: Omnibus Press.

Fevret, Christian. 1991. Comme un Guerrier [Interview with Leonard Cohen]. *Les Inrockuptibles*, August 21. https://www.lesinrocks.com/1991/08/21/musique/comme-un-guerrier-11223522/. Accessed 6 Jan 2019.

Glazer, Aubrey. 2017. *Tangle of Matter & Ghost: Leonard Cohen's Post Secular Songbook of Mysticism(s) Jewish & Beyond*. Brighton, MA: Academic Studies Press.

Gwyer, Kirstin. 2014. *Encrypting the Past: The German-Jewish Holocaust Novel of the First Generation*. Oxford: Oxford University Press.

Holt, Jason (ed.). 2014. *Leonard Cohen and Philosophy*. Chicago: Open Court.

Idel, Moshe. 2013. The Tsadik and His Soul's Spark: From Kabbalah to Hasidism. *Jewish Quarterly Review* 103: 196–240.

Kierkegaard, Sören, trans. Douglas V. Steere. 1956. *Purity of Heart Is to Will One Thing: Spiritual Preparation for the Office of Confession*. New York: Harper & Row.

Liebovitz, Liel. 2014. *A Broken Hallelujah*. New York: Norton.

Light, Alan. 2012. *The Holy or the Broken*. New York: Simon & Schuster.

Nadel, Ira B. 1996. *Various Positions: A Life of Leonard Cohen*. New York: Random House.

Pleshoyano, Alexandra. 2014. Leonard Cohen: Viens guérison: La quête spirituelle d'une vie. In *Croire aujourd'hui*, ed. Elizabeth Parmentier, 105–124. Strasbourg: Université de Strasbourg.

Rashin, Esther. 1992. *Family Secrets and the Psychoanalysis of Narrative*. Princeton: Princeton University Press.

Ringuet, Chantel, and Gérard Rabinovitch. 2016. *Les révolutions de Leonard Cohen*. Québec: Presses de l'Université du Québec.

Scheil, Andrew. 2016. *Babylon Under Western Eyes*. Toronto: Toronto University Press.

Scholem, Gershom. 1954. *Major Trends in Jewish Mysticism*, 3rd ed. New York: Schocken Books.

Scobie, Stephen (ed.). 2000. *Intricate Preparations: Writing Leonard Cohen*. Toronto: ECW Press.

Simmons, Sylvie. 2012. *I'm Your Man: The Life of Leonard Cohen*. New York: Harper Collins.

Wolfson, Elliot R. 2006. New Jerusalem Glowing: Songs and Poems of Leonard Cohen in a Kabbalistic Key. *Kabbalah: Journal for the Study of Jewish Mystical Texts* 15: 103–152.

Yeats, W.B. 1938. *A Vision*. New York: Macmillan.

Leonard Cohen Recordings Cited by Date of Issue

Songs of Leonard Cohen. New York: Sony/ATV USA, 1967.
Songs from a Room. New York: Sony/ATV USA, 1969.
Songs of Love and Hate. New York: Sony/ATV USA, 1971.
New Skin for the Old Ceremony. New York: Sony/ATV USA, 1974.
Various Positions. London: Sony/ATV UK, 1984.

I'm Your Man. London: Sony/ATV UK, 1988.
The Future. London: Sony/ATV UK, 1992.
Cohen Live. London: Sony/ATV UK, 1994.
Ten New Songs. London: Sony/ATV UK, 2001.
Dear Heather. New York: Old Ideas LLC, 2004.
Old Ideas. New York: Sony/ATV USA, 2012.
Popular Problems. New York: Sony/ATV USA, 2014.
You Want It Darker. New York: Sony/ATV USA, 2016.

CHAPTER 12

Springtime for Defaults: *The Producers* as the Ruin of History and the Triumph of Hystery

Christina Dokou

Say, what do I care about Napoleon? What do we care about what they did 500 or 1,000 years ago?... It means nothing to me. History is more or less bunk. It's tradition. We don't want tradition. We want to live in the present...

> Henry Ford, May 25, 1916, *Chicago Tribune* interview with Charles N. Wheeler

The above dismissal of history as defaulted, as a set of facts not just past, but ruined, useless, "bunk," coming from the American tycoon who single-handedly changed the world's industrial system through his "assembly line," seems to haunt American cultural thinking fundamentally. The etymological associations of "bunk" with falsity and waste twist the idea of the ruin, that helpful, even picturesque remnant of the past upon which the narrative of history is (more or less imaginatively) reconstructed, into a useless piece of burdensome debris, which, moreover, is inherently mendacious. It is then no surprise that more than a

C. Dokou (✉)
National and Kapodistrian University of Athens, Athens, Greece

© The Author(s) 2019
E. Mitsi et al. (eds.), *Ruins in the Literary and Cultural Imagination*,
https://doi.org/10.1007/978-3-030-26905-0_12

few cultural critics and historians have opined that, in the last fifty years, Americans' sense of history is, in Noam Chomsky's words, at "a level of superficiality that's beyond belief" (2014), while for Jean Baudrillard, "History and Marxism are like fine wines and haute cuisine: they do not really cross the ocean" (1996, 79). On the one hand, capitalism, the ruling ideology of America, runs on a perpetual present and "doesn't play by the rules of critique, the true game of history" (Baudrillard 1996, 80), erasing origins as unprofitable, inflexible and hence retardant of consumption, unless reinvented as marketable vintage-retro nostalgia; on the other, America, as Gerry Coulter notes, "is a country with little history and one that quickly obliterates what history it has—the violence of its founding and westward expansion" (in Ruiz 2005). Baudrillard concludes that "Octavio Paz is right when he argues that America was created in the hope of escaping from history, of building a utopia sheltered from history, and that it has in part succeeded in that project, a project it is still pursuing today" (1996, 80). Even a champion of American historicism like David Glassberg is careful to specify that the average American's love of history is about localized "communal identity," completely divorced from an "academic" and "impersonal" idea of history (2001, xiii). One could well argue, however, that it is precisely this *ur*-view of history that allows its precious causality to emerge best, and that

> … even if professional historians were to reach out beyond the walls of the academy to bring history to the masses, they face what the historian Michael Wallace has termed a "historicidal" American culture. The nation's rapid pace of technological innovation, insatiable hunger for novel forms of mass entertainment and relentless transformation of the physical environment inevitably work against its citizens' sense of the past… (Glassberg 2001, 5)

But also within the academia, Jean Mayer, President of Tufts University, notes the disastrous effects of the lack of a unified/unifying "sense of history" among college students: "Without a student's knowledge of the facts and chronology of historical events—world, regional and national—it is almost impossible to teach in any meaningful fashion not just specific periods in history but any other subject…There is no conceptual skeleton on which to hang the information" (1983). Hence, the massive affective powers of American-style show business, as well as the advances of techno-virtuality may increasingly allow unchecked misconceptions to become the popular norm, in "the constant and terrifyingly successful effort to build a post catastrophic, globalizing mass-mediated consumerist consensus" (Coulter in Ruiz 2005). Baudrillard and Louis Marin have repeatedly spoken about the dangers of spectacularized "recycling" or "disneyfication" of history, whose "fantasmatic" distortions in the eyes of children easily displace any honest attempt at depicting historic relations (Baudrillard 1996, 55).[1] The synergy of fragmentation and spectacle— in whose instantaneous nature of information transmission, according to Kip Kline, "any sense of history or historical evidence disappears" (2016, 72)—thus produces a grey, innocuously sanitized area of pseudo-historical "modality" where traumas are profitably expunged.

What is the mechanism, however, by which history—the narrative of events past in order to determine causalities and effects, keeping in mind the complications arising from the term "narrative"—is so ruined? To explain it, I shall use a paradigm drawn from one of US pop culture's "cult classics," Mel Brooks's famous 1967 satirical film *The Producers*. An analysis of the original film, which was converted into a Broadway mega-hit musical in 2001 only to end as a lacklustre film rendition of the said hit in 2005, will hopefully demonstrate what I term here the conversion of history into *hystery*. This neologism is intended to conjoin two meanings of the adjective "hysteric/al": first, in the sense that Josef Breuer and Sigmund Freud coined, that is, an individual suffering from a variety of psychologically originated physical symptoms as an unconscious reaction to traumatic stress (2000, xi, 6); and second, indicating something so wildly funny, that a person is physically overwhelmed by laughter. I propose that the film captures the seduction of the historically conscious subject by the mechanism of the American profitable spectacle, i.e. "the media's way of replacing any event, any idea, any history with any other," thus annulling the authenticity of "the concentration camps or Hiroshima" (Baudrillard 1993, 91). This is achieved specifically by disassembling the text of history into a number of fragments decontextualized, a heap of signifiers without a chain of signification, thus vulnerable to arbitrary reinterpretation or substitution—in other words, to recall Ford, a turning of history into an assembly line product. This notion of hystery could be said to take a step further the idea of Baudrillard's "hysteresis," which he defines as "the process whereby

[1] See also Louis Marin (1994).

something continues to develop by inertia, whereby an effect persists even when its cause has disappeared" (1996, 115). According to David Clarke, "[a]lthough etymological connections between 'hysteresis' and 'hysteria' are eschewed by lexicographers, symptomatological resonances abound," linking neurotic aporia to history's "process without a subject" (2010, 97–98). However, unlike hysteresis, which focuses on the missing original, hystery helps us to focus on the refractions and distortions of the missing item's ghost image upon the big screen of public consciousness, not only because of the medium's format (which is Baudrillard's concern), but because the causal sequences upon which meaning is built are themselves ruined.[2] After all, it is only the ruinous state that evokes such a reconstruction—albeit warped—to complete it and fill in the emptiness it so patently signals. In another sense, hystery operates at the end of Baudrillard's "reversibility"[3] of all postmodern thought systems, as it masks the demise of history with an entertaining simulacrum. It thus opens up the question[4]—meriting a much greater discussion—of the suitability of satire as a means of representing history: in a context wherein modern theory has made a seminal point of problematizing *any* representation/textualization as a necessary but false idol, the added variables of entertainment and aggressive humour in satire, aimed ostensibly at revealing truths and moral imperatives, may end up ruining them further.

The Producers tells the story of a Jewish Broadway producer, Max Bialystok, himself so much a ruin of his former illustrious careerist self that he has resorted to romancing octogenarian ladies in exchange for "checkies" that will supposedly finance his next play. Enter Leopold Bloom, another Jew, an insignificant accountant from an auditing firm

---

[2] The idea of the ghost after-image nevertheless aligns itself with Baudrillard's notion of "recyclability" of history which ends up producing a "ghostly" version of "cloned events, farcical events, phantom events" and such distortions and caricatures of the original (1997, 452, 453).

[3] Defining "reversibility … a model that can be detected as an underlying pattern intrinsic to post-modern culture," Botz-Bornstein explains: "All systems based on techniques, science, and logic are bound to run empty sooner or later because technical perfectionism kills the enigmatic surplus or the quantity of the 'unknown' that philosophical investigations should maintain if they want to be interesting and fruitful as *philosophies* and not merely as scientific accounts of realities" (2013, 2).

[4] I thank the anonymous reviewer who suggested this larger possibility to me in her/his astute remarks on my paper.

and a neurotic suffering from hysterical infantile phobias, against which he forms an obsessive attachment to a piece of his blue baby blanket he carries in his pocket. While doing a check of Bialystok's shaky financial records, Bloom offhandedly remarks that a producer could make more money from a flop than from a hit show, if they raised a huge amount of money by overselling the show's profit percentages to separate investors, used only a portion of that to produce a failure, and then, after the show closed on premiere night, ran away with the rest of the money because no investor would expect reimbursement for a default. The hypothesis inflames the avaricious Bialystok, who then seduces the timid, law-abiding Bloom into actualizing this scheme. The two unearth the perfect play for a flop: "Springtime for Hitler" by Franz Liebkind, a practically insane and extremely slow-witted former Nazi who has escaped to the US and hopes to restore the good name of Adolf Hitler to the world. To guarantee failure, Bialystok and Bloom hire Roger DeBris, a flamboyantly gay, clueless director of horribly kitsch and trashy spectacles, as indicated by his "ruinous" surname. He decides to present the drama as a Broadway mega-musical, complete with an SS tap-dancing ballet and a happy ending for Germany. Finally, for the role of Hitler, they pick a stoned, idiotic hippie whose initials spell L.S.D. Unfortunately, on opening night, L.S.D.'s "flower-power" and "yeah, baby" performance is so unwittingly funny, that the audience think the pro-Nazi show is a spoof and declare it a raging comedy hit. Bloom and Bialystok manipulate Liebkind into blowing up the theatre to end the show, but this plan also fails and the trio end up in jail—apparently having learned nothing from their mistake, for the film closes with them trying the same scam on their fellow inmates, exploiting them to produce a sure-fire failure called "Prisoners of Love."

Although *The Producers* was the first feature-length film Mel Brooks directed, his debut became one of the greatest hits in his illustrious comedic career, winning an Oscar for Best Original Screenplay (Crick 2002, 16). However, the 1967 film suffered a lukewarm reception: as Kirsten Fermaglich notes, "Jews in 1967 were still anxious about anti-Semitism, fearful of fascism, and just beginning to express rage publicly about the murder of millions of Jews during World War II," ergo "the idea of a play produced by Jews glorifying Nazis was not only tasteless but also despicable and even dangerous" (2007, 60). Not only was the aforementioned danger of satirical interpretations of history perceptible at the very beginning, but what made reception harder was that Brooks's satire actually targeted certain traits of Americans, American Jews and show business: "just about every aspect of the film makes fun of something. Max, Leo, DeBris, Giya, L.S.D., even the *Springtime for Hitler* audience—these aren't just characters but types, vehicles through which Brooks sends up the whole Broadway show-biz scene" (Crick 2002, 24). This general offensive was fully intentional, since Brooks wanted "to point out and remind us of what we are—to humble us and expose our foibles…" (Bonnstetter 2011, 19). Geoffrey Cocks points out that American showbiz frequently used the evil Nazi as a metaphor, "because the Nazi allowed Hollywood to engage American issues of class, race and power without indicting American culture itself" (2015, 38). However, Brooks's attack on American crypto-fascism was far more overt:

> …in the fantastic musical sequence, "Springtime for Hitler," in *The Producers*, Brooks transgressed another convention of cold-war America by actually equating American society with Nazi Germany. A number of scholars and critics have noted that in his presentation of a Busby Berkeley swastika, jackbooting chorus girls, and elaborate costumes of German kitsch … Brooks made significant and pointed comparisons between Broadway showmanship and fascist pageantry. Brooks's portrait, moreover, of the uptight and tasteless middle-class audience uproariously embracing the play, "Springtime for Hitler," presents the American bourgeoisie as insensitive, tasteless, and so amoral that they might be willing to embrace fascism itself if it were presented in a palatable or funny form. (Fermaglich 2007, 62)

Even if the fault lies not in the amoral stars of "the American bourgeoisie" but in the nature of satire as a dissociative agent (one cannot laugh at Hitler while visualizing documentary Auschwitz images), the choice of the hippie suggests that young America's withdrawal from history into Ut/opiate bliss would offer a foothold to fascism: as Fermaglich reveals, a "good number of liberal intellectuals in the 1960s were convinced that the counterculture's ignorance, intolerance and romanticism would open the door to fascism. Mel Brooks's decision to make an addle-brained hippie his Hitler reflected this intellectual trend" (2007, 63).

Unwittingly, American Jews also contributed to this worrisome situation Brooks satirizes, through their desire to assimilate into middle-class whites and achieve the American Dream. Andrea Most notes how "[i]n the 1920s and 30s Jews were increasingly perceived as un-American—nonwhite, communist, alien—and confronted quotas aimed at keeping the 'foreign' Jew out of 'native' American institutions," redefining Americanness on a racialized rather than politicized basis, same as the Nazis had done (1999, 335). Post-Holocaust Jews became so anxious to dispel that image that they even performed cosmetic surgery to alter their "stereotypical" looks (Schrank 2007, 29). Others, inversely, saw anti-Semitism and the horrors of World War II so firmly past, that they felt safe and even privileged in ridiculing them openly (Ashkenazy 2011, 97), especially, as Brooks indicates, if a production was advertised as "tongue-in-cheek chic, in-joke ironic, and cutting-edge trendy" (Crick 2002, 24). It appears that the satirical lens, while alerting us to our contemporary foibles, might also blunt our sense of history precisely because it offers an alienating distance from the traumatic impact of the event itself. As Dustin Griffin has pointed out, after all, satire only reveals the hidden truth about history being, in its textuality, itself a fiction (1994, 124–126)—and fictions always ruin the fact, or at least its impact. Beth Bonnstetter's remarks on her students' reaction to the film warn against such an effect: "if *The Producers* is 'just entertainment,' as the students argued, and the 'Springtime for Hitler' sequence is simply meant to be funny, then at best, laughing at the Nazis' flaunting of their power misses the point, and at worst, it is potentially anti-Semitic" (2011, 18). All in all, the above attest to the prophetic acumen of Baudrillard's conclusion, as explained by Coulter, that "cinema too plays an important part in the disappearance of history ... Our collective understanding of realities such as the holocaust disappear and are replaced by images from cinema and other media" (Coulter 2010, 19).[5]

Jewish post-war attitudes as portrayed in the film play a major role in the default of history into hysteria, for they fragment historical causality by removing from the Shoah its victims. "The conversion of the Jews" into history-resistant Americans at the core of this film evinces the problematic line historically-oriented satire walks between condemnation and gloss via humour. For many critics, Max Bialystok "epitomizes the money-hungry Jew (he kisses dollar bills in one scene!)" (Baskind 2007, 7), but isn't money also America's "Almighty Dollar," blending religion and capitalism in its "In God We Trust"? Max also combines the

---

[5] For an alternative cinematic representation of the Holocaust through the absence of ruins, see Chapter 13 by Angeliki Tseti.

two seamlessly, as also indicated by his explosive cry, "God, I want that money!" Max, however, is also a synecdoche for Broadway, as he is specifically associated with "New York theatrical life" (Burston 2002, 469), its seductive and deceptive nature. His method of conning his "little old ladies" is engaging each one in her favourite sexual fantasy play, complete with individual stock lines, and he plays a role with everyone else that enters his office—victimized pauper to his landlord, bully and avuncular mentor to Leo—so much so that we doubt a real Max even exists. His conversion of the self-conscious (that is, history-conscious) Leo into an ahistorical funster, moreover, is motivated purely by profit.

On the opposite side of Max stands Leo, a bundle of traumatized nerves. Played by Gene Wilder as an overgrown baby, he is the hypersensitive innocent trapped by his personal past (as his blanket obsession indicates), but also trapped by history in general: he goes into hysterics when he thinks Max will jump on him and squash him flat, because, as he says, that is what Emperor Nero did to his wife Poppaea! At the same time, his cowering, supine posture suggests the Jewish victim of Nazi violence, and in this vein one can read his outburst: "I'm hysterical! I'm hysterical! I'm wet! I'm in pain!" as both hysterically funny (as was intended to be in the film) and an echo of un-erasable concentration camp victimization. Leo's self-casting in the role of Poppaea must, too, be read in racial terms, since in "European antisemitic and racialist rhetoric" that transferred over to the American stage there was an "association of Jewish men with femininity" as defined by "physical weakness, illness, and passive forms of gaining power—dissimulation, intrigues, tricks and lying" (Most 1999, 322). Leo is, significantly, an "accountant" by trade—the one who accounts for history, and holds others accountable for their past errors, as he does with Max (Most 1999, 322). Yet Leo will willingly "bloom" from a hysteric nobody to a con man, a would-be bomber, a convict, a Broadway producer of more lies for dollars. Not only that, but Leo's willing embrace of his conversion redeems retrospectively Max's corruption of him: Crick correctly observes that Max "somehow wins our sympathy even when breaking every law in the book" because "he shows joyless, friendless Leo the best time of his unhappy life" (Crick 2002, 18, 20). Doesn't that, however, invite by analogy the possibility that, if we can retrospectively be entertained by Nazis, they weren't so bad to begin with? In the same way that many objected to Hannah Arendt's 1963 *The Banality of Evil* not for any flaw in its argumentation, but on the grounds of the danger that accepting that "banality" might blunt the sense of evil attributable to the Nazis, it could be said that Brooks's satire against Shoah deniers, ahistorical Americans, or people who would deny the political capacity of satire itself to deal with any issue, no matter how grim, also runs the risk of being misconstrued by the very *hoi polloi* it seeks to educate as glossing over its material (Arendt 2006).

Such dark aspects of Leo's happy fall via entertainment are enabled in the film by the casting of Max as a loveable Jewish Satan, given that the self-declared "King of Broadway" and the Lord of lies have dishonesty, dissimulation and temptation in common, not to mention that the American public opinion often accused "Jewish leftwingers ... of poisoning innocent American youth" (Bruhle 2014, 82). Both Max and the Devil boast of a completely inverted morality, with Max asking in despair "Where did I go right?" like Milton's Satan who declares in *Paradise Lost*, IV:110, "Evil, be thou my good!" (2003, 86). In his first encounter with Leo, Brooks zooms in on Max sitting on his chair, which boasts a pair of carved gilded angel wings, making him appear like a monstrous cherub. Max acts as a tempter throughout, either with the old ladies (whose sexuality constitutes his hell) or with Leo, at whom he roars demonically, "You miserable, cowardly, little wretched caterpillar, don't you ever want to become a butterfly?" New York's Central Park becomes the Garden of Eden/Delights, where Max offers Leo a bite not from an apple, but from a very American hot dog—after which, Leo is re-baptized in the artificial lake into a conscience-free man who suddenly knows happiness for the first time! As Crick aptly puts it, "Leo is Pinocchio becoming a real boy by embracing Pleasure Island, not fleeing it" (2002, 21). The most telling Satanic allusion, however, comes when Max takes Leo on top of a skyscraper, shows him a sprawling vista of New York, "the most exciting city in the world," lists its temptations of luxuries and women and prods him to have it all by crying, "Join me!" Those with a knowledge of the Gospels will recognize in the scene Satan's temptation of Jesus in the desert (Matthew 4: 1–11); and hence, Leo's final outburst—"Where's *my* share? Where is Leo Bloom's share? I want ... I want ... I want everything I've ever seen in the movies!"— casts him as a ruined innocent Jesus and takes on a clear meaning of *non serviam*, with Satan's rebellion against the divine order matching Leo's rebellion against his Jewishness in the land of the *goyim*. Consequently, the end scene of the film with the two producers in prison busy recruiting rough convicts to yet another flop, and the elaborate ritual of Leo stamping on and giving share stubs to each sucker/investor reads like a parody of Christian hell, where the sinners who have been tricked to sign over their souls to Satan receive eternal punishment. Yet at the same time, in tandem with the satire's dubious dialectics of exoneration, the scene reads like a negation of hell and prison: as Leo admits in his court-room scene speech, he had been in prison all his life and Max's influ-ence set him forever free. In jail, he schemes and collects money, while prisoners sing and dance to their new catchy tune, "Prisoners of Love, blue skies above, can't keep our hearts in ja-ail!" Imprisonment with-out chastisement, punishment without remorse, does not result only in burlesque, but in the erasure of the causality lessons for which history is prized.

The fragmentation of the historical picture of the Shoah into hys-tery is compounded next by the removal of the victimizer. Fermaglich observes that "*The Producers* flouted a significant taboo of American popular culture in the 1960s: humor about the Nazi regime. Both before and during World War II, ridicule of the Nazi state and its leaders had been a familiar feature in American popular culture, as people viewed that humor as a weapon in the war effort" (2007, 61); however, this was before the information of the "bestial genocide" of the Shoah became widely known (Fermaglich 2007, 62). Ridiculing an enemy when he is strong shows courage; but ridiculing an enemy when defeated (or, at least, historically far removed) runs the risk of erasing the memory of what it was that made him an enemy originally, since pleasurable humour and a sense of safety can jointly generate complacency. In such a con-text, the portrayal of the mad, unrepentant Franz Liebkind as scared and immensely stupid makes Nazism "so ridiculous that it can no longer be considered a threat. In post-war American society, for Brooks, Nazism is of interest only as a musical, not as an ideology" (Ashkenazy 2011, 100). A breeder of pigeons, so inept he cannot even shoot people without pleading for their cooperation, "Kenneth Mars' Liebkind reveres Hitler as madly as Max loves money, and for this perhaps we should hate him, but he's so tragically misguided and filled with paranoid dread ... we feel for him much as we do the cowardly Leo" (Crick 2002, 23).

Moreover, Liebkind is the vehicle that introduces audiences to his ver-sion of historical Hitler, where the image of the mad dictator, instead of being tied causally to war ruins and concentration camps, is bro-ken up into disjointed fragments showing pleasant personal traits: "the Fuhrer was a terrific dancer," tender and loyal to Eva Brown, "a better dresser than Churchill" with "a great singing voice," plus "a painter" of distinction, since "he could paint an apartment in one afternoon—two coats!" The travesty is compounded with L.S.D. hippie Hitler on opening night, providing the turning point in the plot and the scheme of *The Producers*: the very moment some New Yorker lady says "It's *funny*!" the audience members, initially aghast and enraged at the historical sacrilege, immediately switch their allegiances. As Fermaglich observes, "It was not Bialystock and Bloom, but the bourgeois audience in the film, who demonstrated a frightening abandonment of moral values as they rushed to embrace the hippie Hitler in *Springtime for Hitler*" (2007, 66). The jab was not lost to Brooks's critics; they, "in the 1960s commented on the discomfort and lack of humor in this scene," which "ruined the movie's mood" (Fermaglich 2007, 73). Of course, Brooks intended his shock to have a beneficial result:

> More than anything the great holocaust by the Nazis is probably the great outrage of the Twentieth Century. There is nothing to compare with it. And ... so what can I do about it? If I get on the soapbox and wax eloquently, it'll be blown away in the wind, but if I do Springtime for Hitler it'll never be forgotten. I think you can bring down totalitarian governments faster by using ridicule than you can with invective. (Brooks qtd. in Fermaglich 2007, 67)

This quote encapsulates the combination of factors that ultimately problematize Brooks's vindication of history. Faced with the task of representing the unrepresentable Shoah to a wilfully blithe American public, he makes a risky gesture that catches their attention—but to what effect? What is exactly that "it" which will never be forgotten? Is it the Holocaust, so vaguely invoked that it is never mentioned in the film, "Springtime for Hitler" with its funny lines and catchy tunes, or something else (perhaps the gesture of its ridicule, decontextualized from its historical organicity)? It could thus be a moment of prophetic clarity or self-deconstruction when Brooks has his dumbfounded Max read a congratulatory telegram saying "*Hitler* will run forever!"

The point is ironically echoed in the perspective of Roger DeBris, the musical's disastrous director, who functions as the living manual for converting history to hystery. His cluelessness about history is precisely his fragmented vision of it (he admits he had no idea the Third Reich and Germany were connected). This leads to a frightfully distorted vision of historical events (especially dangerous for a clueless audience), like World War II portrayed as a mashup of historical drama and kitsch musical, or the Russian Revolution as a transvestite chimera: his "Grand Duchess Anastasia" costume that joins a Russian princess's body to an American man's head. DeBris's cluelessness about Nazism makes him so dangerously benevolent towards it, that he wants to literally alter its course of history for laughs: "that whole third act has got to go!" he exclaims, flustered, "They're losing the war! It's too depressing!" Out of such mismatched fragments, "history by Roger DeBris!" comes, inevitably, history as debris, a heap of useless ruins.

Hence, the final triumph of hystery: crowds storming the foyer during the play's break call it "hysterical," focusing exclusively on its comic effect, not the rationale behind it. Prey to psycho-sensory fragmentation, the spectators are blind to any seam, fissure, or fault in the spectacle they have just witnessed, accepting this simulation as perfect in itself instead of flawed history. Their reaction is clinically hysterical, for they have deflected their initial outrage into convulsive laughter, which Freud saw as a ready but crude release from stress (1990, 183).

Certainly, despite the problematizing reading offered above, Brooks's satire is clearly geared to counter Leo's rhetorical question at court, "Whom has Max Bialystok wronged?" Brooks's reply might lie not in the action of one individual, but in the parallel and related ruination of the victims of history/hystery, the pair of Jewish producers. The film chronicles their gradual descent into Nazism, which starts innocently, with Max asking the honest Leo to "move a few decimals around" and cover his financial peccadillo; yet follows with increasingly graver moral lapses. They pretend to like Nazism for Liebkind to the point of going out on the street wearing swastika armbands; they employ the Aryan blonde, Ulla, the brainless *shiksa* of Jewish male transgression, as their personal sex toy and in the end even conspire with Liebkind to blow up their theatre in a parody of the Nazi arson of the German Reichstag in 1933 that signalled the beginning of Nazi dominion. In the film's most hideous moment, a diabolical Bialystok, desperate not to lose his scam money, arms Liebkind's hand and incites him to "Kill! Kill! Kill!" all the actors so as to stop the play, labelling them as subhuman ("animals"), in precisely the same way the Nazis had done to his fellow Jews. This truly chilling instant presents hystery as a drug that harms those it seduces with the false promise of helping them escape their existential burdens, the very victims of history; and it is there that Brooks wagers the weight of his didactic satire.

Ultimately, though, the removal of both victim and victimizer, cause and effect, from the representation of the Shoah and their replacement with liberating yet distortive laughter in *The Producers* perhaps attests to yet another Baudrillardean "absurdity that is obvious" (Botz-Bornstein 2013, 2): the impossibility of extracting any history from its ample ruins, or even any satisfactory meaning from its representational default. What the film suggests is that all history is perhaps eventually doomed to become hystery, its fragmented ruins misunderstood or replaced by simulacra offering the illusion of completeness—at only 100 dollars per Broadway seat!

References

Arendt, Hannah. 2006. *Eichman in Jerusalem: A Report on the Banality of Evil*, introd. Amos Elon. New York: Penguin.

Ashkenazy, Ofer. 2011. Ridiculous Trauma: Comic Representations of the Nazi Past in Contemporary German Visual Culture. *Cultural Critique* 78: 88–118.

Baskind, Samantha. 2007. The Fockerized Jew?: Questioning Jewishness as Cool in American Popular Entertainment. *Shofar: An Interdisciplinary Journal of Jewish Studies* 25 (4): 3–17.

Baudrillard, Jean. 1993. *The Transparency of Evil*, trans. James Benedict. London and New York: Verso.

Baudrillard, Jean. 1996. *America*, trans. Chris Turner. London: Verso.

Baudrillard, Jean. 1997. The End of the Millennium or the Countdown, trans. Chris Turner. *Economy and Society* 26 (4): 447–455.

Bonnstetter, Beth E. 2011. Mel Brooks Meets Kenneth Burke (and Mikhail Bakhtin): Comedy and Burlesque in Satiric Film. *Journal of Film and Video* 63 (1): 18–31.

Botz-Bornstein, Thorsten. 2013. Book Review: *Jean Baudrillard: From the Ocean to the Desert, or the Poetics of Radicality*, by Gerry Coulter. *LSE Review of Books*, April 10: 1–4. http://blogs.lse.ac.uk/lsereviewofbooks/2013/04/10/book-review-jean-baudrillard-from-the-ocean-to-the-desert-or-the-poetics-of-radicality. Accessed 6 Nov 2017.

Breuer, Josef, and Sigmund Freud. 2000. *Studies on Hysteria*, trans. James Strachey. Basic Books Classics. New York: Basic.

Bruhle, Paul. 2014. Review of *Theatrical Liberalism: Jews and Popular Entertainment in America*, by Andrea Most. *American Jewish History* 98 (2): 81–82.

Burston, Jonathan. 2002. Review: *The Producers*. *Theatre Journal* 54 (3): 467–469.

Chomsky, Noam. 2014. Interview: Why Americans Know so Much About Sports but so Little About World Affairs. *Alternet*, September 15. http://www.alternet.org/noam-chomsky-why-americans-know-so-much-about-sports-so-little-about-world-affairs. Accessed 6 Nov 2017.

Clarke, David B. 2010. Hysteresis. In *The Baudrillard Dictionary*, ed. Richard G. Smith, 97–99. Edinburgh: Edinburgh University Press.

Cocks, Geoffrey. 2015. Hollywood *Über Alles*: Seeing the Nazi in American Movies. *Film & History: An Interdisciplinary Journal* 45 (1): 38–53.

Coulter, Gerry. 2010. Jean Baudrillard and Cinema: The Problems of Technology, Realism and History. *Film-Philosophy* 14 (2): 6–20.

Crick, Robert A. 2002. *The Big Screen Comedies of Mel Brooks*. Jefferson and London: McFarland.

Fermaglich, Kirsten. 2007. Mel Brooks' *The Producers*: Tracing American Jewish Culture Through Comedy, 1967–2007. *American Studies* 48 (4): 59–87.

Freud, Sigmund. 1990. *Jokes and Their Relation to the Unconscious: The Standard Edition*, trans. James Strachey. The Complete Psychological Works of Sigmund Freud. New York: Norton.

Glassberg, David. 2001. *Sense of History: The Place of the Past in American Life*. Amherst: University of Massachusetts Press.

Griffin, Dustin. 1994. *Satire: A Critical Reintroduction*. Lexington: The University Press of Kentucky.

Kline, Kip. 2016. *Baudrillard, Youth, and American Film: Fatal Theory and Education*. Lanham: Lexington.

Marin, Louis. 1994. Disneyland: A Degenerate Utopia. In *Contemporary Literary Criticism: Literary and Cultural Studies*, 3rd ed., ed. Robert Con Davis and Ronald Schleifer, 283–295. New York and London: Longman.

Mayer, Jean. 1983. Young Americans with No Sense of History. *The New York Times*, April 24. http://www.nytimes.com/1983/04/24/opinion/l-young-americans-with-no-sense-of-history-118262.html. Accessed 6 Nov 2017.

Milton, John. 2003. *Paradise Lost: A Poem in Twelve Books*, ed. Merrit Y. Hughes. Indianapolis and Cambridge: Hackett.

Most, Andrea. 1999. "Big Chief Izzy Horowitz": Theatricality and Jewish Identity in the Wild West. *American Jewish History* 87 (4): 313–341.

Ruiz, Nicholas, III. 2005. Interview with Gerry Coulter. *Kritikos* 2 (September). https://intertheory.org/coulter.htm. Accessed 6 Nov 2017.

Schrank, Bernice. 2007. "Cutting Off Your Nose to Spite Your Race": Jewish Stereotypes, Media Images, Cultural Hybridity. *Shofar: An Interdisciplinary Journal of Jewish Studies* 25 (4): 18–42.

CHAPTER 13

In the Absence of Ruins: The "Non-sites of Memory" in Claude Lanzmann's *Shoah* and Daniel Mendelsohn's *Lost: A Search for Six of Six Million*

Angeliki Tseti

In 1943 and 1944, the Nazis planted trees at Sobibór, Belzek and Treblinka to conceal all evidence of their atrocious acts; the sites in question are but links in the vast chain of ghettos, transit and extermination camps across Europe, unfailingly intended for annihilation and consistently hidden behind high walls or thick vegetation. When defeat was imminent, the Nazis sought to eliminate all evidence of their acts, whether by demolishing and burning material traces, or by initiating the death marches that would make the remaining witnesses disappear in the dense forests surrounding the camps. These acts are posterior to the "Holocaust-by-bullets": the term describes mass shooting operations most commonly executed in public, that were organized between 1941 and 1944 across Eastern Europe by German police and military forces, and locally recruited collaborators. Neighbours of the victims were forced to witness but also provide services as gravediggers, van

A. Tseti (✉)
National and Kapodistrian University of Athens, Athens, Greece

© The Author(s) 2019
E. Mitsi et al. (eds.), *Ruins in the Literary and Cultural Imagination*,
https://doi.org/10.1007/978-3-030-26905-0_13

213

drivers and so on. As indicated by the United States Holocaust Memorial Museum archives, approximately 40% of the Jews who perished during the Holocaust were victims of these mass shootings; their graves span across an estimated 2500 locations in Ukraine, Russia, Belarus, Poland, Moldova, Lithuania and Romania, of which only two thirds have been identified to date.[1] These shootings are posterior to the gas vans which constituted an earlier version of the crematoria; and contemporaneous to the innumerable killings taking place upon discovery of hiding places across urban areas—all atrocious acts that, by definition and in practice, remain clandestine and untraceable.[2] In effect, and despite its historical specificity, the Holocaust is geographically non-specific; the event is marked by a notable placelessness, manifest not only in the vast scale and expanse of the destruction but also in, precisely, this lack of traces, the occasional absence of ruins and debris that would allow us to literally "place" the staggering crimes within a specific location.

As nature soon took over and eventually completely covered these sites, and as scholarship turned to the microhistory of the genocide and attempted to shed light on the innumerable individual stories of the victims, the unrepresentability and indescribability of the event were invested with a new meaning: much more than an "event without a witness" (Felman and Laub 1992, 80–82),[3] whose magnitude cannot be grasped and whose representation can "no longer be reduced to a single, authoritative story" (Fogu et al. 2016, 19), the Holocaust narrative is fraught with gaps and absences. It is marked with erasure, obliteration and, literally, spaces of nothingness. Thus, the unrepresentability and unassimilability of the Holocaust are renewed with an added problematic. How can the story of the extermination be reconstructed when its traces have been erased? How can one expose dimensions of the catastrophe that cannot be fully retrieved through material evidence? How can the memory of the genocide surface in the absence of ruins? And,

---

[1] See "Holocaust by Bullets," the USHMM's online exhibition; or "What is the Holocaust by Bullets?"—in Unum's website.

[2] Numerous archives and documents attest to the Nazi's tactics of concealment. Despite their meticulous recording of their operations, they never made direct references to their actions, but used euphemisms and code words instead. The "Final Solution" is, perhaps, the most obvious case in point.

[3] The Holocaust is "an absolute historical event whose literally *overwhelming evidence* makes it, paradoxically, into an *utterly proofless event*" (Felman and Laub 1992, 211).

eventually, how can this memory be preserved in the present and disseminated into the future independent of mnemonic sites and monuments?

Claude Lanzmann's *Shoah* (1985) and Daniel Mendelsohn's *The Lost: A Search for Six of Six Million* (2006), a film and a photo-textual memoir, respectively, stand in alliance with a series of works by other artists[4] and writers attempting to tackle these issues and seeking to produce a type of memory work that does not rely on empirical evidence or, rather, a type of memory work that ensues precisely *in the absence* of ruins or material traces. While turning the void and the gap into their all-informing principles, the works discussed here (re)turn to the sites of torture and seek to reconstruct the past in and through the present, by centring on erasure, absence and inference. Significantly, this endeavour unfolds from spaces that bear little or no traces of the crimes committed there and, thus, constitute "non-sites of memory"; in other words, spaces where memory, to recall Nora, literally "takes root in the concrete, in spaces, gestures, images and objects" (1989, 9), yet does not secrete itself through the visibility of the ruin or the symbolism of the memorial.

Defined by anthropologist Marc Augé as non-relational, non-historical and unrelated to identity spaces of the anonymous where meaning is absent (1992), these sites are devoid of any sense of individuality; there, the traces of the past are but a hypothesis. This is particularly relevant to genocide overall,[5] but it is also of special interest to Lanzmann who uses the term in his eponymous article to speak of traumatic sites that challenge memory work by restricting the Holocaust to a distant, historicized past, and depriving it of its "present-ness."[6] It is this insistence on grounding the genocide on the present that constitutes the connecting thread which brings Lanzmann and Mendelsohn's works together. More importantly, it is the chosen modus operandi, namely the combination of verbal—specifically testimonial—and visual elements that distinguishes these two endeavours from many others.

To be more specific, as both Lanzmann and Mendelsohn suggest, memory work performed through "non-sites of memory" depends on situating the viewer (or reader) in the context of the event that eludes

---

[4] See, for example, Mikael Levin and Dirk Reinartz's photographs, or "counter-monuments" such as Esther Shalev-Gerz and Jochen Gerz's *Monument Against Fascism* (Harburg 1986), and Horst Hoheisel's *Aschrott Fountain* (Kassel 1985), among others.

[5] See also Bensoussan (2004).

[6] See Augé (1992) and Lanzmann (2000a).

historical readings, and calling upon their imagination to approach and possibly retrieve it. To this end, both *auteurs* employ visuality alongside the fragments of witnesses' or bystanders' memories as a cardinal aspect of their narration of the catastrophe and destruction of European Jews during World War II. It is important to note, right from the start, that neither of these works' constituent elements takes precedence over the other. The verbal and the visual components engage the viewer by working in complementarity towards the construction of a single narrative, and, therefore, analyses of their separate functions would necessarily overlap and intermingle. Hence, this article embarks upon a presentation of the techniques employed in order to foreground the non-sites of memory and proceeds to discuss the ways in which the reciprocal workings of testimony and the image situate the viewer, or viewer/reader, in the position of a witness.

FRAGMENTS OF TESTIMONY AND NON-SITES OF MEMORY

Claude Lanzmann's *Shoah*, a nine-and-a-half-hour-long[7] "intricate tapestry of real-time interviews with [Holocaust] survivors," perpetrators and bystanders, "proceeds into the heart of evil," as Margaret Olin writes, "beginning with an evocation of pastoral beauty" (1997, 2). In fact, this painstaking and persistent journey into the inferno of the concentration and extermination camps consists solely of mostly unmoving, static stills of featureless, wooden landscapes, predominantly vast expanses of forest and grass-covered railway tracks, significantly shot in the present of the filmmaking: Chelmno, on the Narew river, in Poland; but also Sobibór; Vilna, in Lithuania; and Treblinka. This is obviously akin to the representational and commemorative strategies of the documentary film which speak of a more direct act of testimony when interviews with witnesses and bystanders are conducted in the actual site, the scene of the action. More than this, however, Lanzmann's choice of *Schauplätze*, specifically his decision to depict the terrains of such atrocities in their

---

[7] Lanzmann took eleven years for the completion of his project, the first six of which were spent travelling in fourteen countries across the globe—very much in the same way Daniel Mendelsohn conducted his search for witnesses to his Uncle's life and death—looking for survivors and urging them to remember and share their stories. When the shooting was completed, it took another five years to organize and edit his material, so that 350 hour of footage could be condensed into the 9.5-hour film.

present-time silence and tranquillity, points to the deceptive normalcy instated by the landscape; it denotes the reign of trees and vegetation as evidence of the denial and concealment surrounding the genocide; and it seeks to unearth the occurrence of death and destruction on these very sites by juxtaposing or conjoining the present elusiveness of the "tainted" landscape with the horrific accounts of the past, provided by witnesses and bystanders.

The director's method and intention—to bring the voices of the past into the present—become apparent from the very first scene of the film, with Simon Srebnik's return to Chelmno, and remain consistent throughout. Fillip Müller's account of the victims' final moments before entering the gas chambers offers, perhaps, the most eloquent example of Lanzmann's technique. As the voice-over speaks of the wooden benches in the "undressing rooms," the arrival of the so-called disinfection squad and the pouring in of Zyklon gas crystals, the director's camera presents a visual analogue that consists in a static shot of a snowfall over the Death Wall, in present-time Auschwitz. This is followed by a single-shot passage through the dark, silent and deserted corridors of Block 11 and the preserved crematoria that now make part of the museum.

The entire film, in fact, consists in an elaborate testimonial collage, fragments of fractured memories offered in close-ups, repetitively, often seemingly haphazardly, placed one after the other or sometimes interweaved and mingled. The stories speak of the same experiences, albeit occurring in different locations and phrased in different languages, they narrate the same atrocities, building up overwhelming (both quantitatively and qualitatively) pieces of information. They compose a circular account of the genocide that does not emerge fully fledged until after the end of the film, once the testimonies of all "actors," victims and perpetrators alike, have been placed alongside one another. Voiced against the long stretches of the now devoid of "infernal smells" forests that once hosted and hid these abominable acts, it is these repetitions that solidify the unthinkable conception of the Holocaust, since, as Ruth Franklin notes: "[E]ven when the details differ slightly from person to person, the phenomenon of hearing the same story repeated over and over renders the story undeniable" (2011, 30).

In a similar vein, and while also bringing the issues of third-generation witnesses and postmemory[8] to the fore, Daniel Mendelsohn's *The Lost: A Search for Six of Six Million* seeks to reconstruct the persecution of European Jews, predominantly the "Holocaust-by-bullets," by connecting the singular stories of various witnesses, now scattered around the globe. The book recounts the writer's five-year-long quests and journeys across continents and through nothingness—manifest both in the lack of material traces and in the shortage of archival information—in search of survivors of the genocide, specifically people who knew and might be able to shed some light onto the exact circumstances of the death of his Great-Uncle Shmiel and his family—wife and four daughters that were "*Killed by the Nazis*" (emphasis in the original).

> The latter was, we all understood, the unwritten caption of the few photographs that we had of him and his family, which now lie stored carefully inside a plastic baggie inside a box inside a carton in my mother's basement... *unknown and unknowable*: this could be frustrating but also produced a certain allure. The photographs of Shmiel and his family were, after all, more fascinating than the other family pictures that were so fastidiously preserved in my mother's family archive, precisely because *we knew almost nothing* about him, about them. (Mendelson 2006, 8, emphasis added)

Echoing Lanzmann's fractured *mise-en-scène*, *The Lost* is constructed through a montage of fragments: stories narrated by the people the writer meets; transcribed interviews and historical documents extracted from archives; commentaries on parts of the Book of *Genesis* that bear on different aspects of the writer's quest; fictional episodes during which Mendelsohn imagines the fate of his family; the tale of the writer's travels and search; and, most important, photographs—either old ones, copied from various family albums, or recent, taken by the writer's brother, Matt, during their travels. The barren landscapes that dominate *Shoah* also find a powerful equivalent in the overarching sense of vacancy pervading Mendelsohn's narrative, made manifest in the omnipresent voids, the memory lapses, the occasional dead ends and gaps in information,

---

[8]Coined by Marianne Hirsch the term describes "the relationship that the 'generation after' bears to personal, collective, and cultural trauma of those who came before—to experiences they 'remember' only by means of the stories, images, and behaviours among which they grew up" (2012, 5). See also Hirsch (1997).

but also the structural *lacunae* created by the formal rendition of the quest. As Marc Amfreville observes,

> If we consider the structuring information gaps, the memory lapses, the pits dug during the first Aktion, the telling photograph of the Vienna cemetery,[9] and even the empty places occupied by the lost and their missing descendants, emptiness hollows out every page of Mendelsohn's work. Vacancy hence becomes a motif whose repeated occurrences structure the whole text in the way a metaphor infiltrates a poem. (2016)[10]

Moreover, just like Lanzmann, Mendelsohn returns to the scene of the crime—a small town in Galicia called Bolechow, now Bolekhiv—guided by the people's often misleading or even contradictory stories, seeking to trace the house where his Great-Uncle hid and was killed, only to find a complete lack of traces, one that is eventually transcribed—symbolically, but also literally—as a black hole. Specifically, a cellar that appears as one of the current occupants of the house in question accidentally drags a rug away with her foot and reveals a small trapdoor, from which:

> [A] smell escaped, the dank smell of earth and something else, the failed odor of disuse… The hole was just that: a hole. I had descended maybe eight or nine feet and was at the bottom. Down there, there was no light, and even though the trapdoor above my head was open the space itself was steeped in a profound, inky black. I had to stretch out my hands to locate the walls, which turned out to be very close … it was very cold, surprisingly cold. (Mendelsohn 2006, 613–614)

Thus hidden, forgotten, or—one might say—lost in the depths of an ordinary house Great-Uncle Schmiel's *kestl*—the Yiddish word for box—parallels the film's stretches of forest in that it constitutes a nondescript site of memory, a site of torture that bears no mnemonic signs, a *non-lieu de mémoire* which speaks of a catastrophe of unimaginable extent and magnitude. In a sense, and albeit diametrically opposite in size, the box resonates with Simon Schrebnik's words in the opening scene of Lanzmann's film:

---

[9] The Viennese authorities have decided to leave a vast empty lot where the graves of the Jewish community should have been dug.

[10] Excerpt from a paper titled "The Black Box in Mendelsohn's *The Lost*" which was delivered in the 2016 European Association of American Studies biennial conference, kindly offered by the author.

It's hard to recognize. But it was here. It's hard to recognize, but it was here... No one can describe it...And no one can understand it. Even I, here, now... It was always this peaceful here. Always. When they burned two thousand people—Jews—every day, it was just as peaceful. (Simon Srebnik, in Lanzmann 1985)

The words of the survivors, their sometimes peculiarly dispassionate (or traumatized) yet always staggering descriptions of the atrocities committed during the war, constitute, in fact, the cornerstone of the memory work performed in both these texts. Quite interestingly, even though both the documentary film and the photo-memoir rely exclusively or heavily on their visual component, these salient voices comprise the sole references to the genocide, as both Lanzmann and Mendelsohn shun away from archival images and footage. Lanzmann has justified the exclusion of Holocaust iconography saying that "*Shoah* is about the radicality of death inside the gas chambers. There is not one single picture (of filmed executions) from the extermination camp at Belzec, none from Treblinka, Sobibór or Madjanek ... there are no pictures of what took place inside the gas chambers" (Fuller 2011, 17). Yet, much more than aridly reiterating the vexed issue of the *Bilderverbot*,[11] this disavowal proves paramount in the attempt to address and commemorate the event, since—having thus dismissed understanding through the conventional forms of knowledge—the selection of images employed in these works instigates a viewer-based, affective approach, one that is dependent on a transferential relation to the past that includes both distance and proximity, "an affective aspect of understanding which both limits objectification and exposes the self to involvement or implication," what Dominick LaCapra terms "empathic unsettlement" (2001, 102). It is thus that—once the inconspicuous, placeless, sites of torture have been brought to centre stage—the memory of the Shoah may be approached in the present and, perhaps, carried into the future.

[11] The term refers to the prohibition of Holocaust images which are deemed inadequate to represent the magnitude of the genocide and are highly criticized for the mediation they entail. Lanzmann himself has been a fervent proponent of *Bilderverbot* since, as he claims, archival images petrify thought and kill all power of evocation: "*J'ai toujours dit que les images de l'archive sont des images sans imagination. Elles pétrifient la pensée et tuent toute puissance d'évocation*" (qtd. in Didi-Huberman 2003, 120).

The (Reader/)Viewer as Witness

The landscapes and still images in *Shoah* constitute, as mentioned above, non-distinct, empty settings that enact the absences of the Holocaust in their offering, precisely, *nothing* to see; when asked to assume a viewing position, the audience can only experience the place auratically, that is, their gaze can only be drawn by their knowledge of the site's significance, since, in Ulrich Baer's words, "the invitation to relate to and to enter the site is fused with an equally strong message of exclusion" (2005, 66). Nevertheless, the direct juxtaposition and stark contrast of the tales voiced to the serenity and stillness emanating from Lanzmann's takes operates as a mental trigger for the viewer who, as Guerin and Hallas put it, "takes up the position of the cipher, and thus experiences the witness's address as directed to him/her, an address that apparently takes place in the present" (2007, 38).

Put differently, the silences and pauses permeating the totality of these interviews—whether as a manifestation of the difficulty in articulating the traumatic experience, or an indication of the memory breaks, or simply time lapsing in anticipation of the translation—invite the viewer to focus on the screen before him and search for the minor detail or trace. The viewer is thereby asked to resort to the very images and tropes of the Holocaust that have been excluded from the film, yet form an integral part of our collective memory of the genocide; to ponder on the crimes that have transpired in the barren, traceless landscapes before them; and, eventually, to "transform the past event into a dynamic living present" (Skloot 2012, 264).

The church bell tower in Chelmno, for example, emerging from the top left corner of the background, may lead us to contemplate on the role of the Polish Catholic church in the Holocaust—an impression that is later reinforced by the numerous church spires and crucifixes appearing in the film, or the train tracks that visually accompany testimonies of train transports and convoys leading to the camps may provoke us to think about the bystanders' alleged ignorance of the trains' final destination. Lanzmann's camerawork alerts and invites us to correlate the verbal with the visual, to detect any minor details that may not be apparent at first sight, and to fully grasp and possess the image before us. In other words, it invites us to activate our imagination so that the indescribable may be interpreted and become, perhaps, if only mentally, representable. As Bryan Burns notes, in these uncluttered scenes "every object acquires significance and presence, and we are sensitised to the interpretative role that each may play in the drama of the scene in which it appears" (2002, 86). Hence, apart from an obvious intention to speak of the genocide's traces (or lack of them) in the present, Lanzmann's austere, bare even, landscapes engage his audience in an active process of contemplation that may eventually result in the dissemination of the memory of the Holocaust.

In a similar manner, the passages from the *Genesis* that Mendelsohn includes in his book create *lacunae*, spaces of reflection that not only pertain to the photo-memoir's themes but also decelerate the rhythm and pace of reading.[12] This is more intensely the case when the reader/ viewer encounters the photographs inserted in the narrative, which, whether recent or older, depict exclusively the common and the every-day—faces, and family portraits, objects and landscapes—a choice that undoubtedly reiterates the prohibition of Holocaust-related images, and reminds us of writers' and artists' attempts to instigate their audi-ence's engagement by shunning away from visual documents that may induce what Susan Sontag calls "negative epiphany": the shocking "rev-elation" emerging from a viewer's encounter with an image of atrocity, an image that eludes legibility or comprehensibility precisely because it addresses a horror that cannot be conceived or grasped by the intellect (1977, 19). Yet, more than this, the selection of these photographs is dictated by the desire that drives the quest itself: namely, the desire to explicitly denote the embodied connection underlying the narrator's commitment; to counter the impersonal archives and databases through which Mendelsohn conducts his search with a view to depicting this elu-sive world *wie es eigentlich gewesen* (how it really was); and, eventually, to present Uncle Shmiel's story as a family story, indelibly inscribed in the personal as well as the collective. As Ann Rigney argues, "[t]he narrator has to continuously negotiate his way between the scale of the unique individual, the scale of the family, and the large-scale canvas of the 'six million victims,' so as to depict their lives and deaths as being both incommensurable and statistically significant" (2016, 118).

---

[12] In an interview included in the book, the writer states that "the biblical exegeses are thematically relevant. But I also think they have an important structural role… [T]he bib-lical analyses are a way of slowing down the reader and making her or him stop and think what the *themes* (sic) are" (Mendelsohn 2006, p.s. 8–9).

Literally embedded in the body of the text—rather than placed in the paratext—these stills interlace with the verbal narrative in a relation of complementarity, at times informing the written text while at others destabilizing it. As the two media interact, both formally and semantically, the photo-text is allowed to unfold in its full dynamic. I am referring to the fundamentally viewer/reader-dependent hermeneutics established by this powerful conjunction-in-disjunction performed by the two components, which, as I have argued elsewhere (Tseti 2015, 2016), assigns the task of interpretation to the reader. The stillness emerging from Lanzmann's takes is reiterated in the stasis induced as Mendelsohn's reader/viewers are invited to proceed from their initial encounter with the photo-textual construct—in other words, to move from simply visually and mentally perceiving what lies before them in the grain of paper—to an act of tracing the rules and rationale permeating the photo-textual montage.

At a surface level, reader/viewer engagement is initiated with an invitation to correlate these pictures with their verbal referents which, albeit almost invariably existent, are more often than not pages apart from their visual equivalents. Uncle Schmiel's army photograph (Mendelsohn 2006, 92) would be an obvious case in point, a wrinkled, torn at the edges picture suddenly flashing in the midst of the verbal narrative almost ten pages after reading that "the earliest known photograph of Shmiel is the picture in which he is sitting in his Austrian army uniform next to that other man" (2006, 85). Another example would be the photograph of people standing on the quay (2006, 440), which is much further apart from its verbal description:

> There is one more picture, a photo of a small group of people standing far from the camera lens, perhaps on a pavement, an image it took me years to decipher. This was partly because it's somewhat blurry and the faces are impossible to make out, partly because of the strange angle from which it was taken: an odd diagonal line cuts across the bottom left of the picture. Only recently did I realise that my grandfather took this picture on the day he left Israel, indeed at the moment he was going up the gangplank of the ship that took him and my grandmother back home… only after I understood what that angled bar was could I see that the small group standing below was Uncle Itzhak and his family, waiting on the dock for my grandparents to sail away. (2006, 348)

Indeed, the photograph in question is an oblique, difficult to examine picture that performs a mysterious break in the surrounding narrative, even though, in hindsight, we realize that it is situated right at the point where the narrator announces his decision to depart for Israel. Should the reader/viewer attentively follow and succumb to the dynamics of the photo-text, however—in other words, should he or she pause, remember, retrace and relate the picture to its verbal referent lying almost one hundred pages before—and should he or she place the verbal account and visual document together, he or she will realize that the picture in question encompasses the majority of themes and tropes permeating the book: it reflects the search, the quest, the initial illegibility of documents due to the lack of information, the deciphering and subsequent revelation upon discovery of an added element, the re-contextualization and re-appropriation of the material trace when seen under a different light.

This is true of numerous pictures in the book. Consistently caption-less and sometimes ambiguous or blurry, the photographs reach much further than simply highlighting "the disparity between image and experience",[13] nor do they merely "add this amazing flavor of helplessness to (y)our reading of the book" (Mendelsohn 2006, p.s. 9). Rather, they engage the reader/viewer in a back-and-forth, memory-like movement, in search of a trace that will help them identify their origin and subject matter, even though this is not always possible. The picture of the house (2006, 601), for instance, could either be the photograph given to the writer by one of the survivors so that he could find the house she used to live in, or a shot of the "non-site of memory" housing Uncle Schmiel's *kestl*. Similarly, the picture of a garden (2006, 630) most probably depicts another "non-site of memory," the place where Uncle Shmiel's body was dragged and abandoned after being found and shot. As the writer stands pondering his family's history and the persistently inexpressible "it" looming over their fate, he expresses the feelings of bewilderment and awe generated by this nondescript place, but never explicitly mentions photographing it. Nevertheless, the detailed description of the wild bushes and trees arguably urges the reader/viewer to return to this still:

> At the end of the garden there was an ancient apple tree with a double trunk … That is the place …

[13] See the writer's interview to Wulf Kansteiner in Fogu et al. (2016, 138).

I was standing in the place.

For a while, I stood there, thinking. It is one thing to stand before a spot you have long thought about, a building or a shrine or monument that you've seen in paintings or books or magazines, a place where, you think, you are expected to have certain kinds of feelings that, when the time comes to stand there, you either will or will not have: awe, rapture, terror, sorrow. It is another thing to be standing in a place of a different sort, ... a place of which you might say *the place where it happened* and think, it was in a field, it was in a house, it was in a gas chamber, against the wall or on the street, but when you said those words to yourself it was not so much the *place* that seemed to matter as the *it*, the terrible thing that had been done, because you weren't really thinking of the place as anything but a kind of envelope, disposable, unimportant. Now I was standing in the place itself, and I had had no time to prepare. (2006, 640–641)

In effect, the insertion of these photographs in the midst of the verbal components of the book—and particularly the silences surrounding them—proves to be startling, disturbing, and, eventually alerting. No matter which course of reading the reader/viewer chooses to follow, and no matter what the extent of her/his engagement with the photographs will be, these stills are so pregnant with meaning that they necessitate an arrest. And it is precisely during this arrest, the break ensuing from the passage between media that creates space for the incommensurable to be reflected upon and tackled.

Concluding Remarks

Presenting the Holocaust-in-absence by combining words and images is, of course, nothing new, if not at the time when *Shoah* was released, certainly not in contemporary times. W. G. Sebald's photo-texts as well as numerous artists' work—particularly photographers Mikael Levin and Dirk Reinartz's works with such "contaminated" landscapes[14]—have

---

[14]Levin (1997) and Reinartz (1995) both photograph sites of former camps, using the conventions of landscape art to foreground spaces where Holocaust memory is absent, whether due to the complete lack of traces, or because of the decaying quality of buildings and other physical evidence. They produce aestheticized images of scenery that are denoted as "contaminated" through the accompanying captions and texts which indicate that these sites are, in fact, Holocaust sites.

already been widely published, analysed and acclaimed. If anything, the numerous forests across Europe hosting the ghosts of the "Holocaust by Bullets," or the innumerable basements and cellars where Jews were hidden and/or killed are nothing but an absence in the history of the Shoah. What is particular about explorations such as these is precisely their attempt to bring such non-sites of memory to centre stage, to remind us of the effacement of traces or the absence of ruins, and, subsequently, to discuss the event's placelessness not in terms of a gaping void but in relation to the genocide's magnitude and vastness: in short, to highlight the long-reach of catastrophe across space, time and generations.

The *auteurs'* decision to set their works into the present of their making proves seminal to this effect. After all, as Lanzmann himself wrote in 1979, "a film devoted to the Holocaust can only be a counter-myth, that is, an investigation into the *presentness* of the Holocaust, an investigation into a past whose wounds are so fresh and so keenly inscribed in consciousness that they are present in a haunting timelessness" (1979, 143). Mendelsohn's memoir, actually written as a family story during the Nazi occupation of Eastern Poland in the 1940s, exemplifies the Holocaust's presentness in the most eloquent way: as a spectre post-mnemonically haunting the generations after. Further still, it is precisely by setting their act of storytelling into the present time that these works manage to engage their audience by creating a sense of testimonial address, to remember Guerin and Hallas (2007, 38), and, consequently, by visually inciting them to join in the extrapolation of the past with their own personal knowledge.

The images used by both Lanzmann and Mendelsohn in these works bring nothing new to our historical knowledge of the Holocaust; they neither confirm nor deny the crimes committed, nor do they offer us a way to distinguish the sites and faces depicted in them from countless others. In fact, these images, both the cinematic and the photographic ones, seek to "speak from within erasure" (Lanzmann 2000b, 424), to activate and empathically unsettle us. By employing the image in a manner that actually results in sheer visual blankness, and by filling the gaps with the multi-vocal narrative of the survivors, both these works seek to involve us, their audience, in an act of commemoration in the present. They seek to turn us into true witnesses who, in the absence of ruins, are entrusted with the task of carrying the memory of the Shoah in the way Simone de Beauvoir describes when writing on Lanzmann's film:

In spite of everything we knew, the ghastly experience remained remote from us. Now, for the first time, we live it in our minds, hearts and flesh. It becomes our experience. (1985, vii)

References

Amfreville, Marc. 2016. The Black Box in Mendelsohn's *The Lost*. Paper Presented at the Biennial Conference of European Association for American Studies, Constanta, Romania, April 2016.

Augé, Marc. 1992. *Non-lieux. Introduction à une anthropologie de la surmodernité*. Paris: Éditions du Seuil.

Baer, Ulrich. 2005. *Spectral Evidence: The Photography of Trauma*. Cambridge, MA and London: The MIT Press.

Bensoussan, Georges, ed. 2004. *Génocides. Lieux (et non-lieux) de mémoire*, special issue of *Revue de l'histoire de la Shoah, le Monde juif*, 181.

Burns, Bryan. 2002. Fiction of the Real: Shoah and Documentary. *Immigrants and Minorities* 21 (1–2): 80–88.

De Beauvoir, Simone. 1985. Preface. In *Shoah: An Oral History of the Holocaust—The Complete Text of the Film*, Claude Lanzmann.

Didi-Huberman, Georges. 2003. *Images malgré tout*. Paris: Les Éditions de Minuit.

Felman, Shoshana, and Dori Laub (eds.). 1992. *Testimony: Crisis of Witnessing in Literature, Psychoanalysis and History*. New York: Routledge.

Fogu, Claudio, Wulf Kansteiner, and Todd Presner (eds.). 2016. *Probing the Ethics of Holocaust Culture*. Cambridge, MA and London: Harvard UP.

Franklin, Ruth. 2011. On Film: *Shoah*, by Claude Lanzmann. *Salmagundi* 3 (170/171): 26–34.

Fuller, Graham. 2011. Searching for the Stamp of Truth: Claude Lanzmann Reflects on the Making of *Shoah*. *Cineaste* 36 (2): 16–19.

Guerin, Frances, and Roger Hallas (eds.). 2007. *The Image and the Witness: Trauma, Memory and Visual Culture*. London and New York: Wallflower Press.

Hirsch, Marianne. 1997. *Family Frames: Photography, Narrative, and Postmemory*. Cambridge, MA: Harvard UP.

Hirsch, Marianne. 2012. *The Generation of Postmemory: Writing and Visual Culture After the Holocaust*. New York: Columbia UP.

"Holocaust by Bullets." United States Holocaust Memorial Museum online exhibition. https://www.ushmm.org/information/exhibitions/online-exhibitions/special-focus/desbois. Accessed 31 Dec 2014.

LaCapra, Dominick. 2001. *Writing History, Writing Trauma*. Baltimore: Johns Hopkins UP.

Lanzmann, Claude. 1979. From the Holocaust to the *Holocaust*. *Telos* 42: 137–143.

Lanzmann, Claude. 1985. *Shoah: An Oral History of the Holocaust—The Complete Text of the Film.* New York: Pantheon Books.

Lanzmann, Claude. 2000a. Les Non-Lieux de la Mémoire. *Au sujet de la Shoah: le film du Claude Lanzmann,* dirigeé par Michel Deguy et Claude Lanzmann, 387–406. Paris: Belin.

Lanzmann, Claude. 2000b. Le lieu et la parole. *Au sujet de la Shoah: le film du Claude Lanzmann,* dirigeé par Michel Deguy et Claude Lanzmann, 407–425. Paris: Belin.

Levin, Mikael. 1997. *War Story,* text by Meyer Levin. Munich: Gina Kehayoff Verlag.

Mendelsohn, Daniel. 2006. *The Lost: A Search for Six of Six Million.* London: William Collins Press.

Nora, Pierre. 1989. Between Memory and History: Les Lieux de Mémoire. *Representations* 26: 7–24. Special Issue: Memory and Counter-Memory.

Olin, Margaret. 1997. Lanzmann's *Shoah* and the Topography of the Holocaust Film. *Representations* 57: 1–23.

Reinartz, Dirk, and Christian Graf von Krokow. 1995. *Deathly Still: Pictures of Former Concentration Camps,* trans. Isabel Flett. New York: Scalo.

Rigney, Ann. 2016. Scales of Postmemory: Six of Six Million. In *Probing the Ethics of Holocaust Culture,* ed. Claudio Fogu, Wulf Kansteiner, and Todd Presner, 113–128. Cambridge, MA and London: Harvard UP.

Shoah. 1985. Dir. Claude Lanzmann. Historia. Les Films Aleph, Ministère de la Culture de la Republique Française, British Broadcasting Corporation (BBC).

Skloot, Robert. 2012. Lanzmann's *Shoah* After Twenty-Five Years: An Overview and a Further View. *Holocaust and Genocide Studies* 26 (2): 261–275.

Sontag, Susan. 1977. *On Photography.* New York: Penguin Books.

Tseti, Angeliki. 2015. Historiography in Photo-Textuality: The Representation of Trauma in W.G. Sebald's *The Emigrants. Synthesis: An Anglophone Journal of Comparative Literary Studies* 8: 99–117.

Tseti, Angeliki. 2016. Photo-Textual Narratives, Shared Experiences: The Multidirectionality of Traumatic Memory in Jonathan Safran Foer's *Extremely Loud & Incredibly Close.* In *America: Justice, Conflict, War—European Views of the United States,* vol. 8, ed. Amanda Gilroy and Marietta Messmer, 31–49. Heidelberg: Univesitätsverlag.

"What Is the Holocaust by Bullets?," *Yahad in Unum.* https://www.yahadinunum.org/what-is-the-holocaust-by-bullets/. Accessed 31 Dec 2014.

PART III

Contemplation – Preservation – Resistance

CHAPTER 14

Destruction Preservation, or the Edifying Ruin in Benjamin and Brecht

Vassiliki Kolocotroni

Ruin Value

In 1934, Adolf Hitler "surprised" the architect Albert Speer with his first major commission:

> The temporary bleachers on the Zeppelin Field in Nuremberg were to be replaced by a permanent stone installation. I struggled over those first sketches until, in an inspired moment, the idea came to me; a mighty flight of stairs topped and enclosed by a long colonnade, flanked on both ends by stone abutments. Undoubtedly it was influenced by the Pergamum altar. (Speer 1970, 96)

That collaboration was the first in a number of grand projects in the neoclassical mode through which the fascist leader was to create for his nation a portfolio of monumental constructions that would "transmit his time and its spirit to posterity," representing in perpetuity the growing might of the heroic German spirit in triumphant recovery from the humiliation of the First World War. Speer's recollection of the vision behind the undertaking is a gift to the scholar of ruin:

V. Kolocotroni (✉)
University of Glasgow, Glasgow, UK

© The Author(s) 2019
E. Mitsi et al. (eds.), *Ruins in the Literary and Cultural Imagination*,
https://doi.org/10.1007/978-3-030-26905-0_14

231

> To clear ground for [the Zeppelin Field], the Nuremberg street-car depot
> had to be removed. I passed by its remains after it had been blown up. The
> iron reinforcements protruded from concrete debris and had already begun
> to rust. One could easily visualize their further decay. This dreary sight led
> me to some thoughts which I later propounded to Hitler under the pre-
> tentious heading of "A Theory of Ruin Value." The idea was that buildings
> of modern construction were poorly suited to form that "bridge of tradi-
> tion" to future generations which Hitler was calling for. ... By using special
> materials and by applying certain principles of statics, we should be able
> to build structures which even in a state of decay, after hundreds or (such
> were our reckonings) thousands of years would more or less resemble
> Roman models. To illustrate my ideas I had a romantic drawing prepared.
> It showed what the reviewing stand on the Zeppelin Field would look like
> after generations of neglect, overgrown with ivy, its columns fallen, the
> walls crumbling here and there, but the outlines still recognizable. (Speer
> 1970, 96–97)

Here is a vignette, then, of the workings of fascism as a myth machine,
or, as Philippe Lacoue-Labarthe and Jean-Luc Nancy call it, after the
Platonic model of myth, "a *fictioning*, whose role is to propose, if not
to impose, models or types ... in imitation of which an individual, or a
city, or an entire people, can grasp themselves and identify themselves"
(1990, 297). This exemplary fashioning in Speer's hands (and eyes)
produces monuments that are deferent in their citation of classical and
romantic styles, but also precocious in their ruin-readiness. While they
may partly evoke the "beautiful ruins" of eighteenth-century aristocratic
gardens, these imagined constructions are not merely ornamental, but
rather ideological fancies. Nor are they allegories in the German Baroque
mode, remnant-reminders of the ever-presence of death,[1] but guarantors
of permanence, or at the very least, proud survival. As Speer put it in his
memoirs, like Hitler, "I, too, was intoxicated by the idea of using drawings, money, and construction firms to create stone witnesses to history,

---

[1] See, for instance, Walter Benjamin's account of that mode in *The Origin of German
Tragic Drama* (first published in 1928): "This is the heart of the allegorical way of seeing,
of the baroque, secular explanation of history as the Passion of the world; its importance
resides solely in the stations of its decline" (1985, 166). Benjamin links allegory with the
"baroque cult of the ruin" in an aphoristic double definition that has gained much traction
in studies of his thinking: "Allegories are, in the realm of thoughts, what ruins are in the
realm of things" (1985, 178). For an application of this Benjaminian formula to a reading
of Henry James's use of the ruin as mental analogue, see Chapter 5 by Chryssa Marinou.

and thus affirm our claim that our work would survive for a thousand years" (1970, 69).[2] In a mimetic sense, then, these "stone witnesses" are mock, wannabe allegories and presumptuous figurations of deathless style. While the neoclassical architectural style was already "a manifesto carved in stone, speaking to the inhabitants of towns and cities across the Nazi empire in the language of imperialism," as Johann Chapoutot puts it (2016, 260), the additional feature of its ruin-worthiness literally reinforced the citational, generative power to project the greatness of a fragmented yet persisting neo-antiquity into the future. There is a strong theatrical element to this vision, but also a didacticism—an attempted *Bildung*, a project of identity-formation and cultivation, and a rebuilding of history on mythical foundations.

The instructive value of the future ruin was of course based on the assumption of longevity, at least enough for the passing of time alone to bequeath the magnificent constructions as recognizable remnants to future generations; what happened instead was the near-total destruction of German cities by Allied air raids. Berlin alone endured a reported 363 attacks and 45,517 tons of bombs between November 1943 and the end of the war (Brett 2016, 27), which precipitated the delivery-into-ruin of Hitler's architectural vision. The Speer effect *did* account for the remarkable "verticality" of Berlin ruins, noted, for instance, by the Polish journalist Isaac Deutscher (then a correspondent for the *Economist*), for whom the city "was reminiscent of a strangely well-preserved ruin from the ancient world," as "it [stood] upright in front of the observer to a truly astonishing degree" (Brett 2016, 35); but by the mid-1940s, 80% of historical German city centres was reduced to rubble. For Speer himself, by then Nazi Germany's Minister of Armaments and Munitions, the theory of ruin value was superseded by a different kind of logistics: in a brief interlude between times of captivity in 1945, he was set up at the castle of Glügsburg to help the United States Strategic Bombing Survey accumulate and assess data on the effects of bombings on both sides. As he recalled, "we went systematically through the various aspects of the war in the air ... During the next several days an almost comradely tone prevailed in our 'university of bombing'" (1970, 500). On the "curriculum," undoubtedly, will have been one of the flashpoints of the war, in July 1943, when the British and American air forces mounted

---

[2]For a full account of Hitler's taste for antiquity, see Chapoutot (2016, 265–284).

a week-long campaign of raids on the city of Hamburg. It was at the time the heaviest assault in the history of aerial warfare, later called the "Hiroshima of Germany" by British officials. The attack killed over 40,000 civilians and wounded 37,000, virtually destroying most of the city. Its codename was Operation Gomorrah, its aim "to destroy the city and reduce it as completely as possible to ashes" (Sebald 2003, 26).

We will return to Gomorrah in a moment; for now, I want to broaden the focus to include a project of edification through the anticipation and contemplation of ruin, which may serve as a counterpoint to the type of hubristic exemplarity and mimetic identification through myth envisioned by the fascist model. For this, I turn to the thinking of two German contemporaries of Speer and Hitler.

Amongst the Rubble

> *ZIFFEL*: The best school for dialectics is emigration. The sharpest dialectical philosophers are the refugees. They've been made refugees by great changes and all they study is changes. They sit amongst the rubble in their camps, under the stars, plotting victory from the catastrophe all around them. They study what their enemies have done to them to spot the tiniest contradiction, then wham, they're into the crack with their knives out.
> *KALLE*: Long live dialectics. (Brecht 1986, 13)

A refugee from Nazi Germany since 1933, Bertolt Brecht wrote *Conversations in Exile*, a series of dialogues between a former scientist and a former labourer on the theme of displacement and war, in the early 1940s in Finland and Los Angeles. Back in 1934 and 1938, Brecht was often engaged in conversation with the fellow exile, collaborator and friend, Walter Benjamin. As Erdmut Wizisla notes in a recent account of that important friendship, for Benjamin, Brecht was one of those creative spirits "who begin by clearing a tabula rasa." His "simplifications" were "not agitational but constructive," as Benjamin put it, "and ... [his] work ... allowed theatre 'to take on its most sober and unassuming, even its most reduced, form – to get it, as it were, through the winter in this way'" (2016, 231, 232). Brecht and his work made it through the winter; Benjamin didn't. During those fierce but productive years, they anticipated catastrophe and reflected on ruin in constructive, edifying ways. As the extract from Brecht's *Conversations in Exile* suggests, "dark times" required conceptual rigour and vigilance, with which to address "great changes" and unique contradictions: while exile may have provided a safe distance, however, precarious and troubling in its own right, there remained the clear and present danger of the enemy claims on the future. By 1938, that danger had drawn closer: on the third (and last) summer visit to Brecht and his wife in Denmark, Benjamin recalled in a diary entry the urgency with which Brecht defended his decision to include part of the lyric cycle "Children's Songs" in a new volume of poems:

> Brecht is envisioning an epoch without history; his poem addressed to the graphic artists presents an image of that age. A few days later, he tells me that he considers the advent of this age more probable than a victory over fascism. Soon afterward, something else emerged – yet another justification for incorporating the "Children's Songs" into the "Poems from Exile." Brecht, standing before me in the grass, spoke with rare forcefulness: "In the struggle against them, it is vital that nothing be overlooked. They don't think small. They plan thirty thousand years ahead. Horrendous things. Horrendous crimes. They will stop at nothing. They will attack anything. Every cell convulses under their blows. So we mustn't forget a single one. They distort the child in the womb. We can under no circumstances forget the children." (Benjamin 2002c, 339–340)

Brecht was one of Benjamin's oracles at that moment, sharing some of the features of a particular type, important for his thinking, that he had presciently configured as early as 1931:

> The destructive character sees nothing permanent. But for this very reason he sees ways everywhere. Where others encounter walls or mountains, there, too, he sees a way. But because he sees a way everywhere, he has to clear things from it everywhere. Not always by brute force; sometimes by the most refined. Because he sees ways everywhere, he always stands at a crossroads. No moment can know what the next will bring. What exists he reduces to rubble – not for the sake of the rubble, but for that of the way leading through it. (Benjamin 2005a, 542)[3]

It is worth noting the difference between this type and the character of the "inner emigrant" that Hannah Arendt made famous in her account

---

[3] According to Fredric Jameson, the prototype for this "destructive character" was Karl Kraus. See Jameson (1992, 26).

of the immediate pre-war years: "As its very name suggests, the 'inner emigration' was a curiously ambiguous phenomenon. It signified on the one hand that there were persons inside Germany who behaved as if they no longer belonged to the country, who felt like emigrants; on the other hand it indicated that they had not in reality emigrated, but had withdrawn to an interior realm, into the invisibility of thinking and feeling" (1968, 19). Arendt's model of the virtual or actual "refugee style" as enforced but productive alienation is still the most influential testimony to that historical constellation. For Arendt, that style comprised linguistic and psychological effects that correspond to an oblique, ironic perspective—as summarized by Lyndsey Stonebridge: "speak[ing] double, parrot[ing] oneself ironically … Dreaming of oneself as an enemy alien, or as a remnant; this is the psychopathology of the crisis of international human rights which was inaugurated in the early part of the twentieth century" (2011, 75, 83). It is against this diagnosis of an internalized ironic detachment that I want to position Benjamin and Brecht, however seeing instead in their work a strategic deliberation and deployment of the critical resources of the ruin.

Defunct Forms

In 1939, writing on Brecht's work, in "What Is The Epic Theater? (II)," Benjamin makes an important distinction:

> [According to Brecht], an actor should reserve to himself the possibility of stepping out of character artistically. At the proper moment, he should insist on portraying an individual who reflects on his part. It would be wrong to think at such a moment of Romantic irony …. Romantic irony has no didactic aim. Basically, it demonstrates only the philosophical sophistication of the author who … always keeps in mind that the world may ultimately prove to be a theater. (Benjamin 2006b, 306–307)

Benjamin's clarification suggests that the ironist's position or, put in literary and philosophical terms, Romantic irony, may be too familiar to contemporary (German) audiences, and as an expert on the matter (having completed a doctoral thesis on *The Concept of Criticism in German Romanticism* in 1912), he makes a point of disabusing prospective recipients of Brecht's work. The emphasis on didacticism as opposed to irony interests me here, as it may help identify a shared aim that comes to the fore in the work of the two writers. Already in 1931, Benjamin had drawn a line between the nihilistic "left-wing melancholy" or "know-all irony" of Weimar poets whom he accused of "complacency and fatalism," and Brecht's "political lyricism" (2005c, 424, 426). In later pieces, such as the 1935 account of the *Threepenny Novel*, he returned to the necessary Brechtian treatment:

> There are many who consider the dialectician a lover of subtleties. So it is uncommonly useful when Brecht puts his finger on the "crude thinking" that dialectics produces as its antithesis, includes within itself, and needs. ... The forms of crude thinking change slowly, for they are created by the masses. We can still learn things from defunct forms. (Benjamin 2002b, 7)

There is an important difference, then, between the "hollow forms" of "former spiritual goods," "absentmindedly caressed" by the ineffective, quietist ironists castigated by Benjamin in "Left-Wing Melancholy" (2005c, 424–425),[4] and the "defunct forms" created by the masses from which "we can still learn." Against the emphasis on the "crudeness" of the thinking as opposed to its dialectical impetus, and against the received perception of Benjamin as the emblematic solitary and melancholy thinker, I see a strong current in his work of the 1930s that generates projects of intellectual recuperation within the didactic and empowering frame of a new German *Bildung*, projects of popular cultivation in the classical mode.[5] In that he was not alone; as Jean-Michel Palmier notes in his comprehensive study *Weimar in Exile*, the German intelligentsia of the late 1920s and 1930s identified a common cause in "show[ing] what [the] supposed [fascist] 'Germanity' had falsified, but also to emphasize the extent to which the classical German heritage was indissociable from those values now trampled on by the Nazis" (2017, 290).

Benjamin's individual projects included attempts at popularising, reframing for the moment of danger and thus defending an intellectual

---

[4] Namely, the poet, novelist and journalist Erich Kästner, author of the popular children's book *Emil und die Detektive* (Emile and the Detectives, 1928), the journalist and historian of the German Democratic Party Franz Mehring, and the journalist, poet and essayist Kurt Tucholsky, members of a "left-wing intelligentsia," which in Benjamin's account is presented as "the decayed bourgeoisie's mimicry of the proletariat" (2005c, 424).

[5] On the philosophical and political resonances and cultural contestations of the German *Bildung*, see Kettler and Lauer (2005).

heritage against the enemy. One such example is *Deutsche Menschen* (*German People*), a collection of letters for which Benjamin wrote a preface and commentaries and which was published in Switzerland in 1936 under the (non-Jewish) pseudonym Detlef Holtz. The twenty-five letters featured in the book date from the period 1783–1883 and amongst the authors included are Lichtenberg, Johann Heinrich Voss, Hölderlin, the Grimm brothers, Goethe, David Friedrich Strauss and Georg Büchner. A copy of the book that once belonged to Benjamin's sister and was found in a Zurich antique shop bears the dedication: "This ark, built on the Jewish model, for Dora – from Walter. November 1936." As Peter Szondi notes, "One may well apply to the ark of *Deutsche Menschen* these lines from [Benjamin's] *Theses on the Philosophy of History*: 'Only *that* historian has the gift of kindling the sparks of hope in the past who is thoroughly imbued with this idea: even the dead will not be safe from the enemy if he wins. And this enemy has not ceased to win'" (1978, 505–506).

The selected letters are Benjamin's "conversations in exile" in more than one sense: the letter-form is of course conversational in one respect, but also lends itself and poignantly so to the displaced perspective of the exile. The use of the non-Jewish pseudonym underscored in the dedication to his sister in a very Jewish way adds biographical and intellectual resonances, as does the fact of Benjamin's own exile in Paris at the time. In a literal sense too, the selection is apt as the letters in Benjamin's *Deutsche Menschen* were written by German intellectuals in exile in an era marked by the influence of the Enlightenment on the German bourgeoisie, as well as in three notable cases by witnesses to the French Revolution. According to Patrick H. Hutton, Benjamin collected the letters "as testimony of an enlightened German culture now obscured by the rise of National Socialism" and believed that they "possessed a potentially liberating power" (2008, 239–240). As Theodor Adorno, a fellow exile, collaborator and correspondent put it, though effectively defunct as a high-art form, "letters were for Benjamin natural-history illustrations of what survives the ruin of time" (qtd. in Hutton 2008, 238). In Benjamin's terms, what survived, revealed in his collection, were "the lineaments of a 'secret Germany' that people nowadays would much prefer to shroud in heavy mist" (2005b, 466).

This particular story of "a radical German Enlightenment reduced to exile and obscurity," as Irving Wohlfarth puts it (2005, 38), speaks of the present condition of the storyteller himself, then, but also of an obscured vision in ruins that stands as a counterimage to the presumptuously monumental "Germania" of Hitler and Speer. In this sense, Benjamin's project proposes an alternative theory of ruin value,[6] or a sustained mnemonics and reclamation of the past for future use. What Benjamin preserves here is the destruction of an original vision, but also the conviction that amongst its ruins remain signs of a salutary witnessing, fragments of the past that may be defunct, but also ripe for strategic reconstitution.

LEARNING FROM RUIN

"The Fall of Herculaneum and Pompeii," Benjamin's radio piece for children broadcast on Radio Berlin on 18 September 1931 and Brecht's *War Primer*, a collection of photo-epigrams produced between 1940 and 1944, bookend those ruinous times. In their treatment of the classical trope of the instructive rumination on ruins, the foregrounding of the witness's perspective, and the invocation of the works' pedagogical effect, they share a common purpose. Benjamin's piece, the first in a series of brief accounts of natural-historical catastrophes,[7] introduces an iconic site. The pedigree of Pompeii as prime ruin-gazing material, and as cultural and literary spectacle, is well-established (Blix 2009, Hales and Paul 2011, Thomas 2017): since the first discovery of human remains in 1765 that prompted a series of highly dramatic ruin-reflective visits by scholars, artists and emperors (Dwyer 2010), and the popular success of Edward Bulwer-Lytton's 1834 *The Last Days of Pompeii*, and its numerous filmic adaptations (7 versions alone between 1910 and 1935), the site has been the setting for countless iterations of its visual, allegorical, pedagogical, even (psycho)analytical potential—such as Freud's close reading of Wilhelm Jensen's 1902 novel *Gradiva*, one of his first literary forays into the field of psychic archaeology (Freud [1907] 1959, 3–95).

Pompeii is also a leitmotif in the related themes of ruination and revolutionary discharge in Benjamin's own *Arcades Project*. As Jeffrey Mehlman points out, Pompeii was "a constant reference for Benjamin

---

[6]On this juxtaposition, see also Featherstone (2005, 319) and Stead (2003).

[7]The broadcast on Pompeii was followed on October 31 of the same year by "The Lisbon Earthquake." The series continued with "Theater Fire in Canton" (November 5, 1931), "The Railway Disaster at the Firth of Tay" (February 4, 1932) and "The Mississippi Flood of 1927" (March 23, 1932).

during his work on the Paris Arcades. ... Precision of delineation and apocalyptic ending are the two most charged features of the European imagination's fascination with (and excavation of) Pompeii, and, in a different distribution, ... were central to Benjamin's own excavation of the Paris of the nineteenth century" (1993, 23). Pompeii is a meaningful and strategic analogue for Benjamin's Paris in the Arcades compendium, where, as Esther Leslie puts it, "[r]uin and devastation recur, as motif and historical fact ..., as a natural phenomenon and a social one" (2006, 108); as Benjamin notes in Convolut C [Ancient Paris, Catacombs, Demolitions, Decline of Paris], "Paris is a counterpart in the social order to what Vesuvius is in the geographic order: a menacing, hazardous massif, an ever-active hotbed of revolution. But just as the slopes of Vesuvius, thanks to the layers of lava that cover them, have been transformed into paradisal orchards, so the lava of revolutions provides uniquely fertile ground for the blossoming of art, festivity, fashion" ([C1,6] Benjamin 1999, 83).

The 1931 radio piece for children starts with a mythical reference to the ancient Greek labyrinth where the "hideous monster" Minotaur, half man-half bull, awaited its regular victims:

> Have you ever heard of the Minotaur? He was the hideous monster that dwelt in a labyrinth in Thebes. Every year a virgin was sacrificed by being thrown into this labyrinth, whose hundreds of meandering, branching and crisscrossing paths made it impossible for her to find her way out, so she was eventually eaten by the monster; that is, until Theseus was given a ball of thread by the Theban king's daughter. (Benjamin 2014, 152)

Benjamin stages his listeners' entry into the world of the past in the fabulistic, magical way he used elsewhere as a kind of *coup de mémoire*,[8] or as an image-marker for the primitive urban underworld.[9] He drops the mythical but proceeds with an atmospheric, uncanny effect that serves as a form of caution too:

> How often it happened that, while walking through the dead city with one of my friends from Naples or Capri, I turned to him, pointing out a

---

[8] See "Berlin Childhood Around 1900 (Final Version)" (Benjamin 2002a, 352).

[9] See the entry C1a, 2 ["Ancient Paris, Catacombs, Demolitions, Decline of Paris"], in *The Arcades Project* (Benjamin 1999, 84).

faded painting on a wall or a mosaic underfoot, only to find myself suddenly alone; then anxious minutes would pass as we called out each other's name before finding out each other again. You mustn't think that you can stroll through this defunct Pompeii as if it were a museum of antiquities. (2014, 152)

The eeriness of Pompeii, maze of ruins, induces in the visitor "a strange state" (2014, 153), compounded by the fact that, as Benjamin explains, the city was already partly a ghost: sixteen years before the eruption, a "horrific" earthquake had almost destroyed it. Pompeii's final "fall" is told in dramatic detail through two long quotations from the letters written to the historian Tacitus by Pliny the Younger. "These letters may be the most celebrated in the world. They tell us not only about the events that transpired, but also about how they were understood," Benjamin notes (2014, 154). Pliny the Younger's extraordinary eyewitness experience is contrasted in Benjamin's telling to the short-sightedness of those residents of Pompeii whose "primary concern was saving their possessions, leaving them too little time to save themselves" (2014, 155). The subtle moral lesson is reinforced by Benjamin in a final flourish that forges a link between the then and now:

> Over hundreds of years the city vanished from memory. In the last century, however, as the city reemerged from the Earth with its shops, taverns, theaters, wrestling schools, temples, and baths, the Vesuvius eruption of 79 A.D., which destroyed the city two millennia ago, appeared in a whole new light: what for its contemporaries meant the destruction of a flourishing city, for us today meant its preservation. A preservation so precise and so detailed that we can read the hundreds of small inscriptions that covered Pompeii's public walls the same way leaflets and posters cover ours ... Of these hundreds of inscriptions, we will conclude with one, which we can well imagine was the last; as the menacing, fiery glow fell over Pompeii, a Christian or Jew well versed in such matters must have scrawled this final and uncanny inscription: "Sodom and Gomorrah." (2014, 157)

The writing on the wall is a riddle and an epigraph at once, a last word and a warning. Its preservation spells destruction (as it evokes an archetypal scene of ruination), and a memory image, which persists (and flashes up in a moment of danger) as an interpretative code. The graffito he isolates for commentary presents a visual gag, a snapshot of a petrified, emblematic *memento mori*, capturing and interpellating, forcing the gaze of the visitor (from the future) to enact a "backward look"—such as the look that crystallized Lot's wife and forever deprived Orpheus of his muse, or on which Benjamin's "angel of history" is unable to act as he is blown into the future.[10] Benjamin's inscription may also suggest that ruination is a necessary corrective to memory, or rather, memorialization; its ambivalent temporality (as it is still not clearly established that there were in fact Christians in Pompeii at that time)[11] compounds the prescience of the message: whether carved before or after the eruption, the fragment resonates by establishing its own continuum. What carries meaning and weight here, of course, is the insight the inscription of the Biblical name affords into "how [the events] were understood," rather than the fact of a true or false consciousness of them. It may be argued, then, that the piece ends as it begins, with an evocation of mythical thinking, but if so, it is a frisson and a fear that may be recuperated, harnessed to the cause of edification of future residents of "flourishing" cities.

The myth of Sodom and Gomorrah is subtly weaponized here in an invocation of exemplarity that introduces an ambivalence in the eloquent message of the ruin. In that sense, the inscription is oracular; preserved within this act of citation is the certainty of destruction, an iterative process that may overcome but not silence fully the possibility of critical witnessing. Had he survived the war, one can only speculate on what Benjamin would have thought of the later iteration of destruction wreaked in the name of that mythical site of catastrophe, namely the Allied bombers' Operation Gomorrah in 1943.[12] The date of the broadcast (1931) is a few years away too from the bombings of the Spanish Civil War, another Gomorrah, which he and Brecht followed on the radio while in Denmark, but the thinking of that earlier period already

---

[10] See "On the Concept of History": "His eyes are wide, his mouth is open, his wings are spread. This is how the angel of history must look. His face is turned toward the past. Where a chain of events appears before us, he sees one single catastrophe, which keeps piling wreckage upon wreckage and hurls it at his feet. The angel would like to stay, awaken the dead, and make whole what has been smashed. But a storm is blowing from Paradise and has got caught in his wings; it is so strong that the angel can no longer close them. This storm drives him irresistibly into the future, to which his back is turned, while the pile of debris before him grows toward the sky" (Benjamin 2006c, 392).

[11] See Beard (2012) on this conundrum.

[12] On this hypothesis, see Pensky (2011, 77).

demonstrates a concern with the training necessary for receiving images of the past as infused with present danger (and vice versa).

As edificatory ruin, another "stone witness," Benjamin's Pompeii anticipates the final contribution to a radical *Bildung* for ruinous times to which this essay will now turn. In 1937, Brecht wrote a first series of anti-Nazi epigrams under the title "German War Primer," which were published in the Moscow magazine *Das Wort* and set by the composer Hans Eisler as variations for unaccompanied chorus titled *Against War*. They too were fruits of exile and writings on the wall. The ancient Greek epigram was one of the "defunct forms" Brecht found most relevant for the time spent witnessing from afar the rising tide of war. From the fall of Barcelona, the Spanish Civil War to the Munich agreement and the Nazi onslaught, the period (spent in various places of exile) was a prolonged reflection on the ability of language and art to capture the reality of disaster. The "political lyricism" that Benjamin had celebrated in his account of Brecht, combined with an urgent desire for "concreteness" and a purging of language from fascist propaganda (a "linguistic cleanup," as Brecht put it [2017, 88]), made out of Brecht's personal reportage an ABC of humanity at war. For Benjamin, who commented in late 1938–early 1939 on the collection, Brecht's formal choice was pertinent:

> The "Kriegsfibel" is written in a "lapidary" style. This word comes from the Latin *lapis*, meaning "stone," and refers to the style which was developed for inscriptions. Its most important characteristic was brevity. This resulted, first, from the difficulty of inscribing words in stone, and, second, from an awareness that anyone addressing subsequent generations ought not to waste words. ... Accordingly, the character of the "Kriegsfibel" can be seen as arising from a unique contradiction: words which through their poetic form will conceivably survive the coming apocalypse preserve the gesture of a message hastily scrawled on a fence by someone fleeing his enemies. (Benjamin 2006a, 240)

The composition of the work which would eventually be published as the *War Primer* is recorded partly in the journals Brecht kept meticulously while in exile; on 25 July 1940, he writes of the anthology of epigrams his son had brought to Finland: "the mood of these greek epigrams is set by their marvellous concreteness, together with their sense of how a specific wind (evening wind, dawn wind, April wind, wind off the snows) will stir the leaves and fruit on a given tree" (1993, 80). The journals themselves are a remarkable collagistic text, a scrapbook of diary entries and clippings from contemporary magazines and newspapers, which are then recycled into the mixed medium of the *War Primer*, which comprises a series of 85 "photo-epigrams," or quatrains that epigrammatically comment on, explicate, lament, animate and echo an equal number of photographs from the popular press. This collection of "poor monuments, an aid to critical remembering," as David Evans puts it (2003, 9), completed in 1944 and published after a struggle with various authorities in 1955,[13] can be approached via various entry points: as "the last great achievement of a montage culture focusing on the photograph as historical document" (Evans 2012, 174), as an example of the film-strip technique that Benjamin identified in his analysis of Brecht's theatre (Evans 2003, 8), or as a series of "perfect instants," arranged in the manner of Diderot's didactic tableaux that Brecht (like Eisenstein) greatly admired.[14] For Diderot, as Roland Barthes notes, and in Eisenstein's and Brecht's redeployment, these "crucial" instants are "hieroglyph[s] in which can be read at a single glance … the present, the past and the future; that is, the historical meaning of the represented action" (1977, 73).[15]

The first photo-epigram presents the Führer addressing an invisible crowd in hypnotic, magician mode, as per the established trope of the Cagliostro-type figure that writers like Thomas Mann had configured in prescient tales of dangerous demagoguery in the late 1920s[16]: "Like one who dreams the road ahead is steep / I know the way Fate has prescribed for us / That narrow way towards a precipice. / Just follow. I can find it in my sleep." The second cuts to the material base, "brothers" building

---

[13] For a full account of the text's fortunes, see John Willett's "Afterword," in Brecht (2017, 87–94).

[14] In "Diderot, Brecht, Eisenstein," Barthes reports that "Round about 1937, Brecht had the idea of founding a *Diderot Society*, a place for pooling theatrical experiments and studies – doubtless because he saw in Diderot, in addition to the figure of a great materialist philosopher, a man of the theatre" (1977, 78). For a study of Brecht's theatrical debt to Diderot, see Von Held (2011).

[15] On Diderot's "hieroglyphs," see Berri (2000) and Wettlaufer (2003).

[16] See for instance Mann's 1929 novella *Mario und der Zauberer* (*Mario and the Magician*).

"iron wagons" for the war, while the third photo-epigram fuses the ancient motif of the "sunken ships" with the image of a woman bathing on the Spanish coast, hands and feet coated in "black oil," "the only trace left" of that war that set brother against brother. Subsequent photograms animate natural scenes, agitated by the impending disaster (nos. 6–7), followed by a series on air bombing (nos. 16–19 and 23–25) initiated by a press photograph of bomber pilots, all-too human agents of destruction, that changes the scale and by giving the bombed city a "voice" turns the table on clichéd ruin-gazing; photo-epigram no 22 returns to the material base, offering a poignant comment on war as the continuation of business by other means: a photograph of children gathered around the exits of London air-raid shelters carrying prams with blankets and mattresses available to hire, along with their own reserved places in the shelter, for a price: "For older than their bombers is the hunger / That they've unleashed on us."[17] In the final image, a strong, direct awakening from the trance of the first photogram, a student audience in a place of learning throws up a visual riposte to the image of Hitler as orator-in-a-trance at the very start of the book: "And now don't hide your head, and don't desert / But learn to learn, and try to learn for what."

True to its title, Brecht's "primer" begins with an image of mystification and ends with one of its salutary opposites, a scene of instruction, and perhaps caution. It is interesting to note that the instructor or authority figure is missing from the last photograph, though still present in the formal address of the accompanying epigram. As an ark of images and inscriptions, it preserves destruction concretely, one might say "crudely," as a fable and as a manual for disenchanting it (the German word *fibel* contains both senses). By revisiting the Greek poetic mode and juxtaposing it to the image in mass circulation, Brecht repurposes both. Like Benjamin's Pompeii for children, the seemingly inert ruins (of cities and humans) in Brecht's collection speak of an incomplete, ongoing process of radical awakening. To the phantasmagoria of the fascist

---

[17] The photograph, so evocative of *Mother Courage*, Brecht's prescient war play, written in 1939, is a clipping from an unidentified Swedish paper dated 3 December 1940.

dream and its beautiful ruins-to-be, they issue a warning and a memory flash from the immediate past for present and future edification.

REFERENCES

Arendt, Hannah. 1968. *Men in Dark Times*. San Diego, New York, and London: Harcourt Brace & Company.

Barthes, Roland. 1977. Diderot, Brecht, Eisenstein. In *Image–Music–Text*, ed. and trans. Stephen Heath. London: Fontana Press.

Beard, Mary. 2012. Were There Christians at Pompeii? The Word-Square Evidence. *TLS*, November 30. Last modified 8 July 2018. https://www.the-tls.co.uk/were-there-christians-at-pompeii-the-word-square-evidence/.

Benjamin, Walter. 1985. *The Origin of German Tragic Drama*, trans. John Osborne. London and New York: Verso.

Benjamin, Walter. 1999. *The Arcades Project*, ed. Rolf Tiedemann, trans. Howard Eiland and Kevin McLaughlin. Cambridge, MA and London: The Belknap Press of Harvard University Press.

Benjamin, Walter. 2002a. Berlin Childhood Around 1900 (Final Version). In *Selected Writings, Volume 3: 1935–1938*, trans. Edmund Jephcott, Howard Eiland et al., ed. Howard Eiland and Michael W. Jennings, 344–386. Cambridge, MA and London: The Belknap Press of Harvard University Press.

Benjamin, Walter. 2002b. Brecht's *Threepenny Novel*. In *Selected Writings, Volume 3: 1935–1938*, trans. Edmund Jephcott, Howard Eiland et al., ed. Howard Eiland and Michael W. Jennings, 3–10. Cambridge, MA and London: The Belknap Press of Harvard University Press.

Benjamin, Walter. 2002c. Diary Entries, 1938. In *Selected Writings, Volume 3: 1935–1938*, trans. Edmund Jephcott, Howard Eiland et al., ed. Howard Eiland and Michael W. Jennings, 335–343. Cambridge, MA and London: The Belknap Press of Harvard University Press.

Benjamin, Walter. 2005a. The Destructive Character. In *Selected Writings, Volume 2: Part 2, 1931–1934*, trans. Rodney Livingstone et al., ed. Michael W. Jennings et al., 541–542. Cambridge, MA and London: The Belknap Press of Harvard University Press.

Benjamin, Walter. 2005b. German Letters. In *Selected Writings, Volume 2: Part 2, 1931–1934*, trans. Rodney Livingstone et al., ed. Michael W. Jennings et al., 466–468. Cambridge, MA and London: The Belknap Press of Harvard University Press.

Benjamin, Walter. 2005c. Left-Wing Melancholy. In *Selected Writings, Volume 2: Part 2, 1931–1934*, trans. Rodney Livingstone et al., ed. Michael W. Jennings et al., 423–427. Cambridge, MA and London: The Belknap Press of Harvard University Press.

Benjamin, Walter. 2006a. Commentary on Poems by Brecht. In *Selected Writings, Volume 4: 1938–1940*, ed. Michael W. Jennings et al., 215–250. Cambridge, MA: Harvard University Press.

Benjamin, Walter. 2006b. What Is the Epic Theater? (II). In *Selected Writings, Volume 4: 1938–1940*, ed. Michael W. Jennings, Marcus Bullock, Howard Eiland, Gary Smith, 302–309. Cambridge, MA: Harvard University Press.

Benjamin, Walter. 2006c. On the Concept of History. In *Selected Writings, Volume 4: 1938–1940*, ed. Michael W. Jennings, Marcus Bullock, Howard Eiland, Gary Smith, 389–400. Cambridge, MA: Harvard University Press.

Benjamin, Walter. 2014. The Fall of Herculaneum and Pompeii. In *Radio Benjamin*, ed. Lecia Rosenthal, trans. Jonathan Lutes et al., 152–157. London: Verso.

Berri, Kenneth. 2000. Diderot's Hieroglyphs. *SubStance* 92 (29: 2): 68–93.

Blix, Göran. 2009. *From Paris to Pompeii: French Romanticism and the Cultural Politics of Archaeology*. Philadelphia: University of Pennsylvania Press.

Brecht, Bertolt. 1986. Conversations in Exile. Adapted by Howard Brenton, trans. David Dollenmeyer. *Theater* 17 (2): 8–18.

Brecht, Bertolt. 1993. *Journals 1934–1955*, trans. Hugh Rorrison, ed. John Willett. London: Methuen.

Brecht, Bertolt. 2017. *War Primer*, trans. and ed. John Willett. London and New York: Verso.

Brett, Donna West. 2016. *Photography and Place: Seeing and Not Seeing Germany After 1945*. New York and London: Routledge.

Chapoutot, Johann. 2016. *Greeks, Romans, Germans: How the Nazis Usurped Europe's Classical Past*, trans. Richard R. Nybakken. Oakland: University of California Press.

Dwyer, Eugene. 2010. *Pompeii's Living Statues: Ancient Roman Lives Stolen from Death*. Ann Arbor: University of Michigan Press.

Evans, David. 2003. Brecht's *War Primer*: The "Photo-Epigram" as Poor Monument. *Afterimage* 30 (5): 8–9.

Evans, David. 2012. *A Spectre Is Leaving Europe* (1990): Appropriation in a Post-Communist Photobook. In *The Photobook: From Talbot to Ruscha and Beyond*, ed. Patrizia Di Bello et al., 163–178. London and New York: I.B. Tauris.

Featherstone, Mark. 2005. Ruin Value. *Journal for Cultural Research* 9 (3): 301–320.

Freud, Sigmund. [1907] 1959. Delusion and Dream in Jensen's *Gradiva*. In *The Standard Edition of the Complete Psychological Works of Sigmund Freud*, vol. IX, ed. James Strachey, 3–95. London: The Hogarth Press.

Hales, Shelley, and Joanna Paul (eds.). 2011. *Pompeii in the Public Imagination from Its Rediscovery to Today*. Oxford: Oxford University Press.

Hutton, Patrick H. 2008. Walter Benjamin on the French Exile of German Men of Letters. *The Proceedings of the Western Society for French History* 36: 235–248.

Jameson, Fredric. 1992. Benjamin's Readings. *Diacritics* 22 (3/4): 19–34.

Kettler, David, and Gerhard Lauer (eds.). 2005. *Exile, Science, and Bildung: The Contested Legacies of German Émigré Intellectuals*. New York: Palgrave Macmillan.

Lacoue-Labarthe, Philippe, and Jean-Luc Nancy. 1990. The Nazi Myth, trans. Brian Holmes. *Critical Inquiry* 16 (2): 291–312.

Leslie, Esther. 2006. Ruin and Rubble in the Arcades. In *Walter Benjamin and the Arcades Project*, ed. Beatrice Hanssen, 87–112. London and New York: Continuum.

Mehlman, Jeffrey. 1993. *Walter Benjamin for Children: An Essay on His Radio Years*. Chicago and London: Chicago University Press.

Palmier, Jean-Michel. 2017. *Weimar in Exile: The Antifascist Emigration in Europe and America*, trans. David Fernbach. London and New York: Verso.

Pensky, Max. 2011. Three Kinds of Ruin: Heidegger, Benjamin, Sebald. *Poligrafi* 16 (61/62): 65–89.

Sebald, W. G. 2003. Air War and Literature: Zürich Lectures. In *On the Natural History of Destruction*, trans. Anthea Bell, 3–105. London: Hamish Hamilton.

Speer, Albert. 1970. *Inside the Third Reich*, trans. Richard and Clara Winston. London: Weidenfeld and Nicolson.

Stead, Naomi. 2003. The Value of Ruins: Allegories of Destruction in Benjamin and Speer. *Form/Work* 6: 51–64.

Stonebridge, Lyndsey. 2011. Refugee Style: Hannah Arendt and the Perplexities of Rights. *Textual Practice* 25 (1): 71–85.

Szondi, Peter. 1978. Hope in the Past: On Walter Benjamin, trans. Harvey Mendelsohn. *Critical Inquiry* 4 (3): 491–506.

Thomas, Sophie. 2017. Pompeii, the Body, and the Imprint of the Ancient World. *Word & Image* 33 (3): 303–312.

Von Held, Phoebe. 2011. *Alienation and Theatricality: Diderot After Brecht*. London: Legenda.

Wettlaufer, Alexandra K. 2003. *In the Mind's Eye: The Visual Impulse in Diderot, Baudelaire and Ruskin*. Amsterdam and New York: Rodopi.

Wizisla, Erdmut. 2016. *Walter Benjamin and Bertolt Brecht: The Story of a Friendship*, trans. Christine Shuttleworth. London: Verso.

Wohlfarth, Irving. 2005. Walter Benjamin's "Secret Germany". In *Exile, Science, and Bildung: The Contested Legacies of German Emigré Intellectuals*, ed. David Kettler and Gerhard Lauer, 27–45. New York: Palgrave Macmillan.

CHAPTER 15

Thinking Like a Ruin

Carl Lavery and Simon Murray

JOINT PREAMBLE

We begin by explaining, or at least reflecting upon, why we decided to deliver this paper as a live conversation at a conference entitled "Beyond the Ruin: Investigating the Fragment in English Studies" in Athens in 2017, and why we have adhered to such a form in print. Our decision seemed to be the most logical and serendipitous outcome of many conversations we have had about ruin and ruination over the last three years. These dialogues, sometimes private, sometimes in more public arenas, are always good-natured though sometimes contestatory. If this was a methodology, it was one which acknowledged pleasure as a guiding principle and which unapologetically recognized conditionality, plurality and open-endedness as the texture and timbre of our arguments and articulations. It was—and remains—an approach which challenges the tyranny and monolithic nature of all too many academic conference papers and essays. It was a form which, we hoped, celebrated both a rejection of closure and a refusal to have "the last word"; an approach to sharing knowledge, feeling and thought which somehow seemed to resonate persuasively with the unstable and perhaps poignant timeliness of the contemporary ruin and a never-ending sense of material and human

C. Lavery · S. Murray (✉)
University of Glasgow, Glasgow, UK

© The Author(s) 2019   249
E. Mitsi et al. (eds.), *Ruins in the Literary and Cultural Imagination*,
https://doi.org/10.1007/978-3-030-26905-0_15

ruination. It also allowed us to affirm what the art historian Boris Groys in his influential essay "Comrades of Time" (2009) sees as the distinctive feature of the "contemporary": namely, its untimeliness, the sense in which we are always outwitted by the ruses of history, never quite in control of our knowledge, perpetually undone and disappointed by the forces of a dynamically disruptive outside:

> The contemporary is actually constituted by doubt, hesitation, uncertainty and indecision—by the need for prolonged reflection, for a delay. And that is precisely what the contemporary is—a prolonged, even potentially infinite period of delay. (Groys 2009)

Groys reminds us here of what James Knowlson describes as the "radical uncertainty" (1996, 416) of Samuel Beckett in his magisterial biography of the man. A disposition which finds in the ambiguity of the "perhaps" a progressive and resistant position in the face of the fixity and rigidity of so much contemporary political utterance and posturing.

As we discussed how best to revise our live conversation for the relative fixedness of the printed essay, we made various decisions: to retain the essential dialogic form; to keep the occasional vernacular of "Carl this" or "Simon that" (so as to give the reader an inkling of or feeling for our original endeavour); to avoid any major post hoc re-thinkings and re-articulations; and to preserve the open-ended, non-declamatory and comradely structures of our thoughts and perspectives. Only in relation to some recent startling news about NVA (*nacionale vita-activa* meaning the right to influence public affairs) and St. Peter's Seminary (see below) have we added any substantially new comment, but even here we have kept this brief and factual.

Carl

Simon, I think we should perhaps explain what, for some at least, might be a strange title, namely what does it mean to think like a ruin? We are certainly not the first to engage in such analogical game playing—one thinks, for instance, of books such as James C. Scott's *Seeing Like a State: How Certain Schemes to Improve the Human Condition Have Failed* (1998) and Eduardo Kohn's *How Forests Think: Towards an Anthropology Beyond the Human* (2013) and, further back, Aldo Leopold's notion of "Thinking Like a Mountain" in *A Sand County Almanac* (1968)—but

I would hope that we might approach it a little differently. As I see it, to think like a ruin is not just to describe, metaphorically, a way of ordering or relating to the world that is based on the imaginative recuperation of the work of non-human eco-systems or expanded notions of mind. Rather, it is to problematize the classic definition of the *anthropos* as the animal that thinks by expanding and redistributing our notion of what thought is and how it works. Like Antonin Artaud, in the middle section of his incendiary 1948 radio piece *Pour en finir avec le jugement de Dieu*, I believe that thinking does not come from the inside, but rather is provoked via an encounter with what Artaud, in Nietzschean fashion, terms the "infinite outside": matter, force, earth, cosmos, etc. (1992, 318).

So to think like a ruin, from this perspective, is to posit a philosophy of the outside, an uncanny, errant philosophy of encounter that serves to undo distinctions between nature and culture, self and other and, ultimately, inside and outside. Perhaps provocatively the ruin is a perfect example of an outside that shows its inside. To think like a ruin, then, is to posit the ruin as a philosopher, someone (or, in this instance, something) whose task, amongst other things, is to gather together, in a dense nexus, politics, ethics, ontology and aesthetics.

Simon

Carl, this "thinking like a ruin" resonates well with one of my previous approaches to ruin writing and that is to pose questions of the ruin under consideration, and I offer some examples of these later. I hope this conversation will map out our respective angles of incidence towards *ruin*, *The Ruin* and *ruination* and mark and reflect upon where we have creative tensions between our approaches. I guess within those old debates on the philosophical and intellectual left I'm more of the "culturalist" than the "structuralist" persuasion. However, in this respect, my thinking is also driven from the "outside," from the material and the social world.

Where we both agree, I fancy, is that ruin and ruination are—and have been perhaps for the past two decades—in the cultural *zeitgeist*, or rather, in a formulation which I prefer, offer a kind of *structure of feeling* in a way that Raymond Williams proposed the term (1977, 128–135). Williams uses a phrase to hint at what he means by structure of feeling: "social experiences in solution" (1977, 133) and a form of thinking which challenges the separation of the social from the personal—that area of tension between "ideology" and "experience." Cultural theorist, Stuart Hall, reformulating both Gramscian notions of hegemony and Williams's "structure of feeling," might have put it something like this: "what is the 'present conjuncture' that drives us to become acutely sensitised to ruin and ruination"? In a conversation with political activist and cultural geographer, Doreen Massey, Hall says:

> It's partly about periodization. A conjuncture is a period during which the different social, political, economic and ideological contradictions that are at work in society come together to give it a specific and distinctive shape. (Hall and Massey 2010, 57)

What the "present conjuncture" seems to enable is the proposition that "thinking like a ruin," and employing the lenses of ruination, provide us with a dynamic set of tools with which to identify and grapple with present catastrophes and discontents. I think "the present conjuncture" not only offers up ruination as a productive lens to examine the material and social world, it also obliges us, in a way that has perhaps never been the case in other epochs, to engage with the force fields of ecology and environmental catastrophe. In addition, I would suggest that other features of this structure of feeling, this "present conjuncture," might include:

- The ubiquity and urgency with which we are confronted by images of ruin through global and social media.
- A reconfiguring of the emotional drivers of melancholy and loss as generative, and not simply sentimental, states through which to investigate ruination.
- The turn to what Jane Bennett calls "vibrant matter" or a "political ecology of things" (2010).
- The rise and rise of the "Heritage Industry" and a revisioning of policies towards ruins and ruination.
- The (postmodern?) embrace of the fragment, the broken and failure as a trope for understanding the world and, more particularly, as a driver for art practices. (Bailes 2010)

I want to return to melancholy in a moment and also share with you and our readers a couple of examples of specific ruin projects I have recently encountered.

Carl

Despite our longstanding friendship and philosophical and political interest in the performance of ruins, until now I have declined, for some reason or other, to ask you to respond to a question posed, so profoundly, by Jacques Derrida in the "Exordium" to *Spectres of Marx*: principally, what does it mean "*to learn to live finally*"? (1994, xvii–viii; italics in original). That is to say, to be worthy of our present and future?[1]

I proffer this question as a theatrical one, since Derrida's book is inspired by Shakespeare's *Hamlet*, or more accurately, the crisis of time provoked by Old Hamlet, the ghost, when he returns to ask for revenge for his murder. "The time is out of joint," Hamlet says.

Simon

Carl, some big questions here and I'm not sure how to answer them in the context of this exchange. Derrida's question, "what does it mean to live well?" probably preoccupies my waking life as a human being who in many respects is an "old fashioned" Socialist, probably a Marxist still over all these years. Over all these years, I've often enjoyed reading Terry Eagleton and particularly what he has to say about the state or condition of "flourishing" (2003, 124–130). How to distil Eagleton's thoughts on this and to offer a pointer on our ruins road map? For Eagleton "flourishing" is neither a private state of interiority, nor the experience of "happiness," but when (and how) we realize our own powers and capacities as human beings. And for me—and Eagleton—we only fulfil our own powers in a relational context—the state in which the flourishing of one individual comes about through the flourishing of others. I'd like to hold on to this, a kind of lodestone for our unfolding ruinous conversation.

Eagleton offers the metaphor of comparing the good and meaningful life to a jazz ensemble. The musicians improvise and do their own thing, but they also are inspired and cooperate with the other members to form a greater whole. My metaphorical landscape might take us into another territory which I know we both enjoy, namely that of team sports such as football or rugby.

---

[1]For more on how we have approached ruins and ruination, see Lavery and Hassall (2015) and Lorimer and Murray (2015).

But what does all this have to do with ruin and ruination, Carl? Perhaps you are inviting us into a kind of existential acceptance that ruination is a condition of living and one that possibly transcends all the normal parameters and "usual suspects" of class, culture, race, gender, identity and so on. Perhaps, you are inviting us to agree that optimism and the projects that it might generate have to build upon a base of inevitable ruination and that this condition can—and I would wish to stress conditionality here—be a force field for affirmation and regeneration. You ask, "Can the ruin … disclose alternative possibilities for living differently on the earth"? I struggle to deal with this conceptually, but want—as I always do—to anchor any response into micro- and concrete practices—for living, for art-making, for education and so on.

I think part of my answer is to sidle up to ruins as vital things, inviting emotional, intellectual and sensual responses. I want to discover what their broken materiality offers, what questions they pose and what kind of thinking they invite. My research and fieldwork in Glasgow, in Mostar, in Athens and in Sicily has led me to some remarkable encounters with such practices and I will explore and share one or two of these in a minute.

Carl

From my perspective, a successful attempt at dealing with ruination was Andy Goldsworthy's piece *Stonehouse Bonnington*, installed at Jupiter Artland on the outskirts of Edinburgh—a location that looks directly on to the airport, on the one side, and, on the other, the extraordinary land-formation known as the Bings: huge red outcrops of deposited slag, from a relatively short-lived period of oil shale mining in West Lothian that ran from the end of the nineteenth century until 1962. The Bings are now valuable ecological sites in themselves, full of rare grasses, plants, mosses, ferns, an example, perhaps, of how to point beyond the ruin, to find ways of living in and with dereliction. As Anna Lowenhaupt Tsing points out in *The Mushroom at the End of the World: On the Possibility of Life in Capitalist Ruins*:

> Global landscapes today are strewn with this kind of ruin. Still, these places can be lively despite announcements of their death; abandoned asset fields sometimes yield new multispecies and multicultural life. In a global state of precarity, we don't have choices other than looking for life in this ruin. (2015, 6)

I had not expected to like Goldsworthy's piece. I had seen much of it documented as photographic images in glossy coffee-table books, and it had often left me cold: yet another example of nature being mobilized in capital's pursuit to sell everything. But actually going to the work itself, experiencing it bodily and attending to it, produced a reaction that has left me dumb-founded, puzzled and full of thought. The work exists as a problem for me, an enigma that I cannot get to the bottom of.

The piece itself is very simple, an example, maybe, of what Gilles Deleuze and Félix Guattari in their chapter on "The Refrain" in *A Thousand Plateaus* call "cosmic art," "sober composition," art that resonates and takes off, de-stratifying, pointing to some essential groundlessness, a "freeing of the molecular" (1987, 344–347). In keeping with its title, the sculpture is a simple stone brick cottage, like the ones that are scattered throughout so much of the western regions of the UK. Places that were once industrialized sites, full of people and machines, and now left abandoned and designated as nature reserves, landscapes for the eye, sites of consolation for stressed-out city dwellers and their families.

Although Goldsworthy's cottage is not in full disrepair—the roof is still on it, for instance, and the brickwork remains solid—there are no window frames, and the doorway is without door, exposing the darkness of the interior, beckoning you in. And, as you accept the invitation to cross the threshold, to enter the house, you lose your footing a little, and perhaps, like me, your equilibrium. I would say I was de-territorialized, shocked, left flabbergasted. For the cottage, has no floor, no flat surface that would conceal the very thing on which the house, the home, the *oikos*, is built: earth.

Rather what we experience, as we enter the dark dwelling, is an uneven surface, full of compacted, smoothed boulders that are folded and twisted in on themselves, as if they had come together in a series of violent collisions, a kind of primordial earthquake, naked geology, an inhumaness that came before us and points beyond us. Something implacable, and ultimately something whose depth is always on the surface.

The strangeness of the encounter is found, then, in the ruination of the foundations of the building. As with Martin Heidegger's essay "The Origin of the Work of Art," the cottage disclosed a fundamental rift between what he calls "world"—the place of the human, of the Open—and "earth," the opaque secret that reveals itself only by concealing itself (2002, 32–38); the thing that remains obscure, and that, for all its bulk and density, is effectively ungrounded, as invisible and light as air. What I am struggling to convey here, Simon, is the sense in which Goldsworthy's built, even "fake" ruin produces a curious type of thinking by revealing a limit to thought, a borderline that one cannot transcend. To encounter the earth at the very heart of the *oikos*—this house—is to trouble what ecology is, to position it as a form of radical thinking (in the proper etymology of that word as radix, root) that sends the subject on a difficult journey on which we are asked to confront our own disappearance. The ruin does that by "unconcealing" (2002, 19) an earth that our immersion in everyday tasks obscures and veils. To use Heideggerian language again, the ruin, in its uselessness, its obsolescence, its lack of "equipmentality" (2002, 12) undoes the reliability of the world. It de-frames, permitting some chaos in. It provokes a noticing, a way of thinking through surfaces, of making connections, of linking things up, a "mechanosphere," Deleuze and Guattari would call it so to circumvent Heidegger's dangerous investment in a decidedly naturalized concept of nature (Deleuze and Guattari 1987, 514). For whereas Heidegger seems to posit "nature" as a kind of primordial essence, a oneness that we may be able to return to, Deleuze and Guattari contend that "nature" is always shot through with culture. For them, there is no such thing as a "natural" disaster; everything is related, mixed up, a matter of machines plugging into each other and mutating in the process.

So in Goldsworthy's case, I drift from the rock, to the cottage, to the *oikos*, to the Bing, to coal, before colliding with the industrial revolution, the steam engine, to James Watt, to capital, to the ruin—an assemblage of noticing. This noticing, this transversal thinking of surfaces, is very different from the type of noticing that Tsing wants us to take. Tsing is looking for a new-found curiosity, a kind of redemptive enchantment that would take us beyond the ruin. For Tsing, "to find pleasures amidst the terrors of indeterminacy" is dependent on a mode of perception that seeks "to bring back curiosity" (2015, 1, 6). Writing about the pleasure affordances discovered via foraging for the Matsutake mushroom, Tsing concludes: "Unencumbered by the simplifications of progress narratives, the knots and pulses of patchiness are there to explore. Matsutake are a place to begin: however much I learn they take me by surprise" (2015, 6).

The noticing that Goldsworthy's ruin provokes, by contrast, is more disturbing. It keeps us in proximity to the ruin, perhaps suggesting that ruination comes first. This is a type of "ruin thinking" that refutes all transcendence that tethers us to an earth which is always in excess of us, and which cannot be managed or restored. For to notice is not only to pay attention to things, to be a phenomenologist of nature, it is, as the phrase to "hand in one's notice" implies, to make the traumatic realization that things are coming to some kind of an end. How then—and this returns us again to the thinking or philosophy of the ruin—are we to make ourselves worthy of such an ending? Can we affirm it? Can we live it? And what might *become* of it?

Simon

Thinking Like a Ruin Made Concrete: St. Peter's Seminary
Carl, as you know, I always have a strong predisposition to render thought into material practice, to allow practice to speak and problematize thought. I have two examples—amongst the many that I could draw upon—which I think would be generative to share here. And it is with and through concrete that I want to start because it is this material, or equally this *medium*, which dominates both sites. Frank Lloyd Wright called it a "mongrel material" (Forty 2012, 10). And I like that, particularly because I have always delighted in claiming theatre as a mongrel art from. Let me first take the case of St. Peter's seminary (Fig. 15.1), very close to our Glasgow home. I know too that we have had some disagreements on how this strange and ambitious project is unfolding.

For our purposes, St. Peter's seminary has two key points of departure, and, perversely perhaps I will begin with the second in 2010 when a group of academics, artists, writers, architects and landscape architects assembled by a Scottish public art organization, NVA (*nacionale vita-activa*, meaning the right to influence public affairs) gathered in Venice during the 12th Architectural Biennale to discuss the historical background of and future potential for this ruined site at Cardross on the mouth of the River Clyde near Glasgow. The various participants in this seminar had perhaps one key feature in common and that was a critical stance towards much of the conventional wisdom and practices of the "heritage industry": how to let the ruin of St. Peter's Seminary have its say.

The NVA's perspective and aspiration is encapsulated in this statement:

Fig. 15.1   St. Peter's Seminary, Cardross. August 2017. Simon Murray

Our vision accepts loss and ruination as part of the history of the place.
The imaginative re-use of this great modernist structure reflects the same
social dynamism and ambition with which it was conceived: a spirit of
working to improve things and imagining a better world. Rather than rub-
bing off the hard edges to create a polished version of the past, the intention is to preserve a raw sense of otherness, excitement and revelation.
(NVA website)

So, what is this beast that so exercised and excited NVA-curated group
during its Venice deliberations? In 1959, Glasgow architects, Gillespie,
Kidd and Coia were commissioned by the Roman Catholic Church in
the Archdiocese of Glasgow to build a seminary to train approximately
100 novice priests. Led by architects Isi Metzstein and Andy MacMillan,
the buildings were eventually completed in 1966 and the seminary
remained functioning until 1980 when it closed as a result of changing
priorities by the Second Vatican Council which decided that the training

of young priests should henceforward take place in urban areas. From 1983, the church briefly used the buildings as a drug rehabilitation centre, but it was finally closed in 1987. In 1993, St. Peter's was listed by the Scottish Office as a "Category A" building of special importance. Why so?

The shortness of its life and ensuing rapid ruination has given what some claim to be Scotland's greatest modernist building a particular cachet of intrigue, romance and the uncanny in this brutally derelict building in the woods above the River Clyde. Reel forward to 2017 and NVA has raised considerable amounts of money to make the building safe and first welcomed paying visitors to an event signed as "Hinterland" in March 2016. Debate continues whether *Hinterland* was a largely empty spectacle of lasered light and ambient sound, or the first steps in a transformation of this brutalist ruin into "a field station for a wilfully experimental, environmentally aware culture..." (Lorimer and Murray 2015, 66). Whilst not totally seduced by *Hinterland* I felt very prepared to see it in the context of a publicity and awareness-raising exercise, an initial invitation—a creative catalyst—to a West of Scotland public to make a secular pilgrimage to this originally faith-full site.

I am attracted to the NVA St. Peter's project perhaps less around the art and performance projects that it may or may not enable over the forthcoming years, but much more for its potential as a site for research, for learning, for experiment—a commons which welcomes and helps to create "active protagonists." The phrase "active protagonist" is one coined by my Glasgow University geographer colleague, Hayden Lorimer who actively participates in "The Invisible College," an organization set up by NVA to frame and organize research, environmental and educational projects at St. Peter's. An institution without walls, "The Invisible College," first imagined and established by seventeenth-century scientist and philosopher, Robert Boyle, was dedicated to furthering knowledge through experimental investigation. I like the idea of reinventing Boyle for the twenty-first century. St. Peter's is a big and ambitious project in its own geographical and social context, but a tiny one in the whole scheme of things. The St. Peter's undertaking deserves healthy and generously critical debate, but I remain engaged with its aspirations, particularly in so far as they continue to test this "field station" for its future functionality, whilst embedding principles and practices of sociality and sociability into the weave of every project it develops.

Let me conclude this short section, Carl, with the proposition that "thinking like a ruin" might suggest some generative questions we might pose to St. Peter's and the "Invisible College":

- How will the ruin of St. Peter's keep performing itself?
- What further "texts" or scripts for action does St. Peter's offer?
- How do we ruin-goers perform in this space?
- How do bodies circulate and move in this space?
- What does moving around St. Peter's do to our bodies, our thoughts and our feelings?

Postscript: June 2018
Eight months on from delivering our paper to the Athens conference, it was announced (5 June 2018) that NVA was to close and with it the ambitions and plans for St. Peter's Seminary. NVA stated that despite huge success in fundraising for work on St. Peter's, it had been unable to secure the level of funding which would have allowed the project to continue. Of course, these Socratic or rhetorical questions I pose above to St. Peter's may now suggest different answers. Nonetheless, this interrogative method to reveal the life and the force fields within sites of ruins remains, I would argue, a productive and generative approach or angle of incidence.

Carl

Sunday 1 October 2017. Gare du Midi. Brussels
The morning after in the city in the heart of darkness. Europe. The time of the ruin. The time when the show I saw last night in the Kaai Theatre, Brussels—Kris Verdonck's *Conversations at the End of the World* (2017)—is reverberating somehow within me, a series of fragments, images that illuminate and radiate when they return, as they will do for a while, into my consciousness as embers, before dissipating into some bedrock of memory, my earth.

As with much of Verdonck's work, *Conversations at the End of the World*, as its title suggests, is about how things come to an end. This is how the dramaturge Kristof van Baarle describes the piece in his programme notes. He cites the Italian Deleuzian, Franco Berardi: "A world ends when it is no longer possible for its inhabitants to describe, influence or make sense of the things and events that surround them through language" (Van Baarle 2017, n.p.). Verdonck's piece is extraordinary—a devised performance, made from the short absurdist texts of the Russian Futurist writer Daniil Charms (1905–1942), who formed the avant-garde Uberiu collective in Leningrad/St. Petersburg in the 1930s. One of the maxims of the group was to give free range to the imagination, permitting it to affirm everything. Nothing was to be negated, no matter how preposterous, and the most whimsical of propositions were explored and debated with the utmost seriousness.

The piece is about ruins. Not just because Charm's writing is based on small chards of text, mere anecdotes that hang together on some fragile, phantom line, or even because it gestures towards a world that is running out of energy, entropically declining like some of the earth sculptures made by land artists Robert Smithson and Nancy Holt. The ruination of the piece starts at the origin. For Charm's texts are haunted by and written in the ruins of Leningrad, a city that underwent the longest and most destructive siege in history from November 1941 to January 1944. Over one million people died at Leningrad, most of them from extreme starvation, especially during the winter of 1942 when things reached their lowest ebb, and more than 2000 people were arrested for acts of cannibalism as bodies littered the streets of the bombed out city. Hitler had no interest in occupying Leningrad. He simply wanted it destroyed, wiped off the map, a city ground to dust.

In Verdonck's piece, none of this is shown or represented directly, even if the stories told certainly allude to it. Rather, the piece creates what we might call an affect or atmosphere of ruination, something that extrudes like a faint mist from the objects and bodies that populate the space and give off what Gernot Böhme terms the "ecstasy of things" (1993, 120): a kind of radiation, the materiality of every iconic sign, its terrestrialism.

The German playwright Heiner Müller once said that theatre is the art closest to ruination, the one most intimate with decay and decline (Müller qtd. in Lehmann 2006, 167). This is because, for Müller, to watch a performer live is to experience the death of a person in action, to see them subjected to the forces of time, the temporalizing play of a cosmic earth, a planet bound up with violent forces that criss-cross and excoriate it and which even theatre, supposedly the most human of all forms, is unable to withstand.

In Verdonck's performance, as with Beckett's work, particularly perhaps *Endgame* and *Happy Days*, nothing really happens. The *agon* of theatre, the thing that provides dramatic conflict, the device that acts as a motor for narrative, has been abandoned, rendered obsolete. What we are left with are five actors, four men, and a single woman, who stand in great dunes of grey snow that falls all around them in increasingly thick cascades. Until, at the end of the piece, when they have run out of stories, and put on in-human dada-like masks, they decide, without histrionics, to simply lose themselves in the snow that now stands in great dunes in front of us. The actors are at various stages of middle age and are elegantly dressed in evening wear, with flowers in their button holes. At the very edge of the stage, there is a grand piano that one of them— the brilliant concert pianist Marino Formenti—plays from time to time, while the others smile and listen. There is a great sense of calm in the piece, but also a kind of helplessness and melancholy that is evoked by the stories, the incessant falling of snow, the beauty of the music and the strange ambivalence transmitted by the face of the actress José Kuijpers.

As the piece continues its two-hour duration, going nowhere, there is a steady decrease in energy, and it feels that we, too, have been subjected to the forces of time, ruined in our seats. There is no anxiety in this ending, this winding down. Rather, as one of the characters says as he recounts the story of Kulakov, we are confronted with a sort of joyful lightness, a pleasure in allowing things—and ourselves—to pass into nothingness, to submit, to go under:

> "I am being buried," Kulakov thought to himself, filling with horror, and suddenly felt a sense of pride, that he, such an insignificant person, was being buried with such pomp, and with such a quantity of flowers.
> Several times I dreamt of dying. As long as death is approaching, it's very scary. But when blood starts to flow out of your veins, dying is easy and not scary any longer.
> I think I dreamt of something even further, of the moment when you are already dead and dissipating in the air. And that too is easy and pleasant … (Verdonck 2017, n.p.)

To sink into the earth, to cross the small stream that separates the living from the dead, is to provide a pedagogy for the Anthropocene, to teach us how to live and die well in ruins, to make us worthy, perhaps, of our fate. Crucially, in this empathy with the performance, in this encounter with an outside, with the earth, there is the possibility that something might happen, a new becoming that is tentative and stuttering and refuses to show itself because it is already here and impossible to destroy. The great irony of *Conversations at the End of the World* is found in how it makes visible an enigmatic thereness, a "this," a "that," a difference that refuses to be destroyed. Not so much the "always already" or the "not yet," but the indestructibility of the "never-ending," a different kind of eternity, perhaps. The beyond the ruin is always in the ruin but nevertheless invisible, a type of "X," a virtuality that refuses to be actualized.

Simon

Gibellina

And so from Belgium to Sicily and to the story of Gibellina (Fig. 15.2), an extraordinary meeting point of natural disaster, utopian thinking, mad optimism and the potentially redemptive power of art and architecture. Chronologically and materially, it shares both time and concrete with Glasgow's St. Peter's. At the start of his essay on Gibellina, David Williams quotes John Berger: "What is the relation of the dead to what has not yet happened, to the future? All the future is the construction in which their 'imagination' is engaged" (qtd. in Williams 2015, 39). Our story of the fourteenth-century town of Gibellina begins with the terrible earthquake of 1968, which devastated settlements in the Belice valley of Western Sicily. Over four hundred people died, one hundred of these in Gibellina, and the town was entirely destroyed. For the next fourteen years, many of the surviving inhabitants of Gibellina lived in tented communities on the hillside near the rubbled remains of the town. As the Sicilian state slowly began to plan the reconstruction of these ruined towns on a single unitary site further down the valley, Gibellina's newly elected mayor Ludovico Corrao emerged as the key protagonist in post-earthquake Gibellina. Corrao, a charismatic, tenacious and provocative communist lawyer, began to lobby and organize around an alternative vision for the Nueva Gibellina. As David Williams says:

Fig. 15.2   Gibellina. Pietro Consagra's unfinished Teatro Nova. October 2017. Simon Murray

> Corrao conceived of the new Gibellina as a garden-city, open to the fields in the surrounding countryside, with art and culture as the generative foundation and "redemptive" catalyst for elaborating new histories and civic identities from the purported tabula rasa enforced by disaster and displacement. (2015, 41)

Over the next three decades, Corrao assembled teams of architects and artists to build Nueva Gibellina materially, culturally and spiritually. By all accounts, it was a magnificent and messianic project, but one which often left the citizens of old Gibellina waiting to be rehoused, or already living in the new town, perplexed or hostile.

For nearly two decades from the early 1980s, Nueva Gibellina hosted annual music and performance festivals of huge ambition and scale. Today they are much smaller. Named the *Orestiadi* in homage to Aeschylus's classical narratives of redemption and emergence leading from abject catastrophe into the early flutterings of civic democracy, the festival attracted a roll call of international high-profile artists, composers and theatre makers such as Joseph Beuys, John Cage, Robert Wilson, Phillip Glass, Christo, Dario Fo, Franca Rame, Ariane Mnouchkine and her Theatre du Soleil and many more. Hugely influenced by classical Greek and North African culture, the *Orestiadi* in the 1980s presented immensely ambitious and large-scale productions by Aeschylus, Sophocles and Hölderlin, for example, and was very much marked as one of the most adventurous events of the European festival circuit during those times. Meanwhile, almost four hundred works of public art were imagined and began to be constructed within and beyond the butterfly structure of the new town, perhaps the most staggering of which is Alberto Burri's *Il Grande Cretto* (the large crack) covering the site of the old, earthquake-ravaged town. Conceived as a "labyrinth of memory" *Il Cretto* has never been fully finished and is now falling into disrepair. For some, *Il Cretto* with its blanket covering of the destroyed remains of old Gibellina, rather than creating a poignant memorial, has instead silenced and erased those memories.

My account of Nuova Gibellina is sparse and partial. I spent four days there in October 2017, beginning to embody its rhythms, marvelling at its insane ambition, feeling its tangible sense of hope, trying to understand its moods and observing how this project constructed out of ruination is now—in parts—becoming ruin again: massive building projects such as Pietro Consagra's Teatro, unfinished as both money and passion became exhausted. Ludovico Corrao himself died in 2011.

Nuova Gibellina and *Il Cretto* seemed to me to be sites of puzzling but energizing contradiction, with all the complex ambiguities associated with projects that claim or aspire to be "redemptive" in both principle and practice. Interestingly, the recent NVA publication on St. Peter's Seminary is subtitled "Birth, death and renewal" (Watters 2016). Despite its theological history, NVA does not speak the language of "redemption" for its activities in St. Peter's, but "renewal" is an aspiration common to both projects. Nuova Gibellina, born out of catastrophe, has been driven by the energy and vision of Corrao and the many artists and architects whom he enlisted to realize the ambitions of the project. For Corrao, art, performance and architectural design were not superfluous adornments to a new life, but the very foundation for an emerging civic identity and sense of place. As Corrao's vision and plans gradually materialized, they became a focus for highly charged debates around the social responsibilities of the architect and planner, and the form and function of urban design and renewal. For some, Nuova Gibellina represents "the cemetery of the avant garde" (Antonio Stella qtd. in Williams 2015, 42). For others, Corrao's failure, or unwillingness to engage with the dispossessed camp dwellers of old Gibellina, in either the built design of their new urban environment or in the programming of multiple art projects and festivals, has been an unforgivable error. For some, the imposition of numerous manifestations of contemporary art both on the site of the old town and embedded within the structure of the new felt like an alien approach to memorializing a way of life that had been destroyed, or of framing the material life they were soon to be leading within the manifest visions of Burri, Consagra and Corrao. For Gibellina researcher and dramaturg, David Williams, although these contradictions remain unresolved and—probably—unresolvable, the ruin is not yet ruined. He writes:

> For all its continuing problems ... its unfinished structures and art works urgently in need of restoration, and for all of its haunting melancholy at times, in reality Nuova Gibellina today is far from the state of "ruinous abandonment" that initial impressions and fleeting contact may suggest. ... I have become increasingly attached to ... this town ... for the warmth of human exchanges it affords, and for its moments of startling layered beauty in the everyday. Perhaps above all, for the enduring possibilities it still seems to contain, somehow and despite everything, as an ambiguous, provisional, slowly unfolding work in progress ... (Williams 2015, 49)

Carl, I would like to finish with a proposition which I might call "the reclaiming of melancholy." I have recently returned to a writer we both respect and admire, namely W. G. (Max) Sebald, and he has helped me to think further around the dangers and possibilities of sentimentalizing the ruin, of embracing ruin melancholia and loss. Let me begin—provocatively perhaps—by again quoting Raymond Williams, who in his book *The Country and the City* writes, "Nostalgia, it can be said, is universal and persistent; only other men's nostalgias offend" (1993, 12). In October 2017, in fact on my way to Sicily to visit Nuova Gibellina with our mutual friend, David Williams, I stopped by at a small exhibition in London called "Melancholia: A Sebald Variation" (Sebald 2017). Always eager to encounter new inflections on Sebald's extraordinary body of work, I was particularly keen to find connections between this exhibition and my wider preoccupations with the ruin. The programme informs us that the exhibition "traces a Sebaldian path from the ruins of 1945 to the present day" (Sebald 2017, n.p.). Taking a cue from Dürer's famous image *Melencolia 1* and from the ruins of post second-world war Europe, the exhibition invites us to embrace melancholy, indeed to celebrate a melancholic disposition, in a generative and creative light. In his 1997 Zurich lectures entitled "On the Natural history of Destruction," Sebald writes:

> Melancholy, the rethinking of the disaster we are in, shares nothing with the desire for death. It is a form of a resistance. And this is emphatically so on the level of art, where its function is far from merely reactive or reactionary. When, with a fixed gaze, melancholy again reconsiders just how things could have gone this far, it becomes clear that the dynamic of inconsolability and of knowledge are identical in function. In the description of the disaster lies the possibility of overcoming it. (2017, n.p.)

I find this helpful since, contrary to Freud's perspective on melancholy (2005) which was to see it as an indulgent and unproductive form of mourning, I think it returns us to "structures of feeling" with a momentary emphasis more on feeling than on structure. I do think that variations around melancholy and loss begin to explain popular fascination and obsession with ruin. And, of course, this is complex and multiple. Here senses of loss may all too easily bleed into the apparently edgy, but ultimately safe thrill of the spectacle. At a profound and usually subconscious level, however, the ruin plays inexorably with our own mortality.

Carl

Simon, there are, as we had perhaps expected but could not predict before we started this dialogue, a number of convergences and divergences. We both want to join the ruin to a type of thinking that would be ethical and political, to see ruins as possessing a possibility for forms of resistance, ways of becoming other, of abandoning the present, remaining true to their evental charge. But as with the cracks that undo Burri's eponymously named sculpture *Il Cretto*, there are fault lines between us, important differences that ought to be acknowledged, as we bring this conversation to some stuttering, botched and, ultimately, artificial end.

I would like to challenge, for instance, what I perceive to be, rightly or wrongly, a form of redemptive and recuperative logic inherent in your ideas of melancholy. For all the power that you grant to melancholy, this "natural history of destruction" (Sebald 2003). I believe that melancholy, as in *Panegyric* (1993) by Guy Debord, is always bound up with a dialectic of abandonment, a kind of hope in despair, an attachment to a lost object that, if returned or rediscovered, would result in the creation of a just world, a world maybe without history, a world even perhaps without ruination. For me, by contrast, there is no melancholy in ruination because I have little interest in restoring anything. Rather I see the ruin somewhat in the vein of the Paris Communards, who showed a brilliant joy in the destruction of imperialist monuments. For them, there was no lost object to recover, just new worlds—a different earth—to create, again and again, and perhaps to infinity. In 1871, there was no desire to return home, no nostalgia, not even of the critical variety that Svetlana Boym is concerned with in her 2001 publication *The Future of Nostalgia*. The Communards did not want one life; they wanted to live a million different lives.[2] I find that temptation appealing, something to affirm, multiplicity not oneness, intensity not recovery. This refusal of melancholy also offers a mode of history that is, perhaps, different to the dialectic one that Raymond Williams adopts. What if things did not always move forward in terms of a triadic movement of dominant, residual and emergent tendencies? Would that leave us with a virtual history, a way of being in time that suggests that nothing has gone because everything remains, percolating away as a type of virtuality to come, a possibility that is still here? This leaves us with a strange ruin, a ruin that would joyfully ruin itself, if and when it ever came to be, because it is aware that every fall of the dice, every actualization, offers new possibilities for existence. Such a ruin would not invest in a single future, some inevitable moment to come; rather, it would simply affirm a becoming, a kind of cosmic inhumanness that would reject the dehumanizations of capital, with its desire to change the status quo in order that everything always remains the same.

---

[2] This phrase has been strongly influenced by Kristin Ross's beautiful concept of abundance, which she terms "communal luxury" (2015, 39–66).

References

Artaud, Antonin. 1992. Pour en finir avec le jugement de Dieu. In *Wireless Imagination: Sound, Radio, and the Avant-garde*, ed. Douglas Kahn and Gregory Whitehead, trans. Clayton Eshleman, 309–329. Cambridge, MA: MIT Press.

Bailes, Sara Jane. 2010. *Performance Theatre and the Politics of Failure*. Basingstoke: Routledge.

Bennett, Jane. 2010. *Vibrant Matter: A Political Ecology of Things*. Durham, NC: Duke University Press.

Böhme, Gernot. 1993. Atmosphere as the Fundamental Concept of a New Aesthetics. *Thesis Eleven* 36: 113–126.

Boym, Svetlana. 2001. *The Future of Nostalgia*. New York: Basic Books.

Debord, Guy. 1993. *Panegyric*. Paris: Gallimard.

Deleuze, Gilles, and Félix Guattari. 1987. *A Thousand Plateaus: Capitalism and Schizophrenia*, trans. Brian Massumi. Minneapolis: University of Minnesota Press.

Derrida, Jacques. 1994. *Spectres of Marx: The State of the Debt, The Work of Mourning & The New International*, trans. Peggy Kamuf. London: Routledge.

Eagleton, Terry. 2003. *After Theory*. New York: Basic Books.

Forty, Adrian. 2012. *Concrete and Culture: A Material History*. London: Reaktion Books.

Freud, Sigmund. 2005. *On Murder, Mourning and Melancholia*. London: Penguin Classics.

Groys, Boris. 2009. Comrades of Time. *E-Flux*, December 11. https://www.e-flux.com/journal/11/61345/comrades-of-time. Accessed 6 June 2018.

Hall, Stuart, and Doreen Massey. 2010. Interpreting the Crisis. *Soundings* 44: 57–71.

Heidegger, Martin. 2002. The Origin of the Work of Art. In *Off the Beaten Track*, ed. and trans. Julian Young and Kenneth Haynes, 1–56. Cambridge: Cambridge University Press.

Knowlson, James. 1996. *Damned to Fame: The Life of Samuel Beckett*. London: Bloomsbury.

Kohn, Eduardo. 2013. *How Forests Think: Towards an Anthropology Beyond the Human*. Berkeley: University of California Press.

Lavery, Carl, and Lee Hassall. 2015. A Future for Hashima: Pornography, Representation and Time. *Performance Research: on Ruins and Ruination* 20: 112–125.

Lehmann, Hans Thies. 2006. *Postdramatic Theatre*, trans. Karen Jürs-Munby. London and New York: Routledge.

Leopold, Aldo. 1968. *A Sand County Almanac*. Oxford: Oxford University Press.

Lorimer, Hayden, and Simon Murray. 2015. The Ruin in Question. *Performance Research: On Ruins and Ruination* 20: 58–66.

Ross, Kristin. 2015. *Communal Luxury: The Political Imaginary of the Paris Commune*. London: Verso.

Scott, James W. 1998. *Seeing Like a State: How Certain Schemes to Improve the Human Condition Have Failed*. New Haven: Yale University Press.

Sebald, W.G. 2003. *On the Natural History of Destruction*. London: Hamish Hamilton.

Sebald, W.G. 2017. *Melancholia: A Sebald Variation*. Exhibition programme (Unpaginated) curated by John-Paul Stonard and Lara Feigel, Inigo Rooms. London: King's College.

Tsing, Anna Lowenhaupt. 2015. *The Mushroom at the End of the World: On the Possibility of Life in Capitalist Ruins*. Princeton: Princeton University Press.

Van Baarle, Kristof. 2017. *Programme Note for Kris Verdonck's Conversations at the End of the World*, unpaginated. Brussels: Kaai Theatre.

Verdonck, Kris. 2017. *Conversations at the End of the World*, unpaginated. Brussels: Kaai Theatre.

Watters, Diane M. 2016. *St. Peter's Cardross: Birth, Death and Renewal*. Edinburgh: Historic Environment Scotland.

Williams, David. 2015. *Terremoto*: Utopia, Memory, and the Unfinished in Sicily. *Performance Research: On Ruins and Ruination* 20: 39–49.

Williams, Raymond. 1977. *Marxism and Literature*. Oxford: Oxford University Press.

Williams, Raymond. 1993. *The Country and the City*. London: The Hogarth Press.

WEB SITE

NVA: St. Peter's. http://nva.org.uk/artwork/kilmahew-st-peters/. Accessed Nov 2017.

CHAPTER 16

Contemporary Ruins, Fragments of the Lives of Others, Critical Intimacies In and Out of Comfort Zones

Apostolos Lampropoulos

In this chapter, I will be walking through contemporary ruins such as empty buildings and abandoned airports. I will also be dealing with fragments of the lives of the numerous others who have recently been in the vicinity of these buildings and of ourselves, leaving behind them material fragments such as musical instruments, toys, bicycles, and clothes, but also snapshots of their faces, voices and odours. I will be doing this in the context of cultural and critical responses triggered by the so-called refugee crisis. These responses are numerous: one can think of initiatives such as the International Cities of Refuge Network (ICORN 2019) which, as explained on the homepage of its website, has been conceived of as "an independent organization of cities and regions offering shelter to writers and artists at risk," or initiatives undertaken by institutional actors such as curators, galleries and museums, but also grass-roots initiatives. The crisis has embedded itself, leaving an ongoing mark, in such diverse initiatives, often above and beyond their conflicting positions

A. Lampropoulos (✉)
University Bordeaux Montaigne, Bordeaux, France

© The Author(s) 2019
E. Mitsi et al. (eds.), *Ruins in the Literary and Cultural Imagination*,
https://doi.org/10.1007/978-3-030-26905-0_16

vis-à-vis the content, the means, and the goals of literary and artistic production. The 2016 Venice Architecture Biennale, for instance, was entitled *Reporting from the Front*, while an exhibition entitled *Insecurities: Tracing Displacement and Shelter* was held at the Museum of Modern Art of New York between October 2016 and January 2017.

Such responses exemplify crucial ideological and social issues that contemporary literature, art and criticism are supposed to tackle. In a similar way, the city of Athens has recently been seen in at least three different ways: firstly, as one of the loci of a multifaceted crisis and of a heated theoretical, ideological and political debate, "the new disaster site on the global capital empire map" (Dimitrakaki 2017, 136); secondly, as the centre of a territory which has resurfaced as one of the liminal spaces of Europe, a key node for refugees seeking a new home; thirdly, as the capital city of a country in which hospitality is considered a national virtue stemming from the figure of "Hospitable Zeus." To a certain extent, all of the above have generated an effervescent art scene and explain why *documenta* (one of the world's largest contemporary art exhibitions, which has taken place in Kassel, Germany, since 1955) decided to expand and include the city of Athens in 2017 for its fourteenth edition under the working title "Learning from Athens."

If the literary and cultural responses to the refugee crisis bring ongoing traumatic experiences closer to a Western public, they also keep these experiences in the relatively safe zone of literary and cultural activity. This is one of the reasons why such responses are said to spectacularize or exoticize the crisis. While this approach is to some extent legitimate, I think it is nevertheless insufficient. Some decades ago, famines or massacres in Africa were imported into art mainly as reconstructions of monstrous disasters which can only be deplored from a distance; one of the most well-known examples is Alfredo Jaar's *Untitled (Newsweek)* (1995), a sequence of seventeen covers of the magazine, dating from April 1994, when the Rwanda genocide began, until 1 August 1994, seventeen weeks later, when *Newsweek* magazine first put Rwanda on its cover. Nowadays, responses to the refugee crisis are often conceived of and composed in a significantly different way: from live testimonies at various events, to clothes, shoes, notepads, photographs or lifejackets which are used as raw material for installations and other forms of political art. They all speak to current forms of activism, not only *reported* from the front (as the Venice Biennial would designate it) in the form of various textual or visual representations, but literally *imported* from it as material fragments of people's ruined lives. Issues of "situatedness, displacement, and emplacement, practices that produce and constrain human intelligibility" are at stake in this trend, essentially because such practices address "dispossessed subjectivities" as well as the conditions of their "assigned disposability" (Butler and Athanasiou 2013, 18–21). Not surprisingly, this same trend problematizes a number of notions that are central to current critical debates: materiality and corporeality; liveability and empathy with hardly saved or lost lives; survival and afterlife; and, of course, hospitality. Survival and afterlife bring to the fore the inevitable oscillation between the two meanings developed by Derrida: "to be still fully alive" or "to live beyond death," and "we are all survivors who have been granted a temporary reprieve" (2007, 24–25). Hospitality is seen as a calculation rather than a merely thoughtless impulse (Brugère and Le Blanc 2017, 195), given that refugees are most often seen, spoken of and heard by non-refugees from positions that are hardly comparable to, or totally incommensurable with, the experience of the refugees themselves.

I will allow myself an additional remark here. Contemporary art, and especially public or satellite programs of art events, have become major sites of a politico-intellectual debate at the crossroads of several political, social, artistic, cultural, anthropological theories. I am inclined to call this phenomenon the "exhibition turn of theory," or perhaps the "curated theory effect," but I will confine myself to recalling the ever-growing intertwinement of contemporary art, theory and activism. Derrida and Dufourmentelle's *Of Hospitality*, published in 1994 as a response to the French debate regarding undocumented immigrants, is very important in this context. In this dialogical essay, Derrida builds on traditional definitions of hospitality, such as receiving, opening one's door, making space for the guest in one's home. He sees conditional hospitality in most kinds of current hospitable practices, in hospitality offered to known others, to relatives, to friends and to non-foreigners; he also attaches conditionality to all the practical, ethical and legal intricacies of hospitality. By contrast, unconditional hospitality, impossible yet necessary, concerns the uninvited guest, the arrival of the anonymous foreigner and the duty to receive someone without even asking his/her name. A part of this text was included in documenta 14's *Reader* (the theoretical companion to the exhibition), while further references to unconditional hospitality abound. The same concept has become the implicit model for many forms of hospitality offered by politically radical groups and is regularly discussed in leftist or anarchist contexts.

In my view, unconditional hospitality tends to be evoked a bit too easily, and in some cases, almost ritualistically. This is symptomatic of the fact that, as has been pointed out, "relations of hospitality tend to be represented as immanently unobjectionable" (Fraser 2016, 43), and that "the lack of alternative readings means that hospitality presently falls under a sort of epistemological hegemony" (Fusi 2016, 118). Maja Ćirić has also spoken of an "abuse of hospitality in curating in terms of curatorial geopolitics" (2016, 210). However, I am not implying that the concept of unconditional hospitality should not be translated into a political project. In fact, I strongly believe it should. Nevertheless, I somehow fear that the manner in which it has functioned lately, almost as an umbrella term, might occlude and obscure potential hostilities inherent in both mainstream and alternative hospitality practices (cf. Brown 2015). I also think that the inevitable conditionality of hospitality should not be regarded as an outright failure or as a wordless and shameful compromise. Rather, it should be nuanced, eventually through ruins and fragments, and rethought as the specificity of a Nancean being-with.

In what follows, I depart from Fusi's position that "unless we accept that a condition-less hospitality is … *something* other than hospitality per se, we cannot but fail to resolve the conditionality that hospitality poses" (2016, 119). Walking a thin line, I will tackle the conditionality of hospitality through the notion of intimacy. I will be arguing that the former often amounts to and is translated into the latter, tacitly and unavowedly. If, as Derrida tells us, "all cultures compete … and present themselves as more hospitable than the others" concluding that "hospitality—this is culture itself" (Derrida 2002, 361), it seems pertinent to me to reverse the question and ask *if* and *how* culture (writing, institutions, cultural projects and practices) is, itself, hospitality too. The intimacy I am referring to (and this is an important distinction for what I will be developing here) is not the intimacy *of* someone; it is not about one's secrets or one's undiagnosed depths. It is about the intimacy *with* someone, *between* two or more people, or *between* people and objects. As Jean-Luc Nancy says, "if intimacy must be defined as the extremity of coincidence with oneself, then what exceeds intimacy in interiority is the distancing of coincidence itself" (2000, 11–12). Following this logic of distancing, I see intimacy as a close encounter without fusion; as a reconciliation of positions, intentions and emotions without consensus; as the opening of an in-between space among two or more subjects, a space that is shared by them without belonging to them; as a closeness that is devoid neither of a certain imbalance or inequality, nor of the possibility of a conflict. In that sense, intimacy is proximity with the other (the beloved other or someone belonging to "the axis of the unloved" [Moyo qtd. in Ćirić 2016, 208]), who nevertheless remains other and, possibly, a stranger. If Derrida's unconditional hospitality seeks receiving without any control at the entrance, creating intimacy is putting together a common space of possibilities without the risk of hosting one another.

In my understanding, hospitality and intimacy do not complement each other. Neither do I see intimacy as a concept offering some kind of trampoline from which to leap forward. In fact, I see a tension between the idea of unconditional hospitality and the kind of intimacy I am referring to. I also see such an intimacy as *critical intimacy*. This is not an entirely new term: Mieke Bal (2002) proposed critical intimacy as a pedagogical strategy and as a way of teaching how to read. Then Gayatri Chakravorty Spivak used it in an interview to describe deconstruction, saying that "you can only deconstruct what you love," "because you are doing it from the inside, with real intimacy. You are kind of turning it around" (Paulson 2016). But my understanding here is significantly different: critical intimacy is about remaining critical vis-à-vis the one I am intimate with, making my intimacy the object of my critical attention, reinforcing it through my criticality, as well as about a mutual embracement with the eponymous other despite the divisions and the distances that could have emerged. Critical intimacy cannot be part of a "presumption of progressivism" (Brown 2015): becoming more and more intimate with the stranger—intimate socially, culturally, politically, ideologically, personally—should not be seen as a more advanced phase of conditional hospitality superseding the previous wrongheaded ones and gradually leading one closer to unconditional hospitality. Critical intimacy could be a way to handle conditionality, or even a condition that one could legitimately opt for.

My analysis will be based on four case studies: an open letter concerning documenta 14 and the ways in which urban ruins and empty buildings are inhabited; two artworks by Guillermo Galindo which recompose fragments of objects belonging to refugees; the screening of a short documentary filmed in the ruined refugee camp of Idomeni; and a written testimony from the abandoned old airport of Athens. In none of my four case studies will I be indicting writers, film-makers or artists for not performing a sufficiently good hospitality, or for not using one or the other term in a rigorous way. However, I will try to spell out what I see as the promise of these approaches. To paraphrase Claire Bishop (2013, 62), I will not be going in the direction of a post-hospitality, but I will be anticipating what positive things can happen in its name. This is also why in my four case studies—all placed, as already said, amidst contemporary ruins and fragments of lives—I will be moving from more critical to more optimistic readings.

SQUATS AND GOOGLE MAPS

During the first weeks of documenta 14 in Athens, an open letter penned by an unidentified group called "Artists against evictions" was published on e-flux conversations on the occasion of some alleged evictions of occupied spaces shared by refugees and artists (2017). The evictions were reported by the website *Enough is Enough*, dedicated to "anti-capitalist and anti-fascist actions" (cf. "#Athens #Greece" 2017; Dimitrakaki 2017, 131), but not much is known about the conditions under which the presumed events took place. Nonetheless, the letter is indicative of a broader tendency in the art field today, namely the elective affinities between the work of the artist and the experience of the precarious individual. As the letter states, "we are those voices, we are inclusive [of] all genders, we are migrants, we are modern pariahs, we are the dissidents of the regime and we are here." This statement came as a response to the public program of documenta 14 called "The Parliament of Bodies" (the first phase of which was called "34 Exercises of Freedom") that aimed "to write a queer anticolonial symphony of Europe from the 1960s, scripting dialogue and giving visibility to dissident, heterogeneous, and minor narratives" (documenta 14, "34 Exercises of Freedom"). The letter pointed out a discrepancy between what a major art institution could achieve, namely opening the floor to speaking subjects who often remain unheard, and the fact that the major art institution supposedly remained silent after "raids of buildings housing refugees in the city."

The letter refers to a simultaneous eviction of artists and refugees who were thrown out of the same building as a result of a decision made by the same state and executed by the same police forces. It therefore incites us to consider that these two groups had shared homelessness equally, albeit for a short time. Again, many artists around the world do experience economic and social precarity, and, if many of them are somehow privileged, they are not privileged in the same and equal way (Dimitrakaki 2017, 131). To my eyes, though, this identification cannot easily work, either conceptually or politically, because it is unlikely that activism functions in terms of a common "we" located within the same seamlessly shared locality ("we are here"). "Artists against evictions" (writing in impeccable English and voiced by a very popular website) seem to underestimate that hospitality is neither offered nor received without hierarchy and inequality, without "a certain injustice, and even a certain perjury, [that] begins right away, from the very threshold of the right to hospitality" (Derrida and Dufourmentelle 2000, 55).

I do not merely suggest this for the obvious reason that most artists, in all likelihood, have the option of living in a place other than the squats, while most refugees might not. This dissymmetry is of importance when some noteworthy rhetoric is used. The letter defines "all Documenta 14 Viewers, Participants and Cultural Workers" as its addressees and, immediately after that, it reads: "We call for your attention, in this immediate moment of 'Learning from Athens,' we are the people who inhabit this city and we are talking to you as our guests." In just a few phrases, "Artists against evictions" perform multiple movements: speaking on behalf of the refugees with whom they have been sharing the same roof, as if this were a categorically public and radically ungovernable shelter, or as if the experience of an autonomous and egalitarian space could do nothing other than perfectly succeed. The shared space is supposedly occupied in a manner that protects it from the risk of becoming the property of anyone in particular, and, consequently, it refuses to attribute the role of the host and guest to one or to another party within the group. "Artists against evictions" present themselves as the true owners of the city among all the homeless and the unprivileged, adopting the position of the host vis-à-vis both those who might have been born in Athens and lived there forever, and those who arrived just prior to documenta 14.

Sidestepping these issues, the letter does not seem to provide sufficient answers to the crucial question, namely, whether "intimate ties could be legally, culturally, and affectively recognized but also lived beyond the normative propriety and exclusionary proprietariness," as Butler and Athanasiou put it (2013, 83). Yet despite this, the letter performs a gesture that brings the artists who speak up for the misrepresented closer to the displaced, the expurgated, and the unfrequentable. Still addressing the people of documenta 14, the letter reads:

We walk with you, we tread the parallel streets, but you don't see us—you have your eyes trained on the blue dotted lines of your Google map. You have been programmed and directed not to see us, to just miss us, reverse and avoid us—our culture has been censored from you. We ask you to recalibrate your devices, we ask you to get lost, to hack your automation, and rewire your cultural viewpoint. ("Artists against evictions")

I find the terms in which this part of the statement is written far more enthralling than the agonistic style of the passages that I quoted earlier. It is not so much the imaginary of self-spectralization that matters here, not even what might sound as a quasi-technophobic yet digitally informed call. This call places emphasis on the invisibility, inaudibility, intangibility and overall undetectability of those who will choose or will have to experience an alternative kind of homeliness. And, in fact, it takes everyone out of the squats, i.e. the sites of hospitality. After that shift in vocabulary, as Marie-Ève Morin would say, there is nothing resembling an "originary experience of the home to be defended and protected" (2016, 126). Once the "Artists against evictions" nuance the idea of a supposedly equal partaking of a home with the refugees—which would also be a home foreign to and threatened by the unwelcoming people of documenta14—they open the path for an extended intimacy among the authors, the refugees and the people of the exhibition.

The intimacy that I have in mind here is not between artists outside the framework of cultural institutions and refugees who are suffering an ongoing displacement. Rather the intimacy that I am considering is a critical intimacy based on an awareness of technologies which not only allow localization and suggest shortcuts, but also discourage detours that blind people to what might be happening right next to them. Intimacy will happen among those who stroll like foreigners and remain outsiders. By getting lost, rebooting and re-striating space, one (the "we" in the letter above) can avoid the access points that are too well defined, thus leading to hosting. Moreover, "we are here" does no longer sound threatening, because it might mean that "we" are potentially everywhere, that there are less inaccessible spaces for "us," because there is no fixed cartography and no real hosts among us. As Morin says, "if we are all passers-by, if we always remain withdrawn even in our most intimate encounters, then the immigrant, the refugee, the real stranger, are not other than those who are familiar to us, but only a mode of withdrawn presence among others" (2016, 126).

A Touch of Blood

The Mexican artist Guillermo Galindo who defines himself as an experimental composer, sonic architect, performance artist and Jungian Tarotist (2017) presented a few pieces at the Conservatory of Athens as part of documenta 14 (Hopkins 2017). Two of them were instruments from the series "Exit" (2016–2017). The first set of exhibited pieces included "JD Bug (2017): Kickboard Scooter tube from a refugee camp near Kassel, trumpet cup, brass tube, clarinet modified for oboe reed, rubber band," and the second consisted of a "Sonophagus (2017): wood, metal frame, bed from [a] refugee camp near Kassel, bicycle tubes, blood, coffee, springs, metal chimes, wooden pallets, cloth." This information was available on a long rectangular piece of cloth paper on the floor of the Conservatory, on which a piece of marble with the name of the artist inscribed upon it was placed, functioning as a signature detached from the artwork itself, a paperweight, an allusion to the material of most Greek ruins, and perhaps a simulacrum of a tombstone.

I wonder if Galindo's work is after all another way of channelling the risk that is represented by the foreigner, a danger that has been repeatedly theorized (Nancy 1991, 33–42; 2000, 28–41; Boudou 2017, 61). The works that I mentioned are obviously just two among many similar others that have been well received by curators, critics and the art public. The artist chose fragments of the refugees' experience and, more specifically, material from the place where refugees are received, namely the city of Kassel which is a temporary Western European home to them. Following a clear analogy, Galindo's work performs the expatriation of the refugees, followed by the expatriation of their property—which echoes the expatriation of the exhibition itself. If the small piece of marble with the name of the artist is a personalized miniature tombstone, then the splashes of blood mentioned in the work's description evoke an active distress, using, exporting and making the traces of the corporeal ruins available. At the same time, a number of connections are performed by Galindo's work: first, between Athens and Kassel as two cities hosting documenta 14 *and* refugees; second, between the displacement of refugees *and* of artists from their homeland to a foreign land; third, between the extreme precarity that several lives have undergone *and* the visitation of the objects as remnants of this precarity, therefore between lives in danger and lives safe or saved. In a sense, this kind of work is an interesting, and mostly anodyne exercise in "thanatopolitical intimacy" or an "intimacy-in-disintegration" (Butler and Athanasiou 2013, 124), because it can be read as a call to intimacy aiming to reunite those who have already been victims of contemporary thanatopolitics—refugees— with its potential victims, the spectators.

These links are based on a fundamental asymmetry between the connected parts, an asymmetry which could undermine the ethical and political legitimacy of the project, if the latter does not look scandalous already. I think that this type of work and curatorial choice takes for granted what it should be questioning: the very possibility of speaking on behalf of the refugees, the conditions and the limits of a non-refugee's responsiveness to the refugees' call, as well as the possibility of contact or exchange (let me repeat here that intimacy with a stranger maintains his/her status as stranger). Such an approach to an extremely delicate issue puts an experience on display as if it were photographable. The experience itself, however, remains hardly representable (Cohen-Levinas 2017, 198),[1] drawing a connection between two positions— that of the refugee, on the one hand, and of the nomad art crowd, on the other—which to a large extent remain unbridgeable, as if they were interchangeable or, at least, comparable. What is more, at first glance there seems to be nothing shocking about this type of art promoted by avant-garde curators and awaited by the contemporary art public.

To offer a more positive reading of the asymmetrical intimacy in Galindo's piece, I could interpret it as asking for the kind of forgiveness that one must ask from the one who is welcomed, namely forgiveness "for one's lack of preparation, for an irreducible and a constitutive unpreparedness" (Derrida 2002, 380–381). Who should not ask for forgiveness for doing no more than hosting a scooter tube or a wooden pallet within a piece of art? If this is true, then no hospitality, unconditional or not, can be seriously considered here. On the contrary, I would tend to think that a hesitant yet developing critical intimacy might be envisaged. I also prefer to think that Galindo's work asks, in the most direct manner possible, questions such as the following: what kind of intimacy can we possibly share with the refugees in the context of contemporary art; who is becoming intimate with whom and what are the limits of this intimacy; in what ways can intimacy, forged through the exhibition of objects, contribute to a rethinking of hospitality? In a sense,

---

[1]The "unrepresentability" of the tragedy of displacement described here is commensurate with the indescribability of the Holocaust, discussed by Angeliki Tseti in Chapter 13.

Galindo's work takes into account the two steps that Morin describes as essential for composing a new world: the first "consists in taking stock of the entities, human and non-human, that are to be assembled," while the second "consists in figuring out whether we can cohabit together or not" (2015, 36). Morin recognizes that there is no pre-given in this and concludes by saying that "the collective remains fragile, always in the process of exploration and experimentation" (2015, 37).

A pale stain of blood on an artwork—the unrecognized yet acknowledged blood of the unknown and the anonymous—points to a whole range of afterlives that should find their space in an exhibition. Galindo's work is an incomplete task, the first potentially controversial act of critical intimacy with those represented or alluded to. If, as Fœssel says, "the tendency to neutralize intimacy is deeply anti-democratic" (2008, 141), then the critical intimacy that emerged from my second reading of Galindo's work is more likely to lead to a democracy-to-come (Derrida 2005, 78–94) than the first official and institutional reading of the same work as an accomplished act of hospitality. Developing a critical intimacy which is indissociable from an embarrassment before the fragments of human lives in ruins, Galindo's pieces remind us that, as Derrida says in *Acts of Religion*, "no forgiveness is reducible to an act of memory" (2002, 382).

Screening of a Home

On 8 April 2017, the first screening of the documentary *Feeling of a Home* by Io Chaviara and Michalis Kastanidis took place at the Astor cinema in the centre of Athens. The documentary was made in Idomeni, a small village on the border between Greece and North Macedonia, where one of the biggest refugee settlements of the last few years was put together: on the chasm between one of the last places in which refugees were somehow received—albeit under abominable conditions—and fortress Europe. After the screening, refugees who had spent a substantial amount of time in Idomeni were invited by the directors for a discussion with the public. Given that refugees are often present at events such as performances, screenings and debates, what happened at the Astor movie theatre was not necessarily original. But their physical presence pointed to—and perhaps concealed—the huge number of refugees who remained voiceless and all those who have been deprived of their lives, functioning as a salute: a farewell, a greeting, and salvation at the same time

(Butler and Athanasiou 2013, 49). If *Feeling of a Home* was the title of the documentary, the event actually meant to *host* some refugees. The dialogue among the refugees who were present (also standing in for the absent and the dead), the film-makers and the audience occurred in a space which was a proper home to nobody.

I suspect that intimacies developed in several if not all the relational vectors between the participants. All of this felt as though it happened all too late, because the desire for this encounter could not have sufficed to attract more people there, or to keep some more alive, or to last longer. The fleetingness of that moment of intimacy became clear upon all parties' arrival at the encounter, that precise moment which was, as Derrida suggests, "contracted into a sort of absolute halt or haste—this is a necessity that cannot be outsmarted any more: it explains why one always feels late, and that therefore, at the same time, one always yields to participation" (2000, 127). The hosts in this case did indeed say to their guests, "'Enter quickly,' quickly, in other words, without delay and without waiting … hurry up and come in" (2000, 123). Their hospitality, as every hospitality, should have been offered and accepted earlier because it occurred in the aftermath of the loss of lives; and when the hosts and the guests were given an appointment at the movie theatre, no one could be truly on time.

It is precisely around this belated, or almost failed, and in any case very short hospitality that intimacy developed. This happened insofar as all the participants shared a language, varying from basic English to a humanitarian discourse, to the mutual expression of a proximity, to different performances of affect, to promises of substantial solidarity such as open invitations to homes and calls for spontaneous fundraising. Sharing the common, hybrid, imperfect language that was spoken on this occasion, failing to realize hospitality but still performing it, the hosts shared an intimacy with their guests through a spacing which separated one from the other. I see this intimacy as a critical one, because it was an intimacy of belatedness (articulated around the exclamation "what have these people gone through!") and an intimacy of brevity (articulated around the question "where are they going now?"), even if no satisfactory answers were provided. It was not the critical intimacy of total powerlessness, but that of insufficient action, making conversation with those who, for a little while, were slightly less voiceless.

Odours by the Sea

Over the last two years, there has been a heated debate over the fate of the old Elliniko airport of Athens, abandoned since 2001, yet located in a coastal zone that can allegedly become one of the most expensive residential areas of Europe. The debate has touched upon the future of the derelict main building of the old airport (another contemporary ruin), a specimen of modernist architecture designed by the Finnish-American Eero Saarinen—and often described as a modern monument—and more recently, upon the archaeological importance of another part of the same area. For several months, these spaces were transformed into an improvised refugee settlement with rudimentary facilities. The biopolitics of the new ruins and the urgency of hosting are the basic elements surrounding the text "Long Lasting Days" published online in 2017 by Mina Karavanta, a scholar working on postcolonialism and democracy, and resident of the broader area of Elliniko. Here is a passage:

> These days in Athens, my days last long. I think about my courses at the university, my students' inquisitive eyes when, while contemplating the meaning of democracy in the present, we try to respond to a photograph of immigrants washed up on the Mediterranean shores; wrapped in thermal blankets, [s]aved but unreal, present but hidden from the lens, these human bundles shimmering in the metallic color of their wraps look like extra-terrestrial waste washed ashore. My mind takes flight to my father's deathbed in the public hospital, how he is too sick to await any other redemption but death … I need some fresh air before my nostrils fill up with the hospital's odours, dirty sweat, urine, decaying flesh … My sea route and the comfort it has offered me over the years … have changed … I gasp for air but I can smell human odours mixed with the familiar scents of the sea; the pungency of sulfur is overcome by sweat, urine and musty clothes. I turn to the sea to make sure I am not dreaming, I am there, I am not in the hospital, and I see their blankets and sheets laid out to dry in the sun. The barbed wire that fences the coast to protect it from the busy highway looks like a long clothes line stretching from one side of the coast to the other covered with blankets, sheets, scarves, clothes, and all kinds of rugs. Early in the morning, the pensioners who live nearby and cannot afford the longer ride to quieter beaches down the coastline, take their swim next to men, women and children who wash their clothes and take their morning baths. (Karavanta 2017)

This captivating narrative brings into sharp relief the relation between a deserted airport and a wrecked hospital, in other words an improvised hospitality that hardly deserves its name, on the one hand, and "a dispositive of care which acknowledges the imperative of reception and of protection" (Brugère and Le Blanc 2017, 201; my translation), on the other. Karavanta experiences the vulnerable bodies, the familiar and the unfamiliar ones, as a "turbulent performative occasion" (Butler and Athanasiou 2013, 179) for her senses and intellect. Squeezed between them, she is bound to face their countability and their "regimes of management" (Butler and Athanasiou 2013, 100), which are also two different regimes of hospitality. She is overtly addressing the fact that she is on the relatively safe side of this encounter, something that was not always obvious in the three previous cases I studied here. And she is struggling with a number of distinctions that are difficult to maintain: between the eponymous intimacy with the close relative (the one who has still access to some hospital thus to the care of hospitality), the quasi-eponymous intimacy with the local pensioners (the look-alikes of her father who can bathe for the joy of bathing), and an anonymous intimacy with the refugees (the too numerous and hospitalless ones, the less cared-for, those who bathe in order to wash).

These regular crossings striate an empty airport, that is to say a spectral space that was once dedicated to scheduled arrivals and departures, and was hence marked by the controlled flows of modernity. The same space today remains somehow open to arrivals but is inept, unprepared and reluctant to accept that, according to Derrida, "allowing to arrive, is not inertia, [but] imposes a demand upon me: 'Prepare for the unexpected, but without anticipating, without trying to see what is coming'" (Morin 2015, 35). Whereas the author was prepared for the uncertain survival of her father, she admits her unpreparedness vis-à-vis the less expected arrival of the refugees and must cope with the even less expected eventuality of their un-reportable deaths. Reflecting upon and teaching the subject of democracy and its limits, impasses and imperatives, she revisits the "extra-terrestrial waste" of the pictures that she discussed with her students. She does so via an image, in a classroom, by virtue of the fact that she is not behind the barbed wire.

In that sense, Karavanta assumes, and as Derrida says, "we are structurally survivors," all of us, "on the side of the *yes*, on the side of the affirmation of life" (Butler and Athanasiou 2013, 50). At the same time, she is willing to critically address her elective intimacies with some of those survivors (the familiar ones), as well as the conditions of the hospitality offered close to her home. She experiences her impossible, or at least unperformed, hospitality through her intimacy with the collective odours of the refugees living on a shore, filtered through the equally collective odours of the hospital where she visits her father. This intimacy is somewhat comparable to that which lies between her and the elderly who share the same sea and beach with those who currently inhabit it, even if this is only temporary. If "intimacy consists in all those links and attachments that constitute and dispossess us: there is no guarantee that we could find ourselves unchanged" (Fœssel 2008, 157). Karavanta is lucid enough to see that the odours, for her, and the sea, for the elderly, are the sites of their shared intimacy with the foreign survivors, or with their upcoming afterlives. These odours, both familiar and repulsive, are precisely what allows intimacy and what prevents her from claiming the role of the host.

Writing on them is what renders this intimacy critical and what makes one realize the limits of both one's own experience of democracy and one's response to the duty of hospitality. Although it does not compensate for it, it is still a way to embrace the grain of the not so extra-terrestrial responsibility that, almost literally, landed in her courtyard. Filtered through theoretical thinking, critical intimacy gives birth to a reflection on the limits of pedagogy, the difficulties of performativity, and the recurrence of one's resistance to one's own ideas. After all, this intimacy is a crucial mode of admitting that the unconditional "yes" of hospitality remains unsaid and pending.

CONCLUSION

As I wrote at the very outset, this essay is an itinerary through contemporary ruins and fragments of people's lives. It is about speaking on behalf of others, exhibiting fragments of the refugees' experience and ruins of human lives, interacting with refugees in secure spaces, and writing on the difficulties of a genuine empathy with them. All this is related to keeping unrepeatable memories alive, forming a political consciousness and breaking with current immigration policies. It is also an affirmation of the always more urgent need for, at least, clusters of hospitality, inclusive spaces which are not, or not yet, subject to restrictive rules. What is at stake in the cases that I have analysed is the atypical bond between those who create art, film or write while remaining within some comfort zone, and those who only scarcely and exceptionally could reach such spaces.

What was at the centre of my concern here is the way in which a popular definition of hospitality (more precisely, its unconditional version) has become either a common currency or the usual subtext for renegotiating and practicing hospitality. It is an attempt to do more than merely remind ourselves of the inescapable conditionality of a purportedly unconditional hospitality and an attempt to elaborate on what a legitimate condition could be. So, I preferred to take a step back and have a closer look at some of the conditions inherent in an act of hospitality which is offered, described or theorized. I chose the concept of intimacy as a way to understand these conditions because, as I explained, intimacy can maintain both proximity with the other, and his/her otherness, strangeness and foreignness. In the cases that I consider in this essay, intimacy is more than mere information on refugees, or building a community with displaced people. It is a grey-zone locatedness, or a close encounter with the *conditionality* of hospitality—an element which risks annulling the very concept of hospitality.

This is why hosting fragments of the lives of others is more about becoming intimate with them, while keeping the memory of the limits of this intimacy, its temporariness and its fragility. Moreover, the intimacy I am advocating here is a critical intimacy. Instead of calling a conditional hospitality "unconditional," and instead of idealizing any act of hosting, critical intimacy turns one's attention towards what remains to be done, as well as towards the power one might be exercising on those one is willing to host, and towards what, despite all effort, remains nevertheless unbridgeable. If I have been critical of a supposedly accomplished hospitality (which after all, could only lead to a self-congratulatory approach to it), I did it for one reason: to show that among contemporary ruins and fragments of the lives of others, critical intimacy emerges as the cautious exercise of moderate political optimism.

References

#Athens #Greece: Cops Attacked Demo Against Evictions of #Squats GR. 2017. https://enoughisenough14.org/2017/03/13/athens-greece-cops-attacked-demo-against-evictions-of-squatsgr/. Accessed 16 Sept 2018.

Artists Against Evictions. 2017. Open Letter to the Viewers, Participants and Cultural Workers of Documenta 14, April 8. http://conversations.e-flux.com/t/open-letter-to-the-viewers-participants-and-cultural-workers-of-documenta-14/6393. Accessed 16 Sept 2018.

Bal, Mieke. 2002. *Travelling Concepts in the Humanities: A Rough Guide.* Toronto: Toronto University Press.

Bishop, Claire. 2013. *Radical Museology, or, What's 'Contemporary' in Museums of Contemporary Art?* With Drawings by Dan Perjovschi. London: Koenig Books.

Boudou, Benjamin. 2017. *Politique de l'hospitalité: Une généalogie conceptuelle* [Politics of Hospitality: A Conceptual Genealogy]. Paris: CNRS.

Brown, Wendy. 2015. Feminist Change and the University, March 6. https://www.youtube.com/watch?v=D2Eop1_T02s. Accessed 16 Sept 2018.

Brugère, Fabienne, and Guillaume Le Blanc. 2017. *La fin de l'hospitalité* [The End of Hospitality]. Paris: Flammarion.

Butler, Judith, and Athena Athanasiou. 2013. *Dispossession: The Performative in the Political.* Cambridge and Malden: Polity.

Chaviara, Io, and Michalis Kastanidis. 2017. *Feeling of a Home.* https://feelingofahome.wordpress.com. Accessed 16 Sept 2018.

Ćirić, Maja. 2016. The (Un)Spoken Abuse: Curatorial Hospitality Through the Lens of Criticality. In *Hospitality: Hosting Relations in Exhibitions,* ed. Beatrice von Bismarck and Benjamin Meyer-Krahmer, 203–212. Berlin: Sternberg Press.

Cohen-Levinas, Danielle. 2017. Une disparition. Plus intime que l'intime, le visage. In *Jean-Luc Nancy. Penser la mutation,* ed. Jérôme Lèbre and Jacob Rogozinski. *Les Cahiers philosophiques de Strasbourg* 42 (2): 185–198.

Derrida, Jacques. 2002. *Acts of Religion.* New York and London: Routledge.

Derrida, Jacques. 2005. *Rogues: Two Essays on Reason,* trans. Pascale-Anne Brault and Michael Naas. Stanford: Stanford University Press.

Derrida, Jacques. 2007. *Learning to Live Finally: The Last Interview by Jean Birnbaum,* trans. Pascale-Anne Brault and Michael Naas. Brooklyn: Melville House.

Derrida, Jacques, and Anne Dufourmentelle. 2000. *Of Hospitality,* trans. Rachel Bowlby. Stanford, CA: Stanford University Press.

Dimitrakaki, Angela. 2017. Hospitality and Hostis: An Essay on Dividing Lines, Divisive Politics and the Art Field. In *Culturescapes Greece/Griechenland— Archaeology of the Future/Archäologie der Zukunft,* ed. Kataryna Botanova and Christos Chryssopoulos, 128–147. Basel: Christoph Merian.

documenta 14. 34 Exercises of Freedom. September 2016. http://www.documenta14.de/en/public-programs/928/34-exercises-of-freedom. Accessed 16 Sept 2018.

Fœssel, Michaël. 2008. *La privation de l'intime* [The Privation of Intimacy]. Paris: Seuil.

Fraser, Andrea. 2016. As If We Came Together to Care. In *Hospitality: Hosting Relations in Exhibitions,* ed. Beatrice von Bismarck and Benjamin Meyer-Krahmer, 37–47. Berlin: Sternberg Press.

Fusi, Lorenzo. 2016. It's the End of Hospitality as We Knew It (And I Feel Fine). In *Hospitality: Hosting Relations in Exhibitions*, ed. Beatrice von Bismarck and Benjamin Meyer-Krahmer, 117–121. Berlin: Sternberg Press.

Galindo, Guillermo. 2017. http://www.galindog.com/wp/. Accessed 16 Sept 2017.

Hopkins, Candice. 2017. Guillermo Galindo. In *Documenta 14: Daybook: Athens, 8 April—Kassel, 17 September 2017*. Munich, London, and New York: Prestel. 13 May 2017.

ICORN. 2019. https://www.icorn.org/about-icorn. Accessed 16 Sept 2018.

Karavanta, Mina. 2017. Long Lasting Days. *Politics/Letters: A Quarterly Journal and Web Zine Dedicated to the Future of the Non-hairshirt Left 7*. http://politicsslashletters.org/long-lasting-days/. Accessed 16 Sept 2018.

Morin, Marie-Ève. 2015. The Spacing of Time and the Place of Hospitality: Living Together According to Bruno Latour and Jacques Derrida. *Parallax* 21 (1): 26–41.

Morin, Marie-Ève. 2016. How Do We Live Here? Abyssal Intimacies in Jean-Luc Nancy's *La ville au loin*. *Parrhesia* 25: 110–128.

Nancy, Jean-Luc. 1991. *The Inoperative Community*, trans. Peter Connor, Lisa Garbus, Michael Holland, and Simona Sawhney. Minneapolis and Oxford: University of Minnesota Press.

Nancy, Jean-Luc. 2000. *Being Singular Plural*, trans. Robert D. Richardson and Anne E. O'Byrne. Stanford: Stanford University Press.

Paulson, Steve. 2016. Critical Intimacy. An Interview with Gayatri Chakravorty Spivak. *Los Angeles Review of Books*, July 29. https://lareviewofbooks.org/article/critical-intimacy-interview-gayatri-chakravorty-spivak/. Accessed 16 Sept 2018.

CHAPTER 17

Afterword: The Consolations of Ruins—From the Acropolis to Epidaurus

Jyotsna G. Singh

A conference entitled "Beyond the Ruin: Investigating the Fragment," organized by the "Hellenic Association of the Study of English" (*HASE*) and the National and Kapodistrian University of Athens, had a literal and iconic resonance for me while staying in the environs of the rock of the Acropolis with the majestic "ruin" of the Parthenon situated high on top. The sight of the Parthenon carried an evocative charge for me, as for any visitor. I draw on my sensory experiences of the Acropolis ruin (and the Acropolis archaeological museum) followed by a visit to the Epidaurus complex (especially the theatre) as my points of entry into this volume entitled *Ruins in the Literary and Cultural Imagination*. Engagements with ruins and fragments in this anthology include themes of destruction, melancholy, preservation, re-edification, hospitality (and intimacy), among others, as they evoke both the ruins of cultures and global preoccupations with the cultures of ruin. In a different, "presentist" theoretical move, I want to reflect on the affective and imaginative

J. G. Singh (✉)
Michigan State University, East Lansing, MI, USA

© The Author(s) 2019
E. Mitsi et al. (eds.), *Ruins in the Literary and Cultural Imagination*,
https://doi.org/10.1007/978-3-030-26905-0_17

impact of these classical ruins during the *immediacy* of my contact with them.[1] The centre of "gravity" of my musings on the Acropolis rock, the Acropolis museum and the Epidaurus complex is "now, rather than then": evoking their materiality—stone, marble, plaster, wood, bronze—I consider how they could trigger the imagination of the past, though not in terms of any concrete history. Instead of inserting and fixing what remained of these monuments within any substantial knowable "facts," I cast my gaze on my own "situatedness." Thus, what I learned about the Acropolis and Epidaurus as iconic edifices was in the "here and now." In 2017, I could not, of course, forget that Greece was now the home of large numbers of refugees from the Middle East and elsewhere (perhaps a reminder of the ancient Hellenic ethos of hospitality)—the refugees turned away by those very European societies who embraced the symbolism and ethos afforded by Hellenic antiquity. Some of these refugees, sadly, now wandered the streets of Athens, not far from the Acropolis. They were reminders of the costs of warfare as well as the failures of capitalist economies to provide social care and refuge. From these initial experiences, looking back at my visit, I see it as an affective journey among the "ruins" of Greece, where I found myself *creating* fragmentary and experiential evocations of story, history and myth at the moments of contact.

What solace could these ruins offer me? I wondered if I could capture some affective plenitude while beholding their broken beauty and grandeur, and in turn create empathetic bonds with the long-dead cultures and languages not wholly intelligible. Traditionally, the "ruin predominantly recalls a classical or distant past and is valued as a silent yet privileged ground for its reconstruction or continued influence" ("Introduction"). But a question on my mind was whether the monuments were only fixed symbols of a singular past, or mutable cultural objects with multiple stories that tell their "affective and archival

---

[1]A presentist theoretical lens is useful in reading "ruins and fragments" without following the impulse of reading them historically, or inserting them into a context of fixity—one that bears the weight of a cultural and/or national consensus. I draw on Terence Hawkes formulation of presentism as it applies to drama to emphasize the "situatedness" of the present. "Placing emphasis on the present can't help but connect fruitfully with the current realignment of critical responses that stresses the *performance* of a play as much as its 'reference': that looks at what the play *does*, here and now in the theatre, as well as—or even against—what it *says* in the world to which its written text refers" (Hawkes 2003, 1–6).

life."[2] Following another, related line of reflection on our human bond with stones, I was also drawn to cultural theorist, Gabriel Teshome's hypothesis:

> It is common knowledge that stones do not lend themselves to speech; but because stones are mute, it does not mean that they do not speak; they actually do, only they speak in a language that we do not recognize, that we do not know. The question then is: can we translate their silences to our language? (n.d.)

I began to question: How could my personal, affective and sensory journey partake of the life of these ruins? How did they speak to me?

Let me return now to the Parthenon. It took me by breathless surprise: whether it was eerily lit up at night, appearing almost magically, as one turned a corner or appearing as a solid, though striated cluster of fragmented walls and pillars in the bright sun, especially while trudging up the Acropolis rock for a more close-up contact. From the west side, different structures of the edifice could be marked: in front, the Propylaia and the temple of Athena Nike, to the left the Erechtheion and to the right, on higher level, the Parthenon. From the huge blocks and pillars close-up and then descending to the modern Acropolis museum far down at the base of the rock, I encountered a world of rich fragments drawn from the architectural ruins on top. The Acropolis Museum brought to life the imaginary flights evoked by the architecture in the materiality of sculptures, friezes, statues, partially embodied, chipped faces, the sweeping flow of stone hair of the majestic Caryatids and virile male bodies frozen in time on horses, on chariots, with spears, armed for battle or even adjusting a sandal. A recurring reminder in these displays were various figurations of Athena originally associated with the Acropolis as its presiding deity, and almost endlessly signifying the city's identity. Summing up this veneration was a label on a bronze statue of Athena, ca. 350 B.C.

> The dominant deity of the Acropolis rock throughout antiquity was Athena, who was worshipped in a variety of aspects: as the City Patron, Athena Polias in the Erechthium; as Athena Pallas and Parthenos with her military aspect in the Parthenon; as Athena Nike in the small temple of

---

[2] I am indebted to Rajagopalan (2017) for this formulation.

the same name; as Athena Argani, patron of the arts and artisans ... and as
Athena Hygiea near the Propylaia. (Servi 2011, 32)

Another distinctive feature of the museum was the many exhibits in
which original marble friezes were placed within plaster casts copies, signalling the gaps left by fragments pillaged and stolen by Lord
Elgin in the nineteenth century, now on display in the British Museum
in London. In the museum brochure, the "theft" is euphemistically
described when the caryatids are mentioned: an "empty gap between the
kore that once occupied the space [on the Parthenon hill] and which in
the nineteenth century became part of the collection of Greek antiquities that Lord Elgin took to Britain, and which eventually ended up in
the British Museum" (Servi 2011, 100).[3] The truncated statuary of the
friezes was caught up in the story of the British Empire and the hubris of
its standard bearers like Lord Elgin.

Despite the museum's detailed contextualizations of the layers of history marking the layout of the exhibits, the world on display lacked a
coherent wholeness. Objects were often only fragments, chipped, broken, headless bodies, partial torsos, horses cut in half, columns and ped-
estals in shards, as if the denizens of antiquity had been dismembered
for us to witness. Yet, ironically, the figures of the statues or carvings,
however broken, *also* seemed to inhabit a theatrical space in which their
presence was palpable and "alive," conveying with some poignancy both
movement (speed) and stillness. The commercial imperatives of their
"presence" were also dominant in the two gift shops with their beautiful renderings of the figures in souvenirs, postcards, books and statues,
among others. Of course, gift shops were doing what cultural production
often does so well, namely represent these fragments as a metonymy of
nostalgic wholeness of Greek antiquity and nationalism that could then
be marketed, not only in museums, but in mass-produced images on
material objects for the milling tourists outside.

The ancient monuments in Athens were refracted through the bus-
tle of urban modernity including tourism for which the Acropolis was
a convenient signifier. The inert stones of the Parthenon (among other

---

[3]For a full account of the complicated and trivial mostly domestic reasons that led to
the "theft" of the Parthenon "marbles" (friezes and sculptures), see Mitsi (2014). Despite
justifications given today that claim the "protection" of the marbles, Mitsi's essay tells a different story of the arrogance of power manifested in a domestic colonial drama.

Athenian monuments) were made to "speak" for and by the tourism industry. In contrast, the edifices of the Epidaurus complex standing by itself in an open, hillside landscape, isolated from markers of modernity like cities, seemed to "speak" in more elemental voices. We drove along the Corinth coast and bypassed Mycenae, with all the Homeric evocations of its name, for another visit, but nothing prepared me for the solid, virtually intact stone structure of the theatre at Epidaurus, described aptly for tourists as follows:

> The theatre of Epidaurus represents the finest and best-preserved example of classical Greek theatre. Even by today's standards, this monument stands out as a unique artistic achievement through its admirable integration into the landscape and above all the perfection of its proportions and incomparable acoustics. It was built in 330-20 BC and enlarged in the mid-2nd century AD. The overall 55 rows of seats rest on a natural slope and face the stage area set against a backdrop of lush landscape. The theatre is marveled for its exceptional acoustics. Any sound on the open-air stage, whether a stentorian voice or a whisper, a deep breath or the sound of a match struck is perfectly audible to all spectators, even in the topmost row of seats, that is, nearly 60 m away... Once again in use today, the ancient monument floods with theatre devotees during the annual summer Festival of Epidaurus. ("Theatre of Epidaurus", n.d.)

All these epithets rang true generally in terms of the sheer size, proportions and acoustics of the stadium-like open-air theatre. But since there was just a sprinkling of visitors the day of my visit, the sheer physicality of stone that comprised the seating with spaces in between them was particularly imposing, especially in its expansive contrast with a fringe of greenery all around and the spreading blue, sunny sky beyond (Fig. 17.1).

Many chipped, broken or crumbled edges on the stone seats told a story of the natural wear and tear of the amphitheatre through the centuries, but escaping total destruction that befell the Asclepius complex surrounding the theatre (which I discuss below). The theatre itself enabled experiences of both stillness—sitting on solid, speckled seating rows—and movement, walking the pathways, up and down or in circles around the theatre. A visitor tried the vaunted acoustics in the empty space while I was there. Strains of a song, possibly in Chinese, wafted up the steps. The glinting sun demystified the singer, possibly from lands afar, but the sound heightened the palpable sense of the performance

Fig. 17.1   Standing between the sweeping rows of seats at Epidaurus

space being "alive." Above all, even in emptiness one could imagine dramatic actions and speeches of actors through hundreds of years, spectacles, masked and costumed actors, their voices, music, dancing and props. Entrances to the stage on the side were simple, stone arches from where the actors could enter and exit to their "skene" or tent in ancient times and to a hidden dressing area as currently used (Fig. 17.2).

I visited Epidaurus off season, but just experiencing the emptiness and stillness forced me to reconsider stones in terms not of their stillness, but of their movement and mobility. Again, Gabriel Teshome's "animation" of stones offered me a frame of understanding my contact with the theatre:

> Movement is not just a spatial displacement, or a matter of sequence, or of a linear history. While stones are generally associated with immobility, those that tend to remain still are in fact the ones that move the most throughout history. By not moving at all, they move in other directions, in other dimensions, in their own curious and often ironic way. (n.d.)

Fig. 17.2 Entrances and exits for actors

The ironic thrust of this reflection seemed particularly salient to me at the theatre in Epidaurus. Movement *on* this performance space through the centuries, leading to the current playing seasons, became in my imagination *movement of the* performance space, both capturing and following with the footfall of millions of spectators over the long span of its existence. Another tiny discovery I made also made me rethink the relation between stone edifices and their natural habitat and accompanying weather conditions. Many of the rows of seats were serrated by patterns of holes resembling pinpricks (stone tattoos). I was curious about how long they had been there. They looked fresh and recent. Anecdotally, I

Fig. 17.3 Patterns on seats

heard they helped to direct the flow of rainwater or to absorb it, hold it? I would have to research this beyond my experiences (Fig. 17.3).

The theatre in Epidaurus is not a "ruin" in the fragmented form of the Parthenon. It is whole and solid, but it nonetheless lacks the international and national symbolic significance of the latter, whereby one single edifice becomes a metonymy of a nostalgic wholeness and a shared Hellenic past within Greece itself—and more ephemerally within the symbolic registers of Western civilization that venerates Greek antiquity. However, standing at the open theatre, made me think of all the places of the world where the theatrical impulses of spectacle, mimicry, dance and affective, cathartic release played themselves out. Specifically, a brief account of the life of theatre in Greece itself lends a rich symbolic value to the Epidaurus theatre. We get the root of the English word "theatre" from the Greek word *Theatron*, which translates as "viewing place" and designated the curved and banked seating area. Remembering the long history of theatres helped me to see Epidaurus as a privileged site, showing the continued influence of the theatre in our imagination.

> Archaeologists have identified a hundred theatres all over the Greek world – stone semicircles (as well as the occasional rectangle) located in rural villages and cities and at religious destinations. Within several of these structures, both ancient and modern, plays are still staged. Country hillsides whose slopes were wide and gentle enough to seat a crowd made perfect settings for dramatic encounters and were the earliest theatres. Ancient roads that widened below the hills, or level ground at the hill's base, provided a suitable performance spaces. Such sites along with every city's agora and a temple dedicated to Dionysus or another god, [as in Athens near the Acropolis] were the main arenas of community activity. Stone pillars and tablets along roads leading to theatres commemorated local victors; athletes, actors, playwrights, singers, and producers of victorious plays. Theatres in every sense were open to all the crosscurrents of civic, [affective], and domestic life. (Bagg 2012, xxix–xxx)

Keeping in mind how theatres were integrated into the everyday lived experiences of people in the ancient world, while affectively connecting them to mythical deities, I was very moved by the monumental and majestic scale of the large amphitheatre at Epidaurus. Seeing the endless rows of rough, uneven stone seating made me appreciate the spectators who lacked our modern, plush comforts (Fig. 17.4).

Leaving the theatre, I wandered down the hillside on its periphery and came across ruined, fragmented remnants of the other parts of Epidaurus complex. Only partial broken walls denoting rooms remained and rubble stuck in the grass in the bare spaces. How was the Asklepieion destroyed, whereas the theatre stood mostly intact? Stories from various sources, some apocryphal, told of an earthquake and of the special structure of the theatre. As for these adjoining ruins, we learn from one blurb about their identity: not only is it "famed for its unmatched theatre," it is

Fig. 17.4   Rough, uneven stone seats

also known for "its Asklepieion, thus named the sanctuaries sacred to Asclepius, the healing god and son of Apollo":

> Epidaurus is famed for its unmatched theatre, as well as for its Asklepieion, thus named the sanctuaries sacred to Asclepius, the healing god and son of Apollo. Combining religious faith with empirical knowledge and occult rituals with actual treatment, the Asklepieia functioned pretty much as

hospitals and, needless to say, they were of great significance to Greeks and Romans alike. The Asklepieion of Epidaurus in particular was the most important therapeutic center of the ancient Greek world, followed by that of Kos, the birthplace of Hippocrates and medicine. ... Developed out of an earlier cult of Apollo, the sanctuary of Asclepius reached its peak in the 4th century BC when it was adorned with its principal monuments seen today, especially the temple of the god, the *tholos,* and the renowned theatre, all three considered masterpieces of the late classical Greek architecture. ("Asklepieion of Epidaurus", n.d.)

It was with a sad shock that I wandered through the broken outline of what looked like the foundations of buildings—stone walls grounded down to mere jutting outlines and rubble of stones and small architectural shards all around. It was a poignant moment to stand among the shattered remains of the sanctuary, a place of hospitality and healing. I could identify with the ancient travellers or pilgrims who came for solace, relief, worship of Asclepius and consolations of companions in similar plights. Among the treatments offered, I read on the information, hypnosis was an option, some surgery with scalpels, and for continuing health, a small athletic stadium. What did we learn of the holistic units of life in the Epidaurus? Healing, companionship, watching and participating in civic and affective rituals like plays, all constituted what at that time must have been experienced as life-affirming, and as an intrinsic part of the healing and curative rituals available to sick people in Epidaurus—all ways of warding off possible decline and temporarily forgetting death. Thus, in buildings long dismembered, the inert stones of the Sanctuary of Asclepius "give rise to what we might call a poetics of life" (Teshome). Could I experience an "intimacy" with the dead, the "other," through a willed empathy across time?[4] The sanctuary of Asclepius was a place of consolation and hospitality in the past, not available to me in its desolation, but I am nonetheless filled with an inner harmony as I try to capture the spirit of its hospitality across time—try to "listen" to the stones.

---

[4]For a rich discussion of the complex relation between hospitality and intimacy, see Apostolos Lampropoulos, Chapter 16 in this volume.

REFERENCES

Asklepieion of Epidaurus. n.d. *Greek Travel Pages*. International Publications Limited. https://www.gtp.gr/TDirectoryDetails.asp?ID=14656. Accessed 17 Mar 2019.

Bagg, Robert. 2012. Introduction. In *The Oedipus Cycle*, ed. and trans. Robert Bragg. New York: Harper.

Hawkes, Terence. 2003. *Shakespeare in the Present*. London: Routledge.

Mitsi, Efterpi. 2014. Commodifying Antiquity in Mary Nisbet's Journey to the Ottoman Empire. In *Travel, Discovery, Transformation, Culture and Civilization*, vol. 6, ed. Gabriel Ricci, 45–59. London: Routledge.

Rajagopalan, Mrinalini. 2017. *Building Histories: The Archival and Affective Lives of Five Monuments in Modern Delhi*. Chicago: University of Chicago Press.

Servi, Katerina. 2011. *The Acropolis: The Acropolis Museum*. Athens: Ekdotike Athenon.

Teshome, Gabriel. n.d. *Stone. Articles and Other Works*. http://teshomegabriel.net/. Accessed 17 Mar 2019.

Theatre of Epidaurus. n.d. *Greek Travel Pages*. International Publications Limited. https://www.gtp.gr/TDirectoryDetails.asp?ID=80329. Accessed 18 Mar 2019.

Index

Printed by Printforce, the Netherlands